Praise for *Fighter Boys*

"An engaging book. *Fighter Boys* does justice to a campaign that became a legend." —*St. Louis Post-Dispatch*

"By any measure, the pilots of the RAF's Fighter Command in the Battle of Britain were heroes. In Patrick Bishop's remarkable book, he portrays them in meticulous, unsentimental detail. I know no more thoughtful nor yet more moving study of their achievement than that which Patrick Bishop has produced." —*The New York Sun*

"A spirited account . . . Bishop adds to the literature [on the Battle of Britain] twofold. Nicely written and rich in detail." —*Kirkus Reviews*

"Bishop chronicles every conceivable aspect of the air warrior's experience . . . Competently and appealingly integrates the minutiae into a coherent narrative . . . [and] commendably evokes what it really was like to fly and die defending Britain from the Nazi menace." —*Booklist*

"Some may ask whether there is any call for yet another book on the legend of The Few. Patrick Bishop has proved that there is, if you are prepared to look beyond the stereotypes and try to catch the authentic voice of an embattled Britain in its finest hour. The author has made good use of the best of the battle memoirs and the surprisingly under-exploited archived taped interviews left by veterans, together with their often poignant, as well as racy, diaries and letters. Their memories are a rich seam of Bishop's tribute to Fighter Command." —*The Sunday Times* (London)

"This is not a tactical history. The thorny questions of military strategy are wisely left to one side—the maddening ambiguities of German strategy and evergreen question of the true scale of both sides' combat losses. Instead, this is about individuals. . . . And they really were heroes: of the 2,917 pilots who fought in Fighter Command during the Battle of Britain, 544 were killed, while 795 of the survivors were also dead before the Second World War finished." —*The Scotsman*

ABOUT THE AUTHOR

Patrick Bishop, associate editor at the *Daily Telegraph* (London), is the originator of the television series *The Irish Empire* and the author of the highly acclaimed book *The Provisional IRA*. A foreign correspondent who has covered the Middle East, Africa, and the Balkans, Bishop has also written books about the Falklands conflict and the Gulf War. He lives in London.

PATRICK BISHOP

Fighter Boys

The Battle of Britain, 1940

PENGUIN BOOKS

PENGUIN BOOKS
Published by the Penguin Group
Penguin Group (USA) Inc., 375 Hudson Street, New York, New York 10014, U.S.A.
Penguin Group (Canada), 90 Eglinton Avenue East, Suite 700, Toronto,
Ontario, Canada M4P 2Y3 (a division of Pearson Penguin Canada Inc.)
Penguin Books Ltd, 80 Strand, London WC2R 0RL, England
Penguin Ireland, 25 St Stephen's Green, Dublin 2, Ireland (a division of Penguin Books Ltd)
Penguin Group (Australia), 250 Camberwell Road, Camberwell,
Victoria 3124, Australia (a division of Pearson Australia Group Pty Ltd)
Penguin Books India Pvt Ltd, 11 Community Centre, Panchsheel Park, New Delhi – 110 017, India
Penguin Group (NZ), cnr Airborne and Rosedale Roads,
Albany, Auckland 1310, New Zealand (a division of Pearson New Zealand Ltd)
Penguin Books (South Africa) (Pty) Ltd, 24 Sturdee Avenue,
Rosebank, Johannesburg 2196, South Africa

Penguin Books Ltd, Registered Offices: 80 Strand, London WC2R 0RL, England

First published in the United States of America by Viking Penguin,
a member of Penguin Group (USA) Inc. 2003
Published in Penguin Books 2004

10 9 8 7 6 5 4 3 2

THE LIBRARY OF CONGRESS HAS CATALOGED
THE HARDCOVER EDITION AS FOLLOWS:
Bishop, Patrick (Patrick Joseph)
Fighter boys : the Battle of Britain, 1940 / Patrick Bishop.
p. cm.
Includes bibliographical references and index.
ISBN 0-670-03230-1 (hc.)
ISBN 0 14 20.0466 9 (pbk.)
1. Britain, Battle of, Great Britain, 1940. 2. Great Britain, Royal Air Force. Fighter Command—History. 3. Fighter pilots—Great Britain—History—20th century. I. Title.
D756.5.B7B54 2003
940.54'4941—dc21 200305322

Printed in the United States of America
Set in Monotype Dante

To Kelly and Bill

Contents

List of Illustrations

Preface

This book is an attempt to answer a question that has fascinated me since I was a child. I grew up in Kent and London in the late 1950s and early 1960s, when the Second World War was still a real presence. There were daily reminders of it in the weed-choked gaps between houses where German bombs had fallen and the muddy Anderson shelters that could still be found in suburban back gardens.

My first years were spent in the village of Charing. One of my earliest memories is of walking with my father, mother and sister through a ground mist of bluebells in Long Beech woods on the ridge above the village, close to the Pilgrim's Way. Not long before the skies overhead had been a battleground. Occasionally my playmates and I found cartridge cases rusting underneath the ferns that we imagined had tumbled from the heavens during the fighting. Later I learned that a fighter pilot had crashed in flames into Long Beech after being shot down in the autumn of 1940.

We boys knew all about the Battle of Britain from small, square comic books, describing the great events of the war, that we bought eagerly as soon as they appeared in the village newsagent. They were our first history books. There, for the first time, we met heroes other than our fathers. It was the fighter pilots who hijacked our imaginations. We acted out their deeds in our games and dreamed about being them when we grew up. Their style and dash made them much more glamorous than the earthbound drudges of the infantry. Adults seemed to think so too.

The Battle of Britain was mythologised before it was even over and those who took part in it were bathed in the glow of the legend.

At adolescence you shed your old heroes and get a new set. For a while it was slightly embarrassing to recall the passion that the silhouette of a Hurricane or the smudged snapshot of a young pilot once provoked. The grown-ups also seemed to have moved on. This was the Sixties. Men in uniform were now the targets of mockery.

Then, in the funny way that the recent past becomes suddenly almost as remote as the Dark Ages, the pilots slipped into history. There were plenty of books about the battles they fought and their crucial importance to the twentieth century. But they themselves grew obscure, blurred and monochrome like the photographs they took of each other, always smiling, as they hung about at dispersal, waiting to take off.

In the pages that follow I have tried to colour in the picture and to answer the question: What were the Fighter Boys really like? My researches have been helped by the generosity of many people. I am particularly grateful to Malcolm Smith of the Battle of Britain Fighter Association for pointing me to the veterans whose reminiscences enrich this story and answering many queries with his celebrated kindness, good humour and patience. The survivors are men of their time. Everyone I approached was unfailingly courteous, helpful and hospitable. Meetings were invariably a pleasure. The Fighter Boys retain their *joie de vivre*. The contribution of individuals is made clear in the text, and to each of them I give my thanks. Without them the book could not have been written. I would like to make special acknowledgment to Group Captain Billy Drake, Air Commodore Peter Brothers and Air Chief Marshal Sir Christopher Foxley-Norris for the repeated calls I made on them. Group Captain John Cunningham, Hugh Heron, Squadron Leader Jocelyn Millard, Group Captain Anthony O'Neill, Wing Commander Harbourne Stephen and Flight Lieutenant William Walker were also generous with their time.

I was fortunate to be given access to several unpublished texts. Among them was Tim Vigors's splendid autobiography, which has yet to appear in print, a situation which I hope will soon be rectified. I am also grateful to the Beaumont family for allowing me to see S. G. Beaumont's

Reminiscences, to the Fenwick family for sending me Charles Fenwick's account of a young pilot's life, *Dear Mother*, and to Michael Butterworth for enabling me to see Group Captain Frank Carey's personal history. Squadron Leader Dennis Armitage supplemented his talk with me with his written account of the summer of 1940. Edith Kup was kind enough to spend a wintry afternoon filling in some of the gaps in the story of her love affair with Denis Wissler and to allow me to see his letters. Valerie Preston shared with me some of her souvenirs of the White Hart and Robin Appleford has allowed me to reproduce some glimpses of off-duty life in 66 squadron.

I would also like to thank Mrs Lesley Kingcome, her mother Sheila, her daughter Samantha and her son Gavin for their hospitality in Devon and for their memories of the late Brian Kingcome, as well as for permission to reproduce the photographs that appear here and to quote from his memoir, *A Willingness to Die*. I am grateful, too, to Sarah Quill for talking to me about her father Jeffery and for showing me letters from the family archive, and to Yvonne Agazarian for sketching in some details of her brother, Noel.

Our understanding of the ethos of Fighter Command has been helped greatly by the work of the Imperial War Museum, which more than 20 years ago set out to record the testimony of many of those engaged in the air battles of 1940 and preserve them in its sound archive. These interviews have provided much fascinating material and I am grateful for permission to reproduce extracts. The staffs of the Sound Archive, Department of Documents and Printed Books, Photograph Archive and Film and Video Archive were always helpful and efficient. I also want to thank Gordon Leith and his team at the Department of Research and Information Services at the RAF Museum, Hendon and the staff of the Public Record Office in Kew for their patience and the hard work they did on my behalf. Jean Buckberry was a gracious guide to the Royal Air Force College, Cranwell and its library. The staff of RAF, Benson, provided me with the records of the Oxford University Air Squadron in the interwar years.

In another, very different, area of research, I would like to thank Rod

Dean, himself a former RAF fighter pilot, for taking me through the basic manoeuvres of a dogfight in a Harvard trainer in the skies above Tangmere and for explaining the principles of air fighting.

My task would have been much more difficult if it were not for the work done by several aviation historians of the period. I am indebted to Ken Wynn for the definitive research contained in *Men of the Battle of Britain* and to Christopher Shores and Clive Williams for the wealth of detail found in their two-volume *Aces High*. The chronology was greatly aided by reference to Francis K. Mason's *Battle Over Britain*. The writings of Norman Franks, H. Montgomery Hyde, John James, Dr Tony Mansell, Dilip Sarkar, Richard C. Smith and John Terraine were always illuminating.

Thanks are due to the Grub Street team, who continue to ensure that the voices of those who fought the Second World War are heard, for permission to quote from Dennis David's *My Biography*, and *Shot Down In Flames* by Geoffrey Page, to Hutchinson for extracts from *Flying Start* by Hugh Dundas, reprinted by permission of the Random House Group Ltd, who also allowed me to use passages from Alan Deere's memoir *Nine Lives*. Wing Commander Paddy Barthropp allowed me to make use of his autobiography *Paddy*. I am also grateful to Cassell Military for letting me reproduce parts of Paul Richey's classic, *Fighter Pilot*.

Franziska Thomas put me in touch with German Luftwaffe veterans and was a skilful translator of my talks with them. My friend Sophia Coudenhove was a model researcher, a shrewd and indefatigable toiler in the archives and a source of cheer. Nick Farrell, Harry de Quetteville and Hugh Schofield gave encouragement and ideas when the going got heavy. Charles Moore, Editor of the *Daily Telegraph*, and Alec Russell, Foreign Editor, were generous and understanding bosses, and my colleague Ian Jones took the author photograph. My gratitude is due to Leslie Bonham Carter for providing a wonderful working environment at Bussento at a crucial stage of writing.

In closing I would like to mention my late father, Ernest Bishop, himself an RAF man, in whose endlessly-leafed through wartime photograph albums the germ of this project perhaps lies. It would have lain dormant, however, were it not for the intervention of my agent David Godwin, who devoted his great talent and energy to getting *Fighter Boys* airborne. The process was helped enormously by the professionals at Harper-Collins. I would like to thank Michael Fishwick for his enthusiasm and backing, Kate Johnson for her intelligent appreciation of the subject, Mary Ore and Peter Ford for their meticulous editing and Melanie Haselden for the care she took over the picture selection.

The last acknowledgement should really have come first. My eternal gratitude, Marie darling, for your support and – how shall I put this? – *tolerance*. Now it is your turn.

Shetland Islands
Sumburgh
Kirkwall
Orkney Islands
Wick
Inverness
Dyce
Aberdeen
Group 13
Grangemouth
Edinburgh
Drem
Turnhouse
Glasgow
Berwick
Usworth
Acklinton
Newcastle
Middlesbrough
Catterick
Church Fenton
York
Leconfield
Hull
Leeds
Liverpool
Manchester
Group 12
Kirton-in-Lindsey
Tern Hill
Watnall
Digby
Nottingham
Coltishall
Wittering
Norwich
Birmingham
Coventry
Cambridge
Duxford
Pembrey
Group 10
Cardiff
Filton
Colerne
Bristol
Box
Oxford
Group 11 see inset
London
Middle Wallop
Boscombe Down
Exeter
Exeter
Southampton
Portsmouth
Hastings
Dover
Warmwell
Brighton
St. Eval
Roborough
Weymouth
Plymouth
ENGLISH CHANNEL
NORTH SEA
N
Group 11
High Street
Dunwich
Martlesham
Bawdsey
Debden
Bromley
Stapleford
Walton
North Weald
FC
Canewdon
Rochford
Northolt
Hendon
Hornchurch
Uxbridge
Gravesend
London
Croydon
Dunkirk
Foreness
Detling
Manston
Kenley
Biggin Hill
West Malling
Hawkinge
Portsmouth
Lympne
Dover
Eastchurch
Southampton
Tangmere
Rye
Brighton
Hastings
Lee-on-Solent
Fairlight
Thorney Island
Truleigh
Pevensey
Gosport
Ford
Poling
Beachy Head
Ventnor
Westhampnett
Basic (Chain Home) Radar Stations
Low Flying (Chain Home Low) Radar Stations
NETHERLANDS
Amsterdam
The Hague
Soesterberg
Rotterdam
GERMANY
Dunkirk
Ostend
Antwerp
Coquelles
Ghent
Brussels
Cologne
Wissant
BELGIUM
Lille
Liège
Arras
LUXEMBOURG
Luxembourg
Amiens
Cherbourg
Dieppe
La Havre
Beauvais
Laon
Berry-au-Bac
Verdun-Sur-Meuse
Reims
Metz
Caen
Bar-Le-Duc
Flers
Falaise
Paris
Brest
Dinard
St. Malo
Villacoublay
FRANCE
RAF Fighter Command Headquarters
RAF Group Headquarters
Sector Airfields
Other fighter Airfields
RAF Group Boundaries
Sector Boundaries
Luftwaffe Boundary
0
50 miles

Prologue: The White Hart

At 9 p.m. on Thursday, 15 August 1940, in a low-beamed, tile-hung pub in the Kentish village of Brasted, the conversation faded as a radio was switched on and the familiar pulse of the electronic time signal counted down the seconds to the main BBC news broadcast of the evening.

The voice of the announcer was calm but the events he described could not have been more dramatic. Throughout the day huge formations of German bombers, protected by large numbers of fighter escorts, had been crossing the Channel unloading cargoes of high explosive on military and industrial targets across south-east England.

The report was heard in silence until the newsreader revealed the day's score. At least 182 enemy aircraft had been destroyed, he claimed, against British losses of only 34 fighters. There was a burst of cheering and a surge to the bar for celebratory drinks. As the radio was switched off the noise in the pub's stone-flagged bars climbed back up to its normal convivial level.

Most of the men in the White Hart Hotel that evening were pilots from the fighter station at Biggin Hill, seven miles away through ragged, dusty-green lanes, across wheat fields ripened to the colour of wet sand. Watching them was an American journalist who had driven down from London that afternoon. In his report he wrote that he 'found it incredible that these noisy youngsters were in fact front-line troops, even then in the thick of battle'.

It was true. The boisterous young men, tankards and cigarettes in hand, the top buttons of their slate-blue uniform tunics undone to show the world they were fighter pilots, had been on duty since the first light of what had been an unusually misty summer morning. Some had been in action three times.

The day had seen the most intense air fighting in history. The pilots had won a remarkable victory, though not as great a one as the official figures suggested. In fact seventy-eight German aircraft had been knocked down. It was less than half the number claimed, but there was no doubt that the Luftwaffe had been made to suffer.

Half of the men were from 32 Squadron. At the centre of the crowd was the new commander, Flight Lieutenant Michael Crossley, thin and dark-haired, with deep-set humorous eyes, who at six foot two was half a head taller than the other pilots. Before leading the men off, as the dusk thickened, for pints of the warm sudsy Page & Overton bitter that the White Hart's landlady Kath Preston served from wooden casks, he had recorded the events of the day.

> Down to Hawkinge 1 p.m. and from then on had a remarkably blitzy afternoon. Chased something up to Harwich and got mixed up with 109s going home. Got none. They got Grubby Grice instead who descended into the sea . . . back to Biggin to refuel. Off to Portsmouth and attacked thousands of 88s and 110s, got three. Refuel again and attack thousands of 17s who were beating up and bombing Croydon. Slapped down seven. 'Polly' Flinders took training flight out and he and Humph slapped down one each. Day's bag twelve.[1]

The 109s mentioned in this laconic entry were the Messerschmitt fighter escorts shepherding the fleets of raiders that arrived in successive waves from late morning. The '88s' were Junkers 88s, twin-engined medium bombers. The '110s' were Messerschmitt 110s, twin-engined fighters, and '17s' were Dornier 17s, another medium bomber. The Germans had come in unprecedented numbers, launching attacks across an 800-mile front that reached from Edinburgh to Exeter in an effort to overwhelm Britain's air defences and prepare the way for invasion.

The main engagement of 32 Squadron came late in the day. Shortly after 6 p.m., as the sun slipped westward, a force of Me 110s and 109s crossed the Kent coast near Dungeness and raced towards what they thought to be the RAF base at Kenley, a vital station in the RAF defensive system. A mistake in navigation meant they dropped their bombs on Croydon aerodrome instead. The effect was devastating. The bombs crashed between buildings. The blast rolled back and forth to maximum destructive effect. The passenger terminal, which before the war had been a symbol of all that was hopeful and positive about the new world of aviation, was wrecked. Sixty-eight people were killed, all but six of them civilians. There had been no warning. The air-raid sirens sounded fifteen minutes after the attack began.

The streets around the aerodrome were full of people. Newspapers had warned that morning that the air fighting of the previous few days had been only a prelude to the real battle. Invasion fears were excited by the discovery of parachutes scattered across the Midlands and Scotland – but no parachutists. The sight of the bombers sent people running to the earth-and-corrugated-iron shelters they had dug in their back gardens. Others were too absorbed in the drama to take cover. Mr H. J. Edgerton of Couldson watched the Messerschmitts flash past, seemingly only a few feet over the roof of his mock-Tudor home, as 'about 20 Hurricanes and Spitfires streaked after them. Our fellows attacked them from below and roared up under them in terrific power climbs.' It was strangely exciting. The engines were 'screaming deafeningly'. The aeroplanes flew perilously close to each other and 'time after time I thought the RAF were going to ram the bombers but they swept past them'.[2]

On leaving, the Luftwaffe raked its nails across Croydon's homely, lower-middle-class face. Bombs tumbled into the streets, ripping up tarmac, blowing out windows and tearing off roofs. A woman emerged from her shelter to find nappies drying on the line shredded by machine-gun bullets. A doomed bomber piled into a row of semis, peeling away the walls, putting on display the modest lives being lived inside.

The Hurricanes of 32 Squadron and Spitfires of 610 Squadron had been unable to block the attack, though they shot down several of the raiders as they ran for home. Despite the deaths and the devastation there were few recriminations about the lack of warning or the level of protection the anti-aircraft defences and the air force had been able to provide. On the contrary, there was intense pride in the sight of the fighters charging in to attack. It seemed to Mr Edgerton that the British pilots had deliberately held their fire for several minutes, 'because of the danger of bringing the bombers down on the thickly populated district'.

In fact no such restraints were imposed either by the controllers directing the defences or by the pilots themselves. The assumption of selflessness was revealing. Already, after only a few weeks of the air war over Britain, the pilots of Fighter Command were bathed in the light of nobility. The organization was just four years old. Before the spring of 1940 fighter pilots were known as a small, vaguely glamorous élite. Their role in the fighting in France had been peripheral, and, in the great drama of the Dunkirk evacuation, somewhat contentious. Now, with Britain facing possible extinction, they were at the centre of the national consciousness, turning day by day into the heroes of a salvation legend. When people spoke about them it was in an increasingly proprietorial way touched with familial affection. First they were 'our boys'. Then, by midsummer, they were 'fighter boys'. The name conveyed everything: their youth, their job, their dash – and the warm regard in which they were held. 'Stuffy' Dowding, the pilots' austere commander, was the first to use it officially, writing in June a letter of congratulation to his 'dear Fighter Boys'.

By the end of the summer everyone in Britain was in love with them. The air battles of 1940 were intimate affairs. Unlike any external war Britain had been engaged in in the previous thousand years, this one was fought in the sight of the inhabitants of the island, over the territory the pilots were giving their lives to defend. Combat took place above the monotonous roofs of London suburbs, the old market towns and villages of Kent, Sussex and East Anglia, the fields and orchards of the Home Counties. Those below had only to look up to see an unprecedented spectacle: huge masses of bombers and fighters skidding across the cerulean summer sky, scribbling white vapour trails on its placid surface and stitching the blue with the red and gold of cannon and tracer. It was thrilling, and from a distance beautiful and unreal. Then a Heinkel would falter, stagger out of formation, slide into a stricken dive; a Hurricane would spurt flame, roll on to its back and spin down in frantic spirals, and with a final flash and boom the violence reached earth in an ugly tangle of scorched metal and roasted bodies.

The pilots fighting the battles lived among those they were defending. At 6.40 p.m. that Thursday, just outside Sevenoaks, Michael Crossley caught up with one of the Me 110s that had raided Croydon and set it on fire, sending it crashing down near the pleasant village of Ightham. Two hours later he was accepting drinks from locals in the pub, a few miles from where workers were clearing the wreckage and retrieving the corpses of the dead.

The Battle of Britain had many of the characteristics of a siege. Everyone inside the enclave, active or passive, soldier or civilian, was a defender. The closeness this engendered could sometimes be almost unbearable. The girlfriend of Flying Officer Douglas Grice, the 'Grubby' of Crossley's report, was a Waaf at Biggin Hill. The buzz that her man had 'gone in' reached her in a break between driving pilots out to their aircraft. Grice was badly burned but recovered. There were much worse stories. On a later occasion another Waaf, Edith Heap, who worked in the Debden control room, froze as a voice over the Tannoy reported 'Blue Four' was falling into the sea in flames. She knew, without waiting for confirmation, that the man she loved and was about to marry was dead.

Looking up at the wheeling Spitfires and Hurricanes, ordinary people imagined their own sons or brothers at the controls. Sometimes it was true. The mother of Tim Elkington, a young pilot with 1 Squadron, watched from the balcony of her flat on Hayling Island as he was shot down, baled out and drifted perilously over the sea before finally landing safely.

But you did not need ties of blood or romance to feel a particular bond with the Fighter Boys. The backgrounds of the few thousand pilots flying Hurricanes and Spitfires in the summer of 1940 reflected the social composition of the nation, a point that was emphasized by official and unofficial propagandists. 'The most striking thing about the fighter pilots is their ordinariness,' wrote a war artist who spent months among them. 'Just you, I, us and co.; ordinary sons of ordinary parents from ordinary homes.'[3] Fighter Command was perhaps the most motley élite ever to exist in the British military. In 32 Squadron, Crossley had been at Eton. John Proctor had left school at fourteen to become an RAF apprentice. Many of those standing in the pub had been in the RAF reserve before the war, training in their spare time from their often mundane jobs. Oliver Houghton had been a fitter in a Coventry factory. William Higgins was a teacher in a Derbyshire village school.

Their interests and attitudes were as broad as their backgrounds. Fighter pilots might be philistines or intellectuals, bon vivants or ascetics, pious or godless, cynical or trusting. There were some whose dominant trait of recklessness or aggression or amiability made them stand out, but most were too ordinarily complex to be pigeonholed. Fighter squadrons were collections of individuals. The nature of the fighting made it so. Once combat began, a pilot was usually on his own, beyond the control of his commander and making fateful decisions alone.

There were, though, strong affinities and common characteristics that bound the bunch together. The most potent was a love of flying. Speaking about flying, and when occasionally they wrote about it, the pilots dropped their usual clipped understatement for the language of passion. It was an obsession and an addiction and aeroplanes were far more than simply machines. They had quasi-human qualities. They could be brutish and heavy or beautiful, fragile and sensitive. If it was love, it was nearly always love at first sight. The pilots' reminiscences are full of lyrical memories of the first encounter, when the flying circus arrived in town or a mysterious figure floated out of the sky to land in the field next door.

Charles Fenwick was a little boy in the Kentish village of Harbledown when Sir Alan Cobham's troupe of itinerant flyers passed through. His aunt took him to see them.

> 'Would you like to go for a flip?'
>
> What a stupendous question! I was on my way to the plane as fast as

> I could go. I was small for my age and flopped into the rear cockpit. The plane was an early Avro, an aerial marvel quite beautiful to behold. Well, my idea of beauty, all struts and wires and canvas with that intoxicating smell compounded from dope and fuel and hot oil. But to beat it all she was alive. She was roaring like a lion and rattling. I was heading for heaven.[4]

Flying requires courage. Going solo in any aeroplane is alarming. Most aviators never lose a faint feeling of insecurity, no matter how great their experience. Flying with an instructor for the first time in a light aircraft, trainees noted queasily how thin the fuselage seemed, how flimsy the wings, how easy it might be to tip out in a turn. The sensations got more alarming as they progressed to more powerful machines. The Harvard trainer, whose 600-horsepower engine provides only half the thrust of the Merlins of the Hurricanes and Spitfires, is disconcerting enough. Clamping into a tight turn, the most basic manoeuvre of dog-fighting, G forces drag your guts to the sump of your stomach and press your head down on your chest as if you are being crushed by a giant hand. A simple half-roll sends the world spinning incomprehensibly, earth and sky alternating in a blur.

When I experienced this as a passenger, fear never felt far away. It is hard to imagine how pilots were able to fling their aeroplanes around in this way without succumbing to disorientation or panic. It is harder still to understand how they could shoot at, and hit, other aeroplanes while they were doing so. To have the reflexes and eyesight needed to do these things you had to be young. Most pilots were aged between nineteen and twenty-six. They tended to be young in their outlook as well. They liked the latest music, films and fashioned and spiced their talk with Americanisms, creating a Hollywood-meets-public-school slang.

The Fighter Boys belonged firmly to contemporary Britain, ideal warriors in what was being shaped as a people's war. To the public it seemed that their technological skill was, comfortingly, fused to old values and traditions. The pilots' fathers had fought and died in a war that had traumatized Europe and stimulated a wave of pacifist, and then defeatist, feeling. Yet the sons were accepting their duty willingly, almost cheerfully, and confronting the horror again.

On that August night, as the blackout shutters were fitted into the leaded windows of the White Hart, as last orders were called and the banter and laughter subsided, unwelcome thoughts of tomorrow edged in. The fighting of the day had brought only an interim victory, one that would have to be won over and over again. No one present, airman or civilian, was now in any doubt that they were in the middle of a struggle which would determine whether or not Britain would survive as a free country. Winston Churchill had set the stakes even higher. The battle, he said, would decide the fate of the civilized world. Many elements were involved in determining the outcome. Chief among them was the skill, morale and courage of the Fighter Boys. It was an extraordinary responsibility. Not since classical times had such a tiny band of warriors been asked to bear such a heavy burden. It was the pilots, though, who seemed the least concerned as they finished the dregs from their pewter mugs and stepped out into the cool, hop-scented Kent night.

I

Sportsmen and Butchers

In the summer of 1940 the art of air fighting was only twenty-six years old. In that time, aeroplanes had moved from the extreme periphery to the centre of modern warfare. The invention of aircraft made air wars inevitable. Innovators moved with depressing speed to fit guns to flying machines. The air shows at Hendon, Brooklands and Rheims held before the First World War emphasized the potential destructive power of the thing they were celebrating, with aviators dropping flour bombs on the outlines of warships traced in chalk on the ground. Writers frightened readers with stories of airships bombarding cities, a prophecy whose accuracy was soon to be confirmed.

For the military, though, it was the information-gathering potential of aeroplanes that first attracted interest. The first aircraft were used as observation platforms. In the war game played in September 1912 at the annual British army manoeuvres, Red Force and Blue Force were each equipped with a supporting air component. Early on, two airborne officers from Blue Force spotted a concentration of opposition troops and correctly guessed their direction. The information helped their side to win.

The victorious commander, Lieutenant-General Sir James Grierson, drew an important conclusion from the exercise. 'So long as hostile aircraft are hovering over one's troops,' he wrote, 'all movements are likely to be seen and reported. Therefore the first step in war will be to get rid of hostile aircraft.'[1]

This was how combat in the air was to develop in the four years of the Great War. The essential role of aeroplanes was to lift the roof off the battlefield, allowing commanders to peer into the enemy's territory, detecting his movements and trying to divine his intentions. At the same time, spotters hovering perilously over the front lines helped to direct the artillery barrages that occupied much of the effort of both sides.

The rival pilots, from the outset, tried to kill each other. One of the first recorded encounters took place on 25 August 1914. Lieutenant C. E. C. Rabagliati of the Royal Flying Corps was cruising with an observer on a reconnaissance mission over northern France when they came across a lone German aeroplane. Rabagliati's aircraft was unarmed, but he had with him a .303 service rifle. The German carried a Mauser pistol, fitted with a wooden shoulder stock. The two machines approached each other and circled, coming within feet of colliding. Rabagliati fired a hundred rounds without success. Then, he reported afterwards, 'to my intense joy, I saw the German pilot fall forward on his joystick and the machine tipped up and went down'.[2]

Such encounters were to be repeated thousands of times in the following years. Technological advances, accelerated by the demands of warfare, meant that the aircraft became faster, more nimble and more sturdy, and the weapons they carried more deadly. But the purpose of aerial fighting remained the same. No bomber heavy enough to make a significant difference on the battlefield or in the rear had emerged by the end of the war. The main function of military flying remained observing the enemy, and trying to prevent the enemy from observing you.

These activities grew to be increasingly important as the war progressed. The RFC went to France with sixty-two aircraft. In April 1918 it became, together with the Navy's air arm, a service in its own right, the Royal Air Force. It finished the war with 1,799 aeroplanes. This transformation was presided over by a particularly forceful and energetic commander, Hugh Trenchard. There were others who played a crucial part in the creation of a separate air force, but Trenchard's passion made him stand out. He became known as 'The Father of the RAF', a label he claimed to detest. The designation had some truth in it, though. He loved the air force with the fierce love of a father; a Victorian father who would not flinch from sending his boy to his death if duty demanded it.

Trenchard combined nineteenth-century mores with a twentieth-century appreciation of the new. He was born on 3 February 1873 in the West Country, and had a difficult childhood. His sister died of diphtheria, his solicitor father was bankrupted and he failed several attempts to enter military schools before scraping a commission as a second-lieutenant in the Royal Scots Fusiliers and being posted to India. He spent the first decade of the new century in southern and western Africa. In October 1900 he was shot in the chest while trying to capture Boers and was expected to die. Trenchard, who 'hated sick people', pulled through, recovering in characteristic fashion by hurtling down the Cresta run at St Moritz.

He was tall, bony, with mournful eyes that seemed to search for faults and slights. His personality was similarly angular: quarrelsome, morose and dissatisfied, ill at ease in the genial atmosphere of mess and gymkhana club. By 1912 it was clear that his career was going nowhere. He was approaching forty, unmarried and not much loved. His salvation came in a letter from one of his few friends, Captain Eustace Loraine, who was learning to fly at the RFC aviation school on Salisbury Plain. 'You've no idea what you're missing,' Loraine wrote excitedly. 'Come and see men crawling like ants.'[3]

Trenchard was not a natural pilot. His tall, long-legged frame looked ridiculous crammed into the narrow seats of the primitive Blériots and Farmans that were used to give instruction to trainees. What fascinated him was not flying itself, but its potential. He sensed he had finally made his rendezvous with destiny and joined the RFC. Three years later, in August 1915, he became its commander.

Trenchard tried to make the RFC indispensable, straining to satisfy every demand made on it by the army no matter how unreasonable, or how limited his resources. The aim was to obtain and maintain control of the air over the trenches. The balance of power shifted constantly as the technological and tactical advantage swung back and forth between the sides. The level of fighting was kept high. The RFC's main business was reconnaissance. Trenchard decided early on that the best way of defending the spotter aircraft and ensuring a steady flow of intelligence to the army was to go on the offensive, reaching over the lines into enemy air space. This was, at best, a logical response to the three-dimensional nature of aerial warfare in which there were no fixed lines to defend and to wait for the enemy to attack was to cede a moral advantage. At times, though, it could seem like an echo of the numb thinking of the terrestrial generals, who, literally stuck in the mud, threw more and more troops into futile attacks because they could think of nothing better to do.

Trenchard did not hesitate to sacrifice men to fulfil the RFC's obligations to the army and maintain the momentum of aggression. The losses among pilots during the great offensives of 1916 and 1917 came close, in proportionate terms, to matching those on the ground. During the Battle of the Somme pilots were in the air for five or six hours a day. The gaps were often filled by novices coming straight from flying school. Cecil Lewis, eighteen years old, was asked by a senior officer when he arrived at No. 1 Aircraft Depot at St Omer how many hours' flying experience he had.

> 'Fourteen hours.'
>
> 'Fourteen! It's absolutely disgraceful to send pilots overseas with so little flying. You don't stand a chance . . . Another fifty hours and you might be quite decent; but fourteen! My God, it's murder.'[4]

The aeroplanes which carried the war to the Germans became known as fighters. The machines were constantly being refined and improved. These efforts produced steady rather than startling increases in performance. The Bristol Scout, in service in 1915, had a top speed of 86.5 m.p.h. at 10,000 feet, to which level it could climb in twenty-one minutes. The Sopwith Camel, one of the most ubiquitous types in the closing stages of the war, could in ten minutes reach 10,000 feet, where it could travel at 112 m.p.h. Aircraft armaments similarly became heavier and more accurate as interrupter devices were refined to allow bullets to pass through the arc of the propeller.

Fighter pilots came to exemplify the character and spirit of the new air force, even though their role was essentially secondary. They were a godsend to propagandists charged with conjuring romance out of the horror of mechanized warfare. They operated in the clean medium of the air, detached from the vileness of the trenches. The nature of their work made it inevitable that they would be linked to an older, nobler fighting tradition. Some aviators believed this themselves, at least at the beginning. 'To be alone,' wrote Cecil Lewis, fresh from flying school, 'to have your life in your own hands, to use your own skill, single-handed against the enemy. It was like the lists in the Middle Ages, the only sphere in modern warfare where a man saw his adversary and faced him in mortal combat, the only sphere where there was still chivalry and honour.'[5]

What was true was that to be a successful fighter pilot required different qualities from those that made a good infantry officer. In the air you were on your own. The business was entirely new. There was no one to teach it, no textbooks to refer to. To survive, the pilot had to make his own decisions and develop his own tactics. The new air service attracted men who were independent-minded, adventurous, often unusual, sometimes to the point of eccentricity. Among the first to emerge on the British side was Albert Ball, in whom the values of the playing field jostled unhappily with the neurosis of the battlefield. Ball was brought up in a middle-class home in Nottingham where his father hauled himself up the class ladder, starting his working life as a plumber and ending up mayor of the city. He was educated at a local fee-paying school, founded to promote Anglican principles and a sense of patriotic duty. There were cold baths, perpetual exercise and an emphasis on technology.

Like tens of thousands of other young men, he joined up as soon as he was able, and was posted to the infantry. Frustrated at the delay in being sent to the front he took private flying lessons to improve his chances of entering the RFC. Ball fell instantly in love with flying, despite the hazards. 'It is rotten to see the smashes,' he wrote in one of his frequent letters home. 'Yesterday a ripping boy had a smash and when we got up to him he was nearly dead. He had a two-inch piece of wood right through his head and died this morning.' He added, without apparent irony, that he would be 'pleased to take you up any time you wish', if his parents felt like a flip.[6]

He arrived in France, now a lieutenant in the RFC, in time for the great Somme offensive. He flew a French Nieuport, one of the new generation of single-seater scouts. His methods marked him out immediately. He would fly straight into packs of enemy aircraft, getting in as close as he could, firing off a Lewis gun at point-blank range, breaking off an inconclusive attack only to change the ammunition drum and bore in again. It was simple, effective and desperately dangerous. He would return from sorties with his machine shredded by enemy fire.

On the ground his behaviour struck his fellow officers as odd. At his first base, Savy Aubigny aerodrome, north-west of Arras, he turned down a billet in the village, preferring first a tent, then a wooden hut he built for himself at the edge of the airfield, two miles from the squadron mess. He sent home for packets of seeds to plant marrows, lettuce, carrots, cress and flowers. He spent hours in the hangars, chatting with the riggers and fitters, making constant adjustments to his aeroplane to improve its capabilities, yet he seemed less interested in flying for its own sake than as a means of fighting. The camaraderie of the mess held little interest for him. Nor did women.

His main relaxation was the violin, which he would play after dinner while walking around a red magnesium flare. Another fellow pilot, Roderic Hill, described him sitting outside his hut, playing his gramophone and brooding. 'He had but one idea: that was to kill as many Huns as possible, and he gave effect to it with a swiftness and certainty that seemed to most of us uncanny. He nearly always went out alone; in fact he would not let anyone fly with him, and was intolerant of proffered assistance.'[7]

For all his oddness, he was respected. A young New Zealander pilot, Keith Caldwell, saw him as 'a hero . . . and he looked the part too; young, alert, ruddy complexion, dark hair and eyes. He was supposed to be a "loner", but we found him to be friendly . . . One felt that it could only be a matter of time before he "bought it", as he was shot about so often.'[8]

Looking now at the photographs of Ball, at the thick, glossy hair and the black eyes set in the taut, uncreased skin, one senses fatalism behind the easy smile. Almost from the beginning the mild bragging in the letters home is matched by disgust at what duty had led him into. By the end of August he was yearning for home. 'I do so want to leave all this beastly killing for a time,' he sighed in a letter.[9] Yet even when complaining of nerves he would still take every possible opportunity to get airborne.

In October his superiors ordered him back to England for a rest and a new posting as an instructor. He was already famous, the most successful pilot in the RFC, with an MC, DSO and bar. The prime minister, Lloyd George, invited him to breakfast. He went to Buckingham Palace, where King George V presented him with his medals.

Despite the peace and the nearness to family that he had yearned for when in France, he was restless and unhappy and soon agitating to go back. The pressure worked. In February he was posted to 56 Squadron, which was being formed as an elite unit to fly the new SE5 fighters against the best of the German air force. While waiting he fell in love, with an eighteen-year-old florist named Flora Young, who a friend had brought with him when he drove over to visit him at the base. The attraction was instantaneous. He offered to take her up in an aeroplane and she gamely accepted. That night he was writing to thank her for 'the topping day I have had with you. I am simply full of joy to have met you.'[10] On 7 April 1917 the squadron left England. Ball's tour was supposed to be for a month only. He sent daily letters to Flora detailing his successes and setting himself a target. Once he had overtaken the German champion Oswald Boelcke, he would come home.

At 5.30 p.m. on Monday, 7 May, he lead a squadron of SE5s on an offensive sweep aimed at seeking out enemy fighters, believed to be led by the German ace Manfred von Richthofen, who were operating in the Arras area.

Cecil Lewis described the chocolate-coloured fighters flying into a 'May evening . . . heavy with threatening masses of cumulus cloud, majestic skyscrapes, solid-looking as snow mountains, fraught with caves and valleys, rifts and ravines'.[11] Suddenly, high over the Cambrai–Douai road, out of these clouds came the Albatross D111 scouts they were looking for. Richthofen was not among the pilots, but his brother Lothar was. The formations rounded on each other in a confused mêlée of individual combats. Lewis described how Ball 'flew straight into the white face of an enormous cloud. I followed. But when I came out the other side, he was nowhere to be seen.' Four German officers on the ground heard aircraft engines and looked up to see Ball's machine slip out from low cloud upside down with its propeller stopped and trailing black smoke. It disappeared behind a stand of trees and crashed into a shoulder of farmland. By the time the officers reached the wreckage a young Frenchwoman had pulled the pilot clear. There were no marks on the fresh features, but Ball was dead.

Lothar von Richthofen claimed the victory, though no one on the British side believed him. The most likely explanation was that Ball became disoriented inside the cloud – a common hazard – and emerged to find he was flying upside down too low and too late to correct the error.

'The mess was very quiet that night,' Lewis wrote. They held a sing-song in a nearby barn to try and raise morale. The squadron band played and the men sang the hits of the time: 'There's a Long, Long Trail', 'Way Down upon the Swanee River', 'Pack Up Your Troubles'. Then Lewis sang the Robert Louis Stevenson 'Requiem'.

Under the wide and starry sky,
Dig the grave and let me lie.
Glad did I live and gladly die,
And I laid me down with a will.

A month after Ball's death the *London Gazette* announced the award of a posthumous VC, noting that 'in all Captain Ball has destroyed forty-three

German aeroplanes and one balloon and has always displayed most exceptional courage, determination and skill'.

A new hero was already emerging from the ranks of the RFC by the time of Ball's demise, a man of very different background and character. Edward 'Mick' Mannock had been in France for just over five weeks when Ball crashed. He knew all about him. Ball's exploits, read about in the newspapers, had been one of the reasons he had applied to transfer to the RFC from the Royal Engineers. By the time he arrived at the main depot in St Omer he was already twenty-seven, oldish to be a pilot. He had reached the air force by an erratic route. He was born on 21 May 1889 to Irish parents. His father had been a non-commissioned officer in the Second Inniskilling Dragoons, who drank, beat his wife and disappeared, leaving her with two sons and two daughters who she brought up in poverty in Canterbury. Mannock left school at fourteen to work as a clerk. His hard early life converted him to socialism and throughout his military career he enjoyed alarming conventional comrades with his views about class and privilege. He was also an Irish nationalist.

When the war came he was working as a labour supervisor in Turkey with a cable-laying company. He was interned until the Red Cross intervened, returned to England and, with his technical background, ended up in the Royal Engineers with an ambition to be a tunnelling officer. But the training bored him and he was irritated by his fellow officers and their talk of cricket, girls and dances. No one was sorry when he applied for the RFC and went off to learn to fly, managing to bluff his way through the medical despite being blind in one eye from a childhood illness.

By the summer of 1917 the brief period of air superiority the RFC had enjoyed during the Somme offensive, when it had been operating with greater numbers of aircraft and using better tactics, was over. Once again the Germans had taken the technological lead with a new breed of Albatros aircraft grouped into Jagdgeschwaders tasked with achieving control of the sky in whichever sectors commanders selected. Richthofen lead Jagdgeschwader 1. The leading pilots painted their machines in glaring colours – blood red for Richthofen – and decorated them with ancient symbols and devices, including the swastika, which had yet to lose its innocence. Some advertised their identity in huge letters on the top wing. One had inscribed underneath his name, *Kennscht mi noch?* – 'Don't you remember me?'

On 7 June Mannock was helping to escort a bombing mission over Lille when 'we met Huns. My man gave me an easy mark. I was only ten yards away from him so I couldn't miss! A beautifully coloured insect he was – red, blue, green and yellow. I let him have sixty rounds at that range, so there wasn't much left of him. I saw him go spinning and slipping down from fourteen thousand. Rough luck but it's war and they're Huns.' On 19 August he ran into one of the leading German pilots, Leutnant von Bartrap, a holder of the Iron Cross. 'He came over for one of our balloons . . . and I cut him off going back . . . The scrap took place at two thousand feet up, well within view of the whole front. And the cheers! It took me five minutes to get him to go down and I had to shoot him before he would land. I was very pleased that I did not kill him.'[12]

On other occasions he was less considerate. Caldwell remembered watching Mannock chasing a German two-seater trying to reach the safety of its own lines. 'The Hun crashed but not badly, and most people would have been content with this – but not Mick Mannock. He dived half a dozen times at the machine, spraying bullets at the pilot and observer, who were still showing signs of life . . . On being questioned as to his wild behaviour after we had landed, he heatedly replied, "the swines are better dead – no prisoners for me!" '[13]

Mannock was full of such contradictions, mixing vindictiveness with bouts of remorse. He seemed to genuinely enjoy air fighting, writing about it unabashedly as 'fun' and 'sport' in the manner of the day. But he also worried constantly that he was going to crack up. Towards the end he became convinced his death would be a fiery one. It was a common sight to see an aeroplane plunging earthwards, trailing an oily wake of smoke. Fifty-five of eighty machines shot down by Richthofen were registered as *gebrannt* (burned). On most aircraft the fuel tank was fitted in the nose, close to the engine. In the event of fire the backwash from the propeller blew the flames into the pilot seated behind. Once an aircraft was alight there was no escape. Efficient parachutes existed but pilots were not allowed to have them. The staff view was that possession of a parachute might weaken a pilot's nerve when in difficulties so that he abandoned his valuable aeroplane before he had to. Anyway, one general reasoned, aeroplanes went down so swiftly there was really no time to jump.[14]

Mannock carried a revolver in the cockpit 'to finish myself as soon as I see the first sign of flames'.[15] The sight of his victims catching fire upset him – 'a horrible sight and made me feel sick', he confided to his diary after shooting down a BFW biplane on 5 September. But he referred to the victory in the mess as 'my first flamerino'.[16] 'Flamerinoes' became an obsession. One day after shooting down his fourth German in twenty-four hours he arrived back in high spirits. 'He bounced into the mess shouting: "All tickets please! Please pass right down the car. Flamerinoes – four! Sizzle-sizzle wonk!"'[17] It seemed to be a case of making light of that which he most feared. In London on leave in June 1918 he fell sick with influenza and spent several days in bed in the RFC club, unable to sleep because of the nightmares of burning aircraft that swamped in every time he closed his eyes. He visited friends in Northamptonshire. When he talked about his experiences he subsided into tears and said he wanted to die.

He returned to France as commander of 85 Squadron. On the evening of July 25 he bumped into a friend from 74 Squadron, Lieutenant Ira Jones, who asked him how he was feeling. 'I don't feel I shall last much longer, Taffy old lad,' he replied. 'If I'm killed I shall be in good company. You watch yourself. Don't go following any Huns too low or you'll join the sizzle brigade with me.'[18]

The following day he set off at dawn with a novice pilot, Lieutenant Donald Inglis, who had yet to shoot anything down, to show him how it was done. They ran into a two-seater over the German lines. Mannock began shooting, apparently killing the observer, and left the *coup de grâce* for his pupil, who set it on fire. Instead of climbing away as his own rules demanded, Mannock turned back over the burning aircraft, flying at only

200 feet. Inglis 'saw a flame come out of the right hand side of his machine after which he apparently went down out of control. I went into a spiral down to fifty feet and saw the machine go straight into the ground and burn.'[19]

Mannock's self-prophecy had been fulfilled. The bullets that brought him down appear to have come from the ground, a danger he had constantly warned against. He was credited with destroying seventy-four German aircraft by the time he died, nearly reaching the eighty victims recorded by his German opposite number, Richthofen.

Where Mannock and Ball manifested in their own separate ways certain facets of Britishness, Manfred von Richthofen was, to the point of caricature, a paradigm of Prussian maleness. He explained himself with jovial arrogance in an autobiography, *The Red Air Fighter*, which appeared in 1917. The von Richthofens were aristocrats, though not particularly martial ones. Manfred joined the 1st Regiment of Uhlans after cadet school and was twenty-two when the war broke out. Stationed on a quiet sector of the Western Front, he got bored and applied to join the flying service. After a mere fortnight's training he was sent to Russia, flying as an observer. By March 1916 he had qualified as a pilot and began operating over Verdun before being transferred back to Russia, where, he confessed, 'It gave me tremendous pleasure bombing those fellows from above'.[20]

Richthofen impressed Boelcke, who was on a visit to the Eastern Front looking for candidates for the new Jasta fighter units, and brought him back to the West. On 17 September 1916 he claimed his first English victim, flying in 'a large machine painted in dark colours. Apparently he was no beginner, for he knew exactly that his last hour had arrived at the moment I got at the back of him.' Richthofen was 'animated by a single thought: "the man in front of me must come down whatever happens".

> At last a favourable moment arrived. My opponent had apparently lost sight of me. Instead of twisting and turning he flew straight along. In a fraction of a second I was at his back with my excellent machine. I gave a short burst with my machine-gun. I had gone so close that I was afraid

> I might dash into the Englishman. Suddenly I nearly yelled with joy, for the propeller of the enemy machine had stopped turning. Hurrah! I had shot his engine to pieces.'

He had also mortally wounded the two occupants. Richthofen 'honoured the fallen enemy by placing a stone on his beautiful grave'.[21]

So Richthofen's memoir continues, like the reminiscences of some grotesque big-game hunter, constantly noting his score, always on the lookout for opportunities to increase the bag. He was a 'sportsman' by nature rather than a 'butcher'. 'When I have shot down an Englishman, my hunting passion is satisfied for a quarter of an hour,' he wrote. 'Therefore I do not succeed in shooting two Englishmen in succession. If one of them comes down I have the feeling of complete satisfaction. Only much later have I overcome my instinct and have become a butcher.'

As a sportsman he was keen on trophies and the mess of his 'Flying Circus' was hung with the debris of his victims' aircraft. It was a habit he shared with Mannock, another inveterate crash-site scavenger. In keeping with the hunter's philosophy, he admired his prey and had strong ideas about what quarry was worthy of him. Between the 'French tricksters' and 'those daring fellows, the English', he preferred the English, though he believed that frequently what the latter took to be bravery 'can only be described as stupidity'. Richthofen, of course, subscribed to the courtly view of air fighting – 'the last vestige of knightly individual combat'. But he was sensible about how it should be practised. 'The great thing in air fighting is that the decisive factor does not lie in trick flying but solely in the personal ability and energy of the aviator. A flying man may be able to loop and do all the tricks imaginable and yet he may not succeed in shooting down a single enemy. In my opinion, the aggressive spirit is everything.'[22] It was an observation that was to prove equally valid when the two sides met again in the air twenty-three years later.

Richthofen's caution meant that in a long fighting career he sustained only one injury before the end. It came on 21 April 1918 when his red Fokker triplane crashed into a beet field at Vaux-sur-Somme. As with Mannock and Ball, the exact circumstances of his death are confused.

The credit for it was contested. Captain Roy Brown of 209 Squadron plausibly claimed to have been shooting at Richthofen when he went in. So, too, did an Australian machine-gun battery in the vicinity. The body was removed from the wreckage and taken to Poulainville airfield fifteen kilometres away. Richthofen was laid out in a hangar on a strip of corrugated metal, staring upwards, in unconscious imitation of the effigy of a medieval knight. In the night soldiers and airmen came in and rifled his pockets for souvenirs.

The notion of 'aces' placed Richthofen, Mannock, Ball and perhaps a dozen others at the pinnacle of their weird profession. Beneath them were thousands of other aviators who, though mostly anonymous, none the less regarded themselves as special. The faces that look back from the old RFC photographs are bold and open. The men have modern looks and modern smiles. Unlike the army types, whose stilted sepia portraits require an effort of imagination to bring to life, you can visualize the flesh and blood. The images pulse with confidence.

Unorthodox, even louche, though the pilots seemed to the military establishment, the ethos of the RFC was public school. Cecil Lewis, on applying to join, was interviewed by a staff officer, Lord Hugh Cecil.

> 'So you were at Oundle?'
>
> 'Yes, sir.'
>
> 'Under the great Sanderson?'
>
> 'Er – yes, sir.'
>
> 'Play any games?'
>
> 'Yes, sir. I got my school colours at fives, and I captained the house on the river . . .'
>
> 'Fives, you say? You should have a good eye, then.'

After a brief discussion as to whether his six foot three inches would be a major handicap, Lewis was in.[23]

But there were plenty of pilots who knew nothing of the school close or the college eight. James McCudden, one of the RFC's greatest pilots, started his career as a boy bugler in the Royal Engineers before transferring to the RFC as a mechanic. Once inside, though, class was always waiting to pounce. John Grider, an American serving with 85 Squadron, recounted how his fellow pilots objected to having McCudden as their commanding officer, 'because he was once a Tommy and his father was a sergeant-major in the old army. I couldn't see that that was anything against him but the English have great ideas of caste.'[24] The technical ability that flying demanded meant that the RFC could not afford to be exclusive, even though some of the attitudes struck by the pilots seemed in the spirit of a cavalry regiment of another, more raffish time.

The airmen liked alcohol and women, though there were notable exceptions. Ball was teetotal, and had no girlfriend until his meeting with Flora. Mannock drank little and seems to have shown a courtly restraint towards females. Like Ball, he was planning marriage before his death, to a Sister Flanagan who was nursing in France. For Lewis and many like him, though, the bar and the brothel provided fun and relief after the appalling strain. Their playful attitude was summed up in a 1915 drinking song, describing the finale to a day in which the squadron has only narrowly escaped a mauling by an Albatros Jasta.

> But safely at the 'drome once more, we feel quite gay and bright.
> We'll take a car to Amiens and have dinner there tonight.
> We'll swank along the boulevards and meet the girls of France.
> To hell with the Army Medical! We'll take our ruddy chance!

In the cafés of Amiens there seemed to be a large supply of young women happy to entertain Allied pilots who were undeterred by the risk of a dose of clap. Then, as later, wings on a tunic exercised a strong attraction, as Lewis discovered (describing the incident rather coyly in the third person) when he removed his greatcoat after returning with an eighteen-year-old to her room and its vast black iron-and-brass bed.

> 'Ah! Tu es pilote! Que j'aime les pilotes!'
>
> 'Yes?'
>
> 'Yais! Yais!' she imitated, deftly catching a handful of his hair and

> tugging at it. 'Tue es beau, tu sais.' She was on his knee again, and under her open blouse the hollow of her young shoulder seemed infinite in its promise.[25]

Squadrons would lay on spectacular 'drunks' at which the participants sucked on a sponge soaked in a cocktail of whisky and champagne, mixed in a bucket. It was drinking to forget. Insouciance was obligatory. Each death in Mannock's diary is recorded in the same carefully offhand way – 'poor old Shaw went West', 'We've lost poor old Davis', etc. Trenchard had a policy of 'no empty chairs at breakfast' to discourage brooding, replacing pilots instantly, often with greenhorns who were themselves propelled straight to death. During the bad times, the mess at nightfall could be a very melancholy place.

> In such an atmosphere you grew fatalistic, and as time went by and left you unscathed, like a batsman who has played himself in, you began to take liberties with the bowling, [Lewis wrote]. You took unnecessary risks, you volunteered for dangerous jobs, you provoked enemy aircraft to attack you. You were invulnerable: nothing could touch you. Then, when one of the old hands, as seemingly invulnerable as yourself, went West, you suddenly got cold feet. It wasn't possible to be sure – even of yourself. At this stage it required most courage to go on – a sort of plodding fatalism, a determination, a cold-blooded effort of will. And always alone! No friends right and left, no crowd morale.[26]

Crack-ups were routine. Pilots got to recognize the signs in each other and were sympathetic. Mannock, who was hard on anyone he suspected of hanging back, was kindly towards those he saw were reaching the end of their tether, and in contrast to the trenches a certain humanity seems to have guided posting policy so the bad cases were sent to less arduous duties.

Whatever their personal dreads, the pilots were always grateful they were not on the ground. They looked down at the 'poor little maggoty men' toiling in the churned and polluted earth below and blessed their luck. From time to time, they saw the lines at close quarters and the reality was sickeningly brought home. The 20th of July 1917 was a bad day for Mannock. Having shot down a two-seater, he went to inspect the wreckage and discovered a 'little black and tan terrier – dead – in the observer's seat. I felt exactly like a murderer. The journey to the trenches was rather nauseating – dead men's legs sticking through the sides with putties and boots still on – bits of bones and skulls with the hair peeling off, and tons of equipment and clothing lying about. This sort of thing, together with the strong graveyard stench and the dead and mangled body of the pilot (an NCO), combined to upset me for a few days.'[27]

By the last two years of the war, whatever faint notions of nobility and romance may have clung to the business of air fighting had faded. The headlong style of Ball had given way to cold stalking tactics. The general slowness of the aircraft and the narrowness of the speed margins meant that the attacker approached gradually, leaving plenty of time to reflect on what he was doing as he overhauled his prey.

The most successful pilots spent hours synchronizing their guns and sights. McCudden would seek out the sluggish two-seaters on reconnaissance and, taking great care not to be seen, approach slowly to attack from the blind spot behind the enemy plane, finishing the job with a single carefully aimed burst. 'My system was always to attack the Hun at his disadvantage if possible,' he wrote before his death in a crash.[28]

Mannock dinned into his pilots a basic rule of survival: always above; seldom on the same level; never underneath. The huge tactical advantage of invisibility, gained by having the sun at your back, was quickly understood by both sides, but all light conditions carried their advantages and disadvantages. Allied pilots would lurk in the dusk falling in the east to catch Germans on their way home.

Richthofen, despite his fantasies of knightly combat, made sure he had every advantage possible when he went out to deliver death, protected by his fellow pilots when the odds were in the German favour, allowing him to attack without fear of ambush and breaking off if he felt his opponent was getting the upper hand.

It was all a long way from Rabagliati's gentlemanly airborne duel in

August 1914. Yet when the end came the survivors felt a sort of regret at the passing of what they already saw as aerial warfare's heroic era. Cecil Lewis was in a village near Ypres when the news of the Armistice came through. 'So it was over. I confess to a feeling of anticlimax . . . when you have been living a certain kind of life for four years, living as part of a single-minded and united effort, its sudden cessation leaves your roots in the air, baffled and, for the moment, disgruntled. But the readjustment was rapid and soon we began to explore the possibilities of peace. Where should we go? What should we do?'[29]

2

Fighters *versus* Bombers

The possession of an air force the size of the RAF was an affront to the peacetime mood of economy and war-weariness. Under Trenchard it had grown huge. By the end of the war it had 30,122 officers, 263,410 men and 188 combat squadrons.[1] Shortly after the Armistice a decision was taken to prune back the service to a modest force of thirty-three squadrons. The Northcliffe press and air-power enthusiasts in Parliament denounced the myopia of the policy and warned that German quiescence was only temporary. But hardship, public disgust with war and a belief in Britain's ability to rise to the occasion in a future crisis ensured, until the rise of Hitler forced a change of mind, that a frugal attitude to air spending was maintained. In August 1925, the belief that there was no war on the horizon became official policy with the Cabinet's adoption of the 'ten-year rule', which stated that, in revising defence estimates, it should be assumed that the Empire would not be involved in a major conflict for a decade.

Trenchard was put in charge of supervising the new incarnation. He was philosophical about the new restraints. In his brisk memorandum setting out the post-war organization of the RAF he compared the force to 'the prophet Jonah's gourd. The necessities of war created it in a night, but the economies of peace have to a large extent caused it to wither in a day, and we are now faced with the necessity of replacing it with a plant of deeper root.'[2]

The RAF needed roots if it was to resist the grasping hands of the army and navy, who were once again eager now that the war was over to snatch back control of air assets so they could apply them to their own particular needs. They maintained this covetous attitude throughout the inter-war period. Trenchard fought a canny and tenacious defensive campaign. As Chief of the Air Staff, he limited himself to providing 'the vital essentials of a skeleton force while giving way on every possible detail on which he felt expense could be spared'.[3] He reined in his obstreperous nature and tried to make the best use of the tiny resources available. He needed institutions that would provide the foundations of the new force and establish it as an independent reality, and to arrange the limited manpower at his disposal in the most efficient and flexible way.

In this delicate job he had the backing of Winston Churchill, Secretary of State for War and Air, who had, predictably, been enthusiastic about flying since its inception, even trying to qualify as a pilot and almost killing himself in the process. None the less Churchill's support could be fickle and his resolve slacken when faced with the opposition of strong vested interests.

In a paper written for Churchill, Trenchard concluded that the future could be approached in two ways. The first was 'to use the air simply as a means of conveyance, captained by chauffeurs, weighted by the navy and army personnel, to carry out reconnaissance for the navy or army, drop bombs at places specified by them . . . or observe for their artillery'. The other choice was 'to really make an air service which will encourage and develop airmanship, or better still, the air spirit, like the naval spirit, and to make it a force that will profoundly alter the strategy of the future'.[4]

He argued his case for the latter in front of the prime minister, Lloyd George, and the Cabinet, who accepted, with some financial restraints, his and Churchill's main points. The proposals were set out in a 7,000-word White Paper. The document stated that 'the principle to be kept in mind in forming the framework of the Air Service is that in the future the main portion of it will consist of an Independent Force, together with

Service personnel required in carrying out Aeronautical Research'. With that established, the RAF was saved from assimilation by its hungry older rivals, though Trenchard threw them a scrap by allowing that smaller units within it would be specially trained for cooperation work with the army and navy and would probably be absorbed into their organizations in future.

Starved of money, he planned a small versatile service. Twenty squadrons were to be deployed overseas, ready to react rapidly to local unrest. Four squadrons would be held at home in reserve. All the rest of the RAF's resources would be concentrated on training officers and men to provide a pool of expertise which could be drawn on when a crisis arose. New training establishments would have to be set up. Trenchard had rejected the suggestion of the generals and admirals that the RAF should use existing army and navy facilities. The 'air spirit' could only be fostered in places the RAF could call its own.

To solve the problem posed by the youthful nature of military flying, which meant there were many junior officers and comparatively few senior ranks, he proposed a novel system. Only half the officers at any time would hold permanent commissions. Of the rest, 40 per cent would be short-service officers, serving for four or six years with another four on the reserve. The other 10 per cent would be on secondment from the army and navy.

The permanent officers were to be supplied mainly by an RAF cadet college, the air force equivalent of Sandhurst or Dartmouth, and also from the universities and the ranks. Once commissioned, they would be posted to a squadron. After five years they were required to adopt a specialization, such as navigation, engineering or wireless.

The new air force needed a steady supply of first-class mechanics, riggers and fitters. Most of the thousands of skilled tradesmen who had manned the workshops and hangars on the Western Front and at home bases during the war had returned to civilian life. Trenchard's Jesuitical solution was to recruit 'boys and train them ourselves'. They would serve three-year apprenticeships before joining the ranks. There were also plans for a staff college, at Andover, to train future commanders, and centres for research into aircraft development, armaments, wireless and aerial photography.

Cranwell, in Lincolnshire, was chosen for the cadet college. Halton Park, in Hertfordshire, was selected for the main apprentice school. Cranwell was flat, windy and had a large existing airfield. Trenchard liked the fact that it was a long way from London. He hoped that, 'marooned in the wilderness, cut off from pastimes they could not organize for themselves, they would find life cheaper, healthier and more wholesome'. This, he reckoned, would give them 'less cause to envy their contemporaries at Sandhurst or Dartmouth and acquire any kind of inferiority complex'.[5]

Halton, on the other hand, was chosen for the apprentices – 'Trenchard brats', as they became known – because of its proximity to the Smoke. Homesick adolescents would be in easier reach of their metropolitan parents and there were dance halls and cinemas nearby to keep them entertained when the working day was over.

Cranwell is scoured in the winter by freezing winds that race in from the Wash, sunny in the summer. It had been a training base for the Royal Naval Air Service. With the amalgamation of the RNAS and the RFC it had passed into RAF ownership. It opened as the Royal Air Force College in February 1920, the first military air academy in the world. The entrance examination was essentially the same as that for the Sandhurst and Woolwich army cadet colleges, testing applicants on a broad range of subjects, including English, history, languages ancient and modern and sciences – though you could be selected without tackling a science paper.

In the bleak late winter it was a dispiriting place. The first fifty-two cadets arrived, one of them wrote afterwards, to a 'scene of grey corrugated iron and large open spaces whose immensity seemed limitless in the sea of damp fog which surrounded the camp'.[6] The new boys lived in single-storey wood and iron huts, scattered on either side of the Sleaford road, linked by covered walkways to keep off the rain and snow. It was not until 1929 that money was available to start work on the main college building, which was specially designed to look old and respectable.

Despite its ramshackle origins, the college was confident from the beginning that it would be great. Writing in the first issue of the college magazine in September 1920, Churchill set the tone.

> Nothing that has ever happened in the world before has offered to man such an opportunity for individual personal prowess as the air fighting of the Great War. Fiction has never portrayed such extraordinary combats, such hairbreadth escapes, such an absolute superiority to risk, such dazzling personal triumphs . . . It is to rival, and no doubt to excel these feats of your forerunners in the Service that you are now training yourselves and I, for one, look forward with confidence to the day when you who are not at the College will make the name of the Royal Air Force feared and respected throughout the world.[7]

The RAF thought hard about the sort of boy it was looking for. In 1919 a committee chaired by Lord Hugh Cecil, the staff officer who had waved Cecil Lewis into the RFC on the basis of his fives prowess, was set up to try and define the educational and human qualities needed for the officer corps. The architects of the new service accepted, in theory at least, that it should be open to all talents. It had been clear since the end of the previous century that social exclusivity was ultimately incompatible with the technological competence modern warfare required. The first senior military figure to understand this was Admiral Fisher, who insisted all his officers had a degree of technical understanding, a move that challenged the class structure of the Navy.[8]

The Cecil Committee decided that all officers must be able to fly, though the qualification was not so rigid as to exclude good technicians who were poor aviators. It wanted boys who exhibited 'the quality of a gentleman'. It was careful, though, to emphasize that by this they meant 'not a particular degree of wealth or a particular social position but a certain character'.[9] Even so, the new cadet college must have seemed to any ambitious lower-class boy and his parents as cold and daunting as the old ones. Air Ministry officials set out to recruit people like themselves. They wrote to public-school headmasters, advertising the benefits of a service career and claiming that flying training was not the hair-raising activity it had been in the war years (though this was far from the truth and accidents at the college were frequent).[10] An Old Etonian officer was dispatched to the Alma Mater to act as a liaison officer.

Unlike the public schools, few state schools had the resources to provide coaching for the entrance exam. Fees were prohibitive. Parents were expected to pay up to £75 a year plus £35 before entry and £30 at the start of the second year towards uniform and books; this at a time when a bank manager earned £500 a year. Despite the Cecil Committee's wish that selection should be 'free of the suspicion of partiality in favour of either individuals or classes', most cadets in the interwar years were public schoolboys.

The curriculum at the beginning was a mix of academic and practical subjects interspersed with drill and PT. In the first year there was little flying, though much time was spent in the workshops and hangars. Cadets lived five to a hut until their fourth, senior, term, when they got their own cubicles. They received £2 15s. (£2.75) a week and each day was packed with activities from reveille at 6.45 a.m. to dinner in the mess. Sports were a fetish, particularly rugby, which Trenchard considered 'the best game for making an officer and a gentleman out of any material'.[11] Keenness on boxing was admired. The life was clean, spartan, boisterous. Women were nowhere to be seen, except at the end-of-course dance, and the limited delights of Sleaford, the local town, were out of bounds. Cadets were allowed motorcycles but not cars and the lanes round about buzzed with souped-up Broughs and Rudges.

Fun was bruising. First-termers were forced to sing a song for the other cadets. Failure to perform well earned a punishment called 'creeping to Jesus'. The victim was stripped almost naked, blindfolded and forced to sniff his way along a pepper trail that ended at an open window, where he was tipped outside and drenched in cold water.[12] The first commandant, Air Commodore C. A. H. Longcroft, was a hunting man and cadets were encouraged to ride to hounds, though a shortage of mounts meant beagling was more practical. The college had its own pack.

Intellectual activity was limited. There was encouragement from an early teacher, S. P. B. Mais, who left Tonbridge School to become Professor of English at Cranwell. He felt cadets should be treated as undergraduates and founded a play-reading circle and a debating society. The response was initially hesitant. The cadets had gone to Cranwell to fly. Yet at the outset, at the end of their two-year courses, this was something they were still not fully qualified to do. A shortage of aircraft and the demands of the curriculum meant graduates left without their wings, or even a high standard of airmanship. One cadet spent less than nine hours in an aeroplane in his first year, and then only as a passenger. The Avro trainers were equipped with a compass and a bubble indicator like a spirit level to show whether they were flying straight. Navigation was primitive and many flights consisted of simple hops to neighbouring airfields. Cranwell cadets were awarded their wings after leaving once they had satisfied their first squadron commanders that they could indeed fly.

But Cranwell succeeded from the start in generating an air force spirit. The cadets knew what was wanted. Aerial warfare, they understood, had created the need for a hybrid warrior who combined mastery of the latest technology with the mental bearing of a classical champion. It was a new military caste and Cranwell was its spiritual home.

The same aspiration to excellence was encouraged at Halton. Five thousand applicants responded when the scheme was announced. They were mostly boys from the lower middle and upper working classes who saw the RAF as a means of advancement and a gateway to the intoxicating world of aviation. The entrance exam tested applicants on mathematics, experimental science and English. To pass, boys were essentially expected to be up to school certificate level, a tough examination taken at sixteen that qualified the successful candidate for higher education. It was also the entry requirement for Cranwell. Many of those who sat for entrance to Halton and its sister technical schools therefore, had parents who were sufficiently comfortably off to keep them on past the normal school-leaving age of fourteen. Or sufficiently self-sacrificing. In January 1921 a photographer was present as 300 new recruits set off from a

London terminus to begin their course. The boys are cheering. Many wear shabby suits and flat prole hats that make them seem miniature versions of their fathers. The caption notes that 'the variety of class of boys was very striking, many of them having quite an imposing kit, whilst not the least pleased with the whole proceedings were those whose belongings were kept within bounds in brown paper parcels'.[13]

The high standard at entry meant that many of the mechanics servicing the aeroplanes would be educationally equal, and superior in mechanical skill, to the men flying them.[14] RAF other ranks showed less deference to their officers than was customary in the army, where most privates and NCOs came from the uneducated working class. In the RAF, the path from the Naafi to the officers' mess was wider and more frequently trodden than in any of the other services, and many a rigger and fitter ended up a pilot. The system was constructed to allow, if not exactly encourage, the process. The best three apprentices each year were offered a cadetship at Cranwell, with the expectation, frequently fulfilled, that this would lead to the highest reaches of the service. A new class of airman pilots was announced in late 1921 that offered flying training to outstanding candidates from the ranks. They served for five years before returning to their own trade, but kept their sergeant's stripes gained by being in the air. The policy meant that by the time the war started about a quarter of the pilots in RAF squadrons were NCOs – a tough, skilful difficult-to-impress élite within an élite.[15]

There were 300 places in the first intake. The regime followed the same hardworking lines as at the cadet college, with classes and workshop sessions from Monday to Friday and Wednesday afternoons off for games. Discipline was milder than in the army or navy, but firm none the less. Only over-eighteens were allowed to smoke, and then when off-base. Trenchard was as proud of Halton as he was of Cranwell. He was aware that by engineering a new class of educated other ranks, the first in British military history, he was doing something radical, almost revolutionary.

Cranwell and Halton formed the human nucleus for the new air force, but the manpower they provided fell far short of requirements. The short-service commission scheme helped reduce the deficit. It started in 1924 when the Air Ministry advertised for 400 young officers for flying duties. It wanted British-born men of pure European descent[16] who would serve up to six years and spend four more on the reserve list. Despite the lack of long-term career security, there were many takers. The universities seemed another promising recruiting ground. The idea started with RFC veterans, who went up to Cambridge after the war to study engineering, and was encouraged by Trenchard during a visit in 1925. It spread to Oxford, and later to London.

Trenchard had raised the notion of a territorial air force of weekend fliers in his 1919 proposals. Churchill rejected it. It won the backing of the subsequent air minister Sir Samuel Hoare. A bill to set up an Auxiliary Air Force (AAF) was brought in by the short-lived Labour-led government which came to power in January 1924. The first four squadrons were formed in October 1925: No. 600 (City of London), No. 601 (County of London), No. 602 (City of Glasgow) and No. 603 (City of Edinburgh). The pilots were amateurs who flew in their own time on aeroplanes supplied and maintained by the RAF, and the units were intended to have a strong local character. Trenchard considered they would be a success 'if it was looked upon as as much of an honour to belong to one . . . as it is to belong to a good club or a good university'.[17]

This suggested a degree of social exclusivity. There was a strong snobbish tinge to some of the first formations. Flying had always been fashionable and rich amateur airmen were numerous. The Auxiliary Air Force provided an opportunity for some of them to band together in a patriotic cause, with friends from club, links and office. No. 601 Squadron was, according to its own legend, founded in White's, the grandest address in Clubland, on the initiative of the son of the first duke of Westminster. Lord Edward Grosvenor, after Eton and a spell in the French Foreign Legion, had served as a pilot in the RNAS in the First World War. Like several forward-looking grandees he believed air power would decide future conflicts. Auxiliary squadrons, he felt, would allow men to go to war surrounded by comrades with whom they shared ties of place and friendship. Seriousness of purpose was overlaid with thick layers of upper-class fun. He recruited from his own circle. The squadron historian noted that he 'chose his officers from among gentlemen of sufficient presence not to be overawed by him, and sufficient means not to be excluded from his favourite pastimes – eating, drinking and White's'.[18] Candidates were invited to his home in Eaton Square and sluiced large glasses of port. If they passed muster it was on to the club bar for gin and tonics. The squadron's town headquarters were at 54 Kensington Park Road, in Notting Hill. They were furnished and equipped to cavalry regiment standards with silver, military prints on the walls, costly vintages and rich food. The gatherings echoed to the sound of broken glass. After dinner it was customary for diners to try and circumnavigate the room without touching the floor. Another game involved persuading some visiting dupe to 'calibrate the table'. One of the company would lie on his back with his legs hanging over the edge of a large oval table while other squadron members tilted it back and made a show of measuring the angle between wood and limb. Then it was the victim's turn. Once he was helpless, his ankles were grabbed, the table was tipped back and tankards of beer poured down his trouser legs.

Members held an annual training camp at Port Lympne on the Kent coast. It was the summer home of their patron, Sir Philip Sassoon, who combined a wild enthusiasm for flying with almost total ineptitude as a pilot. Squadron pride was nourished by manufactured rivalries with other Auxiliary Air Force units, japes designed to annoy the regular RAF, and self-conscious displays of individualism such as the wearing of bright red socks with uniform.

The snobbery was in keeping with the times and provoked indulgent smiles. But this was not what Trenchard had had in mind. At Cambridge he had emphasized that in the AAF and university squadrons, there was room for everyone: 'the man of initiative and the man of action, the methodical man and even the crank. We open our ranks widely to all.'

Despite the gilded image, not all the auxiliary pilots were rich. Applicants to the AAF needed to be able to fly solo and hold an A licence and courses cost £100. It was a considerable investment. The Air Ministry recognized the reality, refunding tuition costs once a trainee had qualified. Altogether there were to be twenty-one auxiliary squadrons drawn from all over the country. From 1934 they were equipped with fighters instead of bombers. When the war came they made up a quarter of Fighter Command's front-line strength.

Trenchard retired at the end of 1929. His energy and advocacy had ensured the survival and growth of the RAF, albeit slowly and painfully. The RAF was undernourished. From 1921 to 1930 the annual expenditure estimates hovered between £19 million and £18 million. In 1923 the government had promised to build a metropolitan air force of fifty-two squadrons for home defence. Six years later, there were only twenty-five home-based regular squadrons in service, augmented by eleven auxiliary and reserve units, and no official hurry to make up the shortfall.

But the service had an existence and an identity. It had a sky-blue ensign, adorned with one of the red, white and blue roundels the First World War pilots had had painted on their aircraft to shield them from 'friendly fire'. It had its own slate-blue uniform and forage cap. It had a good motto – *Per Ardua ad Astra*. A system of squadron organization, evolved in the battlefields of France, had been established and an independent rank structure, painfully worked out in face of mockery from the army chiefs, that climbed from aircraftman to Marshal of the Royal Air Force. There was an apprentice school to ensure a steady flow of skilled technicians to maintain the aeroplanes and a cadet school and a short-service commission scheme to provide pilots and commanders.

Great energy and thought had gone into the work of creating the new service, comparatively little on defining its purpose. The RAF had men, machines, organization and identity. What it did not have as yet was a clear idea of its purpose. A post-war Marshal of the Royal Air Force Sir John Slessor once wrote that 'before 1939 we really knew nothing about air warfare'. It was a frank admission, but Slessor was in a position to know. Twenty years earlier, in May 1937, he had been promoted to the post of deputy director of plans at the Air Ministry and was appalled to discover how unfitted the RAF was to defend Britain.[19]

The state of the air force during most of the inter-war period was a reflection of a general unwillingness, found in every corner of society, to contemplate another bloodbath. Preparing for war seemed more likely to encourage than prevent it. There were clear political, economic and psychological reasons for Britain's reluctance to rearm. The aversion to doing so was reinforced by confusion as to what weapons were required. Everyone agreed that air power would be crucial. No one knew exactly why or how. If there was a consensus it centred on the belief that bombers and bombing would play a predominant role. Something of the effects of aerial bombardment was already known, from the British and German experiences in the First World War and from small wars that had flared up around the world subsequently. Many military and political analysts believed that hostilities would begin in the air and the results, particularly for civilians, would be horrible.

German Zeppelin airships, then Gotha and Giant bombers, had provided a glimpse of what could be expected, from their intermittent and haphazard bombing campaign on British cities and coastal towns that began in January 1915. Altogether, in 103 raids they killed 1,413 people, all but 296 of them civilians. They wounded between 3,400 and 3,900, the vast majority of them non-combatants.

What impressed was not the quantity of the violence but the quality. In one raid carried out in daylight on 13 June 1917, fourteen Gothas, each loaded with a 500-kilogram bomb, reached the centre of London. One bomb struck a school in Poplar, killing 18 children and maiming 27. Zeppelins excited particular terror. Their destruction provoked un-British displays of glee, with crowds clapping, singing and cheering in the streets as the airships sank to earth with their sixty-strong crews roasting in the flames.

Henceforth, civilians could expect to be in the front line and neither military nor political thinking placed much faith in their ability to endure the experience. As the overture wars of the 1930s established the themes of the great symphony of violence to come, it appeared more and more certain that civilian morale would be unable to withstand the coming ordeal. As early as 1925, the Air Staff were predicting casualties of 1,700 dead and 3,300 injured in London alone in the first twenty-four hours of hostilities, resulting in 'the *moral* [original italics] collapse of the personnel employed in the working of the vital public services'.[20] The Japanese bombing of Shanghai in 1932, the German Condor Legion's destruction of Guernica in April 1937, the Italian bombardment of Barcelona, all reinforced notions of aerial warfare's crucial, possibly decisive, importance.

There were two obvious approaches to countering the danger. One was to improve Britain's defences to a point where the enemy – always Germany, apart from a brief, fantastical moment in 1922 when France was identified as the threat – would be deterred from launching an attack or would suffer severely if it did. Proponents of this view believed that the war had shown that fighters mustered to defend British airspace were, after a slow start, competent to handle raiding airships and bombers. At the same time, the experience had accelerated the development of effective anti-aircraft gunnery and searchlights. The second approach was to concentrate on building up a strong offensive bomber force. That, too, would have a deterrent effect. But if deterrence failed, it left Britain with the means of striking back.

It was the second view that took hold, both in air force and political thinking, although never to the point where alternative reasoning was suppressed. The strategic debate of the inter-war years was dominated by two phrases. They were slogans rather than expressions of profound thought. One was the idea of the 'knock-out blow', which could bring victory in a single action. The other was the conviction that 'the bomber will always get through' – a phrase popularized by Baldwin in November 1932 in a Commons speech which sent a spasm of foreboding through the country. What that meant, he continued brutally, was that 'the only defence is offence . . . you have to kill more women and children more quickly than the enemy if you want to save yourselves'.[21]

The logic of this bleak conviction was that fighters would have only a secondary role to play. Despite the prevalence of these views, successive governments proved reluctant to invest in building up a bombing force that could both 'get through' and strike the 'knock-out blow'. Money was one problem. But the understandable miserliness of politicians trying to manage a vulnerable economy in shaky times was informed by less easily identifiable and more complex motives. Many of the public figures of the 1920s and 1930s had served in the war and knew its horrors at first hand. They shared the ordinary citizen's dread of a recurrence, and shrank away from consideration of the unpopular positions that a reasoned rearmament policy would have required.

The conduct of Britain's defence in the years from 1918 to 1936 looks now to have been extraordinarily negligent and foolhardy. It seemed so to some at the time. But among the victor nations the impulse was to seek idealistic alternatives, exemplified by the great disarmament conference of 1932–4 and the foundation of the League of Nations. Until the threat from Germany was naked and unmistakable, the RAF would lack the sort of carefully planned, sensibly timed and realistically funded programme it needed to develop properly. Progress was jerky and reactive and frequently triggered by panic. The original plan to create fifty-two squadrons for home defence was provoked by alarm at the news that France had an air fleet of 300 bombers and 300 fighters. When that chimerical threat evaporated, so, too, did the will to pursue the scheme.

The arrival of Hitler in 1933, and Germany's withdrawal from the League of Nations and the disarmament conference, produced another spurt of activity, resulting in what was known as expansion scheme A. It was officially announced in July 1934, the first of thirteen such schemes that appeared over the next four years, most of which never got beyond the proposal stage, as Britain tried to achieve some sort of rough parity with Germany. Scheme A was an interim measure designed to signal to Hitler that Britain was prepared to take to the starting blocks in an aerial arms race. It also created a structure to provide training, and the basis for a more ambitious expansion should the message be ignored. The planned level of home squadrons was increased from the original fifty-two to sixty-four. Scheme A also increased the proportion of fighter squadrons. There were to be twenty-five now, against thirty-nine bomber units compared to seventeen and thirty-five in the 1923 plan.

The shift was a political rather than an air force initiative. It was opposed by the Chief of the Air Staff, Sir Edward Ellington, who stuck to the view that a big bomber fleet was central to Britain's security. The well-publicized fact that the increased range of German bombers meant they could now reach well into the industrial north-east of Britain and the Midlands undermined this approach.

The argument that there was no real defence against bombers was being invisibly eroded anyway. Out of sight and far away from the committee rooms where military planners and government ministers and officials met, scientists and engineers worked with RAF officers to develop technologies that would greatly increase the vulnerability of attacking air forces. In the search for scientific means of combating attacking aircraft, attention had been given to a 'death ray' which would neutralize the ignition systems of aircraft, causing them to drop from the sky. Research under the direction of R. A. Watson-Watt, superintendent of the Radio Department at the National Physics Laboratory, suggested the scheme was impractical. However, the experiments confirmed the fact that aircraft interfered with radio waves and radiated a signal back. This suggested the possibility of a detection system that could reveal their position, height and direction. The huge importance of the discovery was recognized immediately and from February 1935 there was strong official backing for the development of what became known as radar.

The RAF's own thinking had been that if enemy aircraft were to fly at more than 200 m.p.h. at over 10,000 feet, and no warning was given of their approach before they reached the coast, it would be impossible to get aircraft airborne in time to prevent them from bombing London. Now radar could provide that warning, a development which, as one historian of the RAF observed, 'indicated the obsolescence of the RAF's whole existing theory of war'.[22] None the less the belief that bombers provided the best security would persist until the end of 1937. The change was led by government figures who were persuaded that there was no longer any hope of equalling the numerical strength of the Luftwaffe before war broke out.

Radar complemented important breakthroughs that were being made in aircraft design. The development of military aviation in Britain had been haphazard. The Air Ministry had no designers of its own and relied on private firms to answer specifications for new types. Perennial money problems made it difficult to establish long-term relationships with private manufacturers, hindering the development of an efficient system of procurement, research and development such as existed in Germany.

There were delays of up to six years between the issue of a specification, acceptance of a design, manufacture and entry into service. The progress of the Hurricane and the Spitfire from drawing board to the skies was quicker, but far from smooth. By the end of the 1920s it was obvious the biplane era was over. The most powerful machine in the RAF's hands, the Hawker Fury, could only manage 250 m.p.h. The 1929 Schneider Cup, a competition of speed and endurance between seaplanes, was won by the Southampton firm of Supermarine with an S6, a monoplane with a streamlined fuselage and metal wings, flying at an average of 328.63 m.p.h. In 1930 the Air Ministry issued specification F.7/30 for a new high-speed fighter, opening the competition to single wing designs. Monoplanes had been around from almost the beginning of aviation but were inferior in terms of manoeuvrability to biplanes, whose twin surfaces provided considerably more lift. Streamlining, metal airframes and new engines powerful enough to keep them airborne removed this restriction and delivered the future to the monoplane.

In August 1933 Sydney Camm, chief designer at Hawker Aircraft Limited, presented two designs to the Air Ministry for a biplane and a monoplane. Both were rejected as too orthodox – evidence of the presence of some radical and imaginative minds at important decision-making levels inside the air establishment. The board of Hawker decided to continue development anyway. When the Air Ministry issued a new specification the following year, Camm's design was close to their requirements, and a prototype, K5083, was ordered. The RAF wanted a fighter capable of 300 m.p.h. which could fly as high as 33,000 feet. To meet these demands the aircraft needed to be streamlined with an enclosed cockpit and a retractable undercarriage. It also had to be capable of bearing a battery of machine guns. Ballistics experts calculated that at the new high speeds an intercepting fighter would have only two seconds to shoot down an incoming bomber. Eight machine guns, each firing 1,000 rounds a minute, were needed to provide the required weight of fire.

The novelty of the project and the high demands of the specification meant that fundamental problems of physics, engineering and design arose at every stage. The crucial question of power had been answered by the appearance of the Rolls-Royce PV twelve-piston engine, later known as the Merlin. It developed 1,030 horsepower, more than twice that of the best engine of the First World War. The thrust it delivered made speeds of 330 to 340 m.p.h. possible – more than enough to satisfy the RAF's demands.

Camm's original design had been called the Fury monoplane, a name that conceded the fact that even after 4,000 blueprints the aircraft was only half-way evolved from its biplane origins. The frame was of metal tubes and wooden formers and stringers. The skin was fabric, heavily painted with dope to reduce drag, and stressed-metal wings were only added fairly late in the development. The outlines of the old Fury were certainly discernible in its profile. But it was definitely something else. They called it a Hurricane. It was not a new name, having belonged to a short-lived aircraft of the 1920s. But it conveyed a note of confidence and aggression that was infinitely more reassuring than the placid Harts, Flycatchers and Grebes of the previous generation.

The Hurricane made its first flight on 6 November 1935 at Brooklands in Surrey. Hawker's chief test pilot, George Bulman, a small, bald, ginger-moustached extrovert who had flown with the RFC in the war, was in the cockpit. The prototype had been developed in great secrecy. When the tarpaulins were stripped away and the hangar doors opened, there were murmurs of surprise. It was painted silver, which emphasized the sleekness of its low, humped lines and the sculptured way the rounded wings fitted beautifully flush to the fuselage below the neat, narrow cockpit. It was big, bigger than any existing fighter, and at more than 6,000 pounds very heavy. It seemed unlikely that a single engine could get it off the ground. Bulman, in overalls and flying helmet, approached the machine and vaulted into the cockpit watched by Camm and other Hawker executives, who stood at the edge of the damp field, smoking nervously. The Hurricane bumped away into the distance then turned into the wind. The rumble of the Rolls-Royce engine deepened into a roar. The machine moved forward, gathering speed, but slowly, so that some thought Bulman would not get airborne before he ran out of field. At the last moment the Hurricane left earth in an abrupt bounding movement and climbed steeply. The spectators watched the undercarriage retract and the muscular shape dwindle into the distance until it disappeared and the sound of the engine faded. Half an hour later the reassuring drone was heard again. Bulman performed a perfect three-point landing and taxied over to where Camm was waiting to report the flight had been 'a piece of cake'.[23]

The Spitfire, the first prototype of which flew in March 1936, was a more modern design, all metal with a monocoque fuselage and thin, elliptical wings, the more sophisticated offspring of the Supermarine C6. It had the same Merlin engine as the Hurricane and carried the same guns, but at 5,180 pounds it weighed 1,000 pounds less and went 30 m.p.h. faster. The name was proposed by the chairman of Vickers, Sir Robert McLean, whose company had taken over Supermarine. R. G. Mitchell, whose designs carried the machine through its various evolutions to become the most beautiful and efficient fighter of its era, was not impressed. 'Just the sort of bloody silly name they would choose,' he is reported to have said on hearing the decision.[24] But in the propaganda film of his life *The First of the Few*, which appeared in 1942, he is portrayed as devising the name himself: 'A curious sort of bird . . . a bird that spits out death and destruction . . . a Spitfire bird.'

The orders came quickly, with the Air Ministry ordering 600 Hurricanes and 310 Spitfires in the summer of 1936. The accelerated pace reflected alarm that the next war might come sooner than expected. Preparations at every level speeded up as successive intelligence reports, and the Germans' own boasts, suggested that Britain's reluctant rearmament programme was insufficient either to deter or defend.

The sense of urgency, and the rapid twists and turns of circumstance, were evident in the brevity of the shelf-lives of the schemes that succeeded Scheme A, as both government and the Air Ministry tinkered with the plan to take account of a situation that always seemed to be changing for the worst. Only one scheme, Scheme F, approved by the cabinet in February 1936, was implemented as planned, coming to fruition in March 1939.

But the expansion was real. From 1935 forty-five new air stations were ordered to be built, most of which were finished by the time war came. Scheme C, which was approved in May 1935, envisaged 123 home squadrons as opposed to the 76 designated in Scheme A. That meant recruiting 1,500 pilots in the next two years. Altogether the RAF was to increase fivefold between 1934, when there were 31,000 officers and men, and the outbreak of war, when the service had an actual strength of 118,000 backed by about 45,000 reserves.

The Air Minister, Lord Swinton, inherited Trenchard's system of short-service officers, who since the early 1920s had supplemented and outnumbered the cadre of permanent RAF officers. He intensified links with public schools, attracting 1,700 entrants. A further 800 pilots were found among RAF non-commissioned officers. Australia, Canada, New Zealand and South Africa were all asked to contribute men. The number of auxiliary squadrons increased from eight to twenty in the run-up to the war. But more radical measures were needed to satisfy the new demand and, equally important, to provide a reserve.

A pool of pilots would be essential to replace the dead and wounded once the fighting started. The Director of Training at the Air Ministry, Air Commodore A. W. Tedder, a Trenchard protégé who had inherited some of his briskness of thinking, conceived the idea of a 'Citizen Air Force'. It was to be democratic in character, and linked to a locality, but to the factories, offices and avenues and crescents of semi-detached homes in the new estates springing up around towns rather than to the shires to which the army's territorial units attached themselves. The Air Ministry added that the new force should be 'open . . . to the whole middle class in the widest sense of that term, namely the complete range of the output of the public and secondary schools'. Given its nature it was felt 'inappropriate to grade the members on entry in as officers or airmen according to their social class'. Everyone therefore started out the same, as airmen under training, with commissions being awarded later on ability and leadership qualities.[25] The Royal Air Force Volunteer Reserve, as it was christened, started in August 1936. It gave young men of between eighteen and twenty-five the chance to learn to fly, at no cost, in their spare time. They received £25 per annum and were expected to attend an annual fifteen-day flying course at one of the training centres set up around the country. The aim had been to take on 800 a year over three years, but the potential number of recruits was much greater and by the spring of 1939 there were 2,500 RAFVR pilots in training. When war broke out, 310 had already entered Fighter Command.

The second half of the 1930s saw the RAF transformed from a small, professional élite into a mass force with the potential to fight a major war. The question of how it would go about doing that was not finally resolved until the end of 1938, when the great strategic conundrum of bombers or fighters, offence or defence, was settled, at least for the first stage of the coming war. In December that year the balance shifted decisively in favour of fighters and 'close defence'. The change was initiated not by the air force itself but by the government. Despite radar and the advent of the Hurricane and Spitfire, the Air Ministry pressed for parity with the German bomber force. But the government decided this was no longer possible within the time available. The goal had always been unrealistic. Britain was a democracy, reacting wearily to the threat of a war it had no wish to fight. Rearmament had been late and grudgingly paid for, with the aircraft factories still operating at peacetime levels of production. Germany was a dictatorship, heading at full speed and with no concern for cost towards a conflict of its own making. Britain was not going to catch up before the war was launched. It was the minister in charge of defence coordination, Sir Thomas Inskip, who forced the air force to accept the change in strategic thinking. In a memo to Swinton of 7 December he stated the new thinking crisply:

> I cannot take the view that our Air Force must necessarily correspond in numbers and types of aircraft with the German Air Force. I cannot, therefore, persuade myself that the dictum of the Chief of the Air Staff

> that we must give the enemy as much as he gives us is a sound principle. I do not think it is the proper measure of our strength. The German Air Force . . . must be designed to deliver a knock-out blow within a few weeks of the outbreak of war. The role of our Air Force is not an early knock-out blow – no one has suggested that we can accomplish that – but to prevent the Germans from knocking us out.[26]

The inference was clear. For the time being at least the emphasis would be on defence and making any German attack on Britain too painful to sustain. Despite the strenuous opposition of the Air Ministry and RAF senior staff, the Cabinet backed Inskip's view. The next years would belong to the fighters, and those who flew them.

3

'Free of Boundaries, Free of Gravity, Free of Ties'

The great RAF expansion gave thousands of young men the chance to realize an ambition that had seemed remote and probably unattainable when they first conceived it. That flying was possible was still a relatively novel idea. For most people in the world the thought that they would ever actually do so themselves was fantastical. The banality of aviation has hardened our imaginations to the fascination it excited in the years between the wars. Once, in Uganda in the 1980s, I was at a remote airstrip when a relief plane took some adolescent boys for a joyride. It was the first time they had been in an aeroplane. When they landed their friends ran out to examine them, as if they expected them to have been physically transformed by the experience.

So it was, or nearly so, in the inter-war years. 'Ever been up?' people would ask each other at the air displays that attracted hundreds of thousands in Britain in the 1920s and 1930s. Those who could say 'yes' were admired for their daring, their worldliness, their modernity. The men and women who flew the beautiful treacherous machines were exalted and exotic. In the eyes of many, their courage and skill put them at the apex of human evolution.

Aviators were as popular as film stars. Record-breaking feats of speed, distance and endurance filled the papers. Men were the most avid readers of these stories, young men and boys. Almost every pilot who fought in

Fighter Command in 1940 fell for flying early. Their interest flared with the intensity of a great romance. For some, the first magical taste came with a ten-minute flip in the rear cockpit of one of the rickety machines of the flying circuses that hopped around the country, setting up on racecourses or dropping in at resort towns. The most famous was led by Alan Cobham, a breezy entrepreneur who was knighted for pioneering flights across Asia. Billy Drake was sixteen years old, on holiday from his boarding school in Switzerland, when the circus arrived to put on a display close by his father's golf club near Stroud. It was half a crown to go up. Drake was already intoxicated with aviation, but his parents tried to dissuade him, partly because flying seemed a dead end for a middle-class boy, but also because they feared for his safety. The brief hop over the Gloucestershire fields was enough to set the course of his early life. 'When I got down,' he remembered many years later, 'I knew that this was it.'[1]

Pete Brothers watched aeroplanes in the skies around his home in Lancashire, where his family owned a firm supplying chemicals to the food and pharmaceutical industries. In his spare time he made model aeroplanes. His family were wary of his enthusiasm. In 1936, on his sixteenth birthday, he was given flying lessons at the Lancashire Aero Club in the hope that the draughty, dangerous reality of flying would cool his ardour. 'My father said, "You'll get bored with it, settle down and come into the family business." But I didn't. I went off and joined the air force.' He took his father flying and he, too, became 'flat-out keen'.[2]

Sometimes, unwittingly, parents planted the germ themselves. Dennis David was seven years old and on holiday in Margate when, 'as a special treat, my mother and I went up in an Avro 504 of the Cornwall Aviation Company. Though I was surprised by the din, this . . . sowed a seed inside me.'[3]

Just the sight of an aeroplane could be enough to ignite the passion. James Sanders got up at five one morning, in July 1933, at the villa in Genoa where his wealthy archaeologist father had moved the family, to watch a formation of twenty-four Savoia Marchetti seaplanes, led by Italo Balbo, the head of the Italian air force, heading west on a propaganda visit to the United States, and felt two certainties. 'There was going to be a war, there was no question about it, and I was going to be in the air force.'[4]

Throughout the inter-war years, all around the country, many a flat, boring pasture was transformed into an airfield and became an enchanted domain for the surrounding schoolboys. On summer evenings Roland Beamont would cycle from his prep school in Chichester to the RAF station at Tangmere, climb on to his bicycle to see over the hedge and watch 11 Squadron and 43 Squadron taking off and landing in their Hawker Furies. From the age of seven, when he had been taken up by a barnstorming pilot, he had been entranced with flying. Watching the silver-painted biplanes, the sleekest and fastest in the air force, he decided he 'wanted more than anything else to be on fighters'.[5] Twelve years later he was in the middle of the Battle of Britain, flying Hurricanes from the same aerodrome.

First encounters with aeroplanes and airmen sometimes had the quality of a dream. Bob Doe, a shy schoolboy, was walking home after classes to his parents' cottage in rural Surrey when 'an RAF biplane fighter . . . force-landed in a field close to the road. I was able to walk around it, touch it and feel what was to me [the] beginning of the mystery of aviation.'[6] Thousands of miles away on the other side of the world, near the town of Westport in the Southern Alps of New Zealand, a small, restless boy called Alan Deere had experienced the same revelation. While playing near his father's farm he heard the note of an engine in the sky, looked up and saw a tiny silver machine. He had heard of aeroplanes but never seen one. 'The fact that one was now overhead seemed unbelievable. Where did it come from? Who was the pilot? Where was it going to land?' After the aircraft put down on a beach, he and his friends stood 'for long hours . . . and gazed in silent wonder at the aeroplane until eventually our persistence was rewarded by an invitation to look into the cockpit. There within easy reach was the "joystick" . . . the very sound of the word conjuring up dreams of looping and rolling in the blue heavens.' As he studied the instruments 'there gradually grew within me a resolve that one day I would fly a machine like this and perhaps land on this very beach to the envy and delight of my boyhood friends.'[7]

Almost all of these recorded episodes feel like encounters with fate. Brian Kingcome was making his languid progress through another term at yet another boarding school when, one sunny afternoon, 'there came the drone of an aero-engine overhead – not a common sound in the mid 1930s – and a small aircraft circled the school a couple of times at roof-top height. The whole school rushed out to watch spellbound as the tiny machine throttled back and, in that lovely, burbling, swooshing silence that follows the throttling back of an old fashioned aero-engine, glided in to land in the park in front of the house.' The pilot who emerged, nonchalant and romantic in flying helmet and silk scarf, was a young man, four years Kingcome's senior, whom he had known at one of the several previous schools his mother's whims had directed him to.

> 'Is there a Brian Kingcome here?' he asked. 'Have I come to the right place?'
>
> He had, and there was. My stock soared . . . Basking in the gaze of many envious eyes, I climbed aboard and a moment later found myself for the first time in a world I had never dreamed could exist – a world free from the drag of earth's umbilical cord, free to climb, swoop and dive, free of boundaries, free of gravity, free of ties, free to do anything except stand still.[8]

Whatever their differences of background, all these boys were children of their time. Their enthusiasms were stoked by what they read in the illustrated papers, aimed at the youth market, that sold in millions. These, just as others would do a generation later, leant heavily on the preceding war for their material, and particularly on the doings of the heroes who had emerged from the RFC. The anonymous editors of the comics of the era, with their almost infallible comprehension of the young male psyche, recognized at once the charge that old-fashioned swashbuckling married to modern technology would carry. The example of the first fighter aces fixed itself in the imaginations of a generation being born just as they had met their deaths. Even at nineteen the thoughts of Geoffrey Page as he left his public school to go up to study engineering at London University 'were boyishly clear and simple. All I wanted was to be a fighter pilot like my hero, Captain Albert Ball. I knew practically all there was to know about Albert Ball; how he flew, how he fought, how he won his Victoria Cross, how he died. I also thought I knew about war in the air. I imagined it to be Arthurian – about chivalry . . . death and injury had no part in it.'[9]

Yet the most popular chronicles of the air war were remarkably frank about what was entailed. The deterrent effect appears to have been minimal. Perhaps Fighter Command's single most effective recruiting sergeant was Captain James Bigglesworth, created by W. E. Johns, who had flown with the RFC in the First World War and whose stories began to appear in *Popular Flying* magazine in 1932. The first novel, *The Camels Are Coming*, was published the same year. Biggles seems unattractive now; cold, driven by suppressed anger, a spoilsport and a bit of a bully. He was a devastatingly romantic figure to the twelve- and thirteen-year-olds who went on to emulate him a few years later. Johns introduced them to a

> slight fair-haired, good-looking lad still in his teens but [already] an acting flight commander . . . his deep-set eyes were never still and held a glint of yellow fire that somehow seemed out of place in a pale face upon which the strain of war, and sight of sudden death, had already graven little lines . . . He had killed six men during the past month – or was it a year? – he had forgotten. Time had become curiously telescoped lately. What did it matter, anyway? He knew he had to die some time and had long ago ceased to worry about it.

Many of the stories were based on real events, some relating to Mannock, who appears disguised as 'Mahoney'. Johns made no attempt to hide the grisliness of the business, emphasizing the man-to-man nature of primitive air fighting. In one story he repeats with approval von Richthofen's maxim that 'when attacking two-seaters, kill the gunner first', and goes on to describe his hero doing just that. 'Pieces flew off the green fuselage, and as he twisted upwards into a half roll Biggles noticed that the enemy gunner was no longer standing up. "That's one of them!" he thought coolly. "I've given them a bit out of their own copy-book." '[10] In another, Biggles notes an 'Albatros, wrapped in a sheet of flame . . . the doomed pilot leaping into space even as he passed'.[11]

It is not only Germans who die. Getting killed is presented as almost inevitable. An important and enduring message, one the young readers took to heart, was that there was no point dwelling on it. 'One of the most characteristic features of the Great War,' Johns wrote in the Foreword to *Biggles in France*, 'was the manner in which humour and tragedy so often went hand in hand. At noon a practical joke might set the officers' mess rocking with mirth. By sunset, or perhaps within the hour, the perpetrator of it would be gone for ever, fallen to an unmarked grave in the shellholes of No Mans Land.'[12]

The Biggles stories are practically documentary in their starkness, as good a guide to the air war over the trenches as the non-fictional memoirs. Their audiences were absorbed and inspired by them. They changed lives. Reading them reinforced Pete Brothers's decision to seek a short-service commission in the RAF. He found them 'beautiful stories that enthralled me and excited me and made me want to emulate them'. At the Lancashire Aeroclub before taking up a short-service commission in January 1936, he had been pleased to find his instructor had been a Sopwith Camel pilot in the war.[13]

Cinematic portrayals of the air were equally frank. The most successful was *Dawn Patrol*, starring Errol Flynn, David Niven and Basil Rathbone, which came out in 1938. The 59th Squadron is based on a sticky sector of the Western Front. Sixteen men have gone in a fortnight. Replacements arrive, fresh from a few weeks at flying school. Orders to send them up against hardened Germans come by telephone from senior officers, comfortably quartered miles behind the lines. New names are chalked up on the duty blackboard to be wiped off within an hour. Kitbags are returned home without ever being unpacked. The *Daily Express* praised the film's 'lack of false sentiment or mock heroics' and called it 'one of the best and bitterest melodramas about men and planes'. It was a box-office hit and was seen, often several times, by hundreds of the pilots who fought in 1940. No one was put off. It was the glamour, camaraderie and romance of flying that pulled them back to the local fleapits, not the message of waste and futility. By this time every young man in Britain was facing a prospect of early extinction. Dying in the air might be awful, but it was better than dying on the ground.

With the expansion programme, thousands of young men were now being given a choice in how they would fight the next war. Before it began, the RAF recruited annually about 300 pilots and 1,600 airmen. Between 1935 and 1938 the average RAF intake was 4,500 and 40,000 airmen and apprentices. Air Ministry officials appealed directly to schools for recruits and advertised in the flying magazines and popular newspapers the young men they were looking for might be expected to read. One that appeared on the front page of the *Daily Express*, adorned by a drawing of three Hurricanes, promised 'the life is one that will appeal to all men who wish to adopt an interesting and progressive career . . . leave is on a generous scale . . . applicants must be physically fit and single but no previous flying experience is necessary'. Pay, in cash and kind, was set at between £340 and £520 a year. A £300 gratuity was payable after four years' service, or £500 after six years. Age limits were set between seventeen and a half and twenty-eight. The educational qualification was school certificate standards, although 'an actual certificate is not necessary'.

Pat Hancock, a mechanically minded eighteen-year-old from Croydon, was at Wimbledon Technical College when he saw an advertisement in the *Daily Express*. 'The ministry – bless it – was offering commissions to suitable young gentlemen – four years, and at the end if you survived you got a magnificent lump sum of £300, which was really a lot in those days. I pounced on it and sweet talked my father and mother into allowing me to apply.'[14]

Parental permission was needed if the applicant was under twenty-one, and many pilots seem to have faced, at first at least, family opposition. Flying was undeniably dangerous. In an era when men chose a profession, trade or occupation and tended to stick with it for the rest of their working life, it offered a very uncertain career. Despite popular enthusiasm, commercial aviation had been slow to expand. Air travel was confined to the rich. RFC pilots who hoped to make their livings flying in peacetime were mostly disappointed. Arguments were needed to overcome the objections. Billy Drake misunderstood the terms and thought the RAF would pay him an annuity of £300, a detail which persuaded his parents to grant their approval.

Geoffrey Page's distant and authoritarian father summoned him to his London club when he heard of his plans to apply for Cranwell. Flying was the family business. Page's uncle ran Handley Page, a leading British aircraft manufacturer. Over tea his father told him he had 'spoken to your uncle at length about your desire to be a pilot and he has advised me strongly against it. Pilots, he tells me, are two a penny. Hundreds are chasing a handful of jobs.' He refused to pay for the 'stupidity' of pursuing an RAF career. Page's mother pleaded with him not to take up flying. Page rarely saw his father and resented the intervention strongly. Later he decided it had been motivated by concern. His father had lost a younger brother in the war, shot down and killed over the North Sea while serving in the Royal Navy Air Service.[15] Page eventually made his own way into the RAF, via the London University Air Squadron.

The RAF set out to be meritocratic in its search for recruits, and Tedder, as director of training, decided to cast the net wide in the search for the best candidates. The requirement to have reached school certificate level meant boys from poor families who could not afford to keep their children on until sixteen were theoretically excluded. The rules were not always strictly imposed and officials occasionally used their discretion.

Bob Doe's father was a gardener on the Surrey estate of the editor of the *News of the World*. Doe left school at fourteen without passing any exams and got a job as an office boy at the paper's headquarters in Bouverie Street. One lunchtime he walked over to the Air Ministry headquarters in Kingsway and announced he wanted a short-service commission. 'I was passed from office to office. They were very disapproving when they found I'd passed no exams. Then I found myself in front of this elderly chap with lots of braid on his uniform and he seemed to like me.'[16] When he discovered that Doe had already joined the RAFVR and done seventy-five hours' flying, any lack of formal education was forgotten. Doe sat the entrance exam, and with some coaching from his Air Ministry sponsor, got through. Doe's case was exceptional. Most entrants had passed their school certificate and had gone to fee-paying or grammar schools.

One obvious source for the sort of healthy, uncomplicated, modern-minded young men the RAF was seeking was the Empire. Senior officers were sent overseas to Australia, Canada, New Zealand and South Africa to supervise selection. The decision to leave home to cross the world at a time when war seemed to be stirring again in Europe was a dramatic one. Yet the populations of the colonies felt strong sentiments of loyalty and respect towards Britain. The RAF appeal offered broader horizons to ambitious and adventurous young airmen as well as touching a sense of obligation. The response was enthusiastic. On catching their first sight of the mother country, many of them wondered whether they had made the right choice. Alan Deere left Auckland in September 1937 aboard the SS *Rangitane* and arrived at Tilbury docks at the start of an English winter. 'The cold discomfort of the railway carriage and the flat, treeless acres of southern Essex were depressing reminders of the warmth and sunshine of far-off New Zealand. We stared in amazement at the grim rows of East End houses, pouring their smoke into the clouded atmosphere, and were appalled by the bustle and grime of Liverpool Street Station, so different from the luxurious gateway to the London of our dreams.'[17]

Despite the relative elasticity of the RAF approach, the selection process was thorough and demanding. After the written test and a strict medical, candidates were summoned to a board and questioned by a panel of officers. The examiners were looking for some technical knowledge and evidence of keenness. Enthusiasm for sports was usually taken as strong proof of the latter. At first, short-service entrants were sent off immediately to an RAF flying training centre, but the existing facilities could not cope with the wave of new recruits and Tedder decided to pay civilian flying schools to give *ab initio* instruction.

The new boys learned in two-seaters, Avro Tutors and de Havilland Tiger Moths. A first flight in the flimsy, thrumming trainers left an indelible impression, akin, as some would remember, to their first encounter with sex. Dennis David had his first lesson in a Blackburn B2 at the grandly named London Air Park, near present-day Heathrow. In reality it was a tiny grass field with a clump of trees in the centre, surrounded by houses. Many years later he 'still [found] it hard to find the words to describe my sheer delight and sense of freedom as the little biplane, seeming to strain every nerve, accelerated across the grass and suddenly became airborne'.[18]

Fantasizing about flying aeroplanes was no preparation for the reality. A few, not necessarily the best pilots, found it gratifyingly easy. Johnny Kent, an eighteen-year-old Canadian, had begun learning at the Winnipeg Flying Club, 'and was absolutely thrilled with the experience of actually handling the controls and I managed to cope with all the manoeuvres including an approach . . . at the end of this first lesson I knew I could fly'.[19] But many found flight in a small, sensitive aircraft unnerving. Bob Doe was 'petrified when I first went up. The side of the aeroplane was so thin that when you banked round I was afraid of falling through it. In no way did I have an affinity for it.'[20] On Hubert Allen's first flight as a new candidate for a short-service commission the instructor

> put the Tiger Moth into a bunt [loop] and I was sick. He shouldn't have done that, but perhaps he thought I was over-confident and needed cutting down to size. He was mistaken. I was under-confident so I probably acted the part of extrovert to conceal this. 'Good God,' he said, when after landing and turning off the magnetos he peered into my cockpit and noticed that I was covered in vomit. 'I hope you're not going to be one of those air-sick fellows . . . better give the rigger half a crown for cleaning up the mess.' . . . he strode off to the bar.[21]

Even those who had flown regularly as passengers discovered that the violent manoeuvres essential to military aviation differed dramatically from the pleasant sensations of straight and level flying. Tim Vigors, a sporting young man from a landed Irish family, had been taken flying by his godmother, who was an air enthusiast, and he liked it so much he applied to Cranwell. Starting flying training he felt fearful and nauseous. As the instructor put the aeroplane into a loop, a standard, elementary manoeuvre, a 'queasy feeling engulfed me . . . then the whole weight of my body fell on my shoulder harness as we turned upside down in a slow roll . . . fear of falling out of the cockpit eclipsed all other sensations'.[22]

Initial success did not mean that progress would then be steady. Robert Stanford Tuck was a confident young man whose long face, athletic build and pencil moustache made him look like Errol Flynn. He had lead an adventurous life in his teens, escaping the mundane horizons of Catford in south-east London for a career in the merchant navy before being accepted for a short-service commission. Tuck started off well. But he found it difficult to progress beyond basics and develop the instinctive ease of handling, the *feel* that was essential if one was to become a serious pilot. Tuck's cocky judgement after his first go at the controls was that flying was easy. So it is, if restricted to the basic manoeuvres of take-off, straight and level flight, shallow turns and landing. But after that the learning ladder is steep. Diving, looping and banking tightly are disorientating. Mistakes lead quickly to panic as the actions required to retrieve the situation are usually counter-instinctive. Tuck found he was the dud of his intake, snatching at the controls, over-correcting and suffering potentially fatal lapses of concentration. He began to fear that something he had come to love would be snatched away from him. It was only when he learned that flying did not require great physical effort that his performance started to improve. The secret lay in relaxation, avoiding sharp movements and settling oneself into the fabric of the machine so as to become part of its nervous system. You had to feel the aeroplane. For the fighter pilots of the First World War, buttocks had been an important sensory tool. Pilots felt they lost something when, in 1927, parachutes, which they were obliged to sit on, became standard equipment.

By the time war broke out the RAF was mass-producing officers. The privately run elementary flying training schools dotted around the country taught a basis in practical flying, with a grounding in navigation and gunnery, that prepared pupils for an advanced course at one of the RAF's own flying training schools. The idea was that, unlike in the previous war, when half-trained men were expected to learn while on squadron duty, pilots would now arrive at their units ready for operations.

The initial flying was done in biplanes. Pupils underwent twenty-two stages of instruction, starting with 'air experience' – the first flip – through to aerobatics during the eight- to twelve-week course. Emphasis was placed on learning to recover from a spin, and there was a compulsory practice every week. It was the only manoeuvre, apart from straightforward flying, that was taught previous to the first solo, which came half-way through the course. Most pupils got off alone after between eight and ten hours in the air. Alan Deere was so impatient to do so he forgot the last words of his instructor to fly for only ten minutes and to attempt only two landings. 'I was really straining at the leash by the time he had delivered these homilies and, thinking he had finished, banged the throttle open . . . and so into the air, solo at last. One, two, three landings, around again and again I went, the ten-minute limit completely forgotten in the thrill and excitement of this momentous occasion.'[23]

Aerobatics were promoted to give pupils complete confidence in their machines as well as preparing them for the stomach-churning reality of aerial combat. Flying blind, encased in a hood, relying only on the instruments, was also taught. Later this hair-raising method was replaced by means of an earthbound flight simulation trainer, the Link. The cost of elementary training was expensive at £5 per pupil per hour (double for advanced training) and those who showed little aptitude were weeded out early on. Those who finished the course successfully went on to a stint at the RAF Depot at Uxbridge for two weeks of drilling, physical training, familiarization with the limited administrative duties required of young officers and learning the niceties of mess protocol. During the fortnight, tailors arrived to kit out the fledgling officers and provide an opportunity for a laugh. Blond, raffish Paddy Barthropp remembered the response to the inevitable question, as they were measured up for their uniforms, which included mess kit with very tight-fitting trousers. 'When the cutters asked their customers which side they dressed the reply would come. "Just make them baggy around the kneecaps." '[24] The new officers were given £50 to cover everything, including uniforms, shirts, socks, two pairs of shoes and a cap – not enough if you went to the better outfitters.

Before candidates moved on to the next stage of training, the chief instructor at the elementary flying school made a recommendation as to whether a pupil's abilities best suited him to fighters or bombers. Flying anything required delicacy. Flying fighters required a particular softness of touch. Horsemen, yachtsmen and pianists, the prevailing wisdom held, made the best fighter pilots. The decision was made on the pilot's flying ability but also on his temperament. Success depended on a combination of discipline of the sort needed to maintain the flying formations beloved of the pre-war RAF, with the audacity and nerve inherent in the dazzling aerobatics which the service also prized as an indication of worth and quality.

The pilots themselves had a say in their fate. To some, like Dennis David, it seemed the choice was preordained, feeling from the outset that 'it was inevitable that I was to be a fighter pilot . . . from the start I was a loner. It was just me and my aeroplane hoping that neither of us would let the other down.'[25] Alan Deere felt the same certainty, 'had always determined to be a fighter pilot' and pressed his superiors to be posted to fighters.

Fighters were not the automatic choice for all young pilots. The strategic thinking of the previous two decades had its effect on ambitious trainees. Most of Deere's contemporaries thought bombers offered a better career and he was one of only four to go to a fighter squadron. But for the majority fighters offered a degree of freedom and individuality that was not available in a bomber crew – and, as was clear even before the war began, a greater chance of survival. Brian Kingcome, who after Cranwell was posted to 65 Fighter Squadron, considered that 'only a man brave beyond belief would ever want to go into bombers. Us cards all went into fighters.'[26]

After leaving the depot, the half-formed pilots moved on to one of the flying training schools to learn on service aircraft. In the early days of expansion, trainee fighter pilots started out on biplanes like the Hawker Hart or the Audax. These eventually made way for the Miles Master and the North American Harvard. The latter was a twin-seat, single-engined trainer with half the horsepower of the new breed of fighters, but which none the less gave a taste of what it would be like to handle a Hurricane or Spitfire when the time came.

The instruction was testing. Deere lost his temper after his teacher scolded him for his clumsy performance of the highly difficult manoeuvre of spinning a Hart, first one way, then the other, with a hood over his head to blot out vision. The tantrum nearly lost him his commission and he was told he had been given another chance 'only because the Royal Air Force has already spent so much money on your training'.[27] The pilots were taught set-piece attacks against bomber formations, each one numbered according to the circumstances. There was some gunnery practice, a small part of which involved using live ammunition on towed aerial drogues.

The student pilots lived in the mess and dressed for dinner each night in mess kit, dinner jacket or lounge suit, depending on the day of the week. Saturday was dress-down day, when blazer, flannels and a tie were permitted. After successful completion of the first half of the course, pilots received their wings, a brevet sewn over the tunic pocket that announced their achievement to the world. It was a great moment, 'the most momentous occasion in any young pilot's career', Dennis David thought. Al Deere felt a 'thrill of achievement and pride' as he stepped forward to receive the badge.

Finally, on completion of training, the new pilots were posted to a squadron. In the first years of expansion, units did their best to preserve what they could of the civilized atmosphere that had prevailed before the shake-up. At Hornchurch, where 65 Squadron was stationed, Brian Kingcome enjoyed 'a most marvellous life . . . if I wanted to take off and fly up to a friend of mine who had an airfield or station somewhere a hundred miles away for lunch, I would just go. It went down as flying training. I didn't have to get permission or [check] flight paths. I just went. If you wanted to go up and do aerobatics, you just went.'[28] Hornchurch was a well-appointed station, built, like many of the inter-war bases, in brick to a classically simple Lutyens design. The mess, where everyone except the handful of married officers lived, was separate from the main base across the road and in front of the main gates. It stood in its own grounds, with a large dining room and bedrooms. Kingcome found it 'luxurious beyond belief . . . the food was superb; you had your own batman and quarters. There was no bar in those days so you did all your drinking in the anteroom with steward service. The gardens outside the mess were beautifully kept with pristine lawns and flower beds.' There were also squash and tennis courts and a small croquet lawn. Pilot officers – the lowest commissioned rank – were paid fourteen shillings (70p) a day, from which six shillings (30p) went on the cost of mess living. That covered food, lodging, laundry and a personal batman.

The rest went on drink and cars, which the junior officers clubbed together to buy to visit country pubs and make the occasional trip to London, less than an hour away. The frequency of nights out depended on two considerations: the price of drink and the price of petrol. To initiate a pub crawl, Kingcome and three or four friends would each put half a crown (12½p) into the kitty. They would then board one of the jalopies (cost £10 to £25) held in loose collective ownership by the squadron. Petrol cost a shilling (5p) a gallon for the best grade, or tenpence (a little over 4p) for standard grade. After having downed several drinks costing eightpence (4p) for a pint of beer or a measure of whisky, they would still have some change over to share out at the end of the evening. Ten shillings (50p) would cover a trip to town, including train fare if no car was available, and the bill at Shepherd's, a pub in Shepherd's Market in Mayfair. It was run by a Swiss called Oscar and became one of Fighter Command's main drinking headquarters in London. For a pound the evening could be rounded off in a nightclub.

Biggin Hill, which like Hornchurch originated as a First World War station, was rebuilt in September 1932 to a similar design. It became home to two fighter units, 23 Squadron and 32 Squadron. Pete Brothers arrived in 1936 to a 'nice little airfield, a lovely officers' mess'. The station had a reputation for *joie de vivre*, and its members enjoyed, when they were not flying, a life of sport, of visits to London and being entertained at surrounding country houses. Because of the airfield's location, 600 feet above sea-level, unexpected visitors aboard civil airliners often dropped in when Croydon was closed by fog. One day in 1936 an Imperial Airways airliner landed carrying the American Olympic team, including Jesse Owens, fresh from his triumph at the Berlin Games. On another occasion a party of French models arrived after being diverted there on their way to a London fashion show. Churchill, whose home at Chartwell was only a few miles away, arrived unexpectedly one evening early in 1939. 'We were having a drink in the anteroom when the door opened and in walked Winston,' Brothers, who by then was a twenty-one-year-old flight commander with 32 Squadron, recalled. 'We all got up and said, "Good evening, sir, can we get you a drink?" The waiter brought him a dry sherry and he asked if we could turn the radio on so he could hear the news. We listened, then he said, "Are you enjoying your Hawker Spitfires?" We didn't like to say, "You've got it wrong, they're Hurricanes."'[29]

Behind the military briskness there lurked an atmosphere of fun. Jokes were not always in the best taste. In 1936, at the height of the war in Abyssinia, Biggin Hill, like every other station, put on a display for the annual Empire Air Day. To demonstrate bombing techniques a Hawker Tomtit dropped flour bombs on an old car carrying two 'native' figures. One, disguised in a black beard, dressed in a white sheet and wearing a pith helmet, was unmistakably supposed to represent Haile Selassie, the Emperor of Abyssinia who had lost his throne after the Italian invasion. The crowd loved it but the Air Ministry was not amused. There was jovial rivalry between the Biggin units. A new squadron, No. 79, was formed around a core of pilots transferred from No. 32 while Peter Brothers was there. 'There were games. We decided we'd have a contest to see who could do the shortest landing. We had to pack it up when some chap hit the hedge and turned his aircraft over and smashed it up.'

Tangmere, at the foot of the South Downs, was a particularly pleasant post. A dreamy, prelapsarian atmosphere seems to have permeated the place in the last years of peace. Billy Drake, arriving there aged nineteen in the summer of 1937 as a newly commissioned pilot officer, found life was sweet. The summer routine involved rising at six and flying until lunchtime in Hawker Furies. Afternoons were spent swimming or sailing at Bosham and West Itchenor. Then there would be a game of squash or tennis before dinner and bed. Social life centred on the mess, furnished like the lounge of a luxury liner, where Hoskins and Macey, the white-coated stewards, shuttled back and forth with silent efficiency. There were good pubs nearby; like the Old Ship at Bosham, where on a summer evening you could sit with fellow pilots or a girlfriend and watch the sun going down over the estuary. Conversation concerned aeroplanes, cars, sport and parties, rarely politics. What was happening in Abyssinia, Germany or Italy was hardly mentioned. If the drums of war were beating, the pilots affected not to hear them. Drake had barely considered the implications of his decision to apply for a short-service commission. 'I simply wanted to go flying,' he said. 'The fact that it might involve going to war never occurred to me until 1938 or 1939.'[30]

Life was not so congenial at every fighter base. Conditions around the country were variable. The fast rate of the expansion meant accommodation often lagged behind needs. Desmond Sheen, a nineteen-year-old Australian who joined the RAF on a short-service commission from the Royal Australian Air Force, arrived at 72 Squadron at Church Fenton in Yorkshire in June 1937 to be told he was living in a tent at the end of the airfield while the mess was being built. 'We stayed there until November when the fog and the mists drove us out and we moved into hangars until the building was completed.'[31] When Arthur Banham reported for duty to 19 Squadron at Duxford in Cambridgeshire after finishing his training in August 1936, he was put with nine other junior officers in a hut which acted as a dormitory. 'The whole place was a mess, with trenches all over the place where they were laying foundations for the new buildings. The officers married quarters weren't built and most officers lived out of the aerodrome altogether.'[32]

Arriving at their first posts, the newly qualified pilots learned quickly that henceforth everything would centre on the squadron. It became the focus of their professional and their social lives. Nothing could be more exciting than flying and no one could be more fun to be with than one's fellow fighter pilots. 'It was a wonderful time for most of us,' remembered John Nicholas, who joined 65 Squadron in December 1937. 'It was very pleasant to be with a number of young men of one's own age, most of whom believed in the same things.'[33] Some of the pre-expansion pilots had worried that the influx would dilute the clubby character of the old organization and dissolve its tenderly guarded *esprit de corps*. Peter Townsend, a sensitive, reflective career officer who had passed out of Cranwell as the Prize Cadet, returned to Britain to join 43 Squadron in June 1937 after a posting to the Far East, to find that 'gone were the halcyon days of "the best flying club in the world". Tangmere was now peopled by strange faces, different people with a different style. I resented the new generation of pilots who had answered the RAF's urgent appeal and found heaven-sent relief from boring civilian jobs.'[34] Townsend accepted, almost immediately, that these feelings were unworthy. In a subsequent *mea culpa* he admitted that 'my prejudices against them were ignoble, for they were soon to become the most generous-hearted friends, then, a little later, die, most of them, for England'. The reasoning was, anyway, wrong. At any time in the years before the run-up to the expansion programme, a majority of officers in the admittedly much smaller RAF were serving on short-service commissions.

The newcomers took to the existing traditions quickly, offering no serious challenge to the way things were done. Many were familiar with the routines of sport, joviality and boisterous high spirits from school days. Most of the short-service commission pilots entering in the expansion years had a public-school background of one sort or another. Roland Beamont was at Eastbourne College, Geoffrey Page at Dean Close, Cheltenham, Paddy Barthropp went to Ampleforth and Arthur Banham to the Perse School, Cambridge. Bob Tuck attended a small fee-paying day school, St Dunstan's at Catford, and Pete Brothers a similar establishment, North Manchester School. Billy Drake, James Saunders and John Nicholas were educated abroad. Pat Hancock went to a day school in

Croydon before moving to the technical college. Dennis David had been to a boarding school in Deal before changing to Surbiton County School. Of the Cranwellians, Tim Vigors had been at Eton and Brian Kingcome at Bedford.

Most of the entrants, even if they had not been to a proper public school, knew something of the ethos, if only from the pages of the *Magnet* and the *Gem*. Bob Doe, a secondary-school boy, felt out of place. Of his fellow short-service entrants he was 'probably the poorest of the lot. I hadn't done all the things other people had done. I felt very much an outsider. I was very shy as well, which didn't help. They were friendly enough but I always felt I was inferior.'[35] The barriers were lowered when he was invited to club together with three others to buy a Hispano-Suiza saloon for £20, this enabling them to go on occasional forays into Cheltenham, twelve miles from Little Rissington, where they were based.

The overseas entrants had little difficulty fitting in. Their status as colonials put them beyond the rigid categorizations of the British class system. Desmond Sheen's father was a plasterer, but he found at 72 Squadron that 'everyone got on, with a lot of hilarity and a lot of fun, extremely well. There was no conflict. There was a lot of taking the mickey out of each other, but it was all very friendly. They were all good sports.'[36]

Being a good sport was the essential quality in fitting in. Taken literally, it meant that athletic ability would count in a pilot's favour, a factor which benefited the outdoorsy arrivals from the Empire. Deere found that 'the natural reserve of all Englishmen gave way to a more friendly approach' after a game of rugby in which New Zealanders took on the rest, beating the English pilots by a colossal score. He was a boxer who had taken part in the New Zealand amateur championships. He was reluctant to don the gloves again, but was persuaded to do so by a senior officer who advised him it would be good for his career. The abbreviation of a first name, the bestowal of a nickname, signalled you were in. Alan quickly became Al.

Being a good sport, however, went beyond the observance of the conventions, attitudes and observances of middle-class males of the time.

A mood of tolerance prevailed so that individuality, even eccentricity, was prized. The business of aerial warfare meant that the type of military discipline applied to soldiers and sailors was not appropriate for airmen. Junior officers addressed their squadron superiors as 'sir' on the initial meeting of the day. After that it was first names. Once in combat in the air, everyone was essentially on their own and beyond the orders of a commander. Good pilots, anyway, succeeded by initiative and making their own decisions.

From the earliest days on the Western Front, pilots took a relaxed view of military conventions and often displayed a sceptical attitude towards senior officers, though seldom with their own immediate commanders if they had earned their respect. Pomposity was ruthlessly punished and shyness discouraged. Coy newcomers learned that a certain amount of leg-pulling and practical joking was the price of belonging. Deere, like all new arrivals, spent his first few weeks at 54 Squadron at Hornchurch doing dogsbody tasks like overseeing the pay and clothing parades. He was also required to check the navigation inventory and found to his concern that an item called the Oxometer was missing. On informing his flight commander, he was told that this was a very serious matter and the station commander might have to be notified if it was not found. It was some days before he 'realized that no such item of equipment existed and that it was a trick played on all new pilots and one in which everyone from the station commander down participated'.[37] The joke took on a further refinement when a particularly earnest pilot officer was told that the missing Oxometer had been found. A fake instrument was rigged up and the relieved officer invited to blow in it to check it was working, which resulted in him being sprayed with soot.

The boisterous and extrovert tone of squadron life disguised a level of consideration and fellow feeling that perhaps marked out the RAF from the other services. The testimony of survivors, and what little was written down by those who died, is imbued with an overwhelming affection for fellow pilots and for the units in which they served. The camaraderie that came with membership of a fighter squadron appears to have provided a degree of spiritual sustenance, augmenting the warmth of an absent family or making those with dislocated backgrounds feel they had arrived at a place where they belonged. The simple cheeriness that was the Fighter Boys' chosen style masked some complicated stories. Geoffrey Page's parents were separated. His father frightened him and he resented his miserly attitude toward his mother. Dennis David was brought up by his mother after his father, who drank and had financial troubles, abandoned the family when he was eight. Brian Kingcome's mother had returned to England with her children, leaving her husband to continue working in India. He returned only once every two and a half years. As Kingcome was at boarding school, he barely saw his son during his childhood and adolescence.

The modern assumption is that such experiences must leave a mark. Feeling sorry for oneself lay outside the range of emotions allowed to adolescents in Britain in the 1930s. Kingcome admired and respected his largely absent father. Paddy Barthropp's mother died in childbirth, a tragedy that meant his father 'resented my very existence almost up to the time of his own death in 1953. I never blamed him.' At Ampleforth one day in 1936 'a school bully approached me to say that it would be a good idea if I read page four of *The Times* in the school library. There it was for all to see – "In the High Court of Bankruptcy, Elton Peter Maxwell D'Arley Barthropp" . . . the fact that one was skint was not acceptable and carried a long-lasting social stigma . . . the next few days were the most embarrassing of my life.' He was farmed out to a step-grandfather, 'extremely rich and very nasty', among whose many possessions was the Gresford Colliery near Wrexham. On hearing that there had been a disaster at the mine killing 264 miners, the old man 'replied that he didn't want to be disturbed. He disgusted me.'[38] Barthropp eventually got an apprenticeship with Rover Cars in Coventry before deciding to join the RAF after a visit to the Hendon Air Display.

Barthropp was hopeless academically. He failed the school certificate five times, and only scraped through his RAF board by gaining 'a phoney pass' from a crammer. Roland Beamont also failed his school certificate and had to resort to coaching to get the qualification he needed to be eligible for a short-service commission. Denys Gillam, who joined the

RAF on a short-service commission in 1935, had been kicked out of his prep school, then his public school, Wrekin College, for drinking and exam irregularities. He later joined 616 Squadron and commanded two fighter squadrons. Against the wisdom of the pre-war days his preferred pilots were 'non-athletic men between the ages of eighteen to twenty-three', who had 'better resilience to stress than the successful rugger player or his equivalent . . . all the best pilots that I knew tended to be rather weedy, though there were exceptions. The best pilot were ones that hadn't had much success in other spheres and were determined to succeed.' Teaching a course to a class of wing commanders later in his career, he discovered that 'out of a group of twelve . . . four had been thrown out of their school before they left. This was, I think, fairly typical.'[39] Kingcome was to deliver the opinion later that, 'Fortunately for us, and, I believe, for the RAF in that generation, there were [no] . . . psychological and aptitude tests, which would have failed a majority of candidates for short-service and permanent commissions and I suspect might have cost us the Battle of Britain.'[40]

Expansion increased the flow of men from the lower reaches of the RAF into the ranks of the fliers as candidates were selected from among the ground crews to serve as sergeant pilots. Of the 2,500 pilots originally sought to man the new aircraft and squadrons, 800 were found from among those already serving as aircraftmen or non-commissioned officers. The RAF apprentice schemes allowed a trickle of fitters, riggers and other tradesmen to receive flying training, on the understanding that they would return to their trades after five years. There were also two places set aside for the top performers at Halton to go on to Cranwell to take up a cadetship. Many, perhaps most, apprentices had dreams of flying. Realizing them was difficult. There was an obvious necessity to maintain the supply of highly skilled, expensively trained ground staff to keep the service flying and prevent apprenticeships from turning into a back-door route to a career as a pilot. None the less, in the pre-expansion years, some of the keenest and most talented felt themselves baulked by what was supposed to be a system that worked on merit. George Unwin was brought up in South Yorkshire, where his father was a miner. His mother encouraged his education and he won a scholarship to Wath Grammar School, and aged sixteen passed his Northern Universities matriculation exam. There was no money for him to take up a place. The only work on offer was down the pit. When, a month before he was due to leave, his headmaster showed him an RAF recruiting pamphlet, he decided to join up.

Unwin chose the Ruislip administrative apprentice school rather than the technical school at Halton, as the course there was two rather than three years. It was a spartan life. The food was horrible. They seemed to live on gristly mutton rissoles, and food parcels from the outside world were eagerly received. They shaved in cold water and lived twenty to a billet. Unwin initially had no thoughts of flying, but the sights and sounds of the aerodrome kindled his ambition. After passing out in 1931 as a leading aircraftman, the minimum rank to qualify for pilot training, he applied, but discovered that 'only one per cent per six months was taken'.

He repeated the process twice a year without success. 'I was getting a bit fed up at not being accepted. I had everything else. I was playing for the RAF at soccer, and that was one of the things you had to be, to be very good at sport. I couldn't understand why I wasn't being selected. You went through a very, very tedious process. First of all you saw your flight commander, then your CO, and then your station commander. If you got past him you saw the air officer commanding. I'd reached the point when I was going to see the AOC and I was getting desperate. At the time it was Air Vice-Marshal J. E. A. Baldwin, who loved polo and kept his own polo ponies.' Unwin decided that when the inevitable question about hobbies came up at the interview, he would be prepared. 'I said "horse riding". He pricked up his ears and said, "Really?" I said, "Of course, I can't afford it down here, but the local farmer at home has a pony and lets me ride it." The only time I'd ridden a pony or anything on four legs was in the General Strike when the pit ponies were brought up and put in fields. I was thirteen and we used to catch them and jump on their bare backs and go haring down the field until we fell off.'[41]

It worked. He was on the next course. It was 1935, four years after he first applied. In August 1936 he was posted to 19 Squadron at Duxford as a sergeant pilot, where his flight commander was Flight Lieutenant Harry Broadhurst, an ex-army officer who had joined the RAF in 1926 and flew in the campaigns against unruly tribesmen on India's North-West Frontier. Broadhurst had played a large part in building the squadron's reputation for flying excellence, which had won it many trophies, and he was regarded as the best shot in the RAF.

Unwin, despite his background, fitted relatively easily into the squadron. His best friend was another ex-apprentice whom he had met on the flying course, Harry Steere, who had gone to Halton from his secondary school in Wallasey in 1930. The two were to fly together for six out of the next seven years. Unwin found that 19 Squadron's competitive streak was compatible with a relaxed approach to duty. 'You didn't fly Saturdays, ever. You could take an aeroplane away for a weekend any time you liked. You used to fly away for lunch. You were encouraged to do this because it helped your map-reading. There were no aids at all, so you [navigated] visually. Radio telephony wouldn't work more than three miles from the aerodrome and then the background noise was so terrific you couldn't hear anything anyone was saying.' On annual exercises at Catterick, Unwin would take his aircraft and buzz his home village of Bolton Upon Dearne.

Making the transition from ground to air was a hit-and-miss affair and required the patronage of an interested senior officer. Ronald Brown left Halton in 1932 to be posted to the RAF station attached to Cranwell, where he worked as a fitter overhauling the engines of the aircraft on which the cadets at the college were taught to fly. Every morning 'the instructors would have a ten-minute flight to check the aircraft was safe for the cadets, and as they were dual-control aircraft we were able to jump in the back or the front. Inevitably that meant we were allowed to fly the plane with them, and long before I went on a pilot's course I was looping and rolling aeroplanes to my heart's delight every morning.'

Brown played football for the RAF and the group captain commanding him was a keen sportsman. 'I had the opportunity of flying him around once or twice and I think that, plus my sporting activity, gave me the chance of being selected for pilot training.'[42] Brown was one of only two airmen to be given the opportunity to fly in the three years he spent at the base. Before he could begin his flying training he was, to his disappointment, posted as a fitter to No. 10 Bomber Squadron at Boscombe Down. When he complained to the CO, he was told he could not start the course until the football season was over and the squadron had won the RAF cup. He was sent to 111 Fighter Squadron at Northolt in February 1937.

Sporting prowess got an airman applicant noticed and pushed his name further up the list. George Bennions, from Stoke-on-Trent, arrived at Halton in January 1929. He was a keen boxer and believed that 'they preferred to recommend sportsmen to become sergeant pilots [as] one way of sorting out the wheat from the chaff because there were many, many people at Halton who could equally have done the job'. Bennions was put forward for a Cranwell cadetship, an offer that later fell through, though he did end up joining 41 Squadron as a sergeant pilot and was commissioned in the spring of 1940. Some of Halton's most successful products were outstanding athletes. Don Finlay, who left in August 1928, became a world-class hurdler, winning a silver medal for Britain at the 1936 Berlin Olympics. He was to take command of 54 Squadron in August 1940, during some of the heaviest fighting of the summer.

As the situation worsened and the demand for pilots grew, the process of transformation became easier. George Johns arrived at Halton in January 1934 as an aircraft apprentice and by the end of 1939 was a sergeant pilot with 229 Squadron. 'You immediately said to yourself: I'm working with these aeroplanes. I'm going to fly them some time. That was the attitude you found there.'[43] Airmen who rose from the ranks to become pilots were to play an enormously important part in the air fighting of 1940. Often they had spent more time in the service than the officers and gained more flying experience. Unlike many of the officers, they also had a deep knowledge of the aircraft they were operating. Pre-war conventions created a certain distance between officer and NCO pilots, but this faded with the intimacy brought by shared danger and death.

Boosting the short-service commission system and intensifying internal recruitment ensured the supply of pilots needed to man the new squadrons. But men were also needed to fill the places of those who would be killed and badly wounded in the initial fighting. The Volunteer Reserve (VR) had been created to fill that gap, though this was not how it was presented to the men who turned up at the centres that sprang up around the country to process applicants. There were many of them. The target figure set in 1936 of 800 a year for three years was reached quickly, and in the spring of 1939 there were 2,500 volunteers under training. By then there were thirty-five flying centres, with eight in and around London and three near Bristol, while Manchester and Birmingham were served by two each.

Tedder had decreed that this should be a 'Citizen Air Force', modern and democratic, attracting 'air-minded' young men from factory, shop and office, and this was how it turned out. Frank Usmar was a postman's son from West Malling in Kent, who left school at fourteen to work in an office and spent his evenings studying accountancy at night school. In 1938 the RAF opened a recruiting office in Rochester. Usmar's interest in flying had stemmed from seeing *Dawn Patrol*. He applied, was accepted and thereafter spent two nights a week attending lectures at the VR Hall in Rochester and weekends flying at a local airfield, for which he was paid a shilling an hour. After nine and three quarter hours dual flying on an Avro Tutor, he went solo. The part-time nature of the training meant that it took much longer to get new pilots up to standard, and it was a year before he moved on to service aircraft like the Hart, Hind and Audax.

But the system did identify pilots showing great potential who could be brought to operational level quickly when the time came. Charlton Haw would never have got into the RAF under normal peacetime conditions. He left school at fourteen to become an apprentice in a lithographic works in York, and as soon as he was eighteen applied for the RAFVR. 'I'd always wanted to fly, from when I was a small boy. I never wanted to do anything else, really, but I just didn't think there would ever be a chance for me. Until the RAFVR was formed, for a normal schoolboy it was almost impossible.'[44] Haw went solo in four hours forty minutes, at a time when the average was eight to ten hours, and was considered a natural pilot by his instructor. Not that a slow start necessarily denoted incompetence. There was a school of thought that said that the longer the apprenticeship, the better the pilot.

The reserve offered an escape from dreary jobs in stifling offices. John Beard was working in the Midland Bank at Leamington when a circular arrived saying that employees who joined the VR would be granted an extra week's holiday to allow them to train. Beard began flying at Ansley aerodrome at weekends and going to lectures in Coventry on navigation, meteorology and elementary engineering and aeronautics a few evenings a week. Ron Berry left school at sixteen and got a job as a clerk at an engineering works in Hull. He stayed eighteen months before moving on to the city treasurer's department. Early in 1938 he saw an advertisement for the RAFVR in a local paper and realized how 'keen I was to try something like that'. To prepare for the medical he ran round the local park every morning at seven o'clock. He was interviewed by an impressive squadron leader in a uniform displaying an Air Force Cross. 'He made me feel strongly about doing something other than clerical work in the city treasurer's office.'[45]

The RAFVR also gave young men a say in their own fate, a chance to choose which branch of the services they would be absorbed into before the inevitable seeming processes of conscription took the decision for them. In January 1939, Robert Foster was working at Shell headquarters in London. 'I thought there was going to be a war and I didn't particularly want to be in the army, or a conscript. I never really thought about the problems of being in the air force, but that seemed a better way to fight a war than as a common soldier.'[46]

The RAF seemed to offer a relatively clean way of fighting the coming war. Many of those who joined had fathers who had served in the First World War and whose experiences had left a strong and disturbing impression. Christopher Foxley-Norris, who was commissioned in the RAFVR after leaving the Oxford University Air Squadron, remembered that undergraduates, when 'sitting around in the evening having a beer . . . used to discuss our ability to survive trench warfare. We'd all read

All Quiet on the Western Front and those sort of things. My father was gassed at Loos in 1915. He died after the war in 1923, of cancer. I think most of us doubted we could stand it.'[47]

The expansion programme also brought an influx of new pilots – many originating from further up the social scale than the young men flocking to the RAFVR – into the Auxiliary Air Force (AAF) and University air squadrons buttressing Trenchard's design for the air force. After February 1936 eight new auxiliary units were created and four existing special reserve squadrons were transferred to the AAF. By the beginning of 1939, fourteen squadrons, most of which had started out equipped with bombers, had been redesignated as fighter units, though the aeroplanes for them to fly were often slow in coming. By the time the great air battles began in July 1940, there were twelve auxiliary squadrons operating as day fighters and two as night fighters – a quarter of Fighter Command's strength.

Among the new creations was 609 (West Riding) Squadron, formed in February 1936. Its first commanding officer was Harald Peake, an old-Etonian businessman from a local coal-owning family who had been chairman of large concerns like Lloyds Bank and London Assurance, and a keen amateur flier who took his private aeroplane on summer tours of the Continent. Peake had long been eager to raise auxiliary squadrons in the county when further units were required, and as soon as he was given the go-ahead began recruiting from among the sons of the big industrial and landowning families of Yorkshire. Stephen Beaumont, a junior partner in his family's law firm, which had Peake as a client, was one of the first to join. He was a thoughtful and dutiful man with a strong social conscience. With Hitler's arrival in power he felt a growing conviction that war was inevitable and he decided to fight in it as a pilot. He began flying at the West Riding Aero Club at Yeadon near Leeds, and when he heard that a new squadron was being formed, offered his services to Peake.

Beaumont found Peake 'very capable. He was about thirty-seven and had held commissions in the Coldstream Guards at the end of the First World War and later in the Yorkshire Dragoons Yeomanry. Perhaps because of our professional relationship I was somewhat in his confidence. He wanted officers who were no more than twenty-five, of public-school and university backgrounds and unmarried.' Beaumont was twenty-six and engaged to be married but was accepted none the less. Peake could afford to be choosy. By 8 June he had vetted 80 applications for commissions and 200 for posts as airmen. Despite this response, actual recruitment was slow, only speeding up as war approached. The squadron had a sprinkling of officers from aristocratic and county backgrounds. They included Peter Drummond-Hay, a textile executive who insisted on the use of both barrels of his Scottish name. He was discontented with his work in the cloth trade. Beaumont wrote that 'he liked to give the impression that he would be better employed as the owner of a large country estate, where he would know all the county, and indeed in North Yorkshire he did know a great many of that section of society. Somewhat caustic about and dismissive of most Yorkshiremen, he was very courteous to women.'[48] Dudley Persse-Joynt was an oil executive from an old Anglo-Irish family, and the first auxiliary adjutant was the Earl of Lincoln, who later became the Duke of Newcastle. But most of the members came from families who had prospered in the reign of Victoria and whose wealth was founded on coal and cloth.

Philip Barran's family were textile and coalmining magnates from Leeds. Joe Dawson's father, Sir Benjamin Dawson, was a power in the cloth trade and a baronet. A later recruit, John Dundas, was related to two Yorkshire grandees, the Marquess of Zetland and Viscount Halifax, and was a cousin of Harald Peake. He was academically brilliant, winning scholarships to Stowe and Oxford and taking a first in modern history before going on to study at Heidelberg and the Sorbonne. He had joined the staff of the *Yorkshire Post*, specializing in foreign affairs, and was sent to report from Czechoslovakia at the time of Munich and accompanied Chamberlain and his own kinsman Halifax to Rome. Barran, always known as Pip, was stocky, boisterous, a rugby player, a trainee mining engineer and the manager of a brickworks owned by his mother's family. His commanding officer eulogized him as 'the very best type of AAF officer, a born leader who communicated his enthusiasm to others'.[49] It was he who came up with the nicknames that adorned the members of 609 as they prepared for war.

The last auxiliary squadron to be formed was 616, which officially came into being on 1 November 1938 in Doncaster, South Yorkshire, as an offshoot of 609. Hugh Dundas had left Stowe in the summer of that year and was hoping to follow his brother John to Oxford. His father, however, insisted on him going into the law and he ended up being articled to a firm of Doncaster solicitors. Dundas applied to join 616 Squadron, but mysteriously failed the medical exam three times before finally being passed fit by an ex-Ireland rugby international RAF doctor after 'the most perfunctory examination', for which Nelsonian oversight he was eternally thankful.

Dundas finally joined in the last summer before the war. His CO was the Earl of Lincoln, who had moved on from 609, and other squadron members included Teddy St Aubyn, a Lincolnshire landowner who had moved into the AAF after being forced to resign his commission in the Grenadier Guards following his marriage to Nancy Meyrick, daughter of Kate 'Ma' Meyrick, who presided over the Forty-Three, a nightclub in between-the-wars London whose liveliness shaded into notoriety.

Dundas spent his time divided between Bawtry, the home of his aunt and her husband Bertie Peake – a lakeside house where the décor and routines had not changed since the 1890s – and the mess at the squadron station at Doncaster, where he also had a room and a batman. It was there that he acquired his nickname. 'I was sitting by the fireplace in the mess one evening before dinner. On the wall at my side was the bell button. Teddy St Aubyn and others were there. Teddy felt the need for further refreshment and decided that I was conveniently placed to summon the mess steward. "Hey you," he said pointing at me. "Hey you – Cocky – press the bell." I promptly did his bidding. But why had he described me as "Cocky"? What had I done? Nervously I asked him.' St Aubyn replied that he had forgotten his name, but that Dundas, an elongated figure with a shock of hair, reminded him of a 'bloody great Rhode Island Red'. The name stuck to him for the rest of his life.

He spent the summer days learning to fly in an archaic dual-control

Avro Tutor, probably one of the last RAF pilots ever to do so. Some difficult manoeuvres came quite easily, 'But slow rolls I hated and had great difficulty in achieving. I felt quite helpless when the machine was upside-down and I was hanging on my straps, dust and grit from the bottom of the cockpit falling around me. Again and again, when inverted, I instinctively pulled the stick back, instead of pushing it forward and so fell out of the roll in a tearing dive.'[50]

The search for new pilots also meant an increase in the strength of the university air squadrons. In May 1938 there were three, Oxford, Cambridge and London, which had been set up three years previously. That month they each increased the number of available places from seventy-five to a hundred. It had been hoped that the squadrons would provide a practical link between the air force and aeronautical research, particularly at Cambridge. The Oxford University Air Squadron (OUAS) operations book records its primary object as being 'to provide at the university a means by which interest in the air generally and in particular in the Royal Air Force can be stimulated'. Its second function was to 'provide suitable personnel to be trained as officers for the Royal Air Force in the event of war'. In practice, for most of its life the squadron functioned primarily as a flying club, for which the government paid.

Christopher Foxley-Norris went up to Oxford from Winchester in 1936 and was encouraged to join the OUAS by his brother, who was already a member. The prospect of the £25 gratuity paid on being accepted was also attractive. He wanted to buy a car, which he believed to be a crucial accessory if he was ever to get a girlfriend. OUAS members cut a dash. They were chauffered to their station at RAF Abingdon in two old Rolls-Royces, nicknamed Castor and Pollux, hired from a local firm. Once qualified, one was entitled to wear the squadron blazer with crest and gold RAF buttons. Foxley-Norris regarded it as 'a *corps d'élite*. It was very difficult to get into because there were some very outstanding people. It was a glamorous sort of club to be in, but not like the Bullingdon or something upmarket like that.'

The most immediately noticeable member was Richard Hillary, whose harsh wit, self-regard, good looks and ability as an oarsman made him stand out in a society not short of distinctive characters or large egos. Foxley-Norris met Hillary through friends who had been with him at Shrewsbury, his old school. 'I came across him when we were out on pub crawls and that sort of thing and I got to know him quite well. He was extremely arrogant and conceited.'[51] Hillary was also a poor learner, and his progress was not helped by the amount of time he spent on the river. 'This member proved very difficult to get off solo,' noted his instructor. 'He would not relax on the controls, he just held on like a vice.' Once flying alone, however, he 'improved rapidly'. The chief flying instructor judged that he 'lacked keenness . . . I do not consider that he has any real interest in flying'.[52]

Hillary was to have a powerful effect on British and international perceptions of the character and motivations of the pilots of 1940 through his book *The Last Enemy*, which appeared in 1941 after he had been shot down and badly burned, and became a best-seller in Britain and the United States. It is a book as much about friendship as flying, and those closest to him in the last years of his short life were all products of the University Air Squadrons. Among them was Noel Agazarian, the third son of an Armenian father and a French mother who had bought an old Sopwith Pup biplane and parked it in the garden of the family's Georgian house in Carshalton, Surrey, for the boys to clamber over. Agazarian went from his public school, Dulwich, to Wadham College, Oxford, in 1935, leaving three years later with a boxing blue and a law degree. He joined the air squadron and was commissioned into the RAFVR in January 1939. He was a brilliant linguist, funny and disrespectful. He was also good looking and when it came to attracting women was a match for Hillary, who seems to have rather resented his easy and natural charm. 'We called him Le Roi Soleil,' said his adoring young sister, Yvonne. 'He was always laughing and clowning. Noel was very much loved by everyone who met him.'[53] Peter Pease and Colin Pinckney, both old Etonians, had also joined the Cambridge University Air Squadron and both had been commissioned in the RAFVR by the end of 1938. They met Hillary during training and their subsequent intense and poetic triangular relationship was to be celebrated in the book.

The great variety of backgrounds and schools, the wide divergences of rank, wealth and privilege, made Fighter Command perhaps the most socially diverse élite ever seen in the British military. In a country where minutely defined social gradations conditioned the reactions of human beings to each other, the mingling of the classes caused some discomfort. The situation was described in a condescending *bon mot*: 'Auxiliaries are gentlemen trying to be officers. Regulars are officers trying to be gentlemen. VRs are neither trying to be both.' It was a last, snobbish gasp from a disappearing world. Very soon the distinction would not matter. It was true that many of the men in Fighter Command came from backgrounds that were 'ordinary'. But that did not mean that they themselves were so; and they were about to do extraordinary things.

4

The Fatal Step

The new pilots had been recruited to fly a new generation of fighter aeroplanes, but the machines were painfully slow in reaching the squadrons. The first Hurricanes did not appear in service until January 1938, when 111 Squadron became the first unit to receive them. It was August, and the eve of the Munich crisis, before 19 Squadron took delivery of the first Spitfires. At the end of the year most fighter squadrons were still flying biplanes.

Ronald Brown, the ex-Halton boy who had been selected for flying training, was a sergeant pilot at Northolt with 111 Squadron when the Hurricanes arrived. The squadron commander and flight commanders were the first to test them. Then it was the turn of the junior pilots. They were told to keep the undercarriage lowered in order to reduce speed. The great power of the Merlin engine, twice as potent as anything they had previously known, would take time to adjust to, it was thought. Brown, even though it was the first time he had handled a monoplane, in fact found it 'quite an easy plane to fly'.[1] Most pilots' accounts of their experience of the Hurricane, however, reveal a mixture of trepidation and elation. Roland Beamont remembered 'a feeling of exhilaration with all this power and being able to get up to 300 miles an hour on the air-speed indicator very easily in a shallow dive at any point in your flight. This was a great experience for an eighteen-year-old.'[2] The Gloster Gauntlets and Gladiators, which represented the zenith of biplane fighter design and served as a stopgap with many fighter squadrons while the new monoplanes were brought in, could manage only 230 and 255 m.p.h. respectively.

For pilots used to biplanes, the Hurricane seemed to take a long time to get airborne. Initially it had a fixed-pitch, twin-bladed propeller that only allowed one setting. With variable-pitch propellers, which were soon to come in, the pilot put the airscrew in 'fine' for take-off. This provided less speed but more power, giving maximum thrust – the equivalent in motoring terms of first gear. Once aloft, the pilot changed to 'coarse', altering the angle of the propeller blade so that it was taking bigger bites out of the air, generating less power but more speed. Later both types would be fitted with constant-speed governors that adjusted the blade angles automatically. Beamont thought flying a Hurricane was 'simple, straightforward'. Christopher Foxley-Norris found it reassuring. 'You get into an aircraft and it gives you confidence. You get into another one and it doesn't . . . [The Hurricane] was very stable but at the same time manoeuvrable. If you didn't want it to do a turn it was absolutely rock stable. If you did turn it was very manoeuvrable.'[3]

The Hurricane was slower than a Spitfire but could turn more tightly. Its wide-legged undercarriage, which opened outwards, planting the aeroplane firmly on the ground, made it 'very forgiving', another advantage over the Spitfire, which balanced on a narrow wheelbase. The initial canvas-and-girder construction of the fuselage meant bullets and cannon shells could go straight through it without bringing the aircraft down, and its sturdy wings provided solid bracing for the eight Brownings. It was, everyone said, an 'excellent gun platform', better, in fact, than the Spitfire. The machine guns were arranged in two groups of four, as close in to the fuselage as they could be placed to clear the propeller. The Spitfire's armament was spread out, with the outboard gun a third of the way in from the wing-tip; then a group of two, then an inboard gun on each wing, which could cause some flexing when the guns fired, making them less accurate. The Hurricane was fast and nimble but honest. It was not quite perfect. Pete Brothers discovered 'it could fall out of the air if you mistreated it trying to be too clever'.

The arrival of the new fighters aroused the fervent interest of newspapers and newsreel companies. Brown remembered them making 'an absolute meal of the Hurricane. We were wonderboys, travelling at vast speeds, pulling all this G [the heavy gravitational force exerted when turning]. We were getting constant visits from the press and staff colleges who wanted to see these things in action.'[4] Having appeared before the Spitfire, the Hurricane was the first to plant itself in the public imagination, though its primacy did not long survive the arrival of its more beautiful sister. The public perception that it represented a battle-winning technical advance was encouraged by a government and military establishment anxious to reassure citizens that the criticisms of the rearmament lobby were unfounded. Some pilots, used to the fixed wheels, open cockpits, broad flying surfaces and manageable speeds of the old types, wondered whether they would be able to cope. The difficulties which 111 Squadron had in making the transition were not reassuring. Some pilots simply could not adjust. Several were killed. One Australian pilot took off without realizing the wheel brakes were engaged. He only avoided crashing on take-off and landing because the field was so muddy the aeroplane slithered through the grass. When he made a subsequent landing without lowering the undercarriage, he was rapidly posted away.

Pilots liked the Hurricane's chunky lines and solid profile. The lean, curved elegance of the Spitfire inspired something more profound. There was never 'a plane so loved by pilots', wrote Hugh Dundas.[5] 'Everybody wanted to fly a Spitfire,' said Jeffery Quill. 'Most pilots used to want to fly the best. It certainly was the best.' Quill knew the quality of the machine better than anyone. He was a test pilot at Supermarine and had taken the Spitfire through the most difficult stages of its development, as the design team struggled to overcome profound technical problems that were preventing it from making the evolutionary transition from being a very good aeroplane to a great one.

Quill was intelligent, shrewd and popular in both air force and civilian aviation circles, as much for his good nature as his superb abilities as a pilot. His father was Irish, an engineer who among other things had built Sierra Leone's water system before retiring to Littlehampton in Sussex.

He died in 1926 when Jeffery was thirteen and a schoolboy at Lancing. As a young boy he watched the aeroplanes at the RFC base at Ford, near the family home. He decided early on to go into the air force, but he was the youngest of five children and there was little money. He had to forgo Cranwell, where his family would have had to support him for two years, and applied instead for a short-service commission. His first posting was to 17 Squadron, flying Bulldogs. Then he joined the Meteorological Flight at Duxford, which made daily sorties to take weather-forecasting readings, dangerous work that was given only to very good pilots. He hoped for a permanent RAF commission. But even in 1935, with expansion under way, his prospects were not sure and with some misgivings he accepted an offer to join Supermarine as an assistant to its chief test pilot, Mutt Summers, working on the Spitfire.

Progress was fitful. The prototype could not reach the 350 m.p.h. expected of it, only scraping up to 335 m.p.h. The propeller was one problem. It had been supplied by an outside contractor. A new one was designed by the Supermarine team and added an extra 13 m.p.h. Then the body surface was not smooth enough. Sinking rivets into the skin of the airframe would have brought better aerodynamic efficiency, but doing so would take much time and money. The team stuck split peas on the prototype to simulate round-headed rivets, which were much simpler to punch, then progressively removed them during aerodynamic tests to see which surfaces absolutely required flush rivets and which did not.

Failure to solve these problems and reach the performance levels Mitchell had claimed for his design could have meant the Spitfire never going into service. Quill and the rest of the team knew what was at stake. Later he revealed how close the decision had been. 'A lot of people felt that the Spitfire, although it had a very good performance . . . had been bought at too high a price. In terms of ease of production it was going to be a much more expensive and difficult aeroplane to mass produce. In terms of the ease of maintenance it was going to be a much more complicated aeroplane to look after and service . . . For instance, you could lower the undercarriage of a Hurricane and take the wings off because the undercarriage was in the centre section . . . You could take the wings off, put the tail up on a three-ton lorry and tow it along the road. You couldn't do that with a Spitfire. If you took the wings off . . . it took the undercarriage off as well . . . There were a lot of people who were against the Spitfire for those practical considerations. Therefore if we had not been able to show a really definite advantage over the Hurricane, it probably wouldn't have been ordered. We were well aware of that.'

A final, crucial question had to be settled. In May 1936 a prototype was sent to the RAF Aircraft and Armament Establishment at Martlesham for trials by the service's test pilots. Before the programme was complete, the research and development representative on the Air Council, Wilfred Freeman, asked the establishment's flight commander Flight Lieutenant Humphrey Edwards-Jones, whether the Spitfire could be flown with relative ease by ordinary squadron pilots. 'Old "E.-J." quite rightly said, "Yes, it can,"' Quill said later. On the strength of this judgement, before any performance testing had taken place, the decision to order was made. Quill reckoned there would have been 'an awful delay if he'd hedged about that. It was one of the best things ever done.'[6]

No. 19 Squadron had been chosen as the first unit to receive the Spitfire because of its record of superlative flying, demonstrated at displays around the country by an aerobatic team which performed such impressive but not necessarily militarily useful stunts as flying in rigid formation tied together with ropes. The five pilots selected to put the Spitfire through a 500-hour series of tests included two sergeants, George Unwin, the Ruislip apprentice, and his best friend Harry Steere. Unwin was particularly struck by the sensitivity of the controls. 'There was no heaving or pulling and pushing and kicking, you just breathed on it. She really was the perfect flying machine. She hadn't got a vice at all. She would only spin if you made her and she'd come straight out of it as soon as you applied opposite rudder and pushed the stick forward . . . I've never flown anything sweeter.' The Spitfire's engine note was instantly recognizable to those who had flown it, and distinct from that of a Hurricane, even though they both had the same Merlin power unit. Many years later Unwin was coming out of Boots in Bournemouth with his wife when he heard 'that peculiar throaty roar . . . I said to her, "There's a Spitfire somewhere." A taxi driver was standing there and said, "There she is, mate." It is a noise you will never forget.'[7]

Brian Kingcome believed 'it had all the best qualities an aircraft could have. It was docile, it was fast, it was manoeuvrable, it was gentle . . . it did everything you asked of it.'[8] John Nicholas of 65 Squadron accompanied Kingcome to the Supermarine airfield at Eastleigh, Southampton, where Jeffery Quill showed them the controls. He warned them that 'everything was sensitive . . . it was so light on the controls, index finger and thumb would fly it'.[9]

There were disadvantages, too, the first of which was immediately obvious at take-off. The undercarriage hydraulics were manual and the wheels had to be pumped up by lever with the right hand. There was a natural tendency to waggle the control column back and forth during the manoeuvre, and new pilots were recognizable by the way they pitched and yawed after they got airborne. This problem disappeared with the fitting of a power pump. It was easy to forget the propeller adjustments that had to be made to the Spitfire, the same as they did to the Hurricane. Brian Considine, a trainee executive with Unilever who joined the RAFVR at nineteen, had only flown fixed-pitch propeller biplanes when he was sent to join 238 Squadron at Tangmere. He was given one short trip in a single-wing Master trainer as preparation for his Spitfire debut. He 'took off in fine pitch and promptly forgot to put it back into coarse pitch, and did a few circles round the field thinking how marvellous it was . . . I made a nice landing and as I taxied in I could see the CO jumping up and down like a monkey in a rage. When I got out he told me I had wrecked the thing. I hadn't, but it was all covered in oil.'[10]

The Spitfire had a very long nose, which allowed the pilot virtually no forward vision when tilted on the back wheel in the taxiing position. To see ahead it was necessary to swing the aircraft from side to side. The centre of gravity was also unusually far forward, so a heavy foot on the brakes would tip the machine on to its propeller. But these, the infatuated pilots believed, were foibles not faults. The Spitfire was certainly a better aeroplane than the Hurricane and at least the equal of its German rival, the Messerschmitt 109. The former it could out-climb and out-dive. The latter it could out-turn. It was still in service in its Mark XII incarnation at the end of the war when the Hurricane had been phased out and replaced by the Typhoon. Brian Kingcome judged that 'the Hurricane was already more or less at the peak of its operational and design potential when it first came into service . . . its future was strictly limited by its rugged, uncouth airframe . . . The Spitfire, by contrast, possessed a unique capacity for development.'[11]

None the less the competitive spirit that the RAF, and particularly Fighter Command, fostered meant that the Hurricane pilots were loyal to their machines, maintaining to the last that they would not have swapped them for a Spitfire if given the choice. No. 111 Squadron pilots had had to endure some mockery at the time it took them to master the new fighters and finish the 500 hours of testing. George Unwin remembered that, as soon as they could muster twelve aircraft, the first thing they did was to come down to 19 Squadron at Duxford to 'beat up' the aerodrome, as the RAF called the practice of flying low and fast over bases to impress their rivals – or show off to girlfriends. Once 19 Squadron was able to do so, it flew over to Northolt and returned the compliment.

The re-equipment programme went slowly, moving at the limited pace that peacetime industrial capacity allowed. By the late summer of 1938 it seemed alarmingly out of step with events. The Munich crisis of September 1938 showed how swiftly the RAF might be called upon to act, and how unprepared it was to do so. As it broke, there were just six squadrons equipped with Hurricanes, only half of which were combat-ready. No. 19 Squadron had only three Spitfires, which were armed with machine guns but lacked gunsights. The remaining sixteen operational squadrons had Gladiator, Gauntlet, Demon and Fury biplanes to oppose the sleek, modern might of the Luftwaffe.

As the crisis deepened, officers of 1 Squadron and 43 Squadron joined aircraftmen in the hangars to cover the gleaming silver paint that usually decorated the Furies – to show them to their best advantage in formation flying and aerobatics – with dismal shades of camouflage green and brown. Billy Drake and his comrades were ordered to sleep in the hangars, next to the aircraft to be at full readiness. No one knew quite what to expect. 'I think we had an idea that they would go for us on the airfields, but nobody really seemed to have any strategy in mind – not at our level anyway.'[12]

At Biggin Hill, 79 Squadron was recalled from leave and on 27 September the auxiliaries of 601 Squadron were summoned to move from Hendon to the station, which had been designated their wartime base. At Hornchurch, 54, 74 and 65 Squadrons were called to immediate readiness and some pilots slept in crew rooms close to the aircraft. No. 74 Squadron had to abandon a gunnery practice camp at Sutton Bridge in Lincolnshire and return home, where they obliterated the squadron badges and tiger stripes adorning the fuselages of their Gauntlets and Gladiators, mixing up the paint from the colours available in the stores when the green and brown ran out. Al Deere, now with 54 Squadron, found it 'a heartrending operation having to desecrate one's beautiful Gladiator'. With the return of Chamberlain, waving his assurance from Hitler, the crisis fizzled out. The sigh of relief that gusted across Britain was not shared by all. 'It is callous and wrong to say it, but when "peace in our time" was agreed, I was horribly disappointed,' Deere admitted later.[13]

The likelihood of the Luftwaffe bombing Britain in the early autumn of 1938 was small, but the scare the crisis engendered was real and had the useful effect of speeding up the delivery of Hurricanes and Spitfires. The episode also blew away the last wisps of complacency that clung to the air force about what the future held. Politicians might maintain that this time Hitler could be trusted and a cataclysm had been averted rather than simply postponed. But many of the young pilots, and those who commanded them, now believed that a clash with the Luftwaffe was inevitable.

By the end of 1938 the Furies disappeared from Tangmere and Hurricanes took their place. Paul Richey arrived there in March 1939. He was in his twenty-third year and had been brought up in Switzerland, France and Albania, where his father, a veteran of the trenches, had helped to organize King Zog's gendarmerie. He was commissioned in 1937 and already knew Tangmere from visits during training. Posted there to join No. 1 Squadron, he noted the new atmosphere.

> Half the pilots in each squadron now had to be permanently available on station in case of a German attack. Gone were the carefree days when we would plunge into the cool blue sea at West Wittering and lie on the warm sand in the sun, or skim over the waters in Chichester harbour, in the squadron's sailing dinghy, or drive down to the Old Ship at Bosham with the breeze in our hair and knock it back under the oak rafters. Our days were now spent in our Hurricanes at air drill, air firing, practice battle formations and attacks, dogfighting – and operating under ground control with the new super-secret RDF (the name then given to radar).[14]

It was the same for everybody. The pleasant old arrangements of no flying after 4 p.m., and weekends and Wednesday afternoons off, were dropped and the tempo of practice and training quickened. The activity was intense but lacked direction and seemed curiously disconnected from the realities of aerial warfare as had been demonstrated by the German and Italian air forces in the skies over Spain. The preparations also seemed to lack consistency, with different squadrons following different programmes. It would soon become clear that some skills vital for success and survival in the changed conditions of air fighting were miserably under-taught and in some cases ignored altogether.

Tactical training before the war was based on two premises that would turn out to be fatally mistaken once the conflict began. The first of these was that close, tight formation flying concentrated force in such a way as to make fighters both more destructive and more secure. The second was the expectation that they would be facing fleets of bombers arriving in waves, capable of defending themselves with onboard guns but unprotected by escorting fighters. The logic of the assumption was that the Luftwaffe would be confined to its German bases and its Me 109s would not have the range to accompany the bombers.

Those who survived the war complained that the RAF had a drill-hall mentality, exalting the sort of flying discipline exemplified by 19 Squadron's aerial rope trick. There was a useful point to close formation flying. It helped groups of aeroplanes to move through cloud without colliding or losing contact with each other. But good formation drill was also seen as the basis of good tactics. Al Deere wrote later that 'the majority of our training in a pre-war fighter squadron was directed at achieving perfection in formation with a view to ensuring the success of the flight and squadron attacks we so assiduously practised'. These were known as Fighter Area Attacks, and were numbered from one to five, depending on the fighters' line of approach and the number of bombers. Thus, No. 1 involved a section of three or a flight of six fighters attacking one after the other a single bomber from astern. In No. 2, two or more fighters attacked a single bomber in line abreast, and No. 3 envisaged three fighters coming at a single bomber simultaneously from rear, beam, and rear quarter. It was all very theoretical and, as it turned out, of little use. But theory was all there was to go on.

'The order to attack was always preceded by the flight commander designating the number of the attack, viz. "FAA attack No. 5 – Go!"' Deere wrote later. 'These attacks provided wonderful training for formation drill, but were worthless when related to effective shooting. There was never sufficient time to get one's sights on the target, the business of keeping station being the prime requirement.'[15] Pete Brothers and the rest of 32 Squadron at Biggin Hill prepared for war by following rigid scenarios that proposed set responses to set situations, practising on 'enemy bombers' that flew stolidly on, disdaining to take any evasive action. 'If there was a small number of bombers your twelve aircraft would be divided up into sections of three. Then three of you would have a go at one bomber, one after the other. If there was a large number, you would spread out into echelon starboard [diagonally] setting it all up and giving them plenty of warning you were coming. It must have been all theoretical because no one had actually fought in these conditions before.'[16]

The tactics taught to George Unwin in 19 Squadron were 'more suited to the Hendon air display' than the realities of war. When put into practice for the first time over Dunkirk, the results were to be disastrous. The severe limitations of the pre-war tactical approach was to become apparent almost immediately, but this did not stop it being taught well into the war. Roger Hall, a young, pre-war professional soldier who transferred to the RAF, was posted to 152 Squadron at the height of the fighting in September 1940 after only a week's operational training. He remembered during his instruction being 'briefed on how to attack a bomber, but it was so perfunctory really that it was almost ludicrous.' Three pilots were designated to take off in their newly acquired Spitfires and 'attack' a Wellington which was playing the role of an enemy bomber. Green though he was, Hall knew that 'when you attack a hostile bomber they try to get out of the way. But this particular one was simply flying straight and level . . . The drill was to get above the bomber and the first Spitfire would come down and shoot its port engine and then it would break away. The next one would come and shoot the starboard, then that would break away. Then the third one would come down and shoot the body of the machine and then break away, but all the time the Wellington was just going straight and level, just asking for it . . . I used to laugh about that.'[17]

Brian Kingcome recalled that 'fighter *versus* fighter wasn't really envisaged or catered for', and the assumption was that if they did take place they would be 'pretty much as they were in the First World War except that you had faster, better aircraft and the huge advantage of a parachute'. None the less individual pilots did get in unofficial practice, going off in pairs to chase each other around the sky.[18]

The pilots who went into action for the first time in 1939 and 1940 might have known a lot about flying. They knew little, though, about how to fight in the air and less about how to shoot. Aerial gunnery was supposed to be taught as part of training and each regular fighter squadron was expected to go to an annual camp at one of the armament training stations for practice with live ammunition, shooting at drogues towed behind other aircraft, or at ground targets. This was occasionally supplemented by the use of camera guns, from which theoretical scores could be deduced. It was all a long way from reality.

In retrospect the amount of time spent on what was a fundamental air skill would seem desperately inadequate. 'Looking back,' Al Deere wrote afterwards, 'I can see how dreadfully we neglected gunnery practice, live or by means of cine-films, and what an important part it plays in the part of a successful fighter pilot . . . squadron morale carried us safely through the early fighter battles of the war, not straight shooting.'[19]

Some pilots never fired at an aerial target before going into action. Tony Bartley, the son of a colonial service judge, who was awarded a short-service commission after leaving Stowe school, did his training before the war. Yet the first time he aimed his guns at a flying object was when he shot at an Me 109 in May 1940. George Unwin was fortunate in having Harry Broadhurst, an outstanding shot, as his flight commander. 'Training in shooting was nonexistent. No one ever taught you how to shoot. But he did.' Broadhurst emphasized 'that the key to shooting was to get in close and the closer you got the more chance you had of hitting'. Unwin, who became a gunner instructor later in his career, found that one of the biggest weaknesses among fighter pilots at the beginning of the war was their inability properly to calculate how far they were from the aircraft they were attacking, often opening fire long before they reached what combat experience would teach was the optimum range of 250 yards. In the pre-war days, when aircraft were still equipped with a simple ring sight, Broadhurst taught his charges to work out the distance of the target by measuring it against the diameter of the circle. At 400 yards a bomber the size of a Wellington exactly filled the sight. At 250 yards, the ring was just outboard of the two engines. It was simple and effective, but according to Unwin never taught systematically.

The apparent explanation for the lack of firing practice was that, with tight financial restraints on the expansion programme, the Air Ministry had decided that spending money on the aircraft and pilots needed to man and equip the new squadrons took priority over new ranges, and so allowances for practice ammunition were cut to a minimum. There was no such excuse in 1940. By then shortage of time was to blame for a continuing failure to teach raw pilots how to shoot before throwing them into battle. When Archie Winskill, a softly spoken RAFVR volunteer from Cumberland, reached 72 Squadron at Biggin Hill on 4 October 1940, he was 'well-schooled in formation flying and tactics but regrettably with no air-firing experience. I'd only fired my guns once into the sea off Liverpool . . . We knew nothing about deflection shooting.'[20]

What was needed to attack successfully was the skill to manoeuvre into a favourable position, the ability to judge the correct range to open fire, and finally, and usually equally importantly, the knowledge of how to angle the shot so it stood the best chance of hitting the enemy aeroplane. The latter was deflection shooting. In all but full-on frontal or rear attacks, shooting in a straight line was useless. To strike the target required 'laying off', in the same way that a game shooter aims ahead of the pheasant so that the bird flies into the spread of pellets. The principle was recognized in the clay pigeon range installed at pre-war Tangmere and copied later in the war at many fighter bases. Some of the most deadly pilots, like Bob Tuck and Adolph Malan, attributed at least some of their success to their skill with shotguns. The importance of deflection shooting was obvious. Winskill was not to learn it until he was sent off to a gunnery course long after the 1940 crisis had passed.

The pilots of Fighter Command also went into the war with little idea of what they would be shooting at. George Unwin 'didn't know a thing' about the Germans' strengths, aircraft types and likely *modus operandi* before he met them in the air. At the time of Munich, the British air attaché in Berlin made a tour of squadron bases and delivered a lecture about the Luftwaffe. But detailed intelligence briefings on the enemy were never given on an organized basis before the fighting began, and during the battles of 1940 pilots were seldom allowed a glimpse of the bigger picture. Their knowledge was confined to what had happened to them and their companions on the base, or what they heard on the radio. These shortcomings in training and preparation would only become fully apparent when revealed by the stresses of combat.

The approach of the cataclysm forced the pilots to think about the future. That the crisis was coming to a head seemed surprisingly comforting to some. Watching Europe's tottering, somnambulistic progress once more towards the precipice induced feelings of restlessness and a desire to get the inevitable over with. Peter Townsend, who at the time of the Abyssinian war had been sickened by the thought of the effects of bombs on men, found the sight of the enemy, clear and unambiguous, was a liberation. 'A complete change of mind and heart had by now come over me . . . My pacifism of the previous year had evaporated; I was becoming rather bellicose – at least as bloody-minded as every other Englishman felt towards the swaggering, bullying Germans.'

Townsend also noticed that the imminence of danger broke down whatever barriers remained between the new and the old RAF inside 43 Squadron, so that 'in the growingly tense atmosphere, I was discovering that those parvenu pilots I had once so resented were really the warmest, most generous friends . . . genuine 'fighter boys', who lived for the shining hour, who did not take themselves seriously.'[21]

The attitude cultivated by fighter pilots from the first days on the Western Front had been hedonistic, light-hearted, little concerned with events outside their world. This was to some extent genuine, to some extent affectation. Nobody now could be indifferent to what was happening in Europe. A number of the pilots had first-hand knowledge of the rise of fascism from time spent on the Continent. James Sanders, who was brought up in Italy, had once at the age of nine sung, with the school choir, the slaves' chorus from Verdi's *Nabucco* in front of Mussolini himself. This encounter had induced no sentiments of respect. Later he got into trouble at school for using squares of newspaper, bearing the Duce's photograph, as lavatory paper. Billy Drake had been sent by his father, first to a German-speaking, then to a French-speaking school in Switzerland in preparation for a career in the hotel business. In the first establishment, 'I was the only English boy and all my classmates were Germans or Italians. I got a bit fed up with their sniping at the British Empire all the time. I spoke to the housemaster and told him what was happening and told him I intended to challenge them to a boxing bout every time it happened with him as the referee. And so I was knocked down about twelve times.'[22]

Pat Hancock was sixteen when, in 1935, he went to stay with a family near Hanover and attended the local school. 'I saw enough of the German youth movement to know how strictly disciplined they were and how confident they were that they had a great role to play in the world.' In the streets of Hanover he saw formations of troops marching everywhere. 'They were cock of the walk . . . everything glistened. I thought, my goodness, these are people who are going to have a go, given an opportunity.'[23]

During an air tour of Europe in the spring of 1935 Jeffery Quill had stopped at Berlin. He wrote to his mother that he had arrived at Templehof 'in the middle of a sort of Hendon Air Display – they shot red lights at us to stop us landing but I was hanged if I was going to float round the sky waiting for their air display to finish, so I landed in the middle of it. They were a bit annoyed at first, but as I couldn't understand what they were saying I just laughed and they soon quietened down. They are much too serious up here.'[24]

Tony Bartley decided to visit Germany after being told by the captain of his rugby team, an RAF officer, that war was inevitable. After leaving Stowe school he had joined a City accounting firm to learn the profession, but left after a year. What he saw in the Reich impressed him profoundly. In Frankfurt-on-Main, staying with acquaintances of his parents, he came across a middle-aged man with a shaven head in the city's botanical gardens. He learned he was a distinguished Jew who had just been released from a concentration camp. He told him of his experiences and invited him home to meet his family. When Bartley informed his hosts, they were horrified and told him to sever the new friendship or return to Britain. When he asked for a reason, he was told that 'their son, a Hitler Youth, would denounce his father to the Gestapo for harbouring a Jew fraternizer'.[25]

Ben Bowring, who joined 600 Auxiliary Squadron in 1938, met Germans in Switzerland, where he was at school, and in America, where his father travelled for business, and later through friends in Britain. He 'absolutely loathed them. I knew them socially and they were always asking me to fly over to Germany and one thing and another. I knew perfectly well by their attitude that they were a very cruel type of people . . . [They] had quick tempers and they thought they were masters of everything. Since I was something of an athlete, if I beat them at a game they were quite upset and quite likely they wouldn't talk to you for a day or so. Or else if you beat them very badly they would come cringing to you on their knees (like) bullies, having been very unpleasant to you beforehand.'[26]

The same unsporting tendencies were to strike Richard Hillary when he went with an Oxford boat crew to compete in Germany in July 1938 in the 'General Goering Prize Fours' at Bad Ems. The team's attitude to the race appeared languid, an approach which annoyed their hosts.

> Shortly before the race we walked down to the changing-rooms to get ready. All five German crews were lying flat on their backs on mattresses, great brown stupid-looking giants, taking deep breaths. It was all very impressive. I was getting out of my shirt when one of them came up and spoke to me, or rather harangued me, for I had no chance to say anything. He had been watching us, he said, and could only come to the conclusion that we were thoroughly representative of a decadent race. No German crew would dream of appearing so lackadaisical if rowing in England: they would train and they would win. Losing this race might not appear very important to us, but I could rest assured that the German people would not fail to notice and learn from our defeat.

The Oxford crew won, by two fifths of a second, and took home the cup, a gold shell-case mounted with a German eagle. 'It was certainly an unpopular win,' Hillary wrote afterwards. 'Had we shown any enthusiasm or given any impression that we had trained they would have tolerated it, but as it was they showed merely a sullen resentment.'[27]

Hillary subsequently saw the race as a metaphor for the coming conflict, a 'surprisingly accurate pointer to the course of the war. We were quite untrained, lacked any form of organization and were really quite hopelessly casual'. This was a particularly British piece of mythologizing that was some distance from the truth. Hillary was fiercely competitive on the river, and the pilots of Fighter Command would turn out to be just as aggressive as their Luftwaffe counterparts. As for training, they had prepared for the war as hard as anybody. The problem was that much of the effort had been misdirected.

It was a question of image. The Fighter Boys, like the rowers, wanted to win, and took their superiority for granted. They would rather, though, that victory was attained without too much obvious exertion. The picture was of amused, easy-going Britons triumphing over robotic Germans. It was the view the pilots had taken of themselves and it was the way they wished to be seen. This, very soon, would come to pass.

It was true, however, that deep political thinking, let alone ideological conviction, was rare among the pilots. All the services had a tradition in which political enthusiasms were regarded as both unprofessional and socially undesirable. The RAF was different in that the majority of its members, the tradesmen and technicians, were from the ambitious upper working class or lower middle class and more inclined to question authority than their counterparts in the army. Junior officers could also be vocal about decisions by higher authority, especially where life-or-death matters concerning equipment or tactics were concerned, and the general conduct of the war would later sometimes be criticised.

At Cranwell, the debating society provided a formal arena for political discussion. In November 1938 the motion was that, 'This House considers that an agreement with Germany is in the best interests of Great Britain and of the world at large.' It was only narrowly defeated by thirty-six to thirty-four votes, after an intervention by a cadet who pointed out that 'the persecution of the Jews precluded any decent-minded people from having anything to do with the Germans'.[28]

Among the squadron pilots, though, domestic and international politics and the details of each crisis appear to have excited little interest. Billy Drake and the Tangmere pilots 'bought a newspaper to look at the sporting events, that's all. We didn't read it to find out what Hitler was doing. The attitude in the mess was that the war was inevitable, so why talk about it?'[29] Geoffrey Page's recollection was that 'pre-war and all through the war one never really discussed politics at all. It wasn't an issue . . . Two subjects were taboo in an officers' mess. You never talked politics and you never talked about the opposite sex.' The first prohibition was more strictly observed than the second.[30]

At Oxford, the University Air Squadron appears to have been gripped by the general sense of inexorability. By 1939 its members all assumed they were going to have to fight, despite the continuing optimistic noises being made by Chamberlain and his supporters. Individual political beliefs, where they were held at all, had become irrelevant. Richard Hillary was contemptuous of his bourgeois left-wing contemporaries and impressed but unconvinced by heartfelt pacifists. He and his contemporaries were perceived, he wrote, as superficially 'selfish and egocentric without any Holy Grail in which we could lose ourselves'. The war, by offering up an unmistakable and worthwhile enemy, had provided it. Now they had 'the opportunity to demonstrate in action our dislike of organized emotion and patriotism, the opportunity to prove to ourselves and the world that our effete veneer was not as deep as our dislike of interference, the opportunity to prove that, undisciplined though we might be, we were a match for Hitler's dogma-fed youth'.[31]

These were more complex sentiments than were felt by most of the pilots. Stephen Beaumont, notably decent and intelligent, was probably nearer the feelings of the majority when he reflected on the motives that had pushed himself and his upper middle class Yorkshire comrades to join the auxiliaries. 'Old-fashioned patriotism? Desire to give back to the community something for their – at least in some cases – admittedly favoured social background? Dismay, turning to acute dislike even hatred of the bullying they came to see in Germany? A desire to fly? Probably all these things.'[32]

The overseas pilots were moved by a simple sense of duty that must have seemed slightly anachronistic even in 1939. Asked later what he had been fighting for, Al Deere replied: 'In my generation, as schoolboys, we always thought of [Britain] as the home country, always referred to it as the Mother Country. That was the old colonial tie . . . There was no question that if this country was threatened, New Zealanders wouldn't go to war for Britain.'[33] It was the same for Adolph 'Sailor' Malan, a South African ex-merchant navy officer who settled in Britain in 1935 and applied for a short-service commission. Malan's voyages with the Union Castle line had taken him to Hamburg, where he 'spent a lot of time talking to German harbour officials, sailors and civilians. Their attitude made me realize that war was inevitable.'[34]

The pilots were joined by men who had no strong bonds natural with Britain, such as Billy Fiske, an upper-class American sportsman, captain of the US Olympic bobsled team, who volunteered two weeks after the outbreak of war. Several recruits came from Ireland. The fact that Eire was officially neutral and just emerging from a bitter independence struggle with Britain had made no difference to 'Paddy' Finucane, whose father had taken part in the 1916 Easter Rising, nor to John Ignatius 'Killy' Kilmartin, black-haired and sleekly handsome, who was to fight almost from the first day of the war to the last.

Acceptance, resignation, a certain thrilled apprehension seem to have been the predominant attitudes and emotions as the last days of peace slipped away. Not everyone answered the call of duty. In 609 Squadron one pilot decided to defect. He was, Stephen Beaumont recalled, 'not a particularly attractive man . . . We felt no loss at his going.' The squadron structure and the overwhelming importance of *esprit* meant that only the dedicated were welcome.

At Hornchurch, aircraft were now dispersed away from their hangars and along the far side of the airfield and tents put up to house the ground crews. A readiness system was introduced so that one shift of pilots was always dressed and ready to fly at short notice. It was to last until 1943 when the Luftwaffe no longer posed any serious threat to the country in daylight. Al Deere and the other pilots spent summer days stripped to the waist, filling sandbags to build the walls of U-shaped blast-protection pens that shielded their Spitfires. At Tangmere 1 Squadron and 43 Squadron skimmed their Hurricanes over the Channel waves, firing at splash targets with volleys from their Brownings that kicked up jagged white plumes and churned the water. The effect seemed devastating to old-timers brought up on the spindly fire-power of a single Lewis gun. 'The noise is not so much a rat-a-tat as a continuous jarring explosion,' wrote an RFC veteran.[35] By night they climbed into the Sussex skies, suspended between the stars and the street lighting that provided bearings and allowed them to keep station in the pre-blackout era. On landing, the ground crews would pounce to rearm and refuel in minutes, practising the rapid turnarounds that would prove crucially important in the fighting to come.

It was not all work. Squadron Leader Lord Willoughby de Broke arrived with the other members of 605 Auxiliary Squadron at Tangmere and entertained at Tangmere Cottage, opposite the base. The pilots, Peter Townsend remembered, 'spent wild evenings, drinking, singing, dancing to romantic tunes', with 'These Foolish Things', the hit of the day, revolving eternally on the gramophone.

All around, though, the peacetime landscape was changing. The whitish aprons and parade grounds of Biggin Hill were covered in chippings in a vain attempt to disguise the station from the air. On several nights, the lights of London were extinguished in a trial to test the efficiency of the blackout. A pilot reported that the ground 'looked like space inverted, just space with a few pinpricks of light like stars'. Barrage balloons wallowed in the air over town and suburb. The skies themselves were filled with ominous noises. In August, 200 bombers, fighters and reconnaissance aircraft appeared over London, Liverpool, Bristol, Birmingham, Manchester and Oxford, where they attracted the attention of RAF fighters and searchlight units. The aircraft were French, and the exercise intended as a test of Britain's air defences, but few could have looked up without a *frisson* of apprehension.

Death moved a little closer. The Oxford University Air Squadron and RAFVR summer camp at Lympne in July was overshadowed by a mid-air collision in which Pilot Officer David Lewis, an experienced pilot who was flying solo in a Hawker Hind, crashed into a Gipsy Moth carrying a pupil and instructor from the Kent Flying School. All three were killed. It was, the OUAS log recorded 'the first fatal accident in the squadron since it formed'.

Accidental deaths were commonplace, however, elsewhere in the air force, as pilots stalled, spun in, or flew into 'clouds with a hard centre' – hills obscured by fog. On one murky night at Biggin Hill, Flying Officer

Olding was sent up to report on the state of a practice blackout in the Greater London area. Soon after take-off his engine seemed to cut out, then the pilots in the mess heard an explosion. A fire tender was ordered out, but fearing it would never be able to locate the wreckage in the foul weather, Flying Officer Woolaston took off, intending to drop a magnesium flare near the crash site. A few minutes later a second explosion was heard. His Hurricane was found a hundred yards from Olding's, having flown into the top of Tatsfield Hill.

The effect of such events could be profound, but not necessarily lasting. Brian Kingcome was ordered to go and formally identify the body of a squadron pilot who crashed near Andover. He flew down and was met by a policeman who was concerned at the effect the sight of a mangled body might have on a healthy young man. 'The body had been quite badly battered, he warned me, and I braced myself for the worst. Gently he drew back the sheet . . . I looked at the broken body and felt curiously unmoved . . . On my way back to Hornchurch I briefly wondered whether there was not a lesson here: whether I ought to be more careful, stick more closely to the rule books . . .' The mood, though, 'was short-lived'.[36]

The number of fatal accidents inevitably increased as the 300 m.p.h. plus monoplanes, far harder to control than the biplanes, and in need of more room to recover if a mistake was made, were fed into the squadrons. At Tangmere, one pilot slid too slowly out of a turn and crashed in front of his comrades. Another time they watched as a pilot clipped the top of a tree coming in to land and burned to death before their eyes. Afterwards, Peter Townsend recorded 'we had our own methods of restoring our morale. In the early hours of that morning, in the mess, we mourned our lost comrade in our own peculiar way, which smacked somewhat of the ritual of primitive tribesmen. Fred Rosier took his violin and to the tune of the can-can from *Orpheus in the Underworld*, we danced hilariously round the mess.'[37]

Other atavistic instincts were stirring; the impulses to marry, or at least to have sex. The pre-war RAF discouraged officers from matrimony under the age of thirty. This was partly out of parsimony, partly out of considerations of efficiency and the desire to foster a mess-centred squadron spirit. What the service needed were single men free of family responsibilities, ready to move, at virtually no notice, where and when they were needed. Pilots had to seek the permission of their commanding officers before taking a wife. Failure to secure it meant no married quarters accommodation and no allowances. As the year wore on, the number of requests multiplied. On getting engaged to his girlfriend, Annette, Pete Brothers had to appear before Group Captain Dick Grice, the Biggin Hill commandant, who, 'fortunately . . . was a very charming chap. He was sitting behind a desk smoking a pipe, and he said, "You're very young" – I was just 21 – "what if I refuse?" I said in that case it would be very difficult to send him an invitation to the wedding.'[38] Grice, an immensely popular father figure with Biggin Hill pilots and staff, laughed and gave in.

Tim Vigors, on leave from Cranwell, took advantage of a trip to London to look up Kitty, a girlfriend who was staying in town with an aunt. They spent the evening dancing in a club off Regent Street, leaving at 3 a.m. Vigors daringly suggested that she come back for a drink. To his surprise she agreed and they repaired to the Regent Palace Hotel. He was prevented from taking matters further when a vigilant night porter blocked his path, protesting that Vigors had 'only booked a single and anyway she's far too young for those kind of tricks'. He 'tried to remain calm despite the fact that I had never felt so embarrassed in my life. "None of your business!" I retorted. "Come on Kitty, let's get inside and lock this bastard out!"' Kitty, however, burst into tears. Vigors gallantly drove her home and returned to the hotel 'feeling embarrassed, ashamed, angry and frustrated'.[39]

Senior officers, too, felt youthful stirrings as the great trial approached. Air Vice-Marshal Trafford Leigh-Mallory, the Air Officer Commanding No. 12 Fighter Group covering the Midlands and north, visited his pilots in 616 Squadron at their summer camp at Manston on the Kent coast. A dinner was laid on in his honour in one of the marquees. At the end of the evening the inevitable, well-lubricated games began. One involved climbing up the centre pole, squeezing through a ventilation flap, clambering over the ridge pole and re-entering the tent through the flap on the other side. Several pilots, including Hugh Dundas, did so without mishap.

> Then someone suggested that the AOC should have a go. Very sportingly, he agreed. But he was not really built for that kind of thing. In the course of the passing years his figure had thickened. He got up the pole all right. But he had a terrible job squeezing out through the ventilation flap. We stood below and cheered him on. At last he plopped through and his face, purple with exertion, disappeared out into the night. The tent swayed and the ridge-pole sagged as he struggled across the top. His legs reappeared on the other side. He got half-way and stuck.
>
> Shouting with laughter, we urged him on and his legs and buttocks wiggled and waggled as he fought his way through that canvas flap. Someone shinned up the pole and helped him with a few hearty tugs. He came out like a champagne cork, grabbed desperately at the pole and descended from a height of about ten feet in a free fall . . . He accepted a very large, very dark whisky and soda and left us hurriedly before we started playing something else.[40]

A few days later Dundas was sitting in the mess tent after a morning's flying when the news of the Molotov–Ribbentrop pact came through. 'Teddy St Aubyn, who was sitting opposite me, put down his soup spoon and said in a loud, clear voice: "Well that's . . . d it. That's the start of the . . . g war."' Looking back, Dundas could not say why this pronouncement struck him with such force, given that, as he dryly remarked, 'Teddy . . . was not noted as a political pundit or a serious student of international affairs. But I heard his words and knew they were true.'

The announcement was finally made late on the morning of 3 September, a day that was generally remembered as being exceptionally warm, sunny and redolent of all the promise of young life. At fighter bases the length and breadth of the country the pilots gathered in the mess or clustered round portable radios rigged up at the dispersal areas to hear Prime Minister Chamberlain speak. At Tangmere, the pilots in Peter Townsend's flight were lying on the grass by their Hurricanes when they were told that 'the balloon goes up at 11.45'. They walked over to the mess, covered in pink creeper, and waited while the faithful stewards served drinks in pewter mugs. As the broadcast ended, 'the tension suddenly broke. The fatal step had been taken; we were at war.' Caesar Hull, a brilliant sportsman and aerobatic pilot who had joined the RAF on a short-service commission from South Africa, was the first to rejoice, repeating, 'Wizard!' over and over. He turned to another 43 pilot John Simpson, and laughingly prophesied: 'Don't worry, John, you'll be one of the first to be killed.' Simpson survived the war. Hull died a year and four months later while attacking a large formation of German bombers. That night, after being released, Townsend and his comrades raced to the Old Ship at Bosham. 'What a party we had; at closing time, we went out into the street and fired our revolvers into the air. Windows were flung open, people rushed from their houses, thinking the invasion had started.'[41]

At Cranwell, Tim Vigors and his fellow cadets were ordered to the ante-room to hear the broadcast. When the declaration of war came, 'a shout of excitement rose from all our throats. As one man we jumped to our feet cheering. There was not one amongst us who would not have been bitterly disappointed had the declaration of war not been made.' The same scene was taking place simultaneously in a classroom in Hull, where Charlton Haw and thirty of his fellow RAFVR pilots were gathered after being called up the week before. 'A tremendous cheer went out from all of us. We were very pleased about the whole thing. We didn't think about the danger. We all had visions of sitting in a Spitfire the following day. And then the disappointing thing was we were all sent home.'[42] In Romford, where he worked in the Ind Coope brewery, another reservist, William Walker, switched off the radio, put on his sergeant's uniform and walked out of his block of flats. A group of men were digging an air-raid shelter and he offered to help. 'They said: "No, not at all! You're in uniform. We can't let you do that sort of thing." '[43]

Charles Fenwick, who had recently joined the RAFVR, was one of the few to be surprised by the news. He was so buoyed up by happiness that he had refused to believe war could not be avoided. 'I was in love as only a twenty-year-old can be in love, I was all set for Cambridge, I owned a lovely little car and damn it I was enjoying life. Then this shit-head comes along and puts the lid on everything.' His first reaction was 'one of absolute shock, horrified shock . . . My second reaction was not long in coming. No bloody German was going to hurt those I loved and get away with it if I could stop him.'[44]

The pilots of 56 Squadron were sitting in small groups in the sun on the east side of the aerodrome at North Weald in Essex, listening to radios powered by outsize batteries. Earlier the squadron adjutant had distributed blue will forms to be filled in. 'There were great roars of laughter,' remembered Peter Down, a twenty-three-year-old who had joined eighteen months before. 'All we had to leave really were our golf clubs and tennis rackets and things. We had the odd car and there were shouts of, "Who wants my Lagonda?" or, "Who wants my clubs?" We left them to each other.'[45]

Not everyone was so light-hearted. Brian Kingcome was struck by the flatness of the address, devoid of drama or tension, 'just this, sorrowful defeated voice going on'. He looked around at his companions in the hangar office in Hornchurch, 'thinking to myself, probably the whole lot of us will be dead in three weeks . . . No sooner had Chamberlain finished his speech on the radio than we expected to hear the murmur of hordes of German bombers approaching and that became the norm at dispersal for a while.'[46]

5

Winter of Uncertainty

The war began in a flurry of false alarms. Air-raid sirens sounded almost immediately after Chamberlain's Sunday broadcast, sending civilians hurrying to the shelters. But no Germans came. The defenders were eager for action and trigger-happy. Three days after the declaration of war, a searchlight battery on Mersea Island in the Blackwater estuary spotted what was thought to be a hostile aircraft crossing the Channel coast. This exciting news was passed on to the Northolt headquarters of 11 Group, which covered the south-east of England. They, in turn, ordered the local sector controllers at North Weald to send up fighters to investigate. Hurricanes from 56 Squadron took off from North Weald aerodrome and climbed through the mist into the clear morning sky to hunt for the intruders. As they did so, their traces were picked up by the radar station at Canewdon, on the muddy tongue of Essex that sticks out between the Crouch and Thames estuaries. Even now, the cause of the tragic fiasco that followed is not entirely clear. Air Chief Marshal Sir Hugh Dowding, the Fighter Command chief, said later that the equipment was faulty and the baffle designed to block out electronic echoes from the landward side was not functioning, though this was disputed. To the operators it seemed they had located a big enemy formation coming in over the sea. More fighters were scrambled to deal with the apparent threat, and they in turn registered on the screen and added to the thickening confusion. Among them were twelve Spitfires from 74 Squadron at Hornchurch. 'A'

Flight, commanded by Adolph Malan, took off first. He led one section of three aircraft. Flying Officer 'Paddy' Byrne, an experienced, Irish-born pilot with a reputation for eccentricity, led another. In the adrenaline-charged atmosphere, chaos, then catastrophe, ensued.

Pilot Officer John Freeborn, barely out of Leeds Grammar School but well-freighted with Yorkshire obstinacy, was directly behind Byrne. 'It was a very misty morning but it was a beautiful day,' he said. 'I remember looking down and seeing we had cut a line through the haze where we had taken off. Malan was well in front . . . We saw these aircraft and Malan gave the order: "Number One attack – go!" They made an attack at these aircraft and then pulled away. And so we went and attacked.'[1]

The combat was only too successful. Freeborn, Byrne and the third man in the section, Sergeant Pilot John Flinders, swooped down in line astern. Freeborn and Byrne opened fire and saw two aircraft go down trailing smoke. Freeborn felt 'exhilarated' at their success. On the way back to Hornchurch he saw what he thought was a Luftwaffe bomber and was about to attack when Flinders yelled a warning on the R/T that it was in fact a friendly Blenheim. On landing he was met by his commanding officer, Squadron Leader George Sampson, and told that the aircraft he and Byrne had disposed of were Hurricanes from 56 Squadron. Pilot Officer Montague Hulton-Harrop was dead. He was nineteen years old, a newcomer to the squadron and 'tall, fair-haired and eager', according to Eric Clayton, a ground-crew member who maintained his machine. Pilot Officer Tommy Rose survived and showed up later in the day.[2]

Freeborn was appalled. He tried to find Malan, but he had 'done a bunk completely. Never saw him.' He and Byrne were put under arrest. 'I was sent to my room with a bloke from 54 Squadron to guard me . . . I was eighteen years old, frightened to bloody death.'[3] Coming soon after an incident when he had been severely reprimanded for landing with the undercarriage of his Spitfire up, Freeborn assumed his RAF career was over. The affair was particularly agonizing because, as squadron adjutant, he had previously distributed orders to the pilots telling them under no circumstances to shoot at single-engined planes. The instruction was based on the calculation that no Luftwaffe fighter had the range to reach Britain and that any single-engined machine was bound to be friendly. The speed with which Freeborn forgot the order was proof of the disorienting power of the heat of the moment. Al Deere, who was also scrambled that morning, had felt it too. 'We were all keyed up,' he said. 'You didn't think about the fact that a 109 could never have got as far as England from the then borders of Germany.'[4]

A general court martial was set for 7 October. Sampson, 'an absolute toff' according to Freeborn, put the pair in touch with Sir Patrick Hastings, an intelligence officer at Fighter Command HQ at Stanmore, who had been a leading QC in peacetime. Hastings agreed to act as prisoners' friend and told them to speak to Roger Bushell, another well-known figure at the London bar who was now commanding 600 (City of London) Auxiliary Squadron at Biggin Hill. Bushell, whose charm and indomitable nature made him one of the best-liked men in the air force, agreed to act as junior to Hastings. The proceedings were held at Stanmore and have never been made public. Freeborn claims Malan denied ever giving the order to attack. The defence argued that the case should never have been brought. After about an hour the four-man tribunal, led by the Judge Advocate, acquitted the two. It was the start of a long-running enmity in 74 Squadron. 'From then on,' Freeborn said, 'Malan and I never got on.'

'Sailor' Malan had already established himself as a formidable personality. He was short, with fair hair, blazing blue eyes and a square, impassive face and cleft chin. He was coming up to twenty-nine, considerably older than most of the other pilots. He had done much in a hard life, and spoken little. Adolph Gysbert Malan was born within sight of Table Mountain in Cape Province and brought up on a farm near the small town of Slent. As a child he roamed the veldt with a shotgun, developing a marksman's eye that would serve him well in the war. Aged fourteen he was sent off to a maritime college on board the training ship *General Botha*. The regime was spartan, the bullying institutionalized and the discipline harsh, bordering on the sadistic. Smoking was punished by six strokes of the lash. The victim was first certified as medically fit enough to withstand the punishment. He was ordered to strip to 'No. 1 Duck Trousers' – shorts – and given a rubber disc to bite on. Then he was stretched over a table in the recreation room and roped down to a ring bolt while the punishment was administered in public.

Malan once said: 'The first time I saw this punishment handed out it was to a big chap – an Old Salt (as the senior cadets were known). It was quite a shock to see him break down. Later on I understood why.' Freeborn had seen the scars from the whippings on Malan's back. His biographer wrote that 'in talks with Sailor, during which he described incidents infinitely more dramatic and perilous than anything that happened aboard the *Botha*, I never saw him more emotionally stirred than when he recalled the ceremony of being tied down and thrashed. The memory of it stayed with him vividly as a deed of outrage, an invasion of pride and privacy that helped to fashion a kind of stoicism that became an armour plating for the strenuous days to come.' The experience also made him reluctant, 'in later years, to join in the horseplay of RAF squadron initiating customs'.[5]

The 6 September débâcle was inscribed in RAF folklore as the Battle of Barking Creek, a reference to a nearby landmark which was a joke location beloved of music-hall comedians. It was one of several similar incidents, all efficiently hushed up (an official communiqué was not issued until seven months later), which revealed to the air force and the government the dangerous inadequacies of the country's air defences. On the same day as the 'Barking Creek' episode, Brian Kingcome was with 65 Squadron patrolling at 5,000 feet over the Thames. Every time they passed over the Isle of Sheppey, anti-aircraft guns opened up, even though the undersides of their Spitfires were painted black and white to identify them as friendly. A signal was sent to the batteries telling them to hold their fire, but it did not stop one aeroplane being hit in the wing and fuselage.

The basic problem was one of identification. The aircraft that sparked the panic on 6 September was, according to Dowding, carrying refugees from Holland. Other accounts say it was a Blenheim returning from a patrol over the North Sea, or an Anson from Coastal Command. Unless air traffic could be quickly and accurately recognized as friend or enemy, the potential for disaster was enormous. The problem had already been solved by a system called IFF (Identification Friend or Foe), a transmitter which sent back an amplified signal that established an aircraft's innocent intentions when picked up in a radar beam. But none of the Spitfires or Hurricanes chasing each other around the Thames estuary had yet been fitted with it. After the incident the installation programme was belatedly speeded up, so that by June 1940 it was standard equipment on every fighter.

The fiasco concentrated minds. Al Deere, who was with 54 Squadron at Hornchurch, noted that 'on five out of my next six training flights I was engaged on tactical exercises in cooperation with the control and reporting organization'. In retrospect he felt that some good had come out of 'this truly amazing shambles'. It was, he thought, 'just what was needed to iron out some of the many snags which existed . . . and to convince those who were responsible that a great deal of training of controllers, plotters and radar operators, all of whom had been hastily drafted in on the first emergency call-up, was still required before the system could be considered in any way reliable'.[6]

The mechanisms for identifying and reporting the approach of enemy aircraft, and the command and control structure to counter their attacks, would be refined and tested in the relative quiet of the winter and spring. Radar was at the heart of the system. It was based on the discovery that solid objects reflected radio waves. A projected radio signal, on encountering the metal skin of an aircraft, bounced back and registered as a blip on a cathode-ray tube. The military potential was obvious and the United States, Japan and, above all, Germany worked on applications throughout the 1930s.

Britain got radar late but it had recovered lost time and by the onset of the war was protected by two chains of transmitters covering the upper and lower airspace of the island's eastern and southern approaches. The twenty stations, with their mysterious 350-feet-high transmitters and 240-feet receivers, could locate aircraft a hundred miles away and give an approximate idea of direction, height and numbers. With radar, the historical defensive advantage given to Britain by the sea extended to the air. It was particularly effective over large expanses of water where there was no confusing 'clutter'. Even so it was to remain, for several years, an inexact science.

The electronic information pulsing on the cathode-ray tubes under the intense gaze of the Waafs, who were the most expert operators, was supplemented by the eyes and ears of the spotters of the Observer Corps. These were volunteers who squatted in sandbagged posts, equipped with binoculars, aircraft identification pamphlets and a crude altitude measuring instrument, trying to track enemy aeroplanes as they droned overhead. The blurred picture provided by the two was brought into sharper focus after passing through the filter room at Bentley Priory, an eighteenth-century Gothic mansion in Stanmore on the north-west edge of London, where Dowding and Fighter Command had their headquarters. There the reports were interpreted in the light of other data, and the distances of incoming aircraft reported by neighbouring radar stations subjected to a calculation known as 'range cutting' to provide a more accurate idea of their course.

The graded information was now transferred on to a map with red counters representing enemy aeroplanes and black counters friendly ones. The information was passed on to the operations rooms at each level of the chain of command – sector, group and Fighter Command HQ – where it was translated on to identical map tables. The development of a raid was watched by the controller and his staff from a balcony. The resources at hand to deal with the intruders were indicated on a large board rigged with coloured bulbs, which showed which squadrons would be available in thirty minutes, which were at five minutes' readiness, which were at two minutes' readiness and which were already in the air.

Fighter Command had a simple pyramid command structure, with Dowding, in Bentley Priory, at the top. One step down were the group commanders, each presiding over one of the four quadrants into which Britain's air defence had been divided. The south-west, and half of Wales, were covered by 10 Group, the middle segment of England and Wales by 12 Group, and Scotland and the far North by 13 Group. No. 11 Group, with responsibility for London and the south-east corner of England, was the busiest. Each group was subdivided into sectors that centred on a main fighter base, supplemented by a number of satellite aerodromes.

Raids fell naturally into one or another group's area of activity. When enemy aircraft were reported, the duty controller in the group operations room, in consultation with the group commander, decided which sector would deal with it and which aircraft would be 'scrambled'. Control of the fighters then passed to the sector controller, whose task was to manoeuvre his aircraft into the best position to intercept the raiders. He was helped in this by the IFF reports, which allowed him to keep track of his assets. The signal – 'Tally Ho!' – from the squadron or flight commander, meant that the enemy had been sighted and battle was about to be joined. At this point control of events passed to the pilots.

Orders and information were passed down the command chain and from pilot to pilot in a code that was very soon to enter public parlance and the popular imagination. The enemy were 'bandits' (the Germans called them *Indianer* – 'indians'). 'Angels' indicated altitude, so that 'Angels fifteen' meant 15,000 feet. 'Pancake' was an order to come back and land. 'Vector', plus a number indicating geometric degrees, gave the course a pilot was to steer. 'Buster' meant flat out. The trusty clock system – 'bandits at ten o'clock' – devised on the Western Front, provided an accurate fix on where the trouble was located.

The prevailing jumpiness of the first weeks of the war was partly because few of those involved in air defence had any clear idea of what to expect. The experience of Poland had suggested a blitzkrieg, sudden and pitiless, in which virtually everything was vulnerable. In fact the first German target was logical and conventional: the British Home Fleet, tucked away in the estuaries and anchorages of Scotland, from where it could menace Germany and its navy in relative security. On the morning of 16 October, twelve Junkers 88 fast bombers set off from Westerland on the Island of Sylt just off the Danish coast to attack shipping at the Royal Navy base at Rosyth on the north side of the Firth of Forth. The first group arrived at 2.30 in the afternoon, taking anti-aircraft gunners south of the Forth Bridge – just east of the base – by surprise. The main target was the battleship HMS *Hood*, but to the disappointment of the raiders it was in dry dock. Hitler, apparently anxious to avoid civilian casualties while there was still a chance of a settlement with Britain, had ordered that only ships on the water could be attacked.

Two targets presented themselves: the cruisers HMS *Southampton* and HMS *Edinburgh*, riding at anchor on the eastern side of the bridge. The Junkers were each carrying two 500-kg bombs. At 2,500 feet, several of them dived on the vessels and released their loads. Both ships were hit, but the bombs failed to do significant damage. Ten men were injured, none fatally.

The anti-aircraft batteries now opened up, joined by fire from the cruisers, which had previously been ordered to engage aircraft only if they proved hostile, presumably a precaution taken to counter the reckless gunnery of the first weeks. The action took place on the doorsteps of two RAF stations. Turnhouse, the home of 603 (City of Edinburgh) Squadron, just to the south of the Forth Bridge, and Drem, where 602 (City of Glasgow) Squadron was based. The raid was already several minutes old before Spitfires were in the air. As the bombers headed for home, they were chased out to sea. One was caught by three fighters from 603 Squadron, who opened fire, killing the rear gunner and shutting down the port engine. They were joined by another section from the squadron, who added to the fusillade battering the Junkers. 'He was responding with all his armaments; tracers were shooting past me, and I got a glimpse of a gunner behind twin guns,' one of the pilots, Patsy Gifford, said after the action. 'We went in again and gave him some more and I saw he was hit forward. Bits of fabric were dropping off and I thought I saw a red glow inside the fuselage.'[7] The Junkers hit the sea with bullets from the Spitfires stitching the water. The surviving three from the four-man crew were picked up by a trawler.

Another Ju 88 was shot down by 602 Squadron, also crashing into the sea. In both cases several pilots had been involved in their destruction. The official account recorded that this had been a team effort, but it singled out Gifford and two 602 pilots, George Pinkerton and Archie

McKellar, for special mention. They were identified not by name but by pre-war profession. The squadrons involved were auxiliaries. Gifford, like several others in 603 Squadron, was a solicitor; he spent his weekends driving a Frazer-Nash car very fast, shooting, fencing, taking out girls and flying. Pinkerton was thirty years old, and had left his wife, six-month-old daughter and fruit farm in Renfrewshire behind after the squadron was called up. McKellar was twenty-seven, short, aggressive and fit, and worked in his father's plastering business before joining the squadron full time. Gifford was to be killed the following spring, McKellar in the autumn.

The image they presented of social cohesion, of ordinary men from different walks of life coming together in the defence of their country, was naturally appealing to official propagandists. The fact that it was the amateurs of the auxiliary air force who had drawn first blood was given the maximum emphasis. 'Saturday Afternoon Airmen Shoot Nazi Bombers Down', was the headline in the *Daily Express*.

In other respects the Rosyth raid gave little reason for satisfaction. The fighters had not been able to prevent one of the raiders dropping an opportunistic bomb on a destroyer, HMS *Mohawk*, entering the Firth of Forth as the Luftwaffe was leaving, killing sixteen members of the crew, including the captain. Once again, the warning system had failed. Intelligence reports had predicted an attack, but from ten o'clock on the morning of the raid the local radar station was ineffective, due either to a power failure or a faulty valve. No sirens were sounded to alert the civilian population (though they were activated at military bases). Despite the rejoicing at the downing of two German bombers, the first raiders to be shot down, the Luftwaffe got off very lightly, given the superior speed and firepower of the attackers. That ten escaped was partly owing to the fact that the Spitfire pilots were under orders to go no closer than 400 yards, which was thought to be the most effective range for the Brownings. The pilots immediately recognized that getting in closer would produce more devastating results.

The bomber crews also benefited from a certain caution on the part of the defenders. When Hector MacLean, who had been training to be a solicitor in a Glasgow legal office before moving to Drem with 602 Squadron, was scrambled he 'couldn't believe it wasn't another mess-up because we'd been ordered off so often to intercept things and it had been a Blenheim or an Anson or something like that'. Spotting a bomber, he 'followed it gingerly thinking . . . I must not shoot one of our own fellas down, but there were the crosses so finally I had a go.' Having emptied his ammunition, he hurried back to rearm in preparation for a second wave that never came. Until the squadron moved south in August the following year, the only Germans he saw were 'mainly single aircraft sneaking over to take pictures and drop the odd bomb and attack convoys off the coast. It was easy to do. They could nip in, drop a few bombs around the boats and get out before we could get at them.'[8]

The same pattern of frustration and boredom settled over all the fighter squadrons in England and Scotland. Pilots spent their days at readiness, being ordered airborne to check out incursions by unidentified aircraft, 'X' raids as they were known, that almost always turned out to be friendly or else were too far off to intercept. Then there were the dreary convoy patrols, flying in circles over ships that were rarely attacked. There were occasional brushes with the enemy. On 20 November, 74 Squadron at Hornchurch recorded its first success when three pilots fastened on to a Heinkel 111 heavy bomber and shot it down over the Thames estuary. The following day two Hurricanes from 79 Squadron at Biggin Hill were patrolling over the south coast when they were ordered to investigate a radar sighting that turned out to be a Dornier 17 medium bomber on a weather reconnaissance. They found it, descended on it, opened fire and watched it explode as it hit the Channel.

On 3 February Peter Townsend took part in the destruction of the first German bomber to be shot down on British soil since the First World War, after 43 Squadron had exchanged bucolic Tangmere for the bleak surroundings of Acklington, high up on the north-east coast near Newcastle. He was leading his section on patrol over the sea, keeping at wave level to surprise any German aircraft, which tended to hug the clouds, when he saw a Heinkel. The crew saw nothing 'until the bullets began tearing into their bomber. Only then did red tracer come spurting from their rear guns, but, in the first foolish rapture of combat, I believed myself . . . invulnerable.' The Heinkel staggered over the cliffs at Whitby and crash-landed in snow behind the town. Townsend felt elated at the success – then, on hearing there were two survivors, a touch of remorse. He visited them in hospital. Then he returned to the mess to drink champagne. It was, he thought later, 'a horribly uncivilized way of behaving, really, when you have just killed someone. But an enemy bomber down was proof of our prowess, and that was a legitimate pretext for celebration. For the enemy crew, whom we had shot to pieces, we gave no thought. Young, like us, they had existed, but existed no longer. Deep down we knew, but dared not admit, that we had little hope of existing much longer ourselves. So, meanwhile, we made merry.'[9]

Death was more likely to come through accident than enemy action that winter. The need to have fighters on permanent standby around the clock meant that pilots were called on to do an increased amount of night flying, a skill to which insufficient attention had been paid before the war. George Bennions, now with 41 Squadron at Catterick, found it was 'automatically assumed that they would just send you off at night and there would be no problem'. The Spitfires they were flying were notoriously difficult to operate in a darkness which had deepened considerably with the introduction of the blackout. 'The long nose blotted everything out straight in front of you, and because the engine had very short stubs, all that you saw . . . was a great moustache of flame . . . The only thing you could do was to tuck your head back into the cockpit and take off on the instruments, which was all right for a trained pilot, but for new pilots who hadn't done any night flying, or very little, it must have been terrible.'

A Canadian pilot, Pilot Officer Overall, took off one night, circled round and flew straight into a house. Bennions protested at the stupidity of sending off pilots in pitch darkness without allowing them to first get familiarized in conditions of bright moonlight. A senior officer accused him of being afraid. His suggestion, though, was eventually adopted.[10]

Even the most skilful pilots found themselves in difficulties, especially when sensory deprivation was combined with incompetence on the part of those directing them on the ground. Al Deere nearly got killed while being guided back after a night patrol in total darkness by the Hornchurch controller, who vectored him straight into a clump of barrage balloons. It was no wonder that so many pilots hated and feared night flying.

The winter of 1939 is frozen in the memory of those who lived through it as the bitterest they ever endured. On many mornings, snow had to be shovelled off the aprons and runways and the Merlin engines of the fighters thawed out and run up before any flying could take place. The aircraft were often covered in a crust of ice and had to be scrubbed down with wire-bristle brooms. At Drem, the 'coldest spot on earth', the pilots sat in poorly insulated dispersal huts, clustered around a lukewarm stove, playing 'uckers' – a form of ludo – and waiting for the phone to ring. Very soon everyone could distinguish the tone of the 'ops' phone, announcing a scramble, from that of the 'admin' line. The bad weather would continue to make flying and life in general difficult well into the spring.

Conditions in the cosy brick messes and living quarters of the fighter station headquarters were bearable enough, but existence at the satellite stations could be miserable. The members of 32 Squadron, pilots and ground crew, had to move to Gravesend while Biggin Hill was temporarily closed so deep shelters could be dug and a concrete runway laid – part of a nationwide programme to replace the now embarrassingly anachronistic grass fields with all-weather surfaces. The squadron diarist recorded that 'the wretched troops lived in the utmost discomfort, sleeping on palliases on the floor and being fed from a cooking trailer . . . the NCOs also slept on the floor, and the less lucky of the officers.'

Great ingenuity was used in the pursuit of fun. When the well-connected sportsmen of 601 Auxiliary Squadron found themselves based briefly at Hornchurch around Christmas, the commanding officer, Max Aitken, son of the press magnate Lord Beaverbrook, used his show-business contacts to arrange for the cast of the Windmill Theatre to visit. The men loved the demure striptease for which the Windmill girls were famous. Several members of the Women's Auxiliary Air Force, the

'Waafs', who were now being posted to RAF stations around the country, walked out in protest, however.

For most pilots, though, life was spartan and uncertain, especially for the newcomers and those finishing their training. In letters home they recounted their daily routines, successes and setbacks in a tone of jaunty confidence that seemed designed to calm the fears of anxious mothers and fathers, brothers and sisters. Occasionally, though, a note of doubt or worry breaks through the surface of imperturbability, a reminder that behind the bravado were innocent young men, barely out of adolescence, green, apprehensive and homesick. Paddy Finucane, then at No. 8 Flying Training School at RAF Montrose, still sounds like a schoolboy in a letter to his younger brother, Kevin. 'How did you like *Robin Hood*? I saw it in London when I was at Uxbridge. It was on at the local fleapit and I enjoyed it immensely. The part I liked was when old Guy of Gisborne got a good twelve inches of cold steel in the bread basket. The fighting and shooting scenes were very good . . .'[11]

Noel Benson sent long, regular letters to his mother and doctor father at their house at Great Ouseburn, near York, throughout the winter of 1939 and 1940, detailing his progress. He had gone to Cranwell as a flight cadet in April 1938 after leaving Sedbergh public school. At the end of November 1939 he was with 145 Squadron at Redhill and Croydon and writing home to complain that the letters 'daddy' sends are not long enough. His main concern is the stinginess of the authorities in allocating petrol coupons, which may prevent him from getting home for leave. He seems to have spent much of his spare time quietly, visiting family and friends in the area for lunch and supper, dutifully negotiating the blackout to give lifts home to other guests. The news from the squadron was mostly domestic. A brother pilot was getting married and he would like to give him a dog as a present. A bitch in the Benson household had recently littered. Could they send photos of the pups so he can pick one out? Occasionally he vented his frustration at the inaction of the phoney war. One of his acquaintances was 'one of the lucky ones', who had been posted to one of the four fighter squadrons sent to France. On 11 December he was 'pretty fed up because there is absolutely nothing doing here. But the big bugs do such damn stupid things at times that it is enough to make anyone wild and fed up. If I try and say any more I shall probably choke with rage!!!'

Eleven days later he had been posted to 603 Squadron, now at Prestwick near Glasgow, and was 'busy from the word go. I started flying immediately which suited me fine.' At the end of the month he reported that he was 'having a very busy time here but like it very much. I am "on" from dawn to dusk, so you see I have not much free time. I am afraid there is no hope whatsoever of any leave for the next month or so.'

On the first day of the New Year, Benson was trained up and took his place as a fully operational member of the squadron. He found his comrades 'a very decent crowd', and liked the fact that, despite an influx of outsiders, the unit was still mostly composed of the pre-war amateurs. 'Being an auxiliary squadron they [all] had jobs before the war and this was really their hobby. So there is a lot of red tape brushed aside. The regulars in the squadron are quite often horrified at the irregular things that they do but I must say they get the job done.'

The squadron routine meant that time off was scarce. After three weeks' continual duty, he went with a friend to Glasgow, where they could 'hardly see a thing because just outside the city we ran into the smoke fog that hangs over the place, and although it was mid afternoon it looked like dusk. Everyone seemed to have long faces and I don't blame them if they are always in that muck.' There is no mention of girlfriends or even women. The boyish note, the thank-yous to uncle Reg for a cardigan and unknown donors for mittens to combat the hellish cold, gradually fades, edged out by a mounting confidence. For his birthday, he announced, he would like a car badge, 'in the form of a Spitfire. It must be a Spitfire, no other type will do.' On 8 February he reported 'we chased away another Hitlerite today, two in fact, but they nipped into the clouds before we got a smack at them'. Early in March he once again expressed his frustration, this time because the auxiliaries of 602 Squadron were seeing more action than his own unit. 'There is a good deal of friendly rivalry between us,' he wrote. 'We are rather annoyed because we have not seen any fun lately while this other squadron has been having all the fun.'[12] This fretting at not being in the thick of things earned him the nickname 'Broody', the commanding officer of 603 told Benson's father later, in a letter, 'because he was always so despondent if, for any reason, he was not allowed to fly'. He also 'had a habit of pondering over the many problems confronting him'.[13]

Noel Benson sounds from his letters to have been what was known as a 'keen type'. To be identified as such won a pilot official approval, but it invited mild, affectionate scorn from comrades who considered conspicuous effort to be slightly embarrassing. The truth was that almost everyone was keen. They were just reluctant to appear so.

Denis Wissler seems to have conformed more to the social norm. He was intelligent and warm-hearted to the point of vulnerability. His father was of Swiss origin, and came from the family that invented Marmite, whose London headquarters he ran. Denis joined the RAF on a short-service commission in July 1939 after leaving Bedford School, alma mater of a number of Fighter Command pilots. In January 1940, aged nineteen, he was in the middle of advanced training at 15 Flying Training School Lossiemouth, in the far north of Scotland. Wissler kept a journal, each evening recording the day's events, no matter how tired he was or how much beer had been taken, in a small red leather Lett's diary. It is a lively account: of days flying and fighting and evenings drinking, of flirtation burgeoning into romance. Sounding through it all is one dominant and recurring theme: his desire to succeed as a pilot and be worthy of the Fighter Boy camaraderie that he, like so many, felt with the force of love.

He began the course on 1 January, flying in the morning and 'feeling perfectly fit and quite at home in the air'. On 3 January he spent the day working on perfecting his rolls – the manoeuvre of rotating while flying straight and level. 'I did two and they were grand,' he recorded with satisfaction. 'I even gained height in the second.' Two days later he felt he 'had them taped now. My two best efforts were a roll at 1,000 feet then three rolls in succession'. The following week he had a flying test in which he was put through '(1) a spin (2) a slow roll (3) a loop (3) [sic] steep turns both ways to left and right (4) a forced landing (5) low flying

(6) slow low flying (7) and naturally a take-off and landing. The instructor said that it was quite good, but that my steep turns were split-arse (ragged and wild).' After a few days without flying, partly it seems because of restrictions imposed by the instructors, he was in the air again, but noted disconsolately that he 'flew very badly today, heavens knows why because I really felt on top of the world and was looking forward to flying again, but somehow it didn't just connect'. Despite the off days, Wissler was a good pilot. At one point he writes that he was asked if he would like to go on an armament course, which would mean rapid promotion and the chance of a permanent commission, but as it entailed a long course of lectures and exams and little or no flying, 'I said NO.'

The prospect of dying pointlessly, crashing into a hillside or misjudging a landing, was always present. On his second day he came back late from a session on a Harvard, an aircraft notoriously difficult to retrieve from a spin, to find that his fellow pupils had heard rumours of a crash and assumed 'I was a fried piece of meat . . . everyone was saying "poor old Wissler"'. A week later a pupil and instructor were killed after their aeroplane 'hit something, what, we don't know yet but it brought the plane down'.

Lossiemouth was an isolated spot, stranded on the chilly extremities of the Morayshire coast, but there were cinemas and pubs a few miles away in Elgin. Given the town's isolation, there seems to have been a variety of films to see. On 19 January Wissler and his friend 'Wootty' – Ernest Wootten, another short-service entrant – saw *The Ghost Goes West*, which he judged a 'grand film and really comes up to what everyone says about it'. In the next nine days he took in *Wuthering Heights*, *Jesse James*, *The Four Feathers* and *The Lion Has Wings*, a stirring story featuring Bomber and Fighter Command based on the raid on German warships in North Sea harbours at the beginning of the war, directed by Alexander Korda and starring Ralph Richardson. Sequences of it had been shot at Hornchurch using 'B' Flight of 74 Squadron the day after Barking Creek. The hard work in the air was supplemented by hearty drinking. On 2 February he wrote, 'we did no flying today as the weather wasn't good enough . . . In fact I did nothing until the evening when Wootty and I went out to the "Beach Bar" and met Sergeant Harman, one of the instructors in my flight, and I really got more drunk than ever before, so badly that I couldn't even stand.'

Despite the overall cheeriness that emanates from the faded ink, sometimes his mood faltered and dejection crept in. On 8 February he went down with German measles ('most unpatriotic'), came up in spots and was confined to bed. Four days later he was allowed out. 'I got up and walked down to flights. Wootty wasn't doing anything so he and I walked into Lossiemouth where I posted a letter home and bought a magazine to help while away the time this evening. Our dinner was quite uneatable tonight. Oh God what a hole this is and how glad I shall be to go.'

He was, it is clear, painfully homesick. The laborious procedures and long delays involved in making a trunk call, made worst by wartime restrictions, never deterred him from ringing home. After a night drinking strong ale mixed with draught bitter he none the less remembered his parents were waiting to hear from him and, after a lengthy wait for a line, 'carried on a small conversation. I could never have forgiven myself if I had missed one word Mummy or Pop had said.'

On Friday, 16 February, he and the rest of his class were given a leaving dinner in the mess and got appropriately drunk. The following day he learned he was going to St Athans in Wales to finish his training. He wrote the news in his diary on the train home to ten days' leave in wobbly writing, registering his delight. It meant that he was 'on fighters'.

It took several more weeks and another move to the operational training unit at Sutton Bridge in Lincolnshire before he finally took the controls of the aeroplane that would carry him through the rest of his war. 'I at last went solo in a "Hurricane",' he wrote on Wednesday, 20 March, 'and did five landings in fifty minutes. It is a grand aeroplane and not so very difficult . . . I can now wear the top button of my tunic undone, as is done by all people who fly fighters.'[14]

The remainder of Wissler's time at Sutton Bridge was spent on Harvards and Hurricanes, frequently practising the disciplined formation manoeuvres that were still considered to be the best training for air flying. In the evening there was snooker and darts in the mess or at the Bridge, a local hotel. The war was moving closer. At the end of March a request was made for volunteers to go to France to replace casualties in the four fighter squadrons based there. Wissler put his name forward, then reconsidered after worrying about the effect such a move would have on his parents.

At the end of April there was another flap when it appeared that one of the pilots was being posted to Norway. His order to move was cancelled at the last minute. It was a small example of the chaos surrounding an enterprise that was ill-organized and amateurish from start to finish. Dowding had been asked to provide fighter cover for an expedition to secure the iron-ore fields of northern Sweden and provide help for the Finns, who had been showing unexpectedly strong resistance to the Russian invaders in their 'Winter War'. Following the capitulation of the Finns to Moscow in March, the Germans had taken the opportunity on 9 April to seize ports and airfields in Norway as bases for an escalated war against Britain and the objective changed. The force was now charged with seizing them back and 263 Squadron was assigned to help them. The squadron had only been reformed six months previously and was equipped with Gladiators, which now had the look of museum pieces. It was facing 500 Luftwaffe combat aircraft, including 330 bombers. The pilots arrived near Trondheim on the evening of 24 April, having flown in from the aircraft carrier *Glorious*. Their base was to be on the ice of Lake Lesjaskog. The following morning the wheels of all the machines were frozen to the ice, the controls locked solid, and it was impossible to start the engines. To compound a hopeless situation, supplies supposed to have been waiting at a nearby port failed to arrive so there was no mobile radar, only two light guns for airfield defence and no petrol bowser or acid for the accumulators in the starter trolleys used to fire up the engines.

In the end these deficiencies were academic. The base was attacked by Heinkel 111s, which swept over, bombing and machine-gunning the Gladiators as they sat glued to the ice. The already demoralized ground crews, many of whom were new to the squadron, ran for the cover of the surrounding forest. By the end of the first day the squadron was reduced to five serviceable aircraft. By the end of the second day there were three, and on the third there were none. The squadron was withdrawn to re-form and re-equip. On 22 May it was back in Norway with its Gladiators as part of the force trying to capture Narvik, where it was joined by 46 Squadron, equipped with Hurricanes. This time it managed to operate on twelve days, flying 389 sorties and claiming to have shot down twenty-six enemy aircraft.

No. 46 Squadron also flew on twelve days and claimed eleven aircraft destroyed. It arrived in Norway from the *Glorious*, but had to return to Scapa Flow when the first airfield selected, near Harstad, turned out to be unusable. On their return they had to abandon a second base at Skaanland after two Hurricanes, including one flown by Squadron Leader Cross, ploughed into the soft ground and went tail-up, and the rest of the squadron was diverted to Bardufoss, sixty miles to the north. Flight Sergeant Richard Earp, who had gone to Halton from his Warrington grammar school before being selected for flying training, managed to land safely. He remembered Skaanland as 'nothing but a strip by a fjord. The troops had been working very hard out there and they'd covered the place with coconut matting and wire netting. Poor Cross came along to land on it and it just rolled up in front of his wheels.'[15] They washed in melted snow and lived six to a tent. 'All I had was a groundsheet and two blankets. You couldn't sleep. It was daylight all the time. It was terribly bloody cold.' As the decision was taken to abandon the campaign, the squadron was withdrawn.

Earp left on a fishing boat and was picked up by a destroyer that took him back to Scotland. When he returned to the base at Digby he found that 'there was hardly any of the rest of the squadron left'. On 7 June ten exhausted pilots of 46 Squadron managed to land their Hurricanes on the *Glorious*, despite the absence of arrester hooks, supposedly an impossible feat. No. 263 Squadron was already embarked. On the way back the carrier was sighted by the battlecruiser *Scharnhorst*, which opened fire at long range. The second salvo smashed into the ship, setting it ablaze. It sank within an hour, taking with it 1,474 officers and men of the Royal

Navy and 41 members of the RAF, including all but two of the pilots. It was the final disaster in a doomed campaign. From the cold perspective of Fighter Command, it was also a terrible waste of men and machines which would be badly needed in the months ahead.

6

Return to the Western Front

In Britain the Fighter Boys waited for the real battle to begin. Across the Channel a handful of pilots were getting a foretaste of what lay ahead. When, in September 1939, the British Expeditionary Force was sent to France, the air force inevitably went too. Four fighter squadrons were sent in the first week of the war to support the army and protect a small fleet of bombers, the Advanced Air Striking Force. This token deployment had been agreed earlier in the year. Dowding none the less protested, claiming he had been promised that no fighters would be sent until 'the safety of the Home Base had been assured'. His fear, justified as it was to turn out, was that once the war started in France, the RAF would be committed to providing more and more aircraft and pilots to fight someone else's battle, leaving the country's air defences fatally weakened when the Germans moved on to attack Britain.

The squadrons flew off to bases that would have been familiar to their RFC predecessors. Their daily patrols took them over shell-ploughed earth, splintered forests and shattered villages that were only just recovering from four years under the hammer of war. No. 1 Squadron arrived in high spirits in Le Havre, flying low over the town in a display of exuberance that impressed both the locals and the Americans crowding the port in search of a passage home. They spent their first night in a requisitioned convent, and their first evening drinking in the Guillaume Tell, the Normandie, the Grosse Tonne and La Lune. The latter was a brothel where the carousing could go on until dawn. The following day they blew away their hangovers with a choreographed 'beat up' of the town, looping and rolling in tight formation at rooftop height. While waiting to move to their forward base, the pilots spent the non-flying hours of the day playing football and writing letters home, and the evenings cruising the boulevards. 'We all felt that our first taste of service in France would probably be our last of civilization and peace for a long time and we wanted to make the best of it,' wrote Paul Richey, who had joined the squadron six months earlier. He took the opportunity to make his peace with God. The old *curé* at the church of St Michel heard his confession, 'giving me the strength and courage to face whatever was to come'.[1]

The No. 1 pilots had a rich variety of temperaments and backgrounds, typical of the established squadrons going into the war. The unit had served on the Western Front from 1915 and got through the inter-war years without suffering disbandment or amalgamation. Its leader was P. J. H. 'Bull' Halahan, whose Irish father had been an RFC pilot. His flight commanders were Peter 'Johnny' Walker from Suffolk, a member of the unit's acrobatic team at the 1937 Hendon Air Pageant; and Peter Prosser Hanks from York, who had been with the squadron since September 1936. There was an American, Cyril Palmer, known as 'Pussy'; a Canadian, Mark 'Hilly' Brown; an Australian, Leslie Clisby, who had been an RAAF cadet, and a New Zealander, Bill Stratton. There was also an Irishman, John Ignatius Kilmartin. 'Killy' was a romantic figure with black wavy hair and chiselled good looks who had been born in Dundalk in 1913, one of eight children of a forester. His father died when he was nine and he was dispatched to Australia under a scheme for orphans known as 'Big Brother'. As soon as he was old enough to work, he was sent to a cattle station in New South Wales, where he lived for five years. He moved on to Shanghai, where he had an aunt, and got a job as a clerk in the Shanghai gasworks. In his spare time he rode as a jockey for Sir Victor Sassoon. Seeing an advertisement offering short-service commissions, he applied, was summoned for an interview and made his way to London via the Trans-Siberian Railway in company with a group of Sumo wrestlers heading for the 1936 Berlin Olympics.

There were four sergeant pilots: Arthur 'Taffy' Clowes and Fred Berry, both of whom had begun their careers as aircraft apprentices in 1929 and volunteered for pilot training, and Frank Soper and Rennie Albonico. The best-known member of the squadron was to be Paul Richey, whose *Fighter Pilot*, based on his diaries and published in 1941, was one of the best books ever written about the experience and ethos of air fighting, and still rings with unalloyed authenticity. Richey was educated at the Institut Fisher in Switzerland and at Downside. He was intelligent and amusing and a good linguist. He was also tall, blond and strikingly good-looking. Cuthbert Orde, who had been a pilot in the RFC before he became a war artist, found him at first 'rather quiet, shy and serious minded', while acknowledging his enthusiasm for a party. Richey's comparative sophistication disguised a strong humanitarian streak and an unusual ability to analyse his feelings. He sympathized with the victims of the war, whoever they might be. It was a quality he shared with Billy Drake, another middle-class Catholic boy in 1 Squadron who displayed a marked sense of decency.

By the middle of October, after several moves, the squadron settled down at an airfield near Vassincourt, perched above a canal and a railway line amid lush and watery cow pastures near Bar-le-Duc where Champagne meets Lorraine. No. 73 Squadron was based not far away at Rouvres, on the drab Woevre plain, east of the heights of Verdun. Their duties were to protect the Advanced Air Striking Force, deployed around Reims and made up of Fairey Battle and Blenheim light bombers in support of the French army holding the Maginot Line along the Franco-German frontier.

To the north were 85 and 87 Squadrons, equipped with Hurricanes, who formed the fighter element of the air component of the British Expeditionary Force (BEF). They were joined on 15 November by two auxiliary squadrons, 607 (County of Durham) and 615 (County of Surrey), in response to persistent demands from the French government for British forces in France to be strengthened. They would have to make do with their Gladiators until Hurricanes arrived. The Hurricanes' wide undercarriage made them less likely to come to grief on the rough grass airfields of northern France than the Spitfire with its narrower wheelbase. There was also a strategic reason for the decision not to send Spitfires. Dowding's vision of a French campaign turning into an unstoppable drain on resources had made him determined not to risk his most valuable weapon in the enterprise.

The pilots of 1 Squadron were billeted in Neuville, a few miles from the airfield, a village accustomed to being washed by the tides of war, having been twice occupied by the Germans, in 1871 and 1914. The squadron flew patrols whenever the poor weather permitted. On a clear day the view from the cockpit was sublime, with the Rhine winding in the distance, beyond it the Black Forest, and way off, glittering on the far horizon, the white battlements of the Swiss Alps. As in Britain, friends were at first to prove more dangerous than enemies. Richey, mistaken for a German, was attacked by two French pilots in Morane-Saulniers, the relatively slow and underarmed standard fighter of the Armée de l'Air. Fortunately his Hurricane's superior performance allowed him to shake them off.

On the afternoon of 30 October 1939, a gloriously sunny day, the unfamiliar drone of bombers was heard high over the airfield, sending the pilots scrambling to get airborne and give chase. Ten miles west of Toul, Pilot Officer Peter 'Boy' Mould, an ex-Cranwell cadet who joined the squadron in June, caught up with a Dornier 17 cruising along at 18,000 feet. Mould approached from behind, hosing the bomber nose to tail with his Brownings. The Dornier, according to the squadron operations record book, 'appeared to have been taken by surprise as no evasive tactics were employed and no fire was encountered by PO Mould'. It caught fire immediately, plunged into a vertical dive and exploded into the French countryside. The only discernible remnants of the crew of four were five hands recovered from the wreckage, along with a mangled gun and an oxygen bottle with a bullet hole in it, which were taken off to the mess as trophies in an echo of old RFC practices. The human debris was buried with full military honours but Mould felt bad about his victory, getting very drunk that night and telling Richey: 'I'm bloody sorry I went and looked at the wreck. What gets me down is the thought that *I* did it.'[2]

For much of the time there was little to do, apart from patrol and practice attacks on 'enemy' Battles. The problem, from the fighter pilots' point of view, was not that there were too many Germans, but too few. When they did appear, usually flying high on cautious reconnaissance missions along the frontier defences, there was a rush to get at them that could produce moments of black farce. On 23 November, after weeks of fruitless patrols, bad weather and exercises, there was, for a change, plenty of activity. Between them 1 Squadron and 73 Squadron accounted for five Dorniers and a Heinkel 111. The Heinkel was heading home when it was spotted at 20,000 feet between Verdun and Metz by a section of three Hurricanes from 1 Squadron, who chased it over the German frontier. The effect of their repeated attacks was limited owing to the fact that at least eleven of the Hurricanes' guns were frozen because of the altitude, a fault later remedied when engine heat was fed to the gunports. The last bursts, which finally brought the Heinkel down, were fired by Taffy Clowes, the ex-Halton boy who was one of the squadron's most dogged and skilful pilots. As he was breaking away, six French Moranes rushed in, firing wildly. One of them smashed into his tail, destroying half the rudder and one of the elevators. The French pilot was forced to bale out and it was only by an extraordinary display of virtuosity that Clowes was able to nurse his machine back to Vassincourt, where he crash-landed. Richey noticed that, when he emerged from the cockpit, 'though he was laughing he was trembling violently and couldn't talk coherently'.[3]

Clowes's experience was one of several dramas on an eventful day. Earlier Pussy Palmer had led a section from 'A' Flight against a Dornier, setting it on fire. The rear gunner and navigator escaped by parachute, but the pilot flew on. As Palmer drew alongside, the German throttled back, causing the Hurricane to overshoot. Then he fastened on to Palmer's tail and opened up, hitting the aircraft thirty-four times. One round, which punctured the locker behind Palmer's head and smashed the windscreen, would surely have killed him if he had not put his machine into a dive.

With clouds of smoke issuing from the engine, he prepared to bale out, but when they dispersed, strapped himself in again and crash-landed with his wheels up. The others in the flight, Killy Kilmartin and Frank Soper, returned to the attack, and this time the Dornier went down. Miraculously the pilot seemed unharmed as he clambered out of his devastated machine, giving them a wave as they circled overhead.

The pilots were reluctant to abandon the notion that a trace of chivalry clung to the business of air fighting. That night, in a gesture the RFC would have recognized and applauded, 1 Squadron decided to honour the pilot who had fought so doggedly and well with dinner in the mess. By now he was in the hands of the French at Ste Menehould gaol, and Billy Drake, who like Richey spoke good French, was sent off to borrow him for the evening. His captors reluctantly let him go, on condition that he was accompanied by a gendarme and delivered to the citadel at Verdun when the evening was over.

His name was Arno Frankenberger, and he had been a glider pilot before the war, when he joined the Luftwaffe, volunteering for special reconnaissance duties. The pilots did their best to help him relax, removing trophies from the mess and insisting on first names. It was hard work. At first he stood up every time he was addressed by an officer. After a while he fell silent and put his head in his hands. Peter Matthews, a twenty-year-old pilot officer from Liverpool who had planned to follow in his father's footsteps and become a vet, but applied for a short-service commission instead, watched what happened next. 'He left rather hurriedly,' he said. 'When he came back in about five minutes' time he was full of beans. He said, "You know, I was told by my officers that the British air force were a bunch of swine, but you're all very nice chaps." '[4] In these improved spirits he boasted that the German maps of Britain were better than the ones of the German frontier the squadron had pinned up on the mess wall, and that the new variation of the Messerschmitt 109 was superior to the Hurricane.

The Hurricane pilots had yet to put this proposition to the test and would not come face to face with the Luftwaffe's most lethal fighter until the spring of 1940. The intervening months were spent patrolling, training and learning what they could from limited experience. Pussy Palmer's narrow escape had demonstrated the vital need for armour plating behind the pilot's back. In front, there was a bullet-proof windscreen insisted upon by Dowding in the face of the objections of cost-conscious Air Ministry officials. The engine block also gave forward protection. The squadron put in a request for steel plates to be fitted behind the seat. Hawker's were consulted, but again there were objections, this time on the grounds that the extra weight would upset the aeroplane's centre of gravity and impair its flying performance. Bull Halahan was not deterred. The bomber pilots had armour. He tracked down a wrecked Battle and had the steel plating removed and fitted on a Hurricane. The squadron record book noted that 'although this alters the flying characteristics . . . to some extent, it most certainly adds to the pilot's confidence'. The benefit greatly outweighed the disadvantage. Hilly Brown, the Canadian short-service officer who at twenty-eight was one of the squadron's most experienced pilots, was sent back to Britain with the modified aircraft and gave a demonstration of aerobatics that persuaded the Air Ministry experts to change their minds. By mid March 1940, all No. 1's Hurricanes had been equipped, and from then on the armour was fitted as standard equipment to RAF fighters, saving many lives.

Halahan's refusal to be baulked was characteristic. He was determined to introduce any innovation that added to the safety and efficiency of his men. Halahan was one of the first to realize that the official range at which fighter aircraft had their eight guns harmonized was misjudged and would significantly reduce their destructive power. Before the war Dowding had decided that concentrating machine-gun fire in a cone 400 yards ahead of a Hurricane or Spitfire was the most effective way of bringing down a big target like a bomber, while keeping his men at the limits of the enemy defensive fire. The decision had been taken in the innocent days when it seemed that bombers were all that Fighter Command were likely to meet. Halahan and his pilots were unconvinced. They doubted that at 400 yards .303 bullets still had the velocity to fly true and penetrate armour, or that the spread would be dense enough to destroy the target, especially if it was a small one like an Me 109. During the squadron's annual month's shooting practice in the spring of 1939, all the guns had therefore been quietly harmonized at 250 yards. The modification meant that pilots had to get in closer. But as events in France were to prove, it made the Hurricanes of 1 Squadron considerably more lethal than those of other squadrons shooting at the official range, and eventually the 250-yard harmonization became standard.

Another innovation was borrowed from the Luftwaffe. British fighters in France had the underside of one wing painted black and the other white, which the pilots felt made them look like flying chequer boards. German aircraft were duck-egg blue, to blend in with the sky and diminish their visibility to attackers lurking underneath. Halahan ordered the squadron machines to be painted the same colour, and this in turn was also adopted by all RAF fighters.

Contrary to his bruiser appearance, Halahan was a thoughtful officer who tried hard to divine the likely nature of the approaching battle and sought to prepare the squadron as best as he could, one evening delivering a lecture on what the war would mean for fighter pilots. He was equally concerned about the well-being of those under his command, introducing rotas to give pilots and airmen regular breaks and arranging diversions and encouraging excursions to make off-duty time as enjoyable as possible. Neuville, a cluster of utilitarian streets relieved by a few rustic half-timbered houses and presided over by a handsome Romanesque church, was welcoming enough. Pilots and airmen were treated with warmth in the houses where they lodged and durable friendships were made. The officers established their mess in the *mairie*. The sergeants set up an English-style pub in a café.

Paulette Regnauld, who was fourteen when the *aviateurs Brittaniques* arrived, remembered them as 'polite and friendly. They mixed in well. There was a certain amount of flirting but they behaved themselves. They were generous and gave us meat and chocolate. At Christmas there was a big party at the *mairie*, where they chased all the pretty girls.'[5] More than sixty years on she still retained some souvenirs. Sitting at the kitchen table in her house in the town square, she produced a postcard from an airman, William Mumford, sent from Uxbridge while on leave in February 1940. A photograph, printed in the dense monochrome of 1940 film, showed Pussy Palmer, Killy Kilmartin and several other pilots standing amiably in front of the church, smiling at the camera. The long shadows cast by the sinking winter sun throw the well-muffled silhouettes of the woman taking the picture and her female companion across the church steps. The pilots are in flying boots and sheepskin jackets. The cold is almost palpable.

Neuville, for all its friendliness, had its limitations. On days off pilots would fly up to Rouvres to meet their friends in 73 Squadron or head off to Nancy, Metz or Bar-le-Duc, where the Hôtel de Metz was their unofficial headquarters and the wife of the owner's son, Madame Jean, welcomed them as if they were family. At Nancy the main attraction was the Roxy, described by Richey as 'low-ceilinged with a dim, religious light. It had a bar at one end and a dance floor at the other. Round the plush-draped walls were crowded tables and comfortable chairs. The bar was invariably surrounded by a throng of British and French air force officers and "ladies of the evening", waiting to be given a drink, a good time and anything else one could afford.'[6] It was a scene that would have stirred memories for Cecil Lewis.

The winter was as cruel in northern France as in Britain. For weeks at a time snow and blanketing cloud made flying impossible. The ground was iron hard, wrecking the tail wheels of the Hurricanes as they taxied out to take-off or touched down after a patrol. The squadron worked hard whenever circumstances allowed. Sightings of enemy aircraft were occasional and usually inconclusive. The pilots found they could not climb quickly enough to reach the high-flying reconnaissance aircraft as they crawled tantalizingly across the sky 20,000 feet overhead. One problem was that their Hurricanes were fitted with early two-bladed wooden propellers. The pitch of the airscrew could not be varied to improve acceleration and achieve the optimum rate of climb the engines were capable of delivering. The problem was solved when the first machine with a three-bladed constant-speed airscrew, which automatically adjusted to the rate of revs to get the best results, was delivered in April 1940. Halahan was the first to fly it, followed by the more experienced pilots, all of whom, the squadron log recorded, 'were greatly pleased by its superior performance'. From then on the old Hurricanes were gradually replaced by the new models, but some pilots were still flying with wooden propellers when the fighting began in earnest.

In March the weather began to improve slightly and patrolling became more intense. Two new pilots arrived at the squadron, Pilot Officer Robert Shaw and Flying Officer Harold Salmon. Shaw, from Bolton, had been one of the first to join the RAFVR and had only been called up to full-time duty at the outbreak of war. Salmon had learned to fly with the RAF in 1933 and was summoned from the reserve in September 1939. Both had done conversion courses to Hurricanes before being posted to France. Halahan was not impressed by their preparations. The record book noted: 'It is observed that new pilots sent out from England are insufficiently trained and [*sic*] too few hours on type to be familiar with its limitations. They also appear to have had little or no practice on R/T [radio telephony] and to have never used oxygen. It means time taken off from squadron duties to give these pilots the necessary training for active service, and also adds to the precious aircraft hours to allow them to do non-operational flying.' Both men were to remain with the squadron throughout the summer, with Salmon claiming an Me 110 and a probable Me 109. Shaw was less successful. In his brief life as a fighter pilot he shot nothing down. He was himself attacked by a British fighter over the Sussex coast in August and forced to land. On 3 September he failed to return from a patrol and was reported missing, one of the many unremarked young pilots among Fighter Command's dead that year.

The pilots of 73 Squadron had seen more action than those of 1 Squadron. This was due partly to their closer proximity to the frontier, partly to a more aggressive approach that sometimes took pilots scores of miles over the German lines in defiance of standing orders. The most willing to take risks was Flying Officer Edgar 'Cobber' Kain, a twenty-one-year-old New Zealander who had first attracted attention when he entertained the crowds at the 1938 Empire Air Day show with a particularly daring aerobatic display. In November 1939 he destroyed two Dorniers and in

January 1940 won a DFC. Kain was regarded by his peers as a 'split-arse pilot', a term that mixed approval with concern, and his approach bordered on recklessness.

Kain soon became known to British newspaper readers through the efforts of correspondents based at Reims, who, after he had shot down five enemy aircraft by the end of March, proclaimed him the first 'ace' of the war. Halahan disliked this development, as did others further up the RAF chain of command. Halahan preached caution, feeling there was no point in risking precious lives and machines before the real battle started. No. 1 Squadron seldom crossed the frontier. When it did it was at high altitude, turning back in a sweep to draw any German fighters out. Halahan was also strongly against publicizing the acts of single pilots, believing it undermined squadron spirit, and he banned newspaper reporters from the base. The Air Ministry had initially seemed to welcome publicity, sending four experienced journalists to act as press officers to France, but it was soon in conflict with the special correspondents. Despite the eagerness of the hacks to produce patriotic material, officials fretted about security and imposed heavy censorship that resulted in dispatches being slashed and rewritten out of recognition. Air Marshal Sir Arthur Barratt, the commander of the British Air Forces in France, also shared the view that creating 'aces' was bad for the morale of ordinary squadron members. When Barratt forbade interviews with pilots and ordered that all information must be filtered through service press offices, news organizations sulked and finally withdrew their men from France.

But the newspapers had recognized that Fighter Command, whose purpose and character were still known only vaguely to the British public, was a rich potential source of stirring copy and were bent on their myth-making mission. In an aggrieved article complaining about restrictions, the *Daily Express* correspondent, O. D. Gallagher, wrote: 'The young men of the RAF who have not yet spread their wings in wartime need their heroes. They're entitled to them, and whatever the policy-makers may say on this score, they're going to have them.' So it came to pass, but at a time when authority had decided that the propaganda benefits of publicizing fighter pilots overwhelmed all other considerations.[7]

The long-awaited encounter with the Messerschmitts came, finally, at the beginning of March. Cobber Kain had the first success, downing an Me 109 on 2 March over the German lines near Saarbrucken. His aircraft was badly shot up in the fight and he was forced to crash-land near Metz. His attacker was probably Oberleutnant Werner Molders, a veteran of the Spanish Civil War, who was himself in the process of acquiring the status of an ace. Kain's standing, and his at this stage rare first-hand experience of the Luftwaffe's machines, pilots and tactics, persuaded the authorities to bring him back temporarily to Britain to lecture to pilots in training. Christopher Foxley-Norris, by then preparing to join an army cooperation squadron equipped with lethally slow Lysanders, was present when Kain gave a talk on fighter evasion. 'At the end, somebody got up at the back and said, "You've told us how to evade one fighter, sir. What happens if you meet two?" To which the answer was, "Oh, most unlikely. They haven't got many aircraft and they're very short of fuel."' The next time Foxley-Norris saw the questioner he was 'being chased around a church steeple by six 109s'.[8]

The Me 109 was to turn out to be the most feared aeroplane in the Luftwaffe's line-up but that was not how it seemed in the spring of 1940. The attention of everyone in the RAF was equally focussed on by the twin-engined Me 110s, which had been designed with the dual roles of clearing the way for the Luftwaffe bomber fleets and attacking incoming enemy bombing raids. The aircraft's boastful nickname, *Zerstörer* (Destroyer), and its nominal top speed of nearly 350 m.p.h. at 21,500 feet – the same as a Spitfire and slightly faster than a Hurricane – made it the subject of apprehensive fascination. Air Marshal Barratt even offered dinner in Paris to the first pilot to shoot one down.

The distinction fell, collectively, to three No. 1 Squadron pilots, who between them on 29 March destroyed three Me 110s. Johnny Walker, Bill Stratton and Taffy Clowes were ordered up in the early afternoon to patrol over Metz at 25,000 feet. Half an hour after taking off they spotted nine Me 110s cruising unconcernedly in sections of three in line astern, east of the city. Once attacked, according to the squadron record, the German machines 'proved very manoeuvrable, doing half-rolls and diving out, coming up in stall turns'. The ensuing dogfight followed the inexorable physical rules of such engagements, with the advantage shifting from attacker to attacked and back again as they followed each other's tails in a downward spiral that in no time brought the mêlée to a bare 2,000 feet. Walker and Stratton ran out of ammunition and returned to Vassincourt, believing they had crippled one machine, the wreckage of which was later found. Clowes meanwhile had disposed of two. After hearing their accounts, the consensus was that the Me 110s were not as fearsome as their name suggested. The record concluded: 'As a result of this combat it may be stated that the Me 110, although very fast and manoeuvrable for a twin-engined aircraft, can easily be outmanoeuvred by a Hurricane.' The pilots also reported that 'it appeared that the rear gunner was incapable of returning fire whilst [the] Me 110 was in combat because of the steep turns "blacking him out" or making him too uncomfortable to take proper aim.' Barratt kept his promise. Two days later he sent his personal aircraft to whisk the three to Paris for dinner at Maxim's.

On the morning of their success, Paul Richey brought down the squadron's first 109. It was a fine day with high, patchy cloud when he took off with Pussy Palmer and Peter Matthews towards Metz. Noticing puffs of smoke from French anti-aircraft fire hanging in the sky, they went to investigate and saw the pale-blue bellies of two single-engined fighters 1,000 feet overhead. As they climbed to reach them, they were attacked from behind by three other 109s that nobody had noticed. Matthews called a warning over the R/T and Palmer jammed his Hurricane into a sharp turn to the left in what was to become the standard, desperate move to escape a pursuing 109. In doing so he lost control and spun down for 12,000 feet before straightening out. Matthews also dived and turned, and as the G forces drained the blood from his head he blacked out, coming to only at 10,000 feet. Richey continued to climb in a left-hand turn. Watching his tail, he noticed an aircraft moving behind him, but was unsure whether it was friend or foe and waited to see if it opened fire. When it did, he twisted down underneath his nose. 'As I flattened out violently,' he wrote, 'either he or one of the other 109s I had seen above dived on my port side and whipped past just above my cockpit. He was so close that I heard his engine and felt the air wave, and I realized that he must have lost sight of me in the manoeuvre. He pulled up in front of me, stall-turned left and dived steeply in a long, graceful swoop with me on his tail.' The German was faster in the dive than Richey. But when Richey pulled up violently and began climbing steeply, he started to gain on him. When, eventually, he was a few hundred yards distant, he 'let him have it. My gun button was sticking and I wasted ammunition, but he started to stream smoke. The pilot must have been hit because he took no evasive action, merely falling slowly in a vertical spiral. I was very excited and dived on top of him, using my remaining ammunition.'[9]

Many pilots were to feel the same rush of elation at the sight of smoke and flame or the first barely perceptible faltering of control that showed a pilot was hit. The temptation to follow the machine down to its fiery end was overwhelming. It was the same instinct that makes a boxer hover over his dazed opponent as he is counted out on the canvas. A pilot had to learn to suppress this impulse if he was to improve his chances of staying alive. By giving in to it he could lay himself bare to another enemy fighter who, unnoticed, may have fastened on to his tail during the intense seconds of combat. Sure enough, as Richey broke away, he noticed another 109 about 2,000 above him. Instead of running for it, he turned to face him. The German, either through caution or lack of ammunition, fled.

That night there was a celebration, first in the officers' then in the sergeants' mess. Toasts were drunk from a special bottle of rum and a 'victory' card signed. Before the party started, Richey 'went across to the village church opposite the mess to say a prayer for the German pilot I had killed, before I got too boozy. The door was locked, so I knelt on the steps and prayed for him and his family and for Germany.' In fact, as he was to discover later, his opponent had crash-landed near Saarburg and survived.

As the countryside thawed out and the days lengthened, it was clear that the Germans were stirring and the fraught boredom of the phoney war was drawing to an end. Until now Luftwaffe activity had mostly been limited to daily reconnaissance flights, with individual or small groups of Dorniers, Heinkels and Junkers 88s snooping over the Maginot defences and the Ardennes sector of the border between France and Germany. The Messerschmitts had been restricted to patrolling their own side of the frontier, only occasionally venturing into Allied air space. From April the reconnaissance missions were more frequent and grew bolder, probing deeper into France, while the fighters came in large formations of up to forty aircraft wheeling brazenly over Metz and Nancy.

The longer hours of daylight meant longer periods at readiness and the day's patrolling now began at 6.30 a.m. when the first Hurricane slithered out across the clayey mud of the thawed-out airfield and took off towards the German lines. In two consecutive days at the beginning of April, the squadron shot down two Me 110s and two 109s. The tactics they had been taught in training were being revised or jettisoned, and new ones invented, with each new experience. One was the designation of one pilot in a section to act as lookout, criss-crossing the sky to cover all possible approaches and shouting a warning if anything was sighted. The value of the 'weaver', or 'Arse-End Charlie' as he became known, was demonstrated on 2 April when Les Clisby, Flying Officer Lorimer, Killy Kilmartin and Pussy Palmer set off after high-flying twin-engined aircraft. As they approached, Palmer, weaving at the back, noticed Me 109s above, waiting to pounce, and alerted the others in time for them to break off the pursuit and face the attackers, shooting two of them down. Palmer was not so lucky and had to bale out after his reserve petrol tank was struck and set on fire.

In mid April it seemed that the war had finally started when the squadron was moved at a few hours' notice to a new base at Berry-au-Bac, thirty miles north-west of Reims. But after a week, during which the log noted that the 'pilots are all fed up with the lack of activity and the long stand-by hours which seem of no avail', they returned to Vassincourt. The first full day back, 20 April, was the busiest they had so far experienced. In one encounter, Berry and Albonico claimed a 109 each, Hanks downed a Heinkel 111 and Mould a Heinkel 112, the first time the type had been engaged. At the same time, Walker was leading Brown, Drake and Stratton on another patrol which ran into nine 109s. Walker and Brown got one each. Billy Drake opened fire on two as they made off and saw one apparently go out of control. The other he followed to the frontier and watched it crash into a hill. Killy Kilmartin had meanwhile set off in pursuit of a high-flying Ju 88 and caught up with it at 26,000 feet, the limit of its altitude. The pilot dived to shake him off, and Kilmartin's Hurricane had a struggle to get within firing range, but eventually managed to score a hit, forcing the Ju 88 to land. It had been a good day for the squadron, the first in which almost all the pilots had seen action. Halahan noted with satisfaction that 'all the original pilots who were with the squadron when it came to France last September, with one or two exceptions, have had combats with the enemy. It is most commendable that the squadron has worked so well and made it a squadron "show" without any publicized individuality'.

By now it was clear that the main threat from the German side came from the Me 109s. The relative merits and shortcomings of the Hurricane and Spitfire compared to the Messerschmitt was to be an eternal subject of debate among pilots on both sides, who were understandably fascinated by the machines opposing them. Like the British fighters, the Me 109 owed much to the engineering prowess of one man. This was Willy Messerschmitt, whose restless creativity was exercised on a broad range of aircraft from gliders to the first jets. In the Me 109 he attempted to wrap a light airframe around the most powerful engine it would carry. The resulting design problems were as daunting as anything faced by Camm and Mitchell. The thin wings that gave the aircraft its superior performance were inefficient when flying slow, requiring a system of slots on the leading edges to increase lift on take-off and landing. Their fragility placed severe restrictions on the way guns could be mounted. Nor were they strong enough to take the machine's weight, a weakness which meant that the undercarriage had to be supported by the fuselage. This made for a very narrow and unstable wheelbase which was the cause of many crashes on landing. According to one estimate, 5 per cent of all Me 109s manufactured were written off in this way.

The Me 109 was smaller and frailer-looking than both its British opponents. It was shorter and sat lower on the ground. Its wingspan was only 32 feet 4 inches compared with 40 feet for the Hurricane and 36 feet 11 inches for the Spitfire. Its total wing area was 174 square feet, whereas the Hurricane's was 258 square feet and the Spitfire's 242 square feet. It had a top speed of 357 m.p.h., the merest shade higher than the Spitfire and perhaps 30 m.p.h. faster than the Hurricane. It carried two machine-guns mounted one on either side of the upper nose decking, each with 1,000 rounds. Each wing housed a 20 mm cannon and 60 shells.

The pilots of 1 Squadron had a chance to examine the German fighter close up when, early in May, they were summoned to Amiens to examine a machine that had been captured intact. Hilly Brown took the controls and, after a practice, mounted a mock dogfight with a Hurricane flown by Prosser Hanks. From this exhibition, the squadron log noted, 'several facts emerged. The Hurricane is infinitely manoeuvrable at all heights and at ground level is slightly faster. The Me 109, however, is unquestionably faster at operational heights and although appearing tricky to fly and not particularly fond of the ground, possesses many fine features to offset its disadvantages.' The report noted enviously that it had 'an excellent view to the rear' – something the Hurricane definitely did not possess. This sober assessment would turn out to be largely accurate. The aircraft was subsequently flown by Brown to the RAF experimental station at Boscombe Down for further testing.

The air force needed all the information it could get. The phoney war had, mercifully, given Britain the lull it needed to accelerate the manufacture of aircraft and the training of pilots, but it had provided little practical experience of modern air warfare such as the Luftwaffe had gained in Spain and Poland. Unlike 1 Squadron and 73 Squadron, the other four fighter units based in France had had little contact with the enemy. Their job was to support the BEF, which was doing nothing, and the buffer zone of Belgium lay between them and the Germans. Squadrons 85 and 87 were based at Lille–Seclin aerodrome, where they fle sector patrols in their Hurricanes. The two auxiliary squadrons, 607 and 615, which arrived in November still equipped with Gladiators, were in no position to inflict much damage on the Luftwaffe even if they had been called on to do so.

Roland Beamont joined 87 Squadron at Seclin in October after a rare moment of excitement. 'Two days before they'd shot down their first enemy aeroplane. It was a Heinkel 111. I arrived just in time to take part in the celebrations with an Air Ministry photographer out there taking pictures of all the ground crew holding on to various parts of the Heinkel that had been sawn off it with black crosses.' Photographs were also taken of the pilots running to their Hurricanes as if they had just been scrambled, a deception that Beamont was required to join in, even though he had never flown with the squadron. The Heinkel was the first enemy aircraft to fall in France in the Second World War and the pilot who destroyed it, Robert Voase Jeff, a twenty-six-year-old short-service commission officer, was rewarded with the Croix de Guerre by a grateful French government.

The moment soon passed. Beamont discovered that normal activity consisted of 'endless patrols looking for enemy reconnaissance but we very seldom saw them. There was no radar to help. It was just a question of eyeballs.'[10] It was not until January that he had his first brush with the enemy. The squadron had been moved to Le Touquet when appalling winter conditions made it impossible to operate from Seclin. It was a miserable day, with rain and scudding low cloud, and none of the pilots expected to be flying when a call came through from the wing operations room ordering two pilots up on an intercept. Beamont took off with John Cock, one of the Australians who had answered the call for recruits, and they were directed over their radio telephones to climb through the cloud, where they saw a 'small speck' a few miles ahead. Beamont 'didn't really know what it was. I could see it had got two engines. Streaks of grey started to come out of the back of it. It suddenly dawned on me that this was a rear gunner firing tracers . . . miles out of range.' The pair finally reached the German at 19,000 feet, whereupon Beamont blacked out, the victim of inoxia or oxygen starvation, caused by the fact that the tube to his oxygen mask had disconnected. He came to, upside down and diving very fast, in time to roll upright and steer for home.

Nos. 607 and 615 Squadrons had also gained little experience from their months at a succession of bleak fields in the Pas de Calais. No. 615 set off from Croydon to its first French base at Merville. One flight was led by James Sanders, who after leaving Italy aged nineteen in 1935, and securing a short-service commission, had risen to the rank of flight lieutenant and acquired the nickname 'Sandy'. He had recently been transferred to the squadron after a display of high spirits landed him in trouble with Harry Broadhurst, the commander of his old unit, 111 Squadron. One September morning at Northolt, with nothing much going on, Sanders had decided to perform a particularly hazardous trick involving taking off, roaring immediately upwards into a loop, then performing a roll at the top. Unknown to him, a meeting of senior officers was taking place at the time. Such exuberance was out of kilter with the stern mood of the times. He was placed under arrest by Broadhurst, who most of the pilots liked, but whom Sanders thought 'a wonderful pilot but an absolute sod'. Broadhurst took him to see the Air Officer Commanding 11 Group, Air Vice-Marshal Gossage, who was more sympathetic and asked him what he would like to do. Sanders mentioned France. 'He said, right, off you go,' Sanders recalled. 'So I was posted to 615 Squadron, demoted from Hurricanes to Gladiators, which were twin wings, and from a regular squadron to an auxiliary.'[11]

With his departure there was an incident that almost altered the course of the war. Winston Churchill had gone to Croydon to see the squadron off, accompanied by his wife, Clementine. The Gladiators were escorting five transport aircraft loaded with fifty-four airmen and stores, and so had their machine-guns, one on either side of the fuselage and one under each lower wing, cocked and ready. The firing system was notoriously unstable. As Churchill inspected Sanders's machine, Clemmie climbed into the pilot's seat and began asking the functions of various knobs and buttons. Just as Churchill stooped to examine one of the wing-mounted machine-guns, his wife reached for the firing button. Sanders moved rapidly. 'I got her out of the aircraft fast,' he said. 'It suddenly dawned on me what an idiot I'd been.'

For much of the winter 615 Squadron was based at Vitry-en-Artois. Sanders was billeted with other officers in the village in the house of an elderly women who still dressed in black in mourning for the husband she had lost in the previous war. After dinner in the mess, which the officers set up in a local hotel, 'they would arrive back and there would be Margot with a tray with some hot bricks with some cloth wrapped round them. I'd always say, "Non, non Margot, ce n'est pas necessaire," but she'd insist. Then at five o'clock in the morning she'd be there with a *café noir*.' When he returned to see her after the war he learned she had performed the same services for the Germans, for which even-handed hospitality she was branded a collaborator by her neighbours.

The pilots found that interaction with their French counterparts tended to be more social than professional. Sandy Sanders and his comrades 'used to go and have parties at Lille with their squadrons, then we would go to a night-club and they would produce the girls. The French were mad keen on that subject, but all we were interested in was the drinking, having a good party. You might say, "Look at that lovely blonde over there," but that's as far as it went. But the French, one by one, would take the girls away and we'd be left, every one of us, drinking until two or three in the morning, having a wonderful time with the French orderly officer waiting for us to finish our fun and go away.'[12] The squadron's enterprising adjutant had arrived with a suitcase full of French letters, as condoms were known to British servicemen, hoping to sell them to pilots and airmen, but custom was non-existent.

The squadron passed its time training on its obsolete aircraft, carrying out 'affiliation' exercises with bomber squadrons and mounting patrols over the Channel. On 29 December Sanders managed to get within range of a Heinkel 111 flying very high above the sea at 26,000 feet and emptied his ammunition at it without visible result. The squadron was told on 1 January, during a visit by the Under-Secretary of State for Air, Captain H. H. Balfour, that it was likely the unit would be re-equipped with Hurricanes within a fortnight. It was not until 12 April that the first machines started to arrive, and the squadron, like 607 Squadron, had only a few weeks in which to get accustomed to them in conditions of relative calm. The transition was still in progress when the frustrations, apprehensions and scares of the phoney war finally came to an end.

As so often on the eve of a great upheaval, the preceding days passed in an unnatural atmosphere of tranquillity. Denis Wissler arrived in France on 2 May to join 85 Squadron at Sacerat. On 6 May he spent the morning sunbathing, went on patrol for one hour forty-five minutes at lunchtime and spent the rest of the day playing pontoon and Monopoly. The following day he did no flying at all and got 'as sunburned as I have ever been before'. On 8 May, as orderly officer, he was deputed to show a visiting actress, Victoria Hopper, and a concert party over a Hurricane, and in the evening went to the show, which on 'the whole was damn good'. On 9 May he was on patrol again when an excited controller directed them to investigate some enemy aircraft. 'However nothing was seen and we returned home,' he recorded despondently in his diary. 'Nothing else happened during the day apart from some patrols and directly after dinner I went to bed.'

It was the last good rest he would get for some time. The same evening Paul Richey was walking with a French girlfriend in the evening sunshine in a park near Metz when they heard a rumbling in the distance. '"Les canons," Germaine said. "Nonsense," I tried to reassure her. "It's only practice bombing. There are lots of ranges round here." It was the guns all right, big ones at that: the guns on the Maginot and Siegfried Lines. We walked back towards the town in silence, thinking our own thoughts.'

7

The Battle of France

Although it had been long expected, the arrival of the blitzkrieg on 10 May still came as a shock. The night before, a perfect summer evening, 87 Squadron had received an order putting all pilots on readiness at dawn. 'There was nothing unusual in that,' the squadron diary recorded, 'or in the accompanying warning that the blitzkrieg would start the following day. People had become a little sceptical. It was therefore with no little surprise that we were wakened before dawn by a tremendous anti-aircraft barrage, the drone of many aero engines and a deep thudding sound we had never previously heard. BOMBS!' Shortly afterwards a Dornier raced in low over the small boggy aerodrome at Senon, near Metz, where pilots and ground crews were living in tents in the woods, and machine-gunned some French aircraft parked on the edge of the field.

There were similar rude awakenings at aerodromes all across northern France that Friday morning. In the Pas de Calais 615 Squadron was in the throes of exchanging its Gladiators for Hurricanes. 'A' flight was at Le Touquet when Heinkels arrived at dawn and bombed the airfield, damaging three Hurricanes. The pilots, billeted in a nearby chateau, assumed at first it was a French air exercise. 'B' flight was up the road at Abbeville, also re-equipping. Their base was attacked as well, but to little effect. The duty pilot, Flying Officer Lewin Fredman, gamely took off in a Gladiator to attack a Heinkel at 20,000 feet but failed to connect.

Peter Parrott, a twenty-year-old flying officer with 607 Squadron, was in the mess at Vitry having a cup of tea while waiting for a lorry to take him and two other pilots to the base to stand by. 'We heard the truck pull up, a three-tonner, the usual transport. But instead of waiting with the engine running, the driver ran into the mess, which was an unheard of liberty by an airman . . . He said, "There are German aircraft overhead, sirs!" Then we started to hear the engines so we hurled ourselves into the truck and went up to the airfield. I didn't stop running. I ran into the crew-room and got my kit on still running out to the aeroplane.'[1] As he took off, a stream of Heinkels was moving over the airfield, and he set off to catch them, firing every one of his 2,250 rounds without doing any visible damage. He would fly four more sorties that day to greater effect, shooting down two Heinkels and damaging another two.

During 10 May, the Luftwaffe launched heavy coordinated raids on twenty-two airfields in Holland, Belgium and north-east France, using more than 300 Heinkel and Dornier bombers. On the ground, the terrestrial component of blitzkrieg, the tanks and motorized infantry battalions, sliced through Holland and Belgium's thin defensive membrane. In the air, the balance of forces and the weight of experience was overwhelmingly in the Germans' favour. Their commander, Hermann Goering, had at his disposal 3,500 modern aircraft, many of them crewed by airmen who had seen action in Spain and Poland. The two air fleets – Luftflottes 2 and 3 – could muster 1,062 serviceable twin-engined bombers, 356 ground-attack aircraft (mostly Ju 87 Stuka dive-bombers), 987 Me 109 single-engined fighters and 209 twin-engined Me 110 fighters. The average daily fighter strength that the RAF could pit against this, consisting of approximately forty Hurricanes and twenty Gladiators, was puny in comparison. The air forces of Holland and Belgium were also negligible. The main deterrent to the Luftwaffe in the West was supposed to be the Armée de l'Air. On paper it seemed equipped to put up a robust defence, with an available strength on the eve of battle of 1,145 combat aircraft. The vast majority of these, 518 of them, were single-engined fighters, supplemented by 67 twin-engined fighters. The bomber feet consisted of only 140 machines, and nearly half of these were obsolete.

Despite the obvious imbalance of the force, France should, in theory at least, have been able to inflict significant damage on the invading German bomber fleets, applying a brake to the momentum that was the essential element of blitzkrieg. But the French fighter strength was illusory. Only thirty-six of their machines, the Dewoitines, which could reach 334 m.p.h., had the speed to compete on anything like equal terms with the Me 109s. Most of the fighters were Moranes, which were underarmed and had a sluggish top speed of just over 300 m.p.h. The French early-warning system was primitive. Britain had let France in on the radar secret before the war, but little had been done to develop it, and on 10 May there were only six mobile sets in place, supplied by London. The main work of locating the direction of a raid and ascertaining numbers was done by a corps of observers who called in their sightings over the public phone system. Then there were the pilots. The men of the Armeé de l'Air were brave enough, and worked hard at their aviator *élan*. But many RAF pilots felt that something more than the spirit they showed in the mess and the night-club was required in the air. There was little attempt to coordinate the two forces or share tactical thinking or intelligence. Once the war began, each air force effectively fought on its own.

Given the Luftwaffe's advantages, the first day of the onslaught in northern France was to turn out disappointing and surprisingly painful for them. The dawn raids failed to do serious damage to any of the airfields and the defenders were immediately in the air and hitting back. The pilots of 1 Squadron were active almost constantly from 5 a.m., shooting down one of a group of Dorniers near Longuyon as they raided a railhead and railway station nearby. Later in the morning they brought down another Dornier. Billy Drake, who had been separated while flying with his section near Metz, saw a condensation trail above him and went to investigate, only to find it was a Spitfire on a photographic reconnaissance mission. 'The next thing I saw was a bloody 109 on my tail,' he said. 'When I tried to evade him he suddenly turned up in front of me and I thought, "Christ! I'd better start shooting at him." Suddenly I looked up and there was a bloody great electricity cable in front of me.

He knew the area and he lead me into it!'' Drake swooped under the high-tension cable and caught the 109 as it climbed away. 'I gave him a couple of bursts and he went in and that was the end.'

It was the first time he had been in action. Even immediately afterwards he found it hard to recount the incident in any detail. 'It was,' he said later, 'rather like having a motor-car accident. You can't remember what the hell happened.'[2] The opening hours, then the whole of the French campaign, were to pass in a blur for many pilots as one sortie merged into another, day melted into day and perpetual exhaustion tinged the whole experience with the quality of a bad dream.

The fighting on the first day did not finish until 9 p.m., when pilots of 3 Squadron, which had been rushed to France that day along with 79 Squadron, knocked down three Heinkels. They were in action within a few hours of arriving at Merville. No. 3 Squadron had left hurriedly from Kenley after lunch. The few maps available were given to the senior pilots and the rest of the squadron followed their lead. No. 79 Squadron at Biggin Hill was given more notice and had time to arrange for mess kit and civvies to follow on in a transport plane so they would be suitably equipped to enjoy themselves in France. It was not to be. The RAF's retreat on the ground had already begun and all subsequent movement would be backwards. During the day 73 Squadron had been pulled from its forward base at Rouvres to the supposedly more secure airfield at Reims–Champagne. No. 1 Squadron also moved hurriedly in the afternoon, from Vassincourt to Berry-au-Bac north-west of Reims. It was stiflingly hot when they arrived and the air was thick with mayflies. As they waited for the next sortie, a lone Heinkel detached itself from a flotilla overhead and dropped fourteen bombs that rippled across the field, sending the pilots diving for cover. No one in the squadron was hurt. A minute earlier, though, four farmhands had been working the neighbouring field. A shout alerted Paul Richey to what had happened.

> We found them among the craters. The old man lay face down, his body twisted grotesquely, one leg shattered and a savage gash across the back of his neck, oozing steadily into the earth. His son lay close by . . .

> Against the hedge I found what must have been the remains of the third boy – recognizable only by a few tattered rags, a broken boot and some splinters of bone. The five stricken horses lay bleeding beside the smashed harrows; we shot them later. The air was foul of the reek of high explosive.[3]

The sight of dead civilians was to have a disturbing effect on many of the pilots who served in France, ruffling their careful nonchalance and stirring up feelings of detestation, even hatred for the enemy. That evening Richey flew the last patrol of the day over the aerodrome, noting the effect of the German visitation on the normally dull and tranquil landscape. 'Smoke was rising from several towns and villages: bombed . . . Here and there farmhouses and barns were burning, and the sight of the lazy red flames licking up nauseated me; it was all so thoroughly evil and hellish.'

The last pilots bumped down on the grass airfields of Champagne, Picardie and the Pas de Calais in near darkness. It had been an extraordinary day. Altogether, the fighters of the Advanced Air Striking Force and the Air Component had flown 208 sorties. Between them, they claimed to have definitely shot down fifty-five bombers – Heinkels, Dorniers and Ju 88s – with a further sixteen probable. British losses amounted to seven Hurricanes shot down and eight damaged. Astonishingly, not one pilot was killed, and only three had been wounded.

The Luftwaffe themselves reckoned they had lost thirty-three bombers. Conflicting claims persisted throughout the air battles of the rest of the year. Wishful thinking, the confusion of battle and propaganda considerations inevitably inflated British figures. The Germans also exaggerated their successes and masked the extent of their losses, employing a system that fudged stark realities by assessing the damage to each aircraft in percentage terms. Whatever the discrepancy, it had been a bad début for the Luftwaffe in northern France. The Hurricane pilots fell asleep believing, or at least hoping, that the Germans were less formidable than they had feared. 'Am I browned off,' complained Denis Wissler, who had missed the action, grounded because of his inexperience.

The first day was to turn out to be the best. Things had for once gone more or less according to plan. All the time put into perfecting the Fighting Area Attacks, precisely numbered and laid out in the pre-war training manuals, appeared to have been justified. 'I have never seen squadrons so confident of success, so insensible to fatigue and so appreciative of their own aircraft,' noted the satisfied Officer Commanding the Air Component, Group Captain P. F. Fullard. But it was beginner's luck. The success which even relatively untested squadrons like 607 had enjoyed was due to the crucial fact that the bombers had arrived without any fighter escort in unconscious fulfilment of the Dowding prophesies as to what sort of war his squadrons would have to fight. The Hurricanes had been able to locate their targets with relative ease, simply because there were so many of them. The pilots arriving from England who were accustomed to Fighter Command's by now reasonably sophisticated ground-control system found themselves operating without direction. Relying on reports of sightings from the French observers, interception orders were transmitted from wing headquarters to aerodromes by field telephone. The sketchy information that could be conveyed to the pilots in the air was often unintelligible because of the short range and poor quality of the R/T.

Setting off from Merville mapless into the dusk, Pilot Officer Mike Stephens of 3 Squadron had soon been separated from the rest of his section, and then lost. 'We took off in whatever direction we happened to be pointing, hoping to catch the Heinkels,' he wrote. 'It was hopeless. There was no radar, no fighter control at all. We were wasting effort and hazarding aircraft in the hope of finding our quarry in the gathering darkness.'[4] The official RAF daily report admitted that the fighters 'had much too little in the way of an effective early-warning system'.[5] In the confusion of the subsequent days, that deficiency could only get worse. Nor were the Luftwaffe to make the same mistake again. On the second day, when the bomber fleets returned, they brought the Me 109s and Me 110s with them.

The very limited strength of the France-based squadrons was to be bolstered by several squadrons from 11 Group, including some equipped with Spitfires, flying from bases in south-east England. The fighters of the AASF and AC, however, were overwhelmed by their workload. The Luftwaffe probed deeper and wider behind French lines. German reconnaissance flights roamed over the forward areas, reporting the progress of the French and British land forces moving by prearranged plan to block the anticipated German advance westwards from the Low Countries. At the same time, bombers began systematically tearing up the defenders' lines of communication attacking aerodromes, railheads and bridges.

The squadrons went into action again at first light on the second day, Saturday, 11 May. Reims–Champagne aerodrome was bombed at 5 a.m. by Ju 88s. They were followed by two Dorniers. One of the raiders was brought down when 73 Squadron scrambled a section. The new arrivals from 79 Squadron at Merville also got into action early, shooting down a Heinkel spotted during a dawn patrol. At Berry-au-Bac, 1 Squadron spent the first hours setting up a new dispersal area, having decided the attack the previous day had probably been aimed at a concrete hut where they had first established themselves. The new arrangement consisted of a tent, a telephone to receive orders from 67 Wing headquarters and a trench and dugout to dive into in the inevitable-seeming eventuality of another raid. Now that the battle had really begun, Bull Halahan took his place at the head of his pilots, leading the first action of the day to confront Heinkel bombers, which turned back when they saw the Hurricanes.

The sound of gunfire and bombs rumbled around the airfields of northern France throughout the day, but the pilots had no clear idea of what they were supposed to do. No. 1 Squadron had been reprimanded by wing headquarters at Reims for taking off and chasing bombers on its own initiative. Their job, the pilots were told, was to await orders to escort Allied bombers trying to stem the German attack and to ignore any overflying raiders. Later on, after three large bombs were dropped outside the chateau where the headquarters staff were based, a request came through to mount a patrol in the vicinity.

The French-based squadrons were supported that morning by fighters which took off from bases in southern England on sorties over Holland and Belgium. Twelve Hurricanes from 32 Squadron were sent off from Biggin Hill to support the Dutch air force. They were directed to the aerodrome at Ypenberg, which they were told was in German hands. Pete Brothers led the attack as the CO had only just arrived at the squadron. 'We arrived, and on the ground there were a large number of Ju 52 transport aircraft,' he said later. 'We dived to set them on fire and to my surprise there was nothing to shoot at. They were all burned out in the middle, though the wing-tips and tails were OK. We thought, that's jolly odd. We whizzed around looking for something and found one parked between two hangars so we set that on fire and climbed back up again.' It was not until several months later that the squadron discovered that Dutch forces had recaptured the aerodrome and had blown up the transports on the ground, saving one for escape to Britain only to see it destroyed by their allies.[6]

No. 17 Squadron, based at Martlesham in Suffolk, was ordered in mid afternoon to patrol the Dutch coast. The whole squadron took off in twelve Hurricanes, crossing into Holland just south of The Hague and turning north. It then split up, with the CO, Squadron Leader George Tomlinson, leading 'A' Flight back to circle Rotterdam while 'B' Flight headed on to The Hague. On the way, 'A' Flight was attacked suddenly by sixteen Me 109s, which swooped on them, breaking up the formation into a series of individual combats in what was probably the first mass dogfight of the war. Something of the hectic confusion was conveyed in the officialese of Flying Officer Richard Whittaker's report. 'Eight [came in] for the first attack,' he wrote. 'Afterwards a dogfight developed and I broke away and saw three 109s on the tail of a Hurricane. I did a quarter attack on his port giving a short burst, but had to carry on past him. I then saw another Me 109 and we circled each other feinting for position and I finally got on his tail. I gave him all I had. We had both been flying at very low speeds, trying to turn inside one another. At this point I commenced to stall and lost sight of the enemy aircraft temporarily.' Breaking away, he flew through the smoke shrouding the coast and headed for home. Looking down he saw that 'The Hague as a whole was on fire'. In the same mêlée, Sergeant Charles Pavey found that, when he did a steep turn to the left, a pursuing Me 109 'could not follow me round. I eventually got on to his tail and the enemy aircraft twisted and turned, diving down. I fired intermittently and finally gave him a deflection shot, finishing my ammunition. He then burst into flames, spinning down to the ground, and I followed him down until he struck the ground.'[7]

This was one of three definite 109s claimed by 17 Squadron on the second day, as well as two army reconnaissance machines. But with the first successes came the first losses. Flight Lieutenant Michael Donne was shot down and killed when his Hurricane crashed south-west of Rotterdam. Pilot Officer George Slee also died after being shot down south of Dordrecht. Two others, Pilot Officer Cyril Hulton-Harrop (brother of Montague, killed by his own side in the Barking Creek débâcle) and Sergeant John Luck, managed to bale out after being hit and were taken prisoner. Squadron Leader Tomlinson's Hurricane was badly damaged, but he managed to crash-land and make his way back to Britain. Every one of them had been the victim of an Me 109.

The hazards of peacetime flying had meant that death was never far away, but now the pilots were encountering it in a new and unfamiliar form. Denis Wissler was at Lille–Seclin when the Luftwaffe arrived at noon. 'I came nearest to death today than I have ever been, when two bombs fell about thirty feet away,' he wrote in his diary. 'I was in the ante-room and my God did I run.' A driver was killed in the attack and a cook injured, and a block of sleeping quarters destroyed. That night Peter Parrot's brother Tim was the co-pilot in a Whitley bomber sent on a reconnaissance mission over the German–Belgian border. In the morning Peter Parrot received a signal saying his brother was missing; later he was confirmed dead.

Mortality concentrated minds. That afternoon Paul Richey had been hurrying over to his Hurricane to intercept a big formation of bombers heading for Reims when he ran into an RAF Catholic chaplain he had met previously and liked. 'He asked me if I wanted absolution, puffing alongside me. I confessed briefly. He asked if there were any other Catholics who might want absolution. I said, "Only old Killy in that Hurricane over there – hasn't wanted it for ten years but you can try!" We laughed and I waved him goodbye. But confess Killy did – sitting in his cockpit with the padre standing on the wing beside him.'[8] Richey was shot down an hour or so later, after an extended dogfight between five members of 1 Squadron and fifteen Me 110s. He baled out and landed in a wood, and after being found by some gendarmes was reunited with the squadron the following day. Five days later he was to take to his parachute again.

The shock of the first casualties was offset, to some extent, by the realization that, despite the high speeds and heavy fire-power now employed in aerial warfare, the chances of surviving a combat in which you came off worse were considerably higher than they had been during the First World War. From the outset it was clear that the news that someone was missing was not necessarily a euphemism for their almost certain death. On the morning of the second day Flight Lieutenant Dickie Lee of 85 Squadron had been injured slightly when his Hurricane was hit by flak near Maastricht and he decided to jump. He landed in a field close to where some tanks were parked on a road. He came across a peasant, who assured him the armour was Belgian. Lee borrowed an old coat to cover his uniform and went to investigate. The tanks were German. Lee was taken by the troops for a civilian, but none the less locked up in a barn, from which he soon escaped and made his way back to Lille, arriving two days later. On the same day his squadron companion, Pilot Officer John 'Paddy' Hemingway, was also badly hit by flak, baled out, and returned unharmed to the unit.

By the end of the second day the fighter squadrons could be reasonably satisfied with their own part in the battle. Together they claimed to have destroyed a total of fifty-five enemy aircraft for the loss of thirteen Hurricanes and eight pilots. It was an overestimate. In one case, 1 Squadron reported that it had shot down ten Me 110s over the village of Romilly near Reims when the real number was two. The discrepancy was caused by confusion rather than wilful exaggeration. Air fighting was disorienting and distorted the senses, a fact acknowledged in the squadron's daily report, which observed that 'questioning pilots immediately after combat, it has been found extremely difficult to obtain [precise] information as to what actually happened as most pilots, after aerobatting themselves into a stupor, were still pressing imaginary buttons and pulling plugs [the override boost mechanism to increase power] an hour or so after landing'. Building an accurate picture was further complicated by the inevitable tendency of several pilots to describe the same incident as if it was their unique experience.

The performance of the British fighters was a welcome piece of good news in an overall story of failure. On the first day the general response of the Allied air forces to the German attack had been hesitant and did almost nothing to slow its advance, which proceeded with the speed and energy of a force of nature. The French commander, Gamelin, displayed a paralysing reluctance to provoke the enemy, fearing that if he authorized bombing raids the Germans would respond with a fury his tiny bomber fleet could do nothing to match. Barratt fumed, argued and finally went his own way, dispatching thirty-two Battle bombers against the Germans advancing through Luxemburg. Only nineteen of them came back, the rest having fallen victim to fighters and the German mobile light flak guns. A second attack was ordered and sixteen bombers flew off. This time nine were shot down from the ground or the air and four limped back badly damaged.

The Fairey Battles were disastrously unsuited to the demands of modern aerial warfare. They were slow, clumsy and poorly armed. The fighter pilots were impressed by the cheerfulness and courage of their crews, but even before the fighting began, no one gave much for their chances. On the first day, their vulnerability had been increased by the fact that no fighter escorts were assigned to them. On 11 May they went into action again in another attempt to blunt the thick black arrows already punching out in all directions across the HQ staff maps.

This time they were occasionally assigned fighters to protect them, but the results were still pitiful and the losses heavy. At 09.30 six Hurricanes from 73 Squadron had taken off from Reims–Champagne to protect a group of eight Battles ordered to attack targets in Luxemburg. Seven of the bombers were shot down. The following day, 12 May, five Battles, crewed by volunteers who were only too aware of the odds they were facing, were sent off again, this time with the mission to destroy two bridges spanning the Albert Canal in an attempt to hold up the German army, which had already captured two vital bridges across the Maas, just to the east. Eight Hurricanes from 1 Squadron led by Bull Halahan were ordered to provide cover. On the way to the rendezvous the fighters ran into a swarm of 109s. In the dogfight that followed they claimed to have shot down at least four 109s and two Henschel spotter planes. Halahan's Hurricane was hit badly and he was forced to land. The Battles pressed on to their doom. Two were knocked down by the 109s before reaching the bridges. Two more were brought down by the flak batteries ringing the target. The remaining bomber crash-landed on the way home. Six crew members died in the raid and seven were captured.

The inadequacy of the support the fighters could offer had already been demonstrated the same morning when Hurricanes from 85 and 87 Squadrons were sent to meet up with twenty-four Blenheims, which had also been sent from RAF Wattisham in Suffolk to attack the bridges. On the way to the rendezvous the fighters ran into a succession of enemy formations. In the mêlée that followed, two 87 Squadron pilots were shot down and one of them, Flying Officer Jack Campbell, a Canadian from British Columbia, was killed. The other, Sergeant Jack Howell, managed to bale out, but his parachute only half-opened and he made a high-speed descent. The squadron diary noted that 'although landing extremely heavily he found on recovering consciousness that he was no more than badly bruised and was flying fit within a week'.

The two were probably victims of a section of Me 109s led by Hauptmann Adolf Galland, who was to shoot down more RAF aircraft than any other Luftwaffe pilot operating in the West. In his memoirs he described closing in on the unsuspecting Hurricanes. 'I was not excited, nor did I feel any hunting fever. "Come on! Defend yourself!" I thought as soon as I had one of the eight in my gunsight . . . I gave him my first burst from a range which, considering the situation, was still too great. I was dead on the target, and at last the poor devil noticed what was happening. He rather clumsily avoided action, which brought him into the fire of my companion. The other seven Hurricanes made no effort to come to the aid of their comrade in distress but made off in all directions.'[9] The Blenheims were equally unsuccessful and suffered heavily at the hands of the fighters and the flak. Out of the twenty-four that set out, ten were lost.

It was now clear that there were nowhere near enough Allied bombers to make a difference, nor fighters to mitigate the devastating effects of the Me 109s and the flak batteries. The French bombing raids were as ineffective as the British and their Moranes and Dewoitines no real deterrent to the Messerschmitts. Even if the Allied air forces had been stronger, the resistance they could offer in the air would not have been enough to counter the fact that, on the ground, the battle was being lost.

A handful of reinforcements arrived in the evening of 12 May. Sixteen Hurricanes of 501 Squadron were sent off from Debden and divided themselves between Bapaume and Vitry-en-Artois. This piecemeal offering was unlikely to do anything to quieten the clamour for more aircraft that was coming from the French government and supported by Winston Churchill, who had become prime minister on the day the blitzkrieg began.

Dowding had always regarded the sovereign strategic objective of Fighter Command as the protection of the British Isles. He seems, from the outset, to have doubted France's ability to defend itself. Well-founded pessimism, a cold streak of realism that contrasted with Churchill's sometimes alarmingly romantic approach and a keen appreciation of the paucity of his resources led him to view the sending of any more fighters to the aid of France as an appalling waste. He would oppose every request for further sacrificial offering of pilots and aircraft. But the battle had already created a vacuum, drawing in pilots and machines in a futile effort to stem a German advance that was now flowing westwards with the inexorability of lava.

On 13 May, the first German tanks crossed the Meuse at Sedan, a psychological as well as political frontier. The more intelligent observers who had grasped the nature of blitzkrieg understood that this, most probably, meant the defeat of the Allies was inevitable. Churchill, by his own admission, had failed to appreciate that warfare now moved at what was a lightning pace by the standards of the previous war. Thus, he was relatively unperturbed by the news of a breakthrough, believing that, as on the Western Front a quarter of a century previously, the thrust could at the least be blocked. That day thirty-two more Hurricanes and pilots were ordered off to France to make up the losses. The Luftwaffe was now concentrating on creating havoc in the rear of the French and British armies, smashing road and rail links to prevent the forward movement of men and supplies and wrecking the already fragile communication network. From now on, chaos was to be the *status quo*.

The Allies' ability to manoeuvre was dictated by the activities of the German bombers. While the Heinkels and Dorniers savaged supply lines, the Ju 87 Stukas moved ahead of the advancing Panzers. They had already proved their destructive power in Spain and Poland. The damage they did was as much to morale as to flesh, bone and metal. The mounting shriek of the sirens as they tipped into their dive was a devastating *coup de théâtre* that terrified even the most cool-headed troops. The Allied pilots, though, felt no concern about meeting them. Stukas could only manage a top speed of 238 m.p.h. and when cruising trundled along at just over 200 m.p.h. They were to prove a gratifyingly easy target for British fighters later on. But now, with the Me 109s in almost constant attendance, there were few chances of getting at them.

Despite the dramatic developments, 13 May was a quiet day. There was one raid by seven Battles over Holland, which was mercifully completed with damage to only one aeroplane. The French also sent seven bombers, with a heavy fighter escort, against troop concentrations in the Sedan area and the pontoons the German engineers had thrown across the Meuse. The effect was negligible. Ten Hurricanes were shot down, six of them, including Billy Drake's, by Messerschmitts. He had been on dawn patrol with five other Hurricanes from 1 Squadron at 22,000 feet when he started 'feeling very woozy. I looked down and sure enough I had no oxygen so I said I was going home. Round about 10,000 feet I saw these four [bombers] and it didn't look as if they were being escorted by anybody. Just as I was firing away, I suddenly heard a bloody great thump behind me and a Messerschmitt 110 had obviously got behind and [blown] me out of the sky.'

He felt as if he had been struck hard in the back and the leg and flames were streaming from his engine. 'I tried to get out but I'd forgotten to open the hood and the aeroplane was really brewing up by this time. I released the hood and went onto my back and that probably saved my life because all the flames that were coming into the cockpit went round the fuselage and missed me so I was able to bale out.'

As he floated down he heard the twin engines of the 110 above him, then tracer twinkled past as the Messerschmitt opened fire, apparently at him. He tried to accelerate his rate of descent by tipping air out of the canopy, but the pain in his back was too great for him to lift his arm. The German veered away and he hit the ground only to face another hazard. Drake was wearing an old white flying overall from pre-war days and his hair was very blond. The French peasants who ran to the scene 'thought I was a German. They all had scythes and pitchforks and they were literally coming for me.'[10] His parents' investment in his Swiss education paid off when he yelled in French that he was a British pilot. When he showed them his wings they became effusively friendly and took him to a field dressing station in a school near Rethel that was crowded with casualties, several of whom died while he was being treated. He had two bullets in his leg, and shrapnel and bullets in his back. He was given morphine that did little to dull the agony as the debris was prised out, then moved to the town hospital.

When he did not return the squadron began to worry. Paul Richey had to collect something from Drake's room after lunch 'and saw his meagre possessions spread about . . . a photograph of his mother, a bottle of hair oil, the pyjamas he would need no more. Poor old Billy!'[11] Then a call came through from the hospital that they had an English pilot. Richey went to see him and plans were made to move him to British care. The next day, though, the hospital was evacuated and Drake began a long and painful journey westwards.

That evening eight pilots and Hurricanes from the new batch of reinforcements landed at Reims–Champagne to shore up 73 Squadron.

They were being thrown in at the deep end. None of them had belonged to a squadron before, let alone seen action, having come directly from No. 6 Operational Training Unit. The following day more machines and men, many of them equally inexperienced, were spread around 607, 615 and 3 Squadrons. No. 1 Squadron also received some welcome arrivals when Flying Officer Crusoe and Sergeants Berry, Clowes and Albonico returned from a gunnery training exercise in Britain, making the last leg of the journey on a train that was bombed several times *en route*.

On Tuesday, 14 May, the Allied air forces made their first and last concentrated effort to stem the German advance now pouring through the gaps in the front around Sedan. Every available British bomber was mustered to destroy bridges on the Meuse on either side of Sedan and crush the heads of the columns thrusting into France, and a mixed batch of British and French fighters were ordered to protect them. Altogether eight attacks were launched on crossing points. The first raiders escaped lightly, protected from the flak batteries by the morning mist rising from the confluence of the Meuse and the Chiers. As the hot day wore on, the German gunners perfected their aim and the sky filled with watchful 109s and 110s. When the biggest raid of the day was launched in mid afternoon, the defences were primed. The first wave of twenty-five Battles, accompanied by French Bloch and Morane fighters, arrived at 4 p.m. local time and flew straight into a wall of flak. Then the hovering Messerschmitts descended to pick off the survivors. Eleven of the bombers and six of the fighters were shot down.

The second wave of twenty-three Battles and eight Blenheims was supposed to be guarded by Hurricanes from 1 and 73 Squadron. On their way to the target, however, the fighters were diverted by the sight of a formation of Stukas grouped over La Chesne, south-west of Sedan, where they had been sent to bomb French troops. The Me 109s protecting the bombers were slow to realize the danger. Killy Kilmartin shot down two, while Hilly Brown, Bill Stratton and Taffy Clowes claimed one each before the Messerschmitts intervened – figures that for once were subsequently broadly confirmed by the German reports. In the clash that followed, four 109s were shot down. No. 73 Squadron also ran into Stukas, destroying two and seriously damaging two more. Pressing on to their rendezvous with the bombers, however, they were ambushed by 109s and Sergeants Basil Pyne and George Dibden were shot down and killed. Earlier another 73 pilot, Pilot Officer Valcourt Roe, had also been killed over Namur. These encounters drastically increased the bombers' vulnerability when they arrived over target. Of the twenty-three Battles that set out, only nine returned and five out of the eight Blenheims were lost.

The day saw the heaviest casualties Fighter Command had yet suffered. Fifteen pilots were killed and two so badly wounded that they subsequently died. Twenty-seven Hurricanes were shot down, most of them by Messerschmitts. The dead ranged from beginners like Flying Officer Gerald Cuthbert and Flight Lieutenant John Sullivan, who had arrived the day before, to some of the most seasoned pilots. Among the latter was Les Clisby and Lawrie Lorimer of 1 Squadron, who had set off at breakfast time from Berry-au-Bac with Prosser Hanks and Boy Mould to chase a large formation of Me 110s which had appeared overhead. On first seeing them, their inclination had been to leave them alone, but they were spurred into action by a fitter who urged them to set off in pursuit for the honour of the squadron.

Clisby was last seen going into a dive, the cockpit of his Hurricane belching smoke and flame after having apparently been hit by a cannon shell. No one saw what happened to Lorimer, who also went down. At first they were posted missing. But when there was no news, the other pilots anticipated the worst. Clisby's unquenchable willingness to attack had persuaded Richey that he had 'bought it'. Some time later French troops discovered two burned-out Hurricanes.

Clisby was a month short of his twenty-sixth birthday. The premature worry lines scoring his forehead made him look older. He had a square, heavy jaw, a wiry moustache and downward sloping humorous eyes. He was extrovert, profane, perpetually cheerful and addicted to flying. He had joined the Royal Australian Air Force as a cadet aged twenty-one, and after being awarded a permanent commission he volunteered to go to Britain in 1937, despite the talk of war. He had turned out to be the most effective of the squadron's pilots, destroying at least nine German aircraft in his time in France, and he died not knowing he had just been awarded the DFC. Lorimer had been posted to 1 Squadron from 87 Squadron and had a reputation for being unlucky. This was the third time he had been shot down in five days.

The losses prompted a debate among the pilots about whether they could continue flying and fighting with such intensity. Pilots were carrying out as many as five sorties a day, of one and a half hours each, against forces that always vastly outnumbered them, taking off from often primitive airfields that were subjected to regular bombardment. Despite the danger, the privations and the exhaustion, morale and the will to engage the Germans remained largely intact. On the evening of 14 May, Flying Officer Frank Joyce and Pilot Officer Chris Mackworth of 87 Squadron were sent off on a reconnaissance mission over Louvain. Mackworth's engine would not start, so Joyce went alone. On the way he ran into a large formation of Me 110s and immediately launched a single-handed attack which he sustained until he was wounded in the leg and had to crash-land. He was rescued by some Scottish soldiers and treated at a field hospital, but had to be constantly shifted as the Germans advanced. Gangrene set in and his leg was amputated.

Mackworth had eventually managed to get his aeroplane started and set off on his mission. He also ran into Me 110s while they were strafing a village close to a tented field hospital, attacked them despite their overwhelming numbers and was shot down. He managed to bale out, but his parachute caught fire and when soldiers found him he was dead. His friend Dennis David received a letter later from Mackworth's father 'to tell me that he had heard from one of the doctors at the hospital. They had buried Chris but had no means of marking his grave other than by writing his name on a piece of paper which they put in a beer bottle on top of it.'[12]

Despite the remarkable mental and physical robustness of the British fighter pilots, fear and exhaustion began to take their toll. Richey, who was sustained by a buoyant reservoir of optimism, admitted that by now 'our nerves were getting somewhat frayed and we were jumpy and morose. Few of the boys smiled now – we were no longer the merry band of days gone by.' After his first parachute jump he had already begun 'to feel peculiar. I had a hell of a headache and was jumpy and snappy. Often I dared not speak for fear of bursting into tears.'[13]

There was to be no lessening of pressure on the pilots in the days to come. On 15 May the French government understood that the Battle of France was lost. This realization did not prevent a passionate request for more fighters. Churchill was woken at 7.30 a.m. by a call from the French prime minister, Paul Reynaud, who 'evidently under stress' announced in English: 'We have been defeated,' and informed him the front line at Sedan had been broken. Churchill candidly recorded that, to his mind, shaped as it was by the memory of the previous war, 'the idea of the line being broken, even on a broad front, did not convey . . . the appalling consequences that flowed from it'.[14] When Reynaud went on to beg for ten fighter squadrons, he was prepared to at least consider the plea.

The request was placed on the agenda of that morning's War Cabinet meeting as the second item. Dowding was present and spoke forcefully to bury a proposal Churchill had already backed away from and which had little or no support elsewhere. It was decided that the prime minister inform Reynaud that 'no further fighter squadrons should for the present be sent to France'.

Dowding understood, though, that the reprieve was likely to be only temporary. Sure enough, the following day, 16 May, his superior, Sir Cyril Newall, the Chief of the Air Staff, decided himself that eight flights – the equivalent of four squadrons – should be detached from Fighter Command and sent to France. His initiative followed a conversation with the BAFF commander, Air Marshal Barratt, who had emphasized the terrible fatigue the fighter pilots were now suffering, and additional plans were made for twenty exhausted men to be rotated out for a rest and replaced with experienced pilots from home squadrons.

Churchill, whose attitude towards the expenditure of fighter reserves chopped and changed with the demands of the hour, agreed and the decision was taken at that morning's War Cabinet meeting. It was not to end there. In the afternoon Churchill flew to Paris, where the extent of the catastrophe became apparent to him. He met Reynaud, his minister of national defence, Alain Daladier, and General Gamelin at the Quai d'Orsay with the smoke hanging in the air from piles of documents being burned in the garden in anticipation of the arrival of the Germans. Commanders and politicians radiated defeat and dejection while simultaneously appealing for yet more British aeroplanes.

Churchill's earlier pragmatism was overwhelmed by a romantic desire 'to give the last chance to the French army to rally its bravery and strength'. With an eye on posterity he also calculated that 'it would not be good historically if their request were denied and their ruin resulted'. The telegram containing these thoughts was sent to the Cabinet, which agreed to send six more Hurricane squadrons to France. The practical difficulties of housing them on battered and vulnerable airfields meant that in fact the squadrons – the last remaining Hurricane units not to have contributed to the French campaign – remained based in England. The plan was that each morning three would fly over to a French airfield and operate there until the afternoon, when the other three would relieve them.

The effect was to reduce further what Dowding, in agreement with the Air Ministry, had set as the minimum number of fighters and pilots needed to defend the country. He had already opposed the earlier decision to send eight flights to France in a letter to the Air Council, reminding them 'that the last estimate which they made as to the force necessary to defend this country was fifty-two squadrons, and my strength has now been reduced to the equivalent of thirty-six squadrons'. He closed by demanding that the ministry decide what level of fighter strength was to be left for the defence of the country and to assure him that, when that was reached, 'not a single fighter will be sent across the Channel however urgent and insistent the appeals for help may be'.

All along the front the French were now in panicky retreat and the fighter squadrons were dragged along with them. At dawn on 17 May Halahan and the 1 Squadron pilots received orders to move immediately from Berry-au-Bac to Condé-sur-Marne, between Reims and Paris. Before leaving they destroyed two Hurricanes damaged beyond immediate repair by pushing them into a shell crater and setting them on fire. Many of the fighters lost in France were to go the same way. As the last Hurricane took off, the German bombers arrived, pounding the next-door village of Pontavert, a place of no military significance. The squadron spent only one night in its new home before being ordered to withdrew again, to Anglure, sixty miles to the south-east.

Passing through Reims on the way to Condé, the road party found the city deserted but the roads round about choked with refugees. The Germans were following a deliberate policy of attacking civilian columns to intensify panic, block the roads and further disrupt the Allied communications. Many pilots witnessed the carnage and felt disgust. One day, when Dennis David's aircraft was unserviceable, he went for a walk near the airfield and met a column of Belgian civilians trudging into France.

> The refugees were pushing prams and small handcarts, with a few horse-drawn carts, and there were even fewer cars. Women were carrying their babies, while toddlers staggered along holding their mother's hand or dress. I borrowed an old motor bike from an army unit, and found a scene of desolation which it was impossible to describe. Old men, women and children, grandparents and babes in arms, not to mention dogs and horses, were strewn over the roadside, mostly dead but a few with just a flicker of life remaining. All had been torn to pieces by the bullets from strafing German aircraft, whose aim was to prevent the road being used by the British army, which was hoping to reinforce the British units already fighting the enemy further east. The whole episode utterly sickened me.[15]

Paul Richey, Sammy Salmon and Boy Mould came across a group of refugees passing through Pontavert. They piled up Salmon's Lagonda with bread, bully beef and jam from the stores and distributed them while listening to their stories: '*This* child's father had been killed by a strafing Hun; *that* young woman's small daughter had had her brains ripped out by a bomb splinter.' When they retold the stories later in the mess, there was at first a shocked silence. 'Then a disillusioned Johnny [Walker] almost reluctantly said, "They *are* shits after all." From this moment our concept of a chivalrous foe was dead.'[16] There could be no comfort in the belief that German fighter pilots were above committing such atrocities. The normally languid Peter Matthews was sent one day to pick up a pilot who had crash-landed and 'got mixed up with a terrible bombing and strafing of the roads. It wasn't just the bomber aircraft who were doing the strafing. It was 109s and 110s. That didn't seem to me a fighter pilot's job in life.'[17]

The additional pilots and machines, and the daily squadron excursions from England, did little to curb the Luftwaffe's freedom of action. The new pilots went up to be knocked down in what was becoming a battle of attrition that could end only one way. The newcomers plunged into an atmosphere of disarray, operating with minimal support and the sketchiest of orders. A pilot officer from 'B' Flight of 253 Squadron, who had just turned nineteen, arrived at Vitry on the evening of 16 May to be immediately confronted with a stark picture of what was happening. 'We got out of our Hurricanes and there were two Lysanders [unarmed army cooperation machines] circling. Suddenly two Messerschmitt 109s came and shot them both down, and instead of rushing away or lying down we just stood there gawping at them.' The flight was led by a forty-year-old Canadian, and comprised a sergeant pilot and four pilot officers, the latter 'with no experience at all'. From the beginning to the mercifully swift end all was confusion. 'We didn't know what we were supposed to do. We were stuck in a field. There was another squadron on the other side of the field and if we wanted to know what was going on, someone had to run across to find out . . . they had a telephone, we didn't.'

On 19 May an order was passed to them to take off and climb to a given height. Most of the pilots had early-model Hurricanes with fabric wings, no armour plating, radios with a range of only two miles and wooden two-bladed propellers. The flight commander's machine was fitted with a new variable-pitch propeller, which allowed a faster rate of ascent. 'He was climbing . . . and we were wallowing about below him.

All the instruction we got from him was, "Get the lead out, you bastards." We couldn't catch him up. He got shot down before we got anywhere near, and so did the sergeant pilot. Suddenly the air was full of aeroplanes all over the place. I shot at one but whether I hit it or not I don't know. Someone was on my tail so I got out of the way. I found myself completely alone. I didn't even have a map. I didn't know where I was. I thought, well, when we took off the sun was over there, so if I go that way I must be going somewhere near [the base]. I saw an airfield and landed and it was Merville. The first bloke I saw was someone who trained with me.' By the time he reached the base, 'the other three had found it and landed . . . We waited and waited and there was no sign of the flight commander or the sergeant pilot.' Both were dead. The next day the surviving pilots were ordered to fly back to England.[18]

Given the small size of the force, the losses of men and aircraft were brutal and unsustainable. On 16 May, thirteen Hurricanes were lost, five pilots were killed, four wounded and two captured. On 17 May, sixteen Hurricanes were destroyed. No pilot died, but one was taken prisoner. The following day thirty-three Hurricanes were shot down, seven pilots were killed and five taken prisoner. On 19 May, thirty-five Hurricanes were shot down or crash-landed, eight pilots were killed, seven were wounded and three taken prisoner. The following day only twelve Hurricanes were lost and three pilots killed, but by then the battle was winding down and the first units were beginning to evacuate back to England.

The squadron hardest hit was 85, which had seven pilots killed in ten days. On one day alone, 16 May, six of their Hurricanes were shot down, with two pilots killed and three burned or wounded. On 20 May three were killed in an engagement with 109s over Amiens, including the new CO, Michael Peacock, who had been in command only for one day, having taken over from the exhausted Oliver. Two more squadron leaders were to die, Lance Smith of 607 and from 3 Squadron Patsy Gifford, the dashing Edinburgh lawyer who had won a DFC for shooting down the first German raider of the war. At least one officer of glittering promise was among the dead, Flight Lieutenant Ian Soden of 56

Squadron, who had been expected to play an important role in Fighter Command's war. He flew his first sortie in France on Friday, 17 May. The following day he was up at dawn, claiming a Dornier and later an Me 109. By 6 p.m. he was dead, shot down by an Me 110 near Vitry. Some pilots just seemed unlucky. Soden's squadron comrade, Flying Officer Tommy Rose, who survived the Battle of Barking Creek, had been killed a few hours earlier.

The return on these losses could not be justified. The habitual over-claiming gave the impression that the fighters were knocking down at least two Germans for each British plane lost. Churchill even claimed the figure was 'three or four to one'. We know now that in reality the ratio was far less advantagous. After the first two days, before the fighter escorts arrived in force, there were only two days, 17 and 19 May, when the balance rose to two-to-one in the RAF's favour. More worryingly for the future, in the crucial contest between fighters, the Messerschmitt 109s and 110s shot down more Hurricanes than Hurricanes shot down Messerschmitts.

The fighters were engaged in a pointless struggle. That was not, however, how some of the pilots saw it. Looking down from the heavens, ranging the length and breadth of the front, the squadrons should have had a better notion of how the battle was developing than the soldiers on the ground whose vision was restricted to the field in front of them. They also knew from bitter experience the strength and ability of the enemy in the air. Yet, despite the evidence, the pilots were anxious to keep fighting. Their morale seems to have been partly sustained by the message in the score sheet, which, although it may have reflected something like the truth in the case of a squadron like No. 1, was far from an accurate portrayal of the overall picture. 'We were sure we had the measure of the Germans,' Richey wrote. 'Already our victories far exceeded our losses, and the squadron score for a week's fighting stood at around the hundred mark for a deficit of two pilots missing and one wounded. We knew the Huns couldn't keep going indefinitely at that rate, but we also knew we couldn't keep it up much longer without help.'[19] Richey pressed in person for reinforcements, telling a visiting senior officer that sending sections of three or flights of six up to protect bombers was useless and that a minimum of two squadrons was needed to provide proper cover.

But the Luftwaffe was far better equipped for a long haul than the air forces facing them. The squadrons in place since the opening of the blitzkrieg had been in a state of exhaustion almost from the second day. 'I have now had six hours' sleep in forty-eight hours and haven't washed for thirty-six hours,' wrote Denis Wissler two days into the hostilities. 'My God am I tired. And I am up again at 3 a.m. tomorrow.' Pilots dozed off in mid-flight. Wissler's squadron comrade Sergeant Sammy Allard was found asleep in the cockpit after landing one evening and it was decided to leave him there until dawn patrol next day. In the morning he was still unconscious, so he was put in an ambulance and sent to hospital. It was thirty hours before he woke up. The chaos and the influx of retreating French troops meant that beds were scarce. The pilots grabbed the precious chance of oblivion wherever it appeared, dossing down in abandoned houses, in barns alongside refugees, beneath bushes and the wings of their aeroplanes, or simply under the stars. Again and again they remarked how it seemed they had only closed their eyes minutes before they were awoken again. Sometimes it was not far from the truth, with warnings and move orders coming through at all hours, ruining the possibility of a clear stretch of undisturbed repose. Often, when they did lie down, sleep would not come easily, and when it finally descended they would be back in the cockpit, twisting, diving and shooting in a dream-replay of the day's combats. They looked forward to sleep with sensuous yearning, noting the experience as a gourmet records a great meal. 'I took off from Cambrai at about 7.30,' wrote Wissler on 14 May, 'after the best night's sleep I have had since this business started.'

Food, by contrast, seemed unimportant. They kept going on bread, jam and bully beef, and drank in great quantities tea that the ground crews thrust into their hands as they clambered out of their cockpits. On the odd occasions when they were able to find a café that was open or not crowded out, the food tasted of nothing. No. 1 Squadron took over a café at Pleurs, next door to the Anglure airfield. 'We all crowded in and mechanically shoved down bread, eggs and wine,' wrote Richey. 'It might as well have been sawdust.' Women were even further from their minds. When the barmaid tried to flirt with Richey, he found her 'quite pretty in a coquettish way but I could scarcely be bothered to look at a woman these days'.[20]

French dread mounted as the Germans pushed closer. Rumours, many of which turned out to be horribly accurate, swirled through the towns and villages, washing over soldiers and civilians alike, saturating the atmosphere in suspicion. In this humid moral climate the pilots found that their allies could be as dangerous as their enemies. German tactics in Holland, where parachute troops had been dropped in advance of the main attack to wreak havoc behind the lines, made anyone descending from the sky an object of distrust, as Billy Drake had already discovered. Now peasants and soldiers were inclined to attack any parachutist without bothering to establish his identity. Pilot Officer Pat Woods-Scawen of 85 Squadron was shot down in a dogfight with 109s in which he accounted for one Messerschmitt himself. He baled out, to be shot at twice on the way down by French troops. British soldiers could be just as edgy. Squadron Leader John Hill, who was flying his first sortie with 504 Squadron after taking over as commander, was forced to bale out and was blasted with shotgun pellets by a peasant as he approached the ground. Having convinced them he was an English airman, he was then arrested by passing British soldiers, who accused him of being a fifth columnist. When he reached into his pockets to show some identification, they opened fire, forcing him to jump into a ditch. This aroused further suspicions and he was pulled out and beaten unconscious, only being saved by the intervention of a passing French officer who knew him.

Fear of fifth columnists was rampant, apparently with some justification. When Pete Brothers first landed with 32 Squadron to fly for the day from Moorsele in Belgium, they found 615 Squadron, who had by now moved there, 'a bit jumpy, looking over their shoulders the whole time'. That morning a sergeant had failed to turn up at readiness. 'They'd gone to kick him out of bed and they found he was lying on his back with a knife in his chest . . . They didn't know if it was a fifth columnist or a refugee come to rob him or what.'[21]

The punishment the German bombers had inflicted on the soldiers and civilians below made them liable to rough justice if they landed behind enemy lines. Bull Halahan came across a crashed Heinkel. He asked some French Senegalese troops what had become of the crew, and was told they had been taken off and shot. Pat Hancock, who had arrived at 1 Squadron at the start of the fighting, was in Sammy Salmon's big Lagonda when they saw a German descending by parachute into a field near Béthienville. 'There was a greeting committee waiting for him,' he said. 'They had been tilling the field and now they wanted to kill him. Sammy said, "We can't have this, Hancock. Bloody French." His car instantly became a tank, through the hedge he went, into the field. We picked up the German. I put my RAF cap on his head and we dispersed the French far and wide.'[22]

By 17 May the Chief of the Air Staff, Air Chief Marshal Sir Cyril Newall, had accepted the hopelessness of the situation. He announced to his peers that he did 'not believe that to throw in a few more squadrons whose loss might vitally weaken the fighter line at home would make the difference between victory and defeat in France'. He concluded that it would be 'criminal' to compromise Britain's air defences further. Churchill agreed and two days later ordered that no more fighter squadrons leave the country whatever the need in France.[23]

What remained of the eight reinforcement flights prepared to withdraw, most of them with only half the aircraft they had arrived with. On 20 May the Air Component squadrons attached to the BEF began to pack up. That evening 87 Squadron set off from Lille to Merville, the thirty-minute journey taking hours because of the blackout and roads clogged with troops and refugees. Roland Beamont described a 'great mass . . . all pouring westwards . . . pushing perambulators, bicycles loaded up with blankets and pots and pans . . . As we tried to get through them in clearly marked RAF vehicles there was a great deal of hostility. I think they felt that here were the British running away.'[24]

Dennis David flew to their new airfield to discover that 'accommodation was nil in the village, and we . . . were thankful to have clean straw to sleep on in a pigsty'. As the morning passed and the traffic outside the airfield was joined by the same retreating Allied troops the squadron had seen at Lille, anxiety grew that they would never get away. All the rumours were bad ones. A young French officer told them 'that Arras had fallen and that the Germans were advancing to the coast. Unbelievable! A battery of 75s stopped at our dispersal point and a harassed *capitaine* told us how Gamelin had been executed by the Paris mob and that the Germans had reached Abbeville [well to the south].'[25] Orders were given for the pilots to carry out strafing attacks on German troops on the road between Cambrai and Arras until troop carriers arrived to evacuate the ground crews, when they would switch to escorting them 'home to England'. These last words, the squadron diary noted, had a profound effect. 'An entirely new atmosphere was noticeable immediately the officers and men read that. A mixed feeling of regret at leaving hospitable France and an unpleasant feeling that should anything happen to the troop carriers or the Hurricanes we should be left very much alone in the world.'

By the following day they were home. Dennis David, who had been shot up in a strafing run, crash-landed but was evacuated in a passenger plane. After months looking down on the plains of northern France he was struck by 'how small and green the fields of Kent looked'. He went home to Surbiton, where his mother sent him to bed. He 'slept without moving for thirty-six hours. She became quite concerned and actually called the doctor, who said I was completely exhausted and should just be left to sleep.'[26] The sister squadron, 85, also made it back. 'I came home last night,' Denis Wissler scrawled in pencil in his diary. 'Bath, bed, booze.'

Bull Halahan decided that his men had now had enough and asked permission for the longest serving pilots to withdraw. The core of the squadron, who had been in France from the first days, left together; including the Bull himself, Johnny Walker, Prosser Hanks, Killy Kilmartin, Bill Stratton, Pussy Palmer, Boy Mould and Frank Soper. Rennie

Albonico, another of the originals, was not with them, having been shot down and taken prisoner on 21 May. Nor was Paul Richey. On the last big day of fighting, 19 May, he had attacked a formation of Heinkels, and after destroying one was caught in return fire. He was hit in the neck by an armour-piercing bullet and temporarily paralysed, only regaining the power in his arms when his Hurricane was 2,000 feet up and locked in a vertical dive. He was found by the French and moved erratically westwards to end up in the American Hospital in the Paris suburb of Neuilly.

Billy Drake also passed through Paris after being collected from hospital in Chartres by an American girlfriend called Helen. Lacking uniform or identity papers, he was again taken for a German at a French roadblock and feared he was going to be shot as a spy until Helen persuaded them to let him go. They went to the Crillon, where she handed over her Buick, its tank miraculously full of petrol, and told him to head for Le Mans, where the British were regrouping. 'The streets were crowded with refugees,' he said, 'and much worse, with soldiers without their rifles, just trudging. They'd had it. It was the most depressing thing I've seen in my life.'[27] At Le Mans there was an emotional reunion with the squadron members who had stayed behind.

Richey, too, eventually joined them after recuperating in Paris, savouring the last days of freedom the city would know for four years. One day, walking down the Champs-Élysées, he came across Cobber Kain sitting at a pavement café with a *Daily Express* journalist, Noël Monks. Kain had chosen to help with the re-forming of 73 Squadron, after those who remained of the surviving pilots returned to England, and was due back himself in a few days. He was young enough to still have acne, but his spirit was frayed. Richey 'noticed that he was nervous and preoccupied and kept breaking matches savagely in one hand while he glowered into the middle distance'.[28]

The following day Kain took off from the squadron base at Echemines, south-west of Paris, and started to perform rolls perilously close to the ground. Among those at the aerodrome was Sergeant Maurice Leng, a twenty-seven-year-old Londoner who was one of the first of the RAFVR pilots to be posted to a fighter unit to replace squadron casualties. 'He'd taken off in . . . the last original surviving Hurricane of 73 Squadron with a fixed-pitch, two-bladed wooden airscrew,' he said later. 'He took off and came across the aerodrome, did a couple of flick rolls and hit the deck. That was it.' The sympathy of the newcomers, who had hardly known him, was muted. 'We all said, "How sad," but we all said, "How stupid."'[29]

The judgement could have served for the whole air campaign. It petered out in a series of withdrawals westwards in ever deepening chaos. Nos. 1 and 73 Squadrons, two of the first four squadrons in, were to be the last out, together with 501, which had been in France since the start of the blitzkrieg, and 242 and 17 Squadrons, which were sent out early in June. No. 1 Squadron was now transformed, with a new commander, Squadron Leader David Pemberton, and an almost entirely new set of pilots. Pat Hancock, one of the replacement pilots, remembered the remaining weeks as 'only retreat, anxiety and lack of knowledge as to what was going on. Communications were almost non-existent. Fighter control, as such, had vanished.'[30] In the first two weeks of June the unit moved four times, in the end taking the initiative to shift itself when it was impossible to contact wing headquarters to obtain orders. They finally left on 17 June. One party departed by ship, boarding two dirty half-loaded colliers at La Rochelle. Another flew from St Nazaire. The squadron had been helping 73 and 242 Squadrons to maintain a continuous patrol over the port to cover the embarkation of the RAF and the remnants of the British army in France. They were unable to prevent the last tragedy of the campaign, the sinking of the *Lancastria*, which went down with the loss of 5,000 lives when a German bomb sailed flukily through an open hatch. Pat Hancock chased after one of the raiders 'for a hell of a way, firing at it but with no success'. Circling over, he saw the victims struggling in the water and threw down his Mae West life-jacket.

No. 17 Squadron was also sent to cover the evacuation, and set up base in tents on the racetrack at Le Mans on 8 June. The same day, Denis Wissler, back with 85 Squadron after a forty-eight-hour leave, was summoned by his commanding officer, Peter Townsend, who had taken over the squadron two weeks before, and told that '17 Squadron had wired and asked for two operational pilots and that he was very sorry but I would have to go, and that at once'. Wissler had only been with 85 Squadron for six weeks, but his first impression on joining was that 'the mob seem damn nice', and he had grown very fond of them. There were only two hours to say goodbye before he left for Kenley. He stopped on the way in London for a solitary, melancholy dinner at the Trocadero, where he 'really got completely plastered and was put to bed by the wing commander'. The same kindly officer woke him up at 3.30 a.m. with some Alka-Seltzer, lent him his bath robe and sent him for a cold shower before he took off.

Wissler left with Count Manfred Czernin, who had been with him in 85 Squadron. Czernin was twenty-seven, born in Berlin, where his Austrian diplomat father was *en poste*. His mother, though, was English, the daughter of Lord Grimthorpe, the polymath who designed Big Ben, and he had been to Oundle public school. There was none the less more than a dash of *Mitteleuropa* in his manner, which made him the object of some teasing. He joined the RAF in 1935 on a short-service commission after a stint farming tobacco in Rhodesia, and served as a bomber pilot before joining the reserve. Unlike Wissler, he had already been in action several times in France and claimed to have shot down four Germans. The pair managed to get lost several times on the way to Le Mans, taking twelve hours over a one-hour journey. The squadron then spent several days patrolling over Rouen and Le Havre, both towns obscured by columns of black smoke coiling up from burning oil tanks. On 12 June Wissler at last had his first taste of fighting when the squadron spotted three Heinkels bombing troopships off Le Havre and attacked. He opened fire on one of the bombers and saw smoke coming from the starboard engine, but modestly did not claim to have shot it down. Czernin, however, fired at another Heinkel in cloud and claimed a 'conclusive casualty'. On a later patrol Wissler had another new and unwelcome experience: coming under heavy ground fire. 'It was most terrifying,' he reported candidly in his diary that evening.

By now the evacuation was almost complete. The squadron returned to Le Mans after a patrol on the morning of Saturday, 12 June, to find the Naafi had gone leaving behind huge quantities of cigarettes and whisky, to which everyone helped themselves. The army had abandoned a batch of Harley-Davidson motor bikes. Pilots and ground staff took the opportunity to ride circuits round the famous track. The same day they moved to Dinard. On 17 June the pilots were at readiness all morning and broke off to eat at a local hotel. Members of a French squadron based at Dinard aerodrome were also there. Peter Dawbarn, a nineteen-year-old pilot officer with 17 Squadron, was among the English pilots who sat down to lunch. There was a radio in a corner of the dining room. When the news came on everyone stopped eating to listen. When the announcement of the capitulation followed there was silence. Then, 'they all burst into tears'.[31]

The newcomers had formed a low opinion of the French. Pilots' attitudes towards their allies differed, depending on when they joined the battle. Many veterans of the phoney war had enjoyed the company of their spirited fellow officers in the neighbouring *escadrilles*, even if they had not found them particularly supportive or even visible during the crucial phase of the Battle of France. No. 1 Squadron had a much-loved Frenchman attached to it as interpreter, Jean 'Moses' Demozay, who was to escape to Britain in an abandoned Bristol Bombay troop carrier and fight bravely and effectively for the RAF and the Free French for the rest of the war. The reinforcement flights and squadrons rarely saw the French. The few recorded encounters were not happy ones. Flight Lieutenant Fred Rosier of 229 Squadron put down at an airfield near Lille, after being nearly shot down in a battle, 'to find the French were there, with brand-new American aeroplanes, fighters, and they were not flying. They were quite friendly, but I was livid . . . They were not participating in the battle at all.'[32]

The French the replacement pilots saw appeared demoralized and apathetic. Peter Dawbarn and the 17 Squadron pilots had come across French fighter pilots on previous trips to Dinard, which they used as a base for patrolling, 'but they never took off as far as I know. We kept taking off, they didn't.' The locals could also seem treacherous. The squadron was convinced that traitors were reporting their movements to the Germans. 'The fifth column is operating here we are sure as Morse code starts every time we take off,' wrote Wissler. The 17 Squadron Hurricanes left from Dinard, fuselages packed with cigarettes and alcohol, and landed at Jersey, where they celebrated their escape in Fighter Boy style with a party. When they left the following day, one Hurricane carried a passenger, a young woman who made the brief journey to freedom with the pilot perched on her lap.[33]

Most of the Hurricanes that went to France never came back. Given the tight margins Fighter Command was working within, the campaign had been ruinously expensive in machines. Of the 452 fighters sent out, only 66 returned when the main force withdrew. Of the missing 386, German fighters and flak accounted for only 208. The rest were abandoned as unserviceable. This was no reflection on the ground crews, who worked continuously while being regularly bombed and strafed, with only a few hours' sleep in tent or field to sustain them before going back on shift. All but intact aeroplanes suffering only light damage had to be set on fire because there were no spares, or the chaotic conditions made repairs impossible. The normally genial tone of No. 1 Squadron diary faltered when it came to describing the waste. 'It has been most noticeable that on a patrol yielding no apparent results as many as two or three aircraft out of six may be struck by shrapnel and on return to aerodrome it has been found necessary to write off all three as u/s, due to lack of proper servicing and maintenance facilities . . . Wastage has so far been in the neighbourhood of thirty-eight, only ten of which have actually crashed. Apparently we in France are the poor relations.'[34]

The pilots of Fighter Command could feel proud of their performance in France. Churchill had claimed that they were 'clawing down two or three' Germans for every British aeroplane lost. It was a vast exaggeration. The Hurricane squadrons reckoned themselves to have definitely shot down 499 bombers and fighters. The true figure was lower but it was at least 299. But with losses of 208 on their own side, it still left the RAF pilots well in the lead. Their success was their own. They were dedicated and aggressive and they made the most of their excellent machines. What they lacked was an effective early-warning system, or any proper control or direction from the ground. The pilots fought using tactics they invented for themselves for objectives that were never explained, if they were ever understood. Given these handicaps, the cost in lives looked relatively low. Altogether fifty-six pilots were killed in the twelve days between 10 and 21 May, and thirty-six wounded, with eighteen taken prisoner. But such losses could not possibly be borne over a long period, and as soon as this battle ended, a new one was beginning.

8

Dunkirk

At Dunkirk some 500,000 British and French soldiers were now penned in, the sea at their backs, awaiting capture or annihilation. The job of finishing them off was given to the bombers and fighters of the Luftwaffe. Goering had proposed the idea. Hitler accepted it, apparently wishing to spare his army for the next stage of the French campaign.

The RAF was given the task of protecting the exhausted lines of soldiers, zig-zagging across the grey North Sea sands waiting to be rescued. This was the heaviest responsibility the air force had yet had to face. The troops were appallingly exposed. Defending them meant not only mounting continuous patrols over Dunkirk port and the beaches on either side. To be effective the fighters would also have to push inland to try to knock down the bombers before they could drop their loads.

Once again, they would be operating at a significant disadvantage in numbers. Despite the losses sustained in the blitzkrieg, the Germans still had 300 bombers and could draw on 550 fighters to protect them. After the depredations of the Battle of France, Air Vice-Marshal Keith Park, whose 11 Group faced Dunkirk, had only 200 fighters at his immediate disposal. The mission, though, had the virtue of clarity and purpose. The pilots knew what they were supposed to do and why they were doing it. The stoicism of the infantrymen as they waited patiently among the bomb bursts was profoundly affecting to the men flying over them, however little this was appreciated on the ground.

The burden of the fighting was to be borne by the squadrons based around London, which would be fully engaged for the first time. Dowding also decided that the time had come to throw his precious Spitfires into the battle. The 11 Group pilots watched the last, painful phase of the BEF's campaign in France with anticipation. To some it seemed to be less of a disaster than an opportunity. 'At Hornchurch,' wrote Brian Kingcome, 'the taste of war at last began to tingle our palates.'[1] 'Operation Dynamo', as the evacuation was code-named, began on the evening of 26 May when a vast flotilla of yachts, pleasure boats, fishing smacks, sailing barges, motor cruisers and dinghies joined more conventional craft in carrying the soldiers back across the Channel.

There had already been some preliminary skirmishing during the previous ten days. The Hornchurch pilots on the evening of 15 May were called to the billiards room of the officers mess for a briefing. There was no briefing room at the base. As Al Deere pointed out, 'there was no need for any; our operations were purely defensive and aircraft were usually launched into the air at a moment's notice, the pilots having only the vaguest idea of what to expect'.[2] Now they were informed that they would be going on the offensive, roaming over the French and Belgian coasts to seek out the Luftwaffe.

When the order came to start patrolling, there was competition among the 54 Squadron pilots as to who would go off first. The honour – for this was how it was seen – went to the twelve most experienced pilots. Al Deere described the excitement, after bumping over the grass at Hornchurch and climbing to 15,000 feet, of crossing the French coast: 'There was a hum in the earphones as the CO's voice crackled over the air, "Hornet squadron, battle formation, battle formation, GO." Symmetrically, like the fingers of an opening hand, the sections spread outwards. As my eyes scanned the empty skies I was conscious of a feeling of exhilaration and tenseness, akin to that experienced before an important sporting event. There was no feeling of fear . . .' When nothing happened, elation soon evaporated. When the squadron returned, the other pilots crowded round to hear about the first real taste of action. Colin Gray, a fellow New Zealander, asked Deere what it had felt like, 'knowing that at any minute a Hun might pop up and take a pot at you?' Deere reported that 'at first I was tingling all over with excitement but when after a time nothing happened I was damn bored'.[3]

It was Johnny Allen, a quiet member of the squadron who stood out because of his strong religious convictions, who scored first, shooting down a Ju 88. Deere's turn came on 23 May. While eating breakfast in the mess that morning, he was called to the phone to speak to his flight commander, Flight Lieutenant James 'Prof' Leathart, so called because he had a degree in electrical engineering. Leathart had just come from a meeting with the station commander, Wing Commander 'Boy' Bouchier, who had learned that the CO of 74 Squadron, Squadron Leader White, had been shot at while patrolling across the Channel and forced down at Calais–Marcq aerodrome. 'Drogo' White was an example of the RAF's fundamentally meritocratic nature. He had started out as a Halton apprentice and been selected for Cranwell, where he won the Sword of Honour. He was regarded as the finest shot in the air force, capable of scoring eighty hits out of a hundred on a towed drogue target, when the average was twenty. None of this had saved him from being shot down on his first sortie, and by a Henschel 126, a relatively slow-moving reconnaissance plane.

Before landing he radioed Johnny Freeborn, who was flying with him, asking him to tell his wife that he was unhurt and would soon be home. This optimistic prediction came true sooner than he could have dared to hope. Bouchier asked Leathart to fly over in a two-seater Miles Master trainer, keep the engine running while White hopped in, then return at sea-level. It sounded to Deere, who with Johnny Allen was asked to fly escort, 'a piece of cake'. They reached Calais without any trouble. Deere sent Allen up to stand guard at 8,000 feet, where Germans might be lurking in the broken cloud. The bright yellow Master landed and taxied over to a hangar, where White was presumed to be waiting. Then Deere heard 'an excited yell from the usually placid Johnny'. Allen had seen a dozen Me 109s heading for the airfield. He attacked, and found himself in the middle of a frantic mêlée, shooting and being shot at.

Deere dropped down to try and alert the Master, which had no R/T, by waggling his wings. As he did so a 109 flashed across his path. He latched on to it and reefed his Spitfire hard over in an attempt to turn inside the Me 109, the crucial manoeuvre in air fighting. If the chasing pilot succeeded in turning tighter, getting inside his opponent, he had the chance to fire a deflection burst, aimed in front for the enemy to fly into. If he failed, the target was always a little ahead, leaving the tracer twinkling harmlessly in his wake. Deere turned inside. He was preparing to fire when Allen's voice again filled his earphones, calling for help. Deere asked Allen to 'hang on while I kill this bastard', and stayed clamped into the turn. Then, 'in a last desperate attempt to avoid my fire, the Hun pilot straightened from his turn and pulled vertically upwards, thus writing his own death warrant. He presented me with a perfect no-deflection shot from dead below and I made no mistake. Smoke began to pour from his engine as the aircraft, now at the top of its climb, heeled slowly over in an uncontrolled stall and plunged vertically into the water's edge from about 3,000 feet.'

Now he went to look for Allen. As he climbed, he was seen by two 109s, which swung round steeply and started after him. Again Deere found that he could comfortably turn inside his pursuers, so that very quickly the roles were reversed and he was chasing them. Deere opened fire on the second 109, causing 'bits to fly off'. Then he and the lead 109 went into an extended dogfight, chasing each other round at high speeds in tighter and tighter circles. Before the end Deere ran out of ammunition, but for reasons he could not later explain he continued the engagement until the German abruptly straightened out and headed east for home. Buzzing with adrenaline, Deere and Allen, whose Spitfire was by now ventilated with bullet holes, did the same. Deere indulged himself with a victory roll over the aerodrome as they came in.

This encounter was the first time a Spitfire had gone up against a Messerschmitt and pilots and ground crew were hungry for details. Deere's account was corroborated by 'Prof' Leathart, who had with White watched the combat from a ditch before they made their escape as soon as the sky was clear. Deere was excited and relieved. It seemed that one of the great questions that the fighter pilots, and those who directed them, had been asking themselves since the start of the war had been settled. Deere believed that as a result of his prolonged fight with the second 109 he had been able to assess practically the relative performance of the two aircraft. The experience of the Hurricanes in France, and the tests carried out on the Me 109 that had fallen into Allied hands, had concluded that the Messerschmitt could out-climb the Spitfire up to 20,000 feet, and always out-dive it, but was less agile at all altitudes. Deere agreed about the dive. The Messerschmitts, unlike the British fighters, had fuel injection, which meant they did not miss a beat at the moment of zero gravity that preceded a rapid descent. That aside, 'the Spitfire was superior in most other fields, and like the Hurricane, vastly more manoeuvrable.'[4] The Spitfire's climbing performance had been significantly improved by the advent of the Rotol constant-speed airscrew.

Later that day there was to be another formative experience for the squadron. That afternoon it took off on cross-Channel patrol and ran into a formation of bombers silhouetted above in the clear sky, heading for Dunkirk. After climbing above, unnoticed, and gaining the maximum tactical advantage, Leathart, who was leading, ordered a No. 5 attack. The four sections of three fanned out into echelon formation, each one tucked into a neat inverted V-shaped 'vic' slanting across the sky in a shallow diagonal, each pilot selecting his target. The flying discipline would have delighted their pre-war instructors. Then a panicked voice on the R/T shouted: 'Christ, Messerschmitts – Break!' The squadron instantly 'split in all directions, all thoughts of blazing enemy bombers momentarily ousted by the desire to survive'.

In the tumbling dogfight that followed, the 54 Squadron pilots claimed to have destroyed eight of the attacking Messerschmitts, but unfortunately no bombers, which were their primary targets. Despite this success, the encounter set off intense discussion of the value of the tactics they had been taught. The criticism was led by George Gribble, a 'very English, very good-looking' twenty-year-old short-service entrant. In Deere's admiring opinion, he 'epitomized the product of the public school; young yet mature, carefree yet serious when the situation required it, and above all possessing a courageous gaity'. Gribble told

Leathart that 'everybody was so damn busy making certain he got into the right position in the formation that we were very nearly all shot down for our pains'. Leathart, who was shortly to take over command, did not argue. He promised that henceforth there would be no more Fighter Area Attacks.[5]

These cross-Channel clashes taught valuable lessons to the 11 Group squadrons. They provided a demonstration of the startling reality of air fighting, but allowed the pilots an opportunity to recover and digest their experiences. Previously no one had known what to expect. During the first days of the Battle of France, 32 Squadron, flying from Biggin Hill, had barely seen the enemy. Michael Crossley noted one day's non-events with typical candour and idiosyncratic punctuation in the squadron diary. 'All set off to France, land at Abbeville, refuel, hear dreadful stories, get very frightened, do a patrol, see nothing, feel better, do another, see nothing, feel much better, return to Biggin Hill, feel grand.'[6]

Mike Crossley was over six feet tall, with jug ears, dark, smiling eyes and a slightly caddish moustache. Between leaving Eton and joining the RAF he had studied aeronautical engineering, worked as an assistant director at Elstree film studios and signed on as an apprentice with De Havilland. He was a natural musician who played the guitar and trumpet brilliantly and had a jokey manner that sometimes appeared to border on the facetious. Crossley, though, could be serious enough when he had to be. Shortly after writing the diary entry he became the first pilot in the squadron to shoot down an Me 109, with a perfect deflection shot, and was to destroy three more in the next four days. Pete Brothers also shot down an Me 109 in the same encounter. In the following week the squadron was in action almost daily, flying offensive patrols and escorting bomber raids, using each sortie to add to its stock of collective and individual knowledge and increase its effectiveness and its members' chances of survival. Its pilots' capacity to learn meant that 32 Squadron remained intact as a fighting force for the next three months and was not withdrawn from the line until the end of August.

Squadron commanders and pilots drew their own conclusions from their experiences and acted on them without waiting to seek approval from above. The nature of the fighting meant that advice or direction from superiors not involved in daily combat carried little authority. To their credit, Dowding and the best of his senior commanders accepted that their own understanding of what was happening could well be inferior to that of even the most junior front-line pilot. They sought their opinions, listened to what they had to say and, when needed, took action.

The new rules of air fighting were being made up with each clash. To succeed, merely to survive, required an adaptability that was found chiefly in the young. In the mayfly span of a fighter pilot's effective life, young meant under twenty-two. The older pilots commanding the squadrons, in whom the parade ground rigidity of the old tactics were strongly ingrained, were for all their experience and flying skills often among the first to go. Roger Bushell, the peacetime barrister who had helped defend Johnny Freeborn and Paddy Byrne and moved up to command 92 Squadron, was shot down on his first day. He would be missed. The squadron was essentially a new creation, having been re-formed only the previous October. Bushell was moved from 601 Auxiliary Squadron to supervise the birth, overseeing training, the switch from Blenheim bombers to Spitfires and infusing the nascent squadron spirit with his personality. He was born in South Africa, moved to England and went to Wellington public school and Brasenose College, Oxford. He was tough, intelligent and warm-hearted, and a good drinker. He was also a sportsman, a superb skier, coaching the British team in the 1936 Winter Olympics. He had a permanently half-hooded eye, the result of a skiing accident, which gave him a truculent look.

Bushell had joined 601 Squadron in the mid 1930s, naturally embracing its credo of taking fun and flying equally seriously, making strong friendships and winning admirers throughout the service. His charm, the squadron chronicler recorded, was 'magnetic and universal'.[7] His forensic talents were at the disposal of all the squadron, fitter and pilot alike. Once he flew himself from London to a distant northern base to defend a ground-crew member, changing out of uniform and into wig and gown to demolish the authorities' case. On the evening of 23 May, 92 Squadron set off on an evening patrol around Dunkirk. Bushell was leading, and when they encountered a formation of Heinkels, heavily protected by Me 109s and 110s, he ordered an attack. Tony Bartley heard him 'swearing on the radio as he plunged into the bomber force' with John Gillies and Paul Klipsch. All three were shot down. Klipsch was killed. Bushell and Gillies were captured. Bushell was last seen standing by his Spitfire, waving his scarf in farewell. He was a troublesome prisoner and was eventually murdered in March 1944 by the Gestapo after being captured in the aftermath of the Great Escape he helped to organize from Stalag Luft 111. He was, Brian Kingcome thought, 'an amazingly great man'.[8] The squadron diary admitted that the losses were 'a very severe blow to us all', and two days later 92 was moved to Duxford to rest and re-equip.

The 19 Squadron commander, Squadron Leader G. D. Stephenson, also went early, on the first day of Operation Dynamo. Once again there were more men than machines, and pilots, with the exception of section leaders, drew lots for who was to go. The twelve Spitfires left at breakfast time and encountered about twenty Stukas over the coast near Calais. They appeared to be unescorted, a circumstance that should have aroused suspicion, but caution vanished as the pilots, most of them going into their first real combat, saw the black crosses and the gull wings crawling unheedingly across the sky and prepared to attack. As they did so, thirty Me 110s came into view. One section, led by Flight Lieutenant G. E. Ball, broke off to engage them. The rest closed in on the Stukas. George Unwin, who had missed out in the draw, heard later what happened from the returning pilots. Stephenson, he said, ordered a Fighting Area Attack No. 1. 'That meant a very slow closing speed in formation "vics" of three, attacking with a very slow overtaking speed so you could get a very good shot at it. That was the idea.'[9] It worked, up to a point. The squadron shot down four, but then the 109s arrived. Pilot Officer 'Watty' Watson was hit by a cannon shell, baled out and disappeared. Stephenson was seen heading inland in a shallow glide, trailing blue smoke. It later turned out he landed safely but was taken prisoner. The squadron claimed five Stukas and two 109s, a reasonable return on their losses, if true. The arithmetic of the squadrons involved at Dunkirk, however, was no more reliable than that of the France-based units. Later they flew another patrol and were again 'bounced' by 109s. Sergeant C. A. Irwin was killed and Pilot Officer Michael Lyne shot in the leg. He nursed his Spitfire back across the Channel and crash-landed on Walmer Beach. This time it seemed that only one 109 had possibly been brought down, and that was unconfirmed.

Stephenson and Irwin were both very experienced men. Irwin was an ex-fitter, typical of the cadre of ground staff who, through ability and ambition, had got airborne and whose professionalism and technical expertise stiffened the pre-war squadrons. Stephenson, like White, had been at Cranwell and was therefore marked out for the RAF's upper reaches. He was regarded as a brilliant pilot and had been an instructor at the Central Flying School. It was a teaching post, but it carried prestige in a service in which skill was of paramount importance. Like the 54 Squadron pilots, 19 Squadron decided after the first day that no matter how flawless the technique, the tactics that Stephenson and his generation epitomized were dead. 'That was the end of going in slow,' Unwin said. 'In fact it was the end of all we knew because we realized we knew nothing. From then on it was get in fast and go out fast. And go close – a hundred yards. Get in close but go in fast and get out fast.'[10]

Some of the younger pilots discovered almost at once that they were good at air fighting. Also that they enjoyed it. 'Prof' Leathart described 'that lovely feeling of the gluey controls and the target being slowly hauled into the sights. Then thumb down on the trigger again and the smooth shuddering of the machine as the eight-gun blast let go.'[11] The best of them were pushed forward to fill the holes in the commanders' ranks. Following the loss of Roger Bushell, Brian Kingcome and Bob Tuck were posted to 92 Squadron as flight commanders. Leathart himself was put in command of 54 to replace Squadron Leader E. A. Douglas-Jones, who had led the squadron on its first offensive patrol on 16 May but had not flown with it since and relinquished command nine days later on grounds of ill-health.

Covering the evacuation meant that pilots were in the air two, three or sometimes even four times a day. Exhaustion set in quickly.

Replacement squadrons arrived at the 11 Group bases to allow the spent units a rest. Some of the new arrivals had seen very little of the war and were slow to appreciate how serious things had become. On 28 May Al Deere returned to Hornchurch after a patrol and noticed that the dispersal areas normally occupied by 65 and 74 Squadrons now had Spitfires with unfamiliar markings. They belonged to 222 Squadron, sent in while 65 and 74 were rotated out for a rest. Later that evening Deere met one of the flight commanders, Douglas Bader, who questioned him closely. Bader, as a pre-war regular and an ex-Cranwell cadet, had become a figure of myth in the RAF by an extraordinary demonstration of will-power, struggling back to serve in a fighter squadron after losing both legs in a flying accident. His biographer wrote that Bader and his pilots were not impressed by their first sight of their Hornchurch comrades and 'gazed, startled, then with mild derision at pilots . . . walking around with pistols tucked in their flying boots and as often as not with beard stubble'. They also noticed that they seemed quiet and preoccupied, but did not consider the significance of this and regarded the guns and the three-day growth as 'line-shooting'.[12]

The accusation of line-shooting could be intended lightly. Jokey boastfulness was an established part of ante-room and saloon bar banter. But it could also be something more grave. It was one thing to shoot a line with no expectation of being taken seriously; another to claim phoney successes or dramatize narrow escapes in an attempt to look heroic. To do so was to break the Fighter Boy code of levity at all times, and with it one of the few social taboos that counted. When Deere read Bader's impressions later, he was not pleased. The Hornchurch pilots' demeanour, he wrote with restraint, 'was no "line-shoot"'.

The experience of the first two days of the evacuation had demonstrated that Fighter Command did not have the resources to mount continuous patrols over the battle area. There were not enough aircraft. Those that were available were limited by the amount of fuel they could carry. Brian Kingcome calculated that the average operational time a Spitfire without overload tanks could spend in the air was between an hour and a quarter and an hour and a half, allowing for five or ten minutes at full throttle (though this could stretch to two hours if the trip was uneventful). It was twenty minutes from Biggin Hill to the French coast. That, theoretically, left the pilots with a good half an hour over the beaches.[13] But, in air fighting, the Merlin engines consumed fuel voraciously, and prudent pilots tried to preserve petrol on the outward journey. Sailor Malan found that 'the only way we could fly to Dunkirk and have enough juice to have a few minutes over the battle area was by coasting and flying at sea-level up from Boulogne'.[14] Even so, the return journey was often fraught with the dread of falling out of the sky.

At first, Park sent patrols off in sixes and twelves – flight and squadron strengths. This ensured that there was a more or less continuous fighter presence in the Dunkirk area from dawn to dusk. But it soon became clear that they did not carry the weight to deter the Luftwaffe bombers and fighters, which always greatly outnumbered the defenders. Fighter Command Headquarters had tried to increase the deterrent effect of the fighters by massing them in 'wings' of two or more squadrons, a tactic which had the drawback of leaving windows in the cover, during which the Germans could bomb unmolested.

On 28 May, 19, 54 and 65 Squadrons were ordered off as a wing from Hornchurch. Al Deere, who had been made up to flight commander, took off, along with 54's eight remaining serviceable Spitfires, on a cold grey morning. It was supposed to be their last sortie before going off for a rest. The formation crossed the coast at Gravelines in rain and mist, when Deere saw a lone Dornier nosing out of a cloud towards the Channel, apparently looking for ships to bomb. He peeled off with his flight to attack. He opened fire at 300 yards, hitting the port engine and setting it on fire. He was about to give another burst when bullets from the bomber's rear gunner struck his engine, hitting the coolant tank. Merlin engines were cooled by a liquid called glycol, which flowed around the block through a vascular skein of metal tubing. Any bullet hitting the nose of the aeroplane was likely to rupture one of these pipes. The glycol drained rapidly away, and the engine seized in a few moments. Deere was enveloped in a fine spray of glycol, which turned to white smoke. He realized he had no hope of making it back to England

and steered landwards, looking for a beach on which to crash-land. The drill was to land wheels up. Wheels down ran the lethal risk of cart-wheeling if the undercarriage hit something. He put the Spitfire, Kiwi 1, down on the water's edge, slithering through sand and spray and knocking himself out when his head hit the windscreen. When he came to, he climbed out and found a café, where he was told he had landed at Oost-Dunkerke, half-way between Dunkirk and Ostend. When he looked back, the tide was coming in and sea and sand closed over Kiwi 1 for ever.

A woman in the café bandaged his eye and he set off walking towards Ostend, where, he had been told, he stood the best chance of getting back to England. Deere, like the rest of the pilots, had no idea of the scale of the drama being played out to the south. They had been told they were participating in a planned withdrawal. The refugee traffic was so heavy on the road north that he turned back and decided to take his chances in Dunkirk. Travelling on a borrowed bicycle, he reached the outskirts of the town, where he began to understand the dimensions of the crisis. Seeing three British soldiers in a café, he asked a corporal if he could speak to someone in authority. 'As far as I know,' the corporal replied, 'there isn't anybody in authority at the moment. Me and my mates here are the only members of our company who have got back this far; where the hell the rest of them are and for that matter the rest of the British army, I haven't a clue.' Deere found them a few miles down the road. His outstanding impression was 'one of discipline and control, despite the obvious exhaustion and desperation of the thousands of troops who, arranged in snake-like columns, stretched from the sand dunes to the water's edge'.

A naval officer eventually arranged for him to be taken off in the destroyer HMS *Montrose*. During the long wait, the Luftwaffe was overhead constantly. There was panic when three bombers swept over the beach, bombing and strafing, pursued by a lone Spitfire, which broke off, badly hit, and glided inland. Deere was now in the position of seeing the air battle from the infantryman's point of view. The waiting soldiers felt that the sky had been handed over to the Germans, from where they could bomb and shoot unmolested by the RAF. Trying to board the destroyer, Deere was pushed back by an army major. When Deere explained he was trying to rejoin his squadron, which was operating overhead, he was told: 'For all the good you chaps seem to be doing over here you might as well stay on the ground.'[15] Deere's experience was not unique. A pilot from 17 Squadron, who was forced to bale out, had to fight his way aboard a departing boat after being told it was for the army only. Flying Officer Anthony Linney of 229 Squadron, who also had to abandon his aircraft over Dunkirk on 29 May, arrived in Dover to be abused by soldiers, who almost reduced him to tears.

The charge that the RAF had let the army down was repeated endlessly over the next months, provoking angry words and punch-ups when blue uniform and brown battledress met in pubs. It spread beyond the military, becoming part of the mythology of the early war. Fred Rosier, who had been badly burned while leading a detachment of 229 Squadron in France in May, told how his wife was travelling by train in a compartment with soldiers returning from Dover. 'They were shouting, "Where was the bloody air force?" and so on. [She] turned to one of them and said, "Well, I can tell you where one of them is – in hospital and I'm just about to visit him." '[16]

The accusation hurt the pilots, sometimes angered them, but they tended to understand. The fortitude of the troops impressed them deeply. Looking down on Dunkirk, they saw a scene they would never forget and thanked God they were not part of it. Brian Kingcome from his cockpit saw 'beaches [that] were a shambles, littered with the smoking wreckage of engines and equipment . . . The sands erupted into huge geysers from exploding bombs and shells, while a backdrop to the scene of carnage and destruction was provided by the palls of oily black smoke rising from the burning harbour and houses . . . and hanging high in the still air. And yet there the orderly lines of our troops stood, chaos and Armageddon at their backs, patiently waiting their turn to wade into the sea.'[17] Much of the smoke climbing into the sky came from oil-storage tanks around the town. George Unwin found that 'you didn't need a compass to get to Dunkirk. You took off from Hornchurch . . . and you just flew down the smoke and you were there. Those tanks were still burning weeks afterwards and it really was desolation, absolute desolation. It was a most incredible sight.'[18]

The pilots knew the effort they were making and the price they were paying. There were several explanations for the belief they were doing little or nothing. One was the smoke itself. Some of the action over the beaches was obscured by the canopy of filth. Another was altitude. Sailor Malan said afterwards, 'We flew too high to be appreciated by our chaps and too low for Spits to operate at their best advantage.'[19] Others disagreed. Tony Bartley claimed that orders had originally been given for the fighters not to venture below 15,000 feet because they would be at risk from the navy and army anti-aircraft guns, which were considered capable of dealing with low-flying raiders, and to stay above 20,000 feet, where they would not be visible from the ground. It was certainly true that British and French gunners could be a menace and many pilots reported being shot at by their own side.

Bartley's new commander, Bob Tuck, had little faith in the anti-aircraft defences and decided to ignore the 20,000 feet instruction. 'We realized that the dive-bombers were at 15,000 feet . . . Finally we disobeyed orders and we came down and started knocking off the Stukas . . . Bobby Tuck said, "Let's go down and catch these fellows." '[20] Another reason for the RAF's apparent absence was that much of the fighting took place away from the beaches as the fighters tried to intercept the German formations before they could reach the target area. In the experience of George Unwin, 'Very little fighting took place over the beaches. What we tried to do was stop these people before they reached the beaches . . . What fighting did go on, most of it was inland.'[21]

Fighter Command's performance was weakened, once again, by the absence of a comprehensive warning system, which made it impossible to predict the approach or strength of the attackers. Hugh Dundas, who had arrived with 616 Squadron to join the battle, thought that 'probably half the times we went to Dunkirk, perhaps not quite as much as that, we didn't actually get engaged at all'. Other squadrons, however, seemed to be in action every time they went up, which meant that the burden of strain and risk was unevenly spread. John Nicholas, a flying officer with

65 Squadron who shot down two 109s, remembered being airborne for 'eight hours a day, beginning with being called about three o'clock by one's batman . . . I must have done fifty-six hours in a week, which is more than you'd do in two or three months in peace time.'[22]

Unable to deploy forces at times of maximum necessity, the controllers were forced into the draining and wasteful tactic of constant patrolling. For this there were simply not enough aircraft or machines. 'In ideal circumstances one should have had five or six squadrons there the whole time,' Dundas said later. 'There wasn't anything like the strength to do that from dawn to dusk.'[23] The pilots were convinced none the less that Dunkirk would have had a different outcome without them. As it was, some 338,000 British and French troops were rescued, against the 45,000 that was all that was hoped for when Operation Dynamo was launched. 'So who got them off?' Tony Bartley asked later. 'Fighter Command – let's not kid ourselves.'[24]

By the end of 4 June it was finished. Tim Vigors, who had joined 222 Squadron after leaving Cranwell, went off on the last patrol. 'The town and its surroundings really did now resemble Dante's inferno,' he wrote later. 'All remaining oil stores, fuel supplies and equipment which had not burnt already were now set on fire . . . Vast clouds of flame and smoke billowed into the air.'[25] When pilots from 610 Squadron flew the final sortie of the day, they did not meet a single enemy aircraft. On the beaches they could see the French troops who had missed the last boat to freedom, who waved farewell to them and awaited the arrival of the Germans. The Fighter Command pilots had flown 2,739 sorties. They went gratefully off on short leaves to family or friends, anywhere that gave them a taste of their former lives.

Churchill, searching to find worth in a humiliating episode, glimpsed one shining thing of value in the smoke, waste and ruin and reached out to grasp it. Addressing a House of Commons glowing with relief at the success of the rescue operation, he warned that it would be a mistake to regard Dunkirk as a victory, as wars were 'not won by evacuations.'. He went on, 'But there was a victory inside this deliverance, which should be noted. It was gained by the Royal Air Force.'

In terms of relative losses, this was a bold claim to make. The number of RAF aircraft destroyed was reckoned to be 106, against 390 on the German side, a highly optimistic calculation. German documents found after the war put their Dunkirk-related losses at 132, some of which were shot down by anti-aircraft fire. On the human side of the ledger, fifty-six Fighter Command pilots were killed and six aircrew, the latter gunners on the Boulton Paul Defiants, which made a brief appearance in the battle. Eight pilots were taken prisoner and eleven pilots and one air-gunner were wounded. The figures could not express the whole truth of the situation. There were other crucial elements, concerning experience, leadership and morale, that statistics could not measure.

9

Doing It

Pilots returning from their first proper sortie were inevitably cornered by even greener members of the squadron with the question: 'What was it like?' By now, the middle of June, many of the pilots in Fighter Command had some idea of the answer. They knew to varying degrees the reality of the things they had so often wondered about: what it was to be shot at and to shoot, how it felt to watch friends and enemies die. They had heard the clatter of flying debris against wings and fuselage and been blinded by the oil spray from an exploding aircraft. They knew now the jolt of panic at the yelled warning, the violent, instinctive reaction, the swirling confusion of a dogfight and the strange emptiness and quiet that suddenly followed. These were universal experiences, but the near impossibility of describing combat meant that the stories of the initiated did not help very much. To understand it, to gauge your ability to withstand it, you had to do it.

At Duxford aerodrome at 4 a.m. on 29 May, Tim Vigors was woken with a cup of tea by his batman. He gave his lurcher, Snipe, a farewell hug, telling him he would see him that evening, and was driven out to dispersal. Under arc lights that cut through the pre-dawn murk, ground crews were making last adjustments to the Spitfires. Then the commander of 222 Squadron, Squadron Leader Herbert 'Tubby' Mermagen, who, girth notwithstanding, had performed acrobatics for the King before the war, gave the eleven pilots flying with him that day their instructions. They were to head to Dunkirk in line astern, then patrol in formation, unless told otherwise, and return to Hornchurch. Vigors, like most of the others, had never been in action before.

> I walked over to my aircraft to make sure everything was in order [he wrote later]. My mouth was dry and for the first time in my life I understood the meaning of the expression 'taste of fear'. I suddenly realized that the moment had arrived . . . Within an hour I could be battling for my life, being shot at with real bullets by a man whose one desire in life was to kill me. Up until now it had all somehow been a game, like a Biggles book where the heroes always survived the battles and it was generally only the baddies who got the chop. I was dead scared and knew I had somehow to control this fear and not show it to my fellow pilots.[1]

He flew eastwards, seeing the sun edge above the horizon. Then the towers of smoke over Dunkirk came into view. As they reached the coast one of the weavers flying behind and above warned there were enemy aircraft below. Mermagen led his flight into a diving attack. Vigors was in the other flight, commanded by Douglas Bader, circling overhead. Bader spotted a formation of Me 109s flying 5,000 feet above that appeared not to have seen the Spitfires. They climbed up behind them and were within 1,000 feet when the Messerschmitts realized the danger and turned round to attack. Vigors banked hard to try and cut inside the turn of one German fighter, but was immediately distracted by the alarming sight of glowing white tracer flowing past his port wing-tip. In that moment his first reaction was 'extreme fear which temporarily froze my ability to think. This was quickly replaced by an overwhelming desire for self-preservation.' Fortunately, unlike many pilots, he had done some practice dogfighting which had taught him that, if he tried to climb away, he would present a steady target to his attacker. Counter to his instincts, he went into a second evasive move and 'pushed violently forward and sideways on the stick, which flung my Spitfire into a sudden and violent dive which threw my whole weight with unpleasant strength against my shoulder harness'. It seemed to have worked. The tracer stopped.

He had lost a lot of height in the manoeuvre, and pulling out of the dive he climbed cautiously back up, glancing around constantly, until he was above the mêlée that had developed. Then he dived down into the action, picking out a 109 that was chasing a Spitfire in a circle, and pulled in behind him.

> Trying to get him in my sights I pulled hard back on the stick and pressed my right thumb on the firing button in the middle of the spade grip on the top of my control column. My aircraft shuddered and tracers shot out from the front of my wings. I could see them passing harmlessly below him. Keeping my finger on the firing button I hauled back even further on the stick, trying to drag the nose of my own aircraft above him. Gradually the tracer came closer to his tail, but just as I thought I had him, he realized his danger and flicked over on his left side and dived.

Vigors followed, still firing, and optimistically thought afterwards that he might have shot a piece off the 109's tail. He broke off when he again came under attack from behind. This time he forgot his training and pulled into an almost vertical climb, blacking out in the process, and came to in time to see the Messerschmitt diving past. Then, as every pilot was to remark in such circumstances, he found to his amazement 'I couldn't see another aircraft in the sky . . . a moment before the whole sky had been filled with circling and diving aircraft and now there was not one of them to be seen'.

In the calm Vigors looked at his watch and saw he had been flying for an hour and a half. He had been hurling his Spitfire about with the throttle wide open, and was in danger of running out of petrol and crashing into the sea. As he turned for home, his first relieved thought was that he was still alive. Also, his Spitfire appeared undamaged. Apart from just possibly having damaged a 109's tail, he had done nothing apart from distracting the enemy.

His biggest concern was 'how deadly scared I'd been when I first saw those enemy bullets streaming past my wing-tip. I had never known any fear like that before in my life . . . I just fervently hoped I could keep it under control.' Vigors met Bader on landing and gave a suitably stiff-upper-lip account of the engagement. But when he reached dispersal, where the returning 222 Squadron pilots were noisily and excitedly discussing the fight, and saw Hilary Edridge, his best friend in the squadron, neither of them hid their feelings.

> 'Glad to see you in one piece,' I exclaimed. 'How did you do?'
>
> 'Never been more scared in my whole bloody life,' he laughed.
>
> 'That makes two of us,' I replied. 'I was shit scared from the word go.'

The next day Vigors completed his baptism. On the second patrol of the day, 222 Squadron ran into a formation of Heinkels. He latched on to one, but his bullets drifted below it and before he could find another the Messerschmitts arrived. Vigors was chased and pulled sharp right as hard as he could, blacking out but bringing himself up behind the German and finding to his satisfaction that he was turning inside him. They were now on opposite sides of the circle in a classic dogfighting position. Vigors kept reefed tight into the turn, on the edge of unconsciousness because of the terrific G forces, until he almost had the target in his sights. In desperation the German dived for the sea, the tactic Vigors had used the previous day. But by now he was right on top of him and at 200 yards opened fire. 'I saw my bullets ripping into his starboard wing and suddenly he burst into a ball of flame. "Got you, you bastard!" I yelled.' This exultation vanished when he 'felt a tug on my right wing and to my horror I saw holes appearing in the wing-tip'. A 109 darted beneath him and then the sky was clear again. A roll of the controls told him that the Spitfire would get him home.

Examining his feelings on the return journey, he was 'more than happy to have made my first kill' and felt the same satisfaction as when, on his family estate near Clonmel, he had 'pulled down a high-flying pigeon flashing across the evening sky with the wind up his tail.' There was a sombre moment at the thought he had just killed a man. He and his adversary would, he pondered, have 'probably got on well together if we'd met drinking beer in a pub'. The mood did not last long. 'But he was on the wrong side,' he concluded. 'He shouldn't have signed up with that bastard Hitler.' Later he was 'surprised that he did not feel more remorse'. In the space of forty-eight hours, Tim Vigors had tasted many of the common experiences of flying a fighter in combat, short of being shot down, wounded or killed. Fifty hours of training was worth less than one hour of the real thing.

By early summer every squadron in Fighter Command except two had clashed with the Luftwaffe on at least one occasion. At this early stage, operations proceeded in an orderly fashion. Standing at dispersal in the rising light of dawn or the glare of an early summer afternoon, the squadron or flight was given its instructions on the ground by the commander. Then, as the riggers and fitters climbed down off the wings, the pilots hoisted themselves up by placing a right foot in the step set into the left side of the fuselage. They then put their other foot on the wing root and swung over into the narrow cockpit, stowing their parachute in the scooped recess of the steel bucket seat. Next came the nerve-calming routine of strapping in, switching on petrol, starting the engine and checking oxygen and instruments. On the order, they took off methodically and flew in formation until they reached the battle zone. The discipline of keeping position had the same effect as infantry drill, creating a feeling of security, a sense of strength in combination, that almost invariably evaporated as soon as the fighting began.

Everyone, at all times, constantly scoured the sky around them for aircraft. Good eyesight was a life-saver. Exceptional eyesight gave a pilot a considerable advantage, enabling him to see his victim before he himself was seen. Pilots twisted their heads up and down, left and right, continuously. In a regulation-wear collar and tie, necks were soon rubbed raw. It was for that reason that they began wearing the silk scarves which in time became their sartorial symbol.

On the outward journey the squadron, flight or section leader could talk to the other aircraft, and his voice and manner over the R/T was an important element in shaping the mood of the pilots behind him. Confident leaders gave confidence to those they led, and commanders could be forgiven many shortcomings if they had the gift of imparting reassurance. Some, like Deere, Kingcome and Bader, did so with a mixture of humour and profanity, using nicknames, reinforcing the ties of intimacy and affection that bound the best squadrons together. The possibility of giving encouragement and direction disappeared, however, in the explosion of confusion that followed engagement.

With the first sighting of Germans, the first 'Tally ho!', the low hum of anticipation jumped to a sharper pitch. Heads swivelled to the bearing as the pilots searched for the enemy aircraft. They went quickly into the last routine of preparation, dropping the seat to get maximum protection from the engine block in front and the armour plate behind, tightening straps, switching on the reflector sight, checking the range and wing-span indicators and flicking the gun button into the firing position. In the distance, the enemy aircraft seem always to have appeared as alien and malign objects, a different species. They looked like 'flies', 'swarms of bees', 'a milling great mass of little insects', never like birds, though flocks of birds could sometimes be mistaken for Germans by nervous pilots. Getting closer, the sight of the black crosses, edged in white, standing out on wings and fuselages, had a profound effect on pilots looking on them for the first time, striking them as sinister, redolent of death, bringing home with unexpected force the seriousness of what they were engaged in.

Once again, training helped to control feeling and instinct as the fighters responded to the designated attack order and manoeuvred into position. Paul Richey found that, on seeing the enemy, 'all the tension and concentration in my body focused in a wild leap of my heart. It always made me swallow hard a couple of times.' Then it was 'into action, body taught against the straps, teeth clenched, thumb on the gun button, narrowed eyes intent on getting that black-crossed Hun in the sights and holding him there.' He felt his 'pounding heart turn into a block of ice. Not in fear. My brain became coldly clear and I was transformed into a cool, calculating killer.'[2]

Shooting a smallish, nimble object travelling at more than 300 m.p.h., when you are moving at a similar speed while diving, turning and rolling, was extraordinarily hard. The difficulties were multiplied by the heavy G forces that crushed the pilots' heads down on their chests, and turned the blood in their veins to the weight of molten metal. Pilots found that when they finally got within range and opened fire, the bullets did not fly with undeviating, linear cleanliness, but wobbled and wavered. It was no wonder that when they spoke of shooting at an enemy they talked of 'giving it a squirt'. The process was more akin to aiming a hose than firing an arrow. The reflector sight, which replaced the old ring sight, projected a dot of red light on the angled underside of the windscreen. It was bracketed by a set of range bars which could be adjusted to the size of bombers or fighters. Kingcome found, 'It was quite helpful in assessing distances, and the red dot simply indicated the line of flight of your bullets . . . if you lined it up on a static target and were also stationary, you scored a hit. What it regrettably did not tell you was where to aim at a moving target, or how much deflection to allow . . . Such judgements only came from experience combined with instinct.'[3]

The first indication that bullets were striking their target was the sight of bits of debris from the air frame or wings tumbling away, sometimes striking the body of the pursuing fighter. If an engine was hit, oil or glycol might suddenly swamp the pilot's windscreen, obliterating vision. The sight of smoke and fire spurting from an engine marked one sort of end. The other came with the death of the pilot. At such speeds, there was little human contact between the men trying to kill each other. A pilot's head might be glimpsed wedged in the narrow cockpit of a 109, more cramped even than that of a Spitfire, as it flashed past, but it was rarely for long enough to register the features or for a look to be exchanged. The most frequent indication of the connection between shooting and killing was during a rear attack on a Heinkel or Junkers, or, particularly, a Dornier, which at this stage of the war carried less armour than the other bombers. The four barrels poking from the rear turret would suddenly slant upwards, a sign that the gunner had been hit and had fallen forward across the breech of his weapon. Some pilots noticed that, after shooting at an aeroplane without apparent effect, they suddenly sensed an invisible change in the aircraft, a loss of vitality as if the spirit had left it, then saw this instinct confirmed as the machine tipped downwards into a dive that its pilot was no longer in any condition to control.

This was the moment of victory, the 'kill'. Richey maintained that aerial combat was not 'a hot-blooded thrilling affair', but he confessed to 'a savage, primitive exaltation' at the sight of an enemy going down that was 'not very edifying'. The point of a fighter pilot's existence was to shoot down aeroplanes, but when Pete Brothers came to do so, his reaction was 'absolute surprise and astonishment [as] the aircraft went over on its back and some bits fell off and it went screaming down into the ground. I followed it down and saw it crash and thought "amazing".' His next response was alarm. 'I thought, "My God, that's really going to make them cross. They'll be after me." I began whizzing around looking behind me, making sure . . . They were probably going to come and do me for this. Maybe I shouldn't have done it.'[4]

Others felt nothing but pleasure at the sight of their opponent going down. Johnny Freeborn ran across a 109 attacking a Spitfire south of Dunkirk and went in to attack it. The Messerschmitt dipped sharply away, a defensive tactic favoured by the German pilots that exploited the fact that the 109's Mercedes-Benz engine had fuel injection, which allowed a steep dive without loss of power. The Merlin engine did not, which meant it missed several beats at the moment of negative gravity as a Hurricane or Spitfire tipped sharply downwards. The way of overcoming this was to flick the aircraft into a half-roll, then straighten out, throwing fuel into the carburettor. Freeborn went into the manoeuvre and plunged down through thick cumulonimbus, emerging to find the 109 right in front of him. 'He went right down to the ground and I shot the hell out of him. The engine stopped and the propeller was just windmilling.' For once, he was close enough to see his enemy's face. 'He looked bloody terrified. I thought, you German bastard, and I gave him another one. He hit a telegraph pole with the prop and went straight into a farmhouse. The farmer was ploughing outside the house . . . I was very pleased about that.'[5] Sailor Malan, shooting down his first Heinkel 111, found 'the release from tension was terrific, the thrill enormous. I'd been wondering for so long . . . how I'd react in my first show. Now I knew. Everything I had learned had come right. There was hardly time even to feel scared.'[6]

Despite the expectation of being shot at, pilots were often slow to realize they were under attack. Flying was noisy. The throb of a 1,175 horsepower engine blotted out the sound of firing, so frequently the first indication of danger was the sight of tracer, floating towards you, gentle and seemingly innocent, 'like a string of light bulbs'. Kingcome described later how 'tracer comes out at you, apparently very slowly to begin with. You see these lazy, long smoke trails coming at you. They get faster as they reach you, then suddenly whip past your ear at the most amazing speed.'[7]

Being fired on for the first time could have a paralysing effect. George Unwin had had four years of flying experience before meeting a 109 over Dunkirk. 'I saw little sparks coming from the front end of him and I knew he was shooting at me and I did nothing, absolutely nothing. I was just, not petrified, but, I don't know, frozen, for ten or fifteen seconds . . . I just sat there and watched him shoot at me.'[8] The Messerschmitt missed and Unwin lived to apply the lesson he had learned.

Frequently, the bullets came without warning, seemingly out of nowhere, arriving with a sudden heart-jolting shock. Peter Parrott was patrolling in France, unaware of any imminent danger, when he 'heard a couple of almighty bangs on the armour plating behind me', and put his Hurricane into a dive. When he landed he found that only two rounds from the 109 that attacked him had hit. One damaged the radio and another struck one of the fuselage formers. Even so, 'it had sounded as if the whole thing was going to break into pieces, the noise they had made coming in'.[9]

The first indication that the engine had been hit was usually the appearance of oil or glycol streaming back over the windscreen. Unless the damage made the aircraft unflyable, a pilot's first instinct was to stay on board as long as possible in the hope of being able to nurse it back to friendly territory, even if this entailed crossing the suddenly very wide-looking expanse of the English Channel. A crash-landing meant finding the nearest piece of flat ground and gliding in, slipping the aeroplane from side to side to increase wind resistance and reduce the impact speed, keeping the wheels retracted to lessen the chances of them catching in an obstacle and somersaulting. Hitting the ground, bouncing and skidding through the topsoil, the pilot faced a last danger in the form of smashing his head on the thick bulletproof glass of the windscreen.

Peter Parrott, who after surviving France had been posted to 145 Squadron, was in the process of shooting down a Heinkel over the coastline of the Pas de Calais when he was hit by return fire from the rear gunner, which damaged the radiator and put a hole in the glycol tank. His cockpit was full of water vapour and the only instrument he could see was the oil temperature gauge, which was dangerously high. Wondering how long the coolant would last before the engine seized, he turned towards England, streaming a long trail of vapour. Half-way across the Channel, the rest of the squadron caught him up and Roy Dutton overtook to try and lead him to a safe landing place. 'We crossed the coast at Deal and within inches of crossing . . . the engine stopped . . . I was around three or four thousand feet and looking for somewhere to put the thing down with the wheels up. Manston was too far to the north and Hawkinge was too far on the south side. Behind Deal there are some downs. It was a Sunday evening and a lot of people were out for their evening walk. I picked out these three fields. One was on the upward slope one was slightly curved – the dome so to speak – and then there was the one on the other side which went downhill fairly sharply.' He chose the top of the hill, expecting to bounce along the turf, but instead came to an almost immediate halt, killing two sheep in the process.

Parrott was soaked in glycol – 'sticky, filthy stuff' – but otherwise unharmed. He and his Hurricane were soon surrounded by strollers, then a policeman arrived and Parrott went off to a farmhouse to phone the base at Manston. On the way he met the farmer arriving in a pony and trap. 'The first thing he said was, "Who's going to pay for them sheep then?" In a lordly tone, I said, "The Air Ministry." He grunted, got back in his cart and went off. So I was faced with going down to the farm, facing this angry man again to ask if I could use his telephone. By the time I got there he and his wife were having high tea. There was a large ham on the table. It looked lovely but I wasn't invited.' Parrott called Manston and a car was dispatched together with a guard for the Hurricane. He left the inhospitable couple to their tea and was back in action next day.

The robustness of Hurricanes and, to a lesser extent, Spitfires meant that even quite badly damaged aircraft could be coaxed back to safety. But if the engine caught fire the only choice was to jump. The decision was instantaneous. The sight of smoke and flame curling backwards, wrapping around the Perspex bubble of the canopy, was enough to settle the issue. Like their First World War forebears, all pilots had a particular horror of burning. When they did bale out, it was, almost without exception, the first time they had been on the end of a parachute. There was no place for practice jumps on the pre-war training curriculum and this did not change when the war started. Parachutes had only become standard equipment in 1928, when the extraordinary argument that possession of them would lead to a diminution of fighting spirit was finally dropped. Pilots were taught the drill for leaving their stricken aeroplane. It required sliding back the canopy, releasing your harness then flipping the fighter on to its back so you dropped free. It sounded easy enough in theory, but in the urgency of the moment things conspired to go wrong.

When Fred Rosier's Hurricane was hit and caught fire over northern France, he went into the drill but found the cockpit hood was jammed. He remembered sitting back 'and thinking that that was that. The next thing I was falling, and I suppose instinctively pulled the ripcord. I saw that my trousers were all on fire. I remember the skin leaving my hands as I tried to put the fire out.'[10] Pilot Officer Ronald Brown of 111 Squadron had not even been taught the theory when he was forced to jump from his Hurricane over Abbeville. Ignorant of what to do, he simply pushed the hood back, stood up and was immediately whipped out of the cockpit by the wind, smashing his legs against the tailplane. 'I always remember it was beautifully warm and I wanted to go to sleep. Then something made me say to myself, pull the ripcord you bloody fool. So I pulled it – a sharp jerk. And there I am on my brolly.'[11]

Prosser Hanks, trying to vacate his Hurricane after being hit and catching fire, had the opposite problem. 'I was suddenly drenched in hot glycol. I didn't have my goggles down and the bloody stuff completely blinded me. I didn't know where I was and somehow got into a spin. I could see damn all and the cockpit was getting bloody hot so I undid the straps and opened the hood to get out but I couldn't. Every time I tried I was pressed back. I started to scream then, but stopped screaming and then somehow or other I got out.'[12]

These dramas sometimes happened in view of other squadron members. Seeing comrades die, frequently at very close quarters, was an eternal part of the infantryman's experience. For pilots, the sensations attached to witnessing the death of a comrade seem to have been muffled slightly by a layer of detachment. Searching for his base in northern France after destroying a Me 110, Flight Lieutenant Ian Gleed of 87 Squadron saw a Hurricane flying serenely along and steered to join up with it. 'Just as I am drawing up to formate on this Hurricane, he dips; I catch a fleeting glimpse of flying brick, and seemingly quite slowly, a Hurricane's tail, with the red, white and blue stripes, flies up past my cockpit. I glance behind and see a cloud of dust slowly rising. He must have had some bullets in him to have hit that house. I wonder who it was?'[13]

The victim went to his end encased in a machine, sparing onlookers the horrible details. There was no body to confront. Death usually occurred at some distance from the home base and dealing with the corpse, or what was left of it, was the responsibility of others. Dead bodies, of friend or foe, were strangely absent from the fighter pilots' war. Peter Townsend never saw a corpse in his entire RAF service, first encountering one when as a journalist he covered the Six-Day War in the Middle East in 1967.

On the other hand, the pause between the appearance of smoke and flame and the end left plenty of time to imagine what was happening inside the cockpit. On several occasions, the doomed pilot's R/T was left switched on and his screams, prayers and curses filled the headphones of his companions.

Crashing into the ground or sea at high speed was often referred to with standard Fighter Boy understatement as 'going in'. The blandness of the term served to soften the hard lines of the reality. The lightness of expression used for the darkest subjects had a very serious purpose: to rob fear of its power. Acknowledged, but only occasionally spoken about, fear tainted every hour of a fighter pilot's working day. It was the second enemy. Levels of fear varied. Different pilots felt it with differing intensity in different circumstances. For all but a handful it was a palpable presence that might be banished during the hours of darkness, driven away by the beer and the company of your companions, then fatigue, but was always up and waiting at readiness next morning. Tim Vigors was right. There really was a 'taste of fear'. It was sour and metallic at the same time, and no amount of swallowing or chewing gum could make it go away. Other physical sensations went with it: mild nausea, a feeling of faintness in the head and a slight tingling of the anal sphincter known to pilots as 'ring twitch'.

Unless a pilot could suppress fear, he was useless, and stood a good chance of getting killed very quickly. Hugh Dundas gave a frank account of the unmanning terror that seized him on his first encounter with Germans during the Dunkirk evacuation. As so often, when he saw an Me 109 turning towards him and noted the ripples of grey smoke and flashing lights coming from the nose of the plane, it took him some time to understand what was happening.

'Red blobs arced lazily through the air between us, accelerating dramatically as they approached and streaked close by, across my wing. With sudden, sickening, stupid fear I realized that I was being fired on and I pulled my Spitfire round hard, so that the blood was forced down from my head. The thick curtain of blackout blinded me for a moment and I felt the aircraft juddering on the brink of a stall.' More 109s attacked and the tail-chasing continued, with Dundas wrenching his machine into the tightest and fastest turn he could squeeze from it. He managed one shot ('quite ineffectual') before the Germans moved off. He was left 'close to panic in the bewilderment and hot fear of that first dogfight. Fortunately instinct drove me to keep turning and turning, twisting my neck all the time to look for the enemy behind. Certainly the consideration which was uppermost in my mind was the desire to stay alive.'

Dundas was to find this feeling never went away. 'When it comes to the point, a sincere desire to stay alive is all too likely to get the upper hand. Certainly, that was the impulse which consumed me at that moment that day. And that was the impulse which I had to fight against, to try and try and try again to overcome, during the years which followed.'

Panic descended again later on in the patrol when he found himself alone just north of Dunkirk. Instead of calmly working out his course to reach the Thames estuary and home, he set off blindly in what he thought might be the right direction. In a few minutes he was lost, high over the empty sea, where there was not even a ship to take as a bearing. He found that the 'need to get in touch with the land pressed in on me and drove out all calmness and good sense. I saw that I was flying almost due north and realized that this was wrong, but could not get a hold of myself sufficiently to work things out. I turned back the way I had come, cravenly thinking that I could at the worst crash-land somewhere off Dunkirk and get home in a boat.' Eventually he sighted the coast of France and worked out the simple navigational problem of finding the course for home. As he crossed the estuary at Southend, heading for the little aerodrome at Rochford, he was soaked in sweat, but 'a sense of jubilation had replaced the cravenness of a few minutes earlier'. He felt 'transformed . . . now a debonair young fighter pilot, rising twenty . . . sat in the cockpit which had so recently been occupied by a frightened child.'[14] He taxied over to the dispersal point where the ground crew were waiting to hear his tales of the battle.

Dundas, like Vigors, had been through a rite of passage. The most testing psychological moments in a fighter pilot's career were those that followed the first experience of coming under fire. The overpowering human impulse, having brushed against death, is to run away. The military impulse is to seek cover, but in the absence of clouds that was not an option in the skies. Dundas had been gripped by 'hot fear', Vigors 'scared shitless', yet both chose to stay and fight however inefficiently. By doing so they crossed a threshold and became warriors.

Dogfights rarely lasted more than a few minutes. Their intensity, though, made them exceptionally draining. The fact that exhaustion could set in very quickly was recognized early on at senior levels of Fighter Command, and intelligent decisions were often – though not invariably – made to move squadrons and pilots out of the line for a rest before their efficiency was so diminished that they became easy targets. Deep fatigue could drag depression and moodiness in its wake. Paul Richey, after being forced to bale out on the second day of the air war in France, 'began to feel peculiar' when he got back to the squadron. 'I had a hell of a headache and was jumpy and snappy. Often I dared not speak for fear of bursting into tears.' He was put to bed by the squadron doctor with some sleeping pills but the sound of bombs on the airfield kept him awake. When he did sleep it was only to relive the day's experiences and he found himself 'in my Hurricane rushing head-on at a 110. Just as we were about to collide I woke up with a jerk that nearly threw me out of bed. I was in a cold sweat, my heart banging wildly.' He went off to sleep again, but the nightmare returned and continued to do so at ten-minute intervals all night. 'I shall never forget,' he wrote, 'how I clung to the bed-rail in a dead funk.'[15]

The question he had asked himself as he lay there was how long he would be able to go on. It was clear from the start that there would be no quick victory. The absence of any sense of progress was potentially particularly demoralizing to pilots who were confronting a future which consisted of the endless repetition of a routine that common sense told them was almost certain to finish in death. As early as 16 June Denis Wissler was writing in his diary: 'Oh God I do wish this war would end.' But for him and the rest of Fighter Command, the real war was only just beginning.

10

Before the Storm

During the morning of 4 June, the pilots of 222 Squadron were stood down from further patrolling duties and given the rest of the day off. Tim Vigors heard the good news after returning to Hornchurch from a sortie over the French coast, during the course of which he and Hilary Edridge narrowly escaped being shot down by 109s. Wondering what to do with their free time, Vigors noticed the date. It was speech day at his old school, Eton. He asked Edridge, his constant companion since they joined the squadron together, to go with him to the celebrations.

Driving through the East End they stopped at a pub. Vigors noticed that they were the only people in uniform and customers 'cast glances at us as if we had come down from the moon'. The woman behind the bar remarked: 'You boys aren't half going to have to look after us now. I just hope that there are enough of you.' Edridge mentioned that they had been airborne only a short time before, and shooting at Germans. The other customers did not believe them at first, then tried to buy them drinks.

At Eton, 'the sky was cloudless and the sun shone down on the brightly coloured scene. Pretty girls in picture hats strolled with their blue blazer-clad escorts under the big shady trees which surrounded the cricket grounds. The peaceful murmur of conversation was broken occasionally by subdued clapping as a boundary was struck or a wicket fell. The war was a million miles away. Could this be the same world in which we had battled so few hours ago? Somewhere God had got this day wrong.'[1]

Several pilots had sensed a reluctance among British civilians to accept that what was happening to the rest of Europe could also happen to them. But after Dunkirk and the fall of France the public's complacency, or studied disregard, had faded. Now that it was no longer possible to treat the danger as remote and theoretical, the sense of detachment from the events that characterized the phoney war gave way to defiance, and in some cases alarm.

Official statements designed to reassure seemed as likely to have the opposite effect. On the morning of 18 June, the Ministry of Information issued a leaflet telling the population how to respond to a German invasion. Citizens were ordered to stay at home to avoid the chaos that had gripped Holland, Belgium and France, when hundreds of thousands of refugees blocked the roads, paralysing supply lines and the defenders' ability to manoeuvre. The second instruction stated: 'When you receive an order make sure that it is a true order and not a fake order . . . if you keep your heads you can also tell whether a military officer is really British or only pretending to be so.'[2] The military correspondent of a newspaper circulating in south-east England warned readers to be on the lookout for parachutists, 'mostly young men of the desperado type' whose task was to 'organize local fifth column members and arm them . . . create panic and confusion and spread false news among the civil population'.[3] Such advice made people panicky. A commercial traveller who failed to stop his car in time at a checkpoint near Wrexham, manned by Local Defence Volunteers, was shot dead. Enemy aliens were moved away from coastal areas and innocents were arrested after tip-offs from neighbours on suspicion of being spies.

But the general mood, as disaster piled up on the Continent, was resolute. The bad news brought with it a sense of relief. Somerset Maugham, docking at Liverpool after fleeing France in a crowded refugee ship, recorded that 'in the officials who came on board, in the porters who took our baggage, in the people in the streets, in the waiters at the restaurant, you felt the same spirit of confidence. Fear of invasion? Not a shadow of it. "We'll smash 'em. It'll take time of course, but that's all right. We can hang on." '[4] On the morning of 18 June, *The Times* quoted from Wordsworth's sonnet 'November, 1806' when England stood in isolation against Napoleon's army, fresh from victories at Austerlitz and Jena.

> 'Tis well! from this day forwards we shall know
> That in ourselves our safety must be sought;
> That by our own right hands it must be wrought;
> That we must stand unpropped, or be laid low

Other newspapers remembered it was the anniversary of the Battle of Waterloo.

That day Winston Churchill laid the foundations of a new British legend. It had dawned hot and clear, another gorgeous morning in a memorable run of fine weather. The prime minister was due to address the House of Commons in the afternoon after the usual Tuesday-afternoon question time. The Cabinet met at 12.30, but Churchill stayed away so he could work on the text, and was still scribbling changes as he sat in the House on the Treasury benches between Neville Chamberlain and Clement Attlee waiting his turn to speak.

He got to his feet at 3.49 p.m. before a packed House and a public gallery overflowing with ambassadors and VIPs. Despite the grimness of the situation, Churchill started off optimistically, presenting catastrophe as a sort of triumph. He stressed the great achievement of the Dunkirk evacuation, not mentioning the fact that the rescued troops had left most of their heavy equipment behind. He emphasized the obstacles facing a German invasion, starting with the Royal Navy, which 'some people seem to have forgotten' Britain possessed.

With the House settled and primed, he moved to the heart of the speech: 'the great question of the invasion of the air and the impending struggle between the British and German air forces'. Churchill conceded that it was 'a very great pity that we have not got an air force at least equal to that of the most powerful enemy within striking distance of our shores'. But this note of caution died as quickly as it had been struck. Then the old certainty returned, and coursed warmly through the remainder of the speech like vintage Armagnac. In the fighting in France in May and June the RAF, he stated confidently, had 'proved itself far superior in quality both in men and in many types of machine to what we have met so far'. Despite the disadvantages of operating from foreign fields and having lost many aircraft on the ground, the air force 'had still managed to routinely inflict losses of two-and-a-half to one'. In the fighting over Dunkirk, he claimed, 'we undoubtedly beat the German air force, which gave us the mastery locally in the air, and we inflicted losses of three or four to one . . . In the defence of this island the advantages to the defenders will be very great. We hope to improve on the rate of three or four to one that we achieved at Dunkirk.'

Churchill went on to predict victory, and calm any fears about the condition of Fighter Command. 'I am happy to inform the House that our fighter air strength is stronger at the present time, relatively to the Germans, who have suffered terrible losses, than it has ever been and consequently we believe ourselves to possess the capacity to continue the war in the air under better conditions than we have ever experienced before. I look forward confidently to the exploits of our fighter pilots who will have the glory of saving their native land, their island home and all they love from the most deadly of attacks.'

And so the speech surged on towards its famous end:

> 'What General Weygand called the Battle of France is over. I expect the Battle of Britain is about to begin. Upon this battle depends the survival of Christian civilization. Upon it depends our own British life and the long continuity of our institutions and our Empire. The whole fury and might of the enemy must very soon be turned upon us. Hitler knows he will have to break us in this island or lose the war.
>
> 'If we can stand up to him all Europe may be free and the life of the world may move forward into broad, sunlit uplands; but if we fail then the whole world, including the United States, and all we have known

> and cared for, will sink into the abyss of a new dark age, made more sinister and perhaps more prolonged by the lights of a perverted science. Let us therefore address ourselves to our duty, so bear ourselves that if the British Commonwealth and Empire lasts for a thousand years, men will say "This was their finest hour."'

The Times parliamentary reporter, numb fingers coming to rest at last, recorded 'loud and prolonged cheers'.

That evening Churchill repeated the speech, which was broadcast by the BBC. Some of the pilots at Biggin Hill listened to it in the mess. 'We were standing in the hall drinking beer and our feeling was one of relief,' said Pete Brothers. 'Thank God we were on our own and not saddled with a craven ally.'[5] This sentiment, though he did not know it, was shared by King George VI. Group Captain Grice, the station commander, had the speech typed up and posted around the base. Most of the pilots, though, seem not to have heard it – too absorbed in the process of recovering from the losses of the previous five weeks to hear the prime minister's dramatic definition of the task awaiting them.

Churchill's analysis had, characteristically, been inaccurate in details but correct in essentials. It was true that the fate of Britain now depended on the fighter pilots. It was also true that, henceforth, flying from their own soil and defending their own homeland, they would enjoy significant practical and moral advantages. But the highly favourable ratio of losses he claimed between British and German aircraft in their encounters to date was, as he must have known, an exaggeration. The RAF did not have more fighters than the Luftwaffe. A month later Goering still had at least 760 Me 109s at his disposal against Dowding's 591 Hurricanes and Spitfires. And Fighter Command was, if not exhausted, depleted in men and machines and in serious need of rest, recuperation and reorganization.

Dowding was now engaged in trying to nurse Fighter Command back to strength before its next great trial, patching up battered squadrons, injecting new blood and replacing the lost fighters. Some units which had been particularly hard hit were moved out of the front line. Among them was 92 Squadron, which had lost six pilots, and was posted to Pembrey in Wales, in the 10 Group area, where it spent most of the rest of the summer. After leaving France at the end of May, 87 Squadron moved north to Church Fenton near Leeds to re-form. There, Roland Beamont found only 'the remnants of the squadron': a few of the Hurricanes that had made it out of France and half the original complement of pilots. The ground crews arrived in 'dribs and drabs', having been left to make their way home by ship. Some aircraftmen who had served in France in other squadrons were not to return to Britain before the middle of July. The squadron diary reported that 'during the first fortnight in June, the task of re-forming went steadily ahead . . . not made easier by the fact that practically all equipment, service and personal, had necessarily been abandoned in France'. Another veteran unit of Fighter Command's French adventure, 73 Squadron, which had only seven pilots fit for operations and half its ground crew, and whose remaining Hurricanes were all in need of repair, also moved to Church Fenton. It spent the next months in the relative calm of 12 Group, practising, patrolling and night flying until it was sent back into the middle of the air battle at the beginning of September.

The fighting in France and over Dunkirk cost the lives of 110 pilots. Another forty-seven were wounded and twenty-six taken prisoner. The losses tore holes in the ranks of virtually every squadron. Of the twenty-two units that served in France, only three had not lost pilots through death, injury or capture. The worst casualties had been suffered by 85 Squadron. Out of its normal establishment of eighteen pilots, it had lost, in the space of eleven days, eight killed or missing in action and six wounded. The commanding officer, Michael Peacock was among the dead. Peter Townsend was moved from 43 Squadron to 85 and given the task of rebuilding the unit's strength and identity around the core of the seven surviving pilots.

Dowding's policy was, wherever possible, to take pilots from the most battle-tested units and spread them through the system to provide a core of expertise that would stiffen performance and morale. But there were few to go around. Many of the most experienced pilots were gone. At

Dunkirk alone, Fighter Command lost three squadron commanders killed and one taken prisoner, six flight commanders killed and one taken prisoner, as well as about twelve section leaders, including two senior NCO pilots. Some veterans were in no condition to return to the battle. Paul Richey spent his convalescence as a sector controller, overseeing fighter operations from Middle Wallop in Hampshire. Billy Drake, also recovering from the wounds he sustained in France, was sent on his return as an instructor to the operational training unit at Sutton Bridge in Lincolnshire, where pilots finished their training before being posted to a squadron, and Killy Kilmartin to another at Aston Down.

It was the young and inexperienced who were pushed forward to fill the gaps, including undertrained pilots just emerging from the ranks of the Volunteer Reserve. Peacetime training was lengthy and intense. The *ab initio* phase to teach the rudiments of flying was followed by forty-four weeks of thorough instruction in every aspect of aviation. The final six-week stage, intended to marry the pilot to the machine he would have to fight in, was carried out by operational training units (OTUs). The shortage of new pilots created by the losses of May and early June led to the setting up of three new OTUs, which raced qualified pilots through the conversion programme in two weeks. But shortages were so acute that promising pilots in training were sometimes posted directly from their flying training schools without passing through an OTU, and by the middle of the year the notional length of time in training was often being cut in half to twenty-two weeks.[6]

Charlton Haw had just turned twenty when he arrived at 504 Squadron. He was born in York and left school at fourteen to become an apprentice in a lithographic works. As soon as he was eighteen he had applied to join the RAFVR but failed the medical. He applied again in January 1939 and was accepted. 'I'd always wanted to fly from when I was a small boy,' he said. 'I never wanted to do anything else really. I just didn't think there would be a chance for me. Most of the people who went into short-service commissions at the time had very high educational qualifications. The chances for any normal schoolboy to get in until the RAFVR was formed [were] almost impossible.'[7] Haw was shrewd and assured despite his lack of advanced schooling. He was also a natural pilot, a talent he partially ascribed to the gentle touch he brought to the controls from playing the piano.

In the eight months before the outbreak of war he spent three nights a week in a classroom in Hull learning navigation and flight theory. At weekends, and during a fortnight's holiday from his firm, he went flying at Brough airfield, the test aerodrome for the Blackburn aircraft works, so that by the time the war began he had eighty hours' experience on biplanes. In September he had been called up, but to his disappointment was sent home almost immediately. A month later he was ordered to report to an initial training wing at St Leonards-on-Sea, Sussex. This was based in a seaside hotel requisitioned by the Air Ministry to provide RAFVR personnel with a taste of service discipline. The routine included drilling on the promenade, lectures, formal warnings of the dangers of VD and marathon PT sessions under the supervision of Len Harvey, the famous British boxer. It lasted about a month and was, almost everybody agreed, a waste of time.

In December he moved on to Sealand, in Cheshire, for intermediate and advanced training, and passed out rated above average. In May he was due to be posted to an OTU to convert to Spitfires or Hurricanes. The shortage of pilots meant that just as he was about to leave he received counter orders to join 504 Squadron, which had lost nine of its members – half its strength – killed, wounded or taken prisoner in France. Five other half-trained pilots went from Sealand with him. The squadron was based at Wick in the far north of Scotland, where its duties included convoy protection patrols, interceptions and the defence of the Fleet, anchored in Scapa Flow. Haw found the surviving members friendly and welcoming, and morale 'fantastically good' despite the losses. The process of getting used to Hurricanes started immediately, but progress was hampered by the delay in delivery of new aircraft to replace those lost in France. By the time he had his first fight he had flown a single-engined fighter for only twelve hours. About a month after joining he was over Scapa Flow in a three-man patrol when the leader spotted a Heinkel 111 and dived after it. Haw, in a state of excitement, followed the attack down. Closing in, he noticed 'red-hot chain links' coming towards him. As he broke away a bullet smashed straight through the narrow cockpit and out the other side. 'When I came back they were all slapping me on the back and saying how lucky I was,' he said later, 'and I was lucky. There as no doubt about it.' Having come through this first, crucial, encounter, he was now better equipped to deal with the next one and his chances of survival had significantly improved.

Frank Usmar also had his training cut short. He was on a few days' leave, awaiting a posting to Sutton Bridge when a policeman arrived at his parents' home in West Malling, Kent, where his father was the village postman, and told him he was to report to 41 Squadron at Catterick. Usmar, too, had left school at fourteen and was working as a clerk while studying at evening school to become an accountant. When an RAFVR recruiting office opened in Rochester he applied to join. He learned to fly, was called up in September and did his stint of square-bashing at St Leonards before passing on to No. 6 Flying Training School at Little Rissington. He remembered later that 'when Dunkirk happened we shot through the final stages at a rate of knots'.[8] Waiting at Catterick station for a ride to the base, he was asked by a corporal whether he was there as a replacement for the pilots the squadron had lost at Dunkirk. It was the first time he heard that the unit had taken part in the action. When he arrived he was pleasantly surprised to find three of his friends from Little Rissington had also been posted directly to the squadron: Pilot Officer Gerry Langley, Sergeant Johnny McAdam, another Kent boy, and Pilot Officer Eric Lock. All of them had come from the RAFVR. Only Usmar was to survive the war.

The four had never flown anything faster than a Harvard. A Spitfire was sent down to a nearby bomber station deemed to have a less tricky runway than Catterick for them to practice on. After three satisfactory landings they were considered competent. From then until the end of July they flew with the squadron on its daily routine, which mostly consisted of convoy patrols.

As new pilots were coming in at the bottom of the squadron structures, changes were also taking place at the top. Before the fighting in France began it was possible to command a squadron without necessarily flying with it. This was a legacy of the First World War, when a squadron leader's duties were not restricted to operations but extended to the whole responsibility of supervising a fighting unit. In the Battle of France, Commanding officers did fly into battle with their men, particularly as the fighting intensified during the blitzkrieg, but initially squadrons were led by their flight commanders. Now it was obvious that, to provide proper leadership, a commander's place was in the air.

The demise of officers like Squadron Leader Stephenson of 19 Squadron and Drogo White of 74 Squadron also suggested that veteran pre-war officers, despite their seniority and flying skills, were not necessarily best suited to lead. Despite the evidence, appointments of senior pilots who were rich in ability but inexperienced in combat continued to be made over the claims of younger pilots who knew the reality of air fighting. The obvious internal choice to replace Stephenson was Flight Lieutenant Brian 'Sandy' Lane. He was twenty-two years old, and had gone to St Paul's public school. He joined the RAF after losing a dead-end job as a supervisor in an electric-light bulb factory. He was tall and good looking with permanent dark circles under his eyes which gave him a misleading slightly dissolute look. His fellow pilots loved him for his energy and cheerfulness. His leadership qualities were recognized in the decision to give him temporary command after Stephenson was shot down, but Flight Lieutenant Philip Pinkham was chosen as the new squadron leader instead. Pinkham had been with the Meteorological Flight, a sure sign of exceptional flying talent. After taking over, though, he played little part in operations until the beginning of September. The squadron had been chosen to test the claims of cannon over machine guns as a more effective fighter armament, and he was preoccupied with supervising what turned out to be a difficult experiment. Barely had the task been completed than Pinkham was dead, shot down and killed by Me 109s over the Thames estuary in a suicidally misconceived attack. This time Lane was given command.

In some cases, commanders demonstrated as soon as they were tested that they were not up to the job. On 30 May, 609 Squadron was detailed to fly off from Biggin Hill to patrol over the Dunkirk beaches. It was led by Dudley Persse-Joynt, a flight lieutenant, the commander having chosen to fly as an ordinary pilot with green section. On the journey out, green section put down at Manston on the North Foreland and proceeded no further. Stephen Beaumont's diary entry noting this incident was followed by the word, 'why?'[9] After this inauspicious debut, the squadron leader played no further part in operations. He had taken over in January as the Air Ministry's second choice after the first candidate was injured in a car crash. He had previously belonged to another auxiliary squadron, and arrived without having done a conversion course to monoplane fighters. Beaumont noticed early on that he demonstrated no great enthusiasm for flying. One spring afternoon he invited him to join him flying two of the squadron Spitfires. 'The CO showed himself to be competent and held formation steadily, but showed no desire to repeat the performance.'

By the end of June he had been quietly shunted out. Beaumont, a charitable man, wrote many years later that 'no leader of a fighting squadron can ever have had less impact on it. We hardly saw him at all either at the flight dispersals or even in the mess.' He added that he could 'now feel sorry for him rather than blame him . . . I can feel some sympathy for him as he must have realized that he was unfitted for his post, but none because he never tried to act to his responsibilities.' Some blamed his lack of leadership for the heavy losses the squadron was to sustain in its disappointing intervention at Dunkirk. Others held the Air Ministry responsible for appointing such an unsuitable officer.

The insouciance of the pre-war days was badly dented by 609's experiences at Dunkirk. Four of the first pilots to join were killed. Persse-Joynt, one of the set of wealthy and well-connected Yorkshire friends at the core of the squadron, failed to return from a patrol on 31 May. John Gilbert, a convivial bachelor known as the 'pink boozer' because of his fresh complexion and taste for beer, disappeared with him. Desmond Ayre, a mining engineer in one of the Peake collieries, crashed to his death after apparently running out of fuel, and Joe Dawson was shot down on 1 June.

It was obvious that the auxiliary ethos of amateurism, albeit of a dedicated kind, and the quasi-familial bonds of place and friendship could not survive the new circumstances for long. On 22 June the squadron got a new commander. George Darley was a great contrast to his hapless predecessor. He was twenty-seven years old, a short-service entrant who had become a regular. Darley had no trouble making the adjustment from peace to war. He already had wide experience, ranging from operations in Aden to controlling duties in Britain and France. He knew the auxiliary system intimately, having been adjutant and flying instructor to two units. He said later that he assumed his appointment arose from his 'awareness of problems peculiar to such squadrons, which were small squadrons of personal friends who had probably grown up together, and in which losses were particularly keenly felt'. On his arrival he found 'the general atmosphere in 609 was depressed, which did not help the younger pilots'. He set about trying to 'restore morale by improving the kill/loss ratio'.[10]

This robust assessment was typical of Darley's approach. Beaumont judged him 'not a man who radiated charm, superficial or not'. Disappointed at their performance and cast down by the loss of friends, the pilots were at first annoyed rather than inspired by Darley's determination to rebuild the squadron spirit and get back into the fighting. Flying Officer Charles Overton remembered that 'initially we couldn't stand the sight of the man'. It was not long, though, before 'our attitude changed to great respect for what he was doing for all of us'.

Darley decided early on that the older pilots would have to go. Beaumont, now over thirty, was 'inwardly relieved' when he heard the news. 'I knew that I was really not suitable as a fighter pilot, let alone a flight commander, but I do not think any of my contemporaries would say I did not try.' The original composition of the squadron had already been altered during the phoney war by the arrival of short-service commission officers and the first of the RAFVR pilots. By the end of the autumn, the core of pre-war members was gone, most of them dead. The same process overtook all the auxiliary squadrons. By the time of the high-summer fighting, death and shared danger had melted most of the pre-war distinctions.

Darley also put his men through a heavy training programme of mock attacks with himself acting the part of the enemy. A lull in the fighting gave the squadrons a chance to practise and to try and apply the lessons of the recent fighting. No attempt was made to pool the hard-won information gathered in combat, let alone to analyse it and use the findings to refine tactics. Intelligence officers restricted themselves trying to establish the veracity of claims. It was up to squadrons to work out their own approaches. Despite the redundancy of the old system, the temptation was to use it as a starting point in coming up with new solutions. 'We practised a wing formation with the Hurricane squadron yesterday, eighteen machines in formation,' wrote Pilot Officer John Carpenter to his parents from 222 Squadron's base in Kirton-in-Lindsey. 'I have been told that it was quite good from the ground.'

Denis Wissler, back from leave after his stint in France and with 17 Squadron at Debden, applied himself with a particular dedication to training, only too aware of his lack of success and touchingly determined to do well. For a week he spent every day practising formation flying and some new attacks evolved by the squadron, which 'did not work out too well'. But it was still air drill that appeared to matter most. On Friday, 28 June, after two flying sessions in front of an audience of senior officers, he thought his formation flying was 'pretty good but apparently the CO and wing commander thought I was the weak link, though the CO didn't say it was really bad'. Wissler confided to his diary that he was 'a bit browned off at the moment. We were suddenly called to readiness at 9.15 p.m. and weren't released until 10.35 and now we have to get up at 3 a.m. tomorrow.' The pattern was to continue until the end of the month.

The heightened state of alert was in response to the resumption of Luftwaffe activity. From the middle of the month Goering launched regular small raids, mostly at night. The bombs did little serious damage. The main purpose seems to have been to unsettle a population which suddenly found itself in the front line, and to probe the effectiveness of the air defences.

As if on cue, several attacks had been mounted on the warm evening that followed Churchill's great speech. As night fell, groups of German bombers set off across the North Sea, arriving in the early hours of the morning, and scattered bombs haphazardly on towns in eight counties in East Anglia and the north, killing twelve civilians and injuring thirty. Blenheim twin-engined fighters from Wittering in the East Midlands went up to meet them. One was shot down by a Heinkel, which in turn was destroyed by Flight Lieutenant Raymond Duke-Woolley, an ex-Cranwellian from 23 Squadron.

To the south the searchlight batteries around Southend at the mouth of the Thames picked up a formation of bombers. Sailor Malan, with 74 Squadron at Rochford, was in bed. He heard the bombs falling from the direction of Westcliff-on-Sea, where his wife Lynda had just given birth to their first son, Jonathan. Malan stood outside, watching the raid and getting increasingly agitated at the rumble of falling bombs. Normally, night interceptions were considered risky from bases in the area because of the danger from anti-aircraft artillery along the coast and around the Thames estuary. But it was a clear night and the moon was nearly full and Malan was worried. He asked for permission to attack the raiders, which was eventually granted. Shortly after midnight he took off and, climbing to 8,000 feet, found a Heinkel 111 held in the beam of the battery searchlights. Closing in from behind he signalled to the ground that he was in a position to attack, and when the anti-aircraft guns stopped he opened fire. There was only time for a three-second burst before he had to break away to avoid collision. As he pushed his Spitfire into a steep dive, the windscreen was smothered in oil from the stricken bomber, which crashed on to the beach. Turning back, he saw another Heinkel caught in a cone of light above him. He approached it cautiously, opening fire at 200 yards. It caught fire and sank from the sky, landing in a vicarage garden near Chelmsford in an eruption of flame that was seen for miles around.

Finding bombers in the darkness on any but the brightest moonlit nights was a near-impossible task. When it happened it was often as much the result of luck as of skill or science. On the evening of 19 June, Tim Vigors invited a Waaf from the Kirton-in-Lindsey control room to dinner at a restaurant in Lincoln. It was a Saturday night. They set off in his Ford 8, with his lurcher, Snipe, in the back. Dinner was followed by drinks at the King's Head, the RAF pub in the area, where he ran into some bomber pilots and 'got seriously stuck into the beer'. Vigors prided himself on his ability to stop drinking before his capacity to walk or drive became impaired. That night this gift failed him. 'With great care, I steered my way on to the dead-straight road which leads north from Lincoln towards Kirton-in-Lindsey,' he wrote later. 'My blacked-out headlights only showed the road about twenty yards ahead. Mercifully the local council had had the foresight to paint a broken white line down the middle of the road. Fixing this line between my right headlight and the mascot of a racehorse on the front of the bonnet, I proceeded slowly and carefully up the road. I didn't talk much and nor did my companion. I knew I was too drunk to concentrate on anything but driving.'

After dropping off his dinner date he donned a pair of bright-red pyjamas and slid gratefully into bed. Sleep was prevented by an attack of what he called 'bedspin', known to non-aviators as 'the phantom pilots'. While he was struggling to control it, a message was broadcast on the Tannoy in the corridor outside his room, calling for one pilot from 222 Squadron to report immediately to dispersal. Vigors, for reasons he was later hard pressed to explain, decided to volunteer. '"Hell," I said to Snipe. "Anything's better than this. Let's go and see what the flap is." I staggered off the bed, slid into my green silk dressing gown, donned my flying boots and weaved my way back to the car. Snipe followed, looking rather bemused. Even with maximum concentration on the drive to dispersal my path was alarmingly erratic.'

His rigger was waiting for him with a parachute. He urged Vigors to get airborne quickly as a large number of 'Huns' had just crossed the coast. 'My rigger jumped on the wing and handed me my helmet. I pulled it over my head, connected the oxygen and turned it on full blast. Somewhere along the line I had learnt that the best cure for a hangover was a strong dose of oxygen. I hoped fervently that it would have the same effect on bedspin.'

Somehow he got airborne and waited for control to vector him towards the raiders. No orders came. The radio was dead. Desperation dispelled the fog of alcohol. Without instructions from the ground there was no hope of intercepting any enemy aircraft. The obvious thing to do was to land as quickly as possible. He started to turn back the way he had come, maintaining the same speed, hoping this would bring him back to Kirton. Swinging round he saw the silhouette of another aircraft crossing the moon. It had two engines and was clearly one of the returning German bombers. Vigors moved behind and underneath the tail and opened fire. Soon its port engine was belching black smoke and it went into a screaming dive towards the cloud below. He had shot down a Heinkel 111.

Elation at this success was dampened quickly by the realization that he was now miles off course with no means of finding his way home. He decided to descend through the thick cloud, hoping that when he emerged he might spot the runway lights of one of the bomber bases in the area switched on to guide its night-flying aircraft home. At 700 feet, still blanketed in murk, he was on the point of climbing again in order to bale out when he broke through the bottom of the cloud. In front of him, glimmering out of the flat black of Lincolnshire, were the lights of a flarepath. He landed, exhausted and deeply relieved, to find he was at Barkston, a grass field he knew from his Cranwell days. The first person to greet him was one of his old instructors, who took his pyjama-clad protégé off for a drink.[11]

Malan's double success pushed him further into the public eye. Fighter pilots had now moved into the centre of the national consciousness as the importance of their role, underlined by Churchill, was recognized. The men of Fighter Command were engaged in the essential warrior task, defending their loved ones and homes from marauders, and they were doing it over the roofs of those they were protecting. This was enough to make them heroes. The stylish way they did their duty added a further layer of lustre.

The Fighter Boys were extraordinarily good for morale. It was important that they were properly rewarded. In the aftermath of the May and June fighting, the medals began to arrive in quantity. On 27 June, King George VI went to Hornchurch to present a batch to a group of pilots who had emerged from the anonymity of their squadrons and were on the way to becoming national figures. Al Deere, Sailor Malan, Bob Tuck and Johnny Allen all received the Distinguished Flying Cross for gallantry in the face of the enemy. James 'Prof' Leathart was awarded the Distinguished Service Order. The ceremony took place on a warm sunny morning. Afterwards the king took sherry with the pilots in the officers' mess and chatted with them about the relative performances of the Spitfire and the Messerschmitt, a subject on everybody's minds. Deere was particularly proud. 'As a New Zealander, brought up to admire the Mother country and respect the King as her head, it was the honour of a lifetime, an ultimate milestone of my flying ambitions – the Distinguished Flying Cross presented by the king, in the field of action.'[12] Afterwards, on the spur of the moment, the pilots rushed from the mess and lined up along the drive leading to the main gates to salute the royal visitor as he drove off. Underneath the top dressing of irony there was simple, solid patriotism.

Malan, Deere and Tuck were now almost famous, following behind the brief comet trail of glory blazed by Cobber Kain. Kain was not forgotten. He had been on the point of getting married, just before his death, to an actress, Joyce Phillips. His mother and sister Judy were on their way by ship to England for the wedding when the accident happened. A photograph in the *Daily Express* showed the two young women meeting for the first time. The caption reported that 'the two girls talked of Cobber and themselves. They played on the piano "Somewhere in France with You".'

Some pilots had put off thoughts of matrimony to avoid just such melancholy situations. Harold Bird-Wilson had never forgotten what happened after five members of 17 Squadron were shot down on their first patrol over northern France. When the unit withdrew to England, 'the wives of the missing people came daily to the officers' mess and hung around waiting for information as to the return of their husbands . . . some of us vowed that we wouldn't marry until things calmed down.' One of the missing made it home. Another was a prisoner. The other three were dead.[13]

The war had come at a very inconvenient time for Charles Fenwick. He was in love with Bunny, a dark-haired girl with smiling eyes whose good nature shines out from the old photographs. Motoring up to London from his boring initial training stint at St Leonards once a month was, he wrote to his mother 'the only thing that makes life bearable . . . then for a few hours everything is heaven'.[14] They went to shows and ate at the Strand Palace Grillroom 'very well indeed'. By the end of July he had made up his mind, and wrote to tell his father.

> Before I joined the war I had little chance of meeting many girls. Since then I have had plenty and have made the most of them to see if I was as completely in love with Bunny as I had thought. To cut a long story short, of all the varied types of girls I have met they one and all either bored me to sobs or made me feel slightly sick, particularly if I kissed any of them, not through any lack of physical attraction on their part but just because I loved somebody else. Now after all this time of 'trial and error' I am completely convinced that my love is no passing breeze. That being so I will tell you what I would be glad to have your opinion on. The desire of both of us is needless to say to get married, the question is when.

The answer, of course, was as soon as possible. He asked his father to let him know 'which side of the balance your vote will go in'. His father wrote back sympathetically, but argued firmly against matrimony. Fenwick was unhappy, but he submitted. 'Dear Pa,' he wrote a few weeks later. 'Thanks. You win, you brought me out of a spin and I've come down to earth all intact although just a bit shaken.'

Women, and wives in particular, complicated things. When Fred Rosier took over 229 Squadron, based at Northolt, later in the year he 'found that the wives of some of the chaps were living in the vicinity . . . It wasn't long before I stopped chaps living out. And I said it would be better if their wives moved, because it was affecting, I thought, morale, in that these wives would count the number of aeroplanes leaving and the number of aeroplanes coming back, and were on the telephone to see if Willy was all right. It was far better when we were all living together and in the mess and developing a first-class squadron spirit.'[15]

June drew to an end in an atmosphere charged with anticipation. The countryside was littered with chopped-down trees and derelict cars pushed into fields to block the arrival of the Germans. Overhead, flabby barrage balloons rolled in the warm air. Odd incidents betrayed the tension. At Debden an aircraftman who had never piloted an aeroplane in his life took off in a Hurricane, flew over the airfield and plunged to the ground, killing himself. In the dispersal hut of 72 Squadron at Acklington a sergeant pilot woke up everyone in the dispersal hut, shouting challenges to the German paratroopers he dreamt had just landed.

It was hot, as memorably hot as another summer month in the not very distant past: August 1914. One bright morning a legendary figure from that era descended on the pilots of 72 Squadron at their base at Acklington on the coast of Northumberland. 'We were honoured by the company of "The Father of the Royal Air Force",' the squadron diarist recorded. 'We were all lined up at dispersal standing there in the blistering sun and his very first gesture was to dismiss the parade – suggesting we all squatted down in the shade of the nearby trees. Sitting on the ground, too, he spoke of [the] activities of World War I, associating the duties and responsibilities of the airmen then with those that faced us at present – with the encouraging conclusion that there was no doubt in his mind that we would win through again.[16]

II

The Channel Battle

A few weeks after Trenchard's visit, three Spitfires from 72 Squadron were ordered off to investigate an unusual aircraft which had appeared near a convoy steaming off Sunderland. It was a Heinkel He 59 biplane, equipped with floats, and was painted white and adorned with red crosses. Undeterred by the innocent-looking markings, Flight Lieutenant Ted Graham led the aircraft into line astern and attacked, spattering the seaplane with 2,500 rounds. It crash-landed close to the beach and its four-man crew was captured by an escorting cruiser. Graham had been right to ignore the red crosses. The aircraft carried cameras and was on a reconnaissance mission.

The little victory of 72 Squadron, though it did not know it, was an indication of the new direction the air war was taking. Trenchard had been wrong on that hot morning when he linked the duties and responsibilities of the First World War airmen with those of the pilots sitting in the shade at his feet. The task facing them was very different from the one carried out by the RFC on the Western Front, and the burden they would have to carry was much greater. The duels over the trench lines in the First World War were an adjunct to the main military effort and decided nothing. Fighter Command was entering a battle that would decide everything.

The German forces had been allowed a short period of relative relaxation after conquering France. It was time now for them to deal with

Britain. The question of how this was to be done had never been clear. Different commanders in different services held strong and conflicting views. Hitler himself had not devoted much time to the subject, having always hoped he could negotiate an agreement with the British government that would leave him free to rule Europe unmolested. When the collapse of France failed to weaken the will to resist, it seemed that Britain would have to be forced into submission.

Hitler announced his intentions in Order No. 16, issued on 16 July, which stated: 'Since England has still not given any sign of being prepared to reach an agreement, despite her militarily hopeless position, I have decided to prepare an operation to invade England and if this becomes necessary, to carry it through. The objective of this operation is to eliminate the English home country as a base for the continuation of the war against Germany and, if this should become unavoidable, to occupy it fully.'

With these words 'Operation Sea Lion' officially came into being. Various invasion plans has been drawn up by the German navy and army since the start of the war. Initial doubts as to the feasibility of the exercise had largely dissolved in the intoxication of victory. Even sceptics like the naval commander Grand Admiral Raeder none the less hoped, as Hitler appeared to, that a combination of blockade and aerial bombardment could, on its own, crack British resistance, removing the necessity for an opposed landing. What the German High Command all agreed upon was that the defeat of Britain, whether through invasion or being battered from the skies, depended on German command of the air. That made the destruction of the Royal Air Force a precondition of success. Hitler spelled it out. A prerequisite of the landing, he wrote in his order, was that 'the English air force must have been beaten down to such an extent morally and in actual fact that it can no longer muster any power of attack worth mentioning against the German crossing'.

The Hitler directive confirmed an operation that had, in fact, already started. The German Armed Forces Supreme Command (the OKW) had anticipated the next stage of the war and had ordered the Luftwaffe to step up operations. By the beginning of July the air force had the use of the entire North Sea coastline from Norway to France from which to spring attacks. The new phase began with an intensified programme of reconnaissance missions, like the one brought to an end by 72 Squadron, probing defences and photographing potential targets. At first these seemed to be no more than a continuation of the harassing missions that had disturbed the sleep of Fighter Command during June.

Then a series of attacks on the convoys, scurrying heavily laden through the Channel to deliver as many cargoes as possible while the going was good, announced the overture to the Luftwaffe's next great symphony of violence. A much earlier Hitler directive issued in November 1939 had envisaged the air force 'waging war against the English economy' once the Anglo-French armies had been disposed of. By bombing convoys, the Luftwaffe was engaging economic targets. But they also hoped to lure Fighter Command into a battle of attrition that would wear it down and weaken it before the opening of the main air attack, which would deliver the fatal blow.

The Luftwaffe operation order of 2 July set two objectives: to close the Channel to British shipping and to clear the air of British fighters. With his usual overconfidence, Goering decided at first that only a limited number of aircraft would be needed. German intelligence, equally inclined to optimism, reckoned it would take between a fortnight and a month to smash the RAF. The job was given to a battle group drawn from Fliegerkorps II, based in the Pas de Calais, and to Fliegerkorps VIII at Le Havre. Oberst (Colonel) Johannes Fink was made Kanalkampfführer, commander of the air battle over the Channel. He was forty-five years old, sombre, religious and intensely patriotic. He had been one of the five pilots allowed each year to receive flying training under the stringent terms of Versailles. When the order came, he was at the head of a bomber wing, Kampfgeschwader 2, equipped with Dornier 17s, based at Arras some way back from the coast. To this force were added two groups of Stuka dive-bombers and two fighter wings, Jagdgeschwaders 26 and 53. The fighter element was led by Oberst Theo Osterkamp, a First World War veteran who had been shot down by Albert Ball. To close the Channel and grind down the British fighters,

Fink had at his disposal seventy-five twin-engine bombers, sixty or more Ju 87 Stukas and about 200 fighters. Down the coast, Fliegerkorps VIII could provide a similar number of Ju 87s and fighters. The unit was commanded by Wolfram von Richthofen, 'the Stuka general', a cousin of Manfred, who had flown in his unit on the Western Front. Later he had become an energetic advocate of dive-bombing as a battle-winning tactic and put his theories convincingly into practice in Spain, where he was responsible for the Guernica atrocity, Poland, Belgium and France.

Fink set up his headquarters in an old bus on Cap Gris Nez within sight of the White Cliffs of Dover. By the end of the month he had radar, known as Freya, to track ship and aircraft movements and an eavesdropping service which listened in to the radio traffic between RAF sector controllers and fighters. The German air force commanders, pilots and crews were in no doubt about the outcome of the battle ahead of them. Their power, as the chief of operations of Luftflotte 3, Werner Kreipe, wrote later, 'was now at a zenith . . . the pilots were highly skilled . . . Their morale was very high and they were confident of victory.'[1] Standing behind the Channel battlegroup, should it prove insufficient for the job, was the weight of Luftflottes 2 and 3, the Luftwaffe deployment in France. Between them, by the end of July, they had 769 serviceable bombers, 656 Me 109 fighters, 168 Me 110 twin-engined fighters and 316 Ju 87 dive-bombers as well as about 100 reconnaissance aircraft. Many pilots had fought in Spain, Poland and the air battles over France and the Low Countries, and replacements were being turned out of training schools at the rate of 800 a month.

Set against this the RAF could muster only 504 battleworthy Hurricanes and Spitfires, as well as 27 two-man Boulton Paul Defiants. The lack of aircraft was matched by a shortage of pilots. On 1 July, Dowding had 1,069 pilots to fly his aeroplanes. That meant two pilots for each aeroplane. This healthy-looking equation took no account of inevitable losses through death and injury. He cast around for volunteers from other branches of the service and borrowed fifty-two pilots from the Fleet Air Arm. But there were far too few to sustain a war of attrition.

The battle for the Channel, the *Kanalkampf* as the Luftwaffe called it, opened on 3 July. The Luftwaffe moved tentatively at first, sending only fifty aeroplanes that day towards Britain. About a quarter of these were on reconnaissance missions, trying to photograph airfields and ports as part of the intelligence preparations for the main attacks. A small group of Dornier 17s appeared over Manston, a forward airfield perched on an exposed patch of flat land on the North Foreland, and dropped a few bombs before being chased away by the arrival of Spitfires from 54 Squadron. In the north, 603 Squadron destroyed three Ju 88 bombers in separate incidents. The day's total of five enemy aircraft shot down was a poor return for the effort involved. Twenty-eight squadrons had flown more than 120 patrols, a total of 570 individual sorties.

The following day the Luftwaffe launched the first serious attack. The opening raid lasted four minutes. Thirty-three Stukas appeared at breakfast time in the misty sky over Portland on the Dorset coast. They were the best known and the most feared of the German aeroplanes. They were the chief symbol of blitzkrieg, howling down in near vertical dives, releasing their one large and four small bombs on bridges, rail junctions or human beings with terrible accuracy. The first doubts about their vulnerability had been raised at Dunkirk, where British fighters found their lack of speed made them relatively easy to knock down. But they seemed impressive enough on the second day of the *Kanalkampf* as they plunged on ships and installations in the naval base, sinking an anti-aircraft ship and setting a tanker on fire in Weymouth Bay.

By the time fighters arrived from the nearest base, Warmwell, they were long gone. At 2 p.m. the Germans came again. Two groups of Dornier 17s escorted by thirty Me 109s pounced on a nine-ship convoy as it moved through the Straits of Dover. Eight Hurricanes from 79 Squadron were scrambled from Hawkinge, another forward field a few miles south of Manston, but as they engaged the raiders they were bounced by the Messerschmitt escort above and one pilot was shot down over St Margaret's Bay and killed. In addition, small groups of German fighters were given the freedom to roam on 'free hunting' sweeps over the coast, looking for targets of opportunity and daring the British fighters to come up and challenge them. A patrol from 54 Squadron was surprised by one such group of Me 109s which appeared out of cloud, shot up two of the aeroplanes and disappeared, anxious to get back to their French airfields within the fifteen to twenty minutes that was all that their fuel capacity allowed them over target.

Patrolling was wasteful and ultimately unsustainable, given Fighter Command's strictly limited resources. Dowding had not expected to have to protect shipping and had told both the Admiralty and the Air Staff that his fighters could provide only limited help. Radar's usefulness in providing a warning and allowing assets to be deployed more effectively was restricted by the fact that the raiders could form up inland beyond the range of the transmitters. It took less than ten minutes to get across the Channel from the Pas de Calais, but Hurricanes and Spitfires needed a quarter of an hour to climb high enough to attack them effectively. One response was to move the squadrons to forward operating bases so they would be nearer the attackers. But this meant they would have even less time to gain vital altitude.

Dowding had guessed the German thinking correctly. He had to avoid being drawn into an engagement that would leave Fighter Command's pilots exhausted and its aircraft depleted before the main attack was launched. Only token cover was provided for the convoys. Park, the 11 Group commander, ordered his pilots to avoid challenging the German fighters roaming provocatively twenty and thirty miles inland from the Channel. But even with this prudent approach, casualties were unavoidable. On Sunday, 7 July, six fighters were shot down and four pilots killed.

The following day a thick cushion of cloud was piled up over the Channel, providing the Luftwaffe with limitless cover for attacks on shipping. With several convoys scheduled to move through the waters off the south and south-east of England, there were plenty of targets to choose from. A large convoy had set off from the Thames early in the morning and was due to pass Dover after midday. Radar reported intense air activity over Calais and Park ordered up patrols in the area. A section from 610 Squadron at Biggin Hill met the convoy in the early afternoon in time to intercept a group of unescorted Dornier 17s, which it attacked, forcing them to drop their bombs harmlessly in the sea. In the encounter Pilot Officer A. Raven was shot down. He was seen swimming away from his Spitfire, but apparently drowned. Nine Hurricanes from 79 Squadron were sent from Hawkinge to take over. Soon after getting airborne, they were swooped on by Me 109s engaged in a free hunt over the Kent coast. Pilot Officer J. Wood was shot down in flames; he managed to bale out but burnt to death while descending. Flying Officer E. Mitchell crashed to earth behind Dover and was immolated in the subsequent fire, which blazed for an hour. No. 79 Squadron had been in action almost continuously since the Battle of France and its men were exhausted. Three days later they were moved far away from the fighting to Sealand, in Cheshire, to recover.

Despite the fact that serious fighting had barely started, some units were already heavily depleted. On 9 July, 54 Squadron lost two pilots, Pilot Officers Garton and Evershed, bringing the total of casualties to six dead and two injured in ten days. The death of Garton had been particularly distressing. 'Prof' Leathart last heard him over the R/T, screaming that he was on fire and being chased by four Germans. Evershed had been considered a promising pilot and a potential leader.

The losses meant, the squadron diary recorded, that it 'could only muster eight aircraft and thirteen pilots'. Al Deere narrowly escaped being killed on the same day Garton and Evershed died. On his fourth trip of the day he was leading his flight out to sea to investigate a report of enemy air activity and saw a silver seaplane apparently on a reconnaissance mission, escorted by Me 109s. He managed to shoot one of the fighters down and turned towards another. The pilot swung round to face him and the two machines powered head-on towards each other. 'We opened fire together and immediately a hail of lead thudded into my Spitfire. One moment the Messerschmitt was a clearly defined shape, its wingspan nicely enclosed within the circle of my reflector sight, and the next it was on top of me, a terrifying blur which blotted out the sky ahead. Then we hit.'[2]

Deere's engine was on fire and seized up, leaving the airscrew immobile. To his amazement he realized that the blades were bent almost double with the impact of the collision. He yanked at the toggle that released the cockpit hood, but it was stuck fast. His only hope lay in a crash-landing. Half-blinded by smoke, he nursed the aeroplane over land and, before coming to rest on the edge of a cornfield, flopped it down in a great rending of splintering timber from the wooden posts planted in the ground to deter Germans landing. With the strength of desperation, he punched at the Perspex hood until it smashed open and then hauled himself out, sucking in lungfuls of fresh air.

His fists were cut and bleeding, his hair and eyebrows singed and both knees badly bruised from where they had been dashed against the instrument panel when his seat broke free in the collision. Rejoining the squadron at Rochford next day, he was asked if he was fit enough to fly. 'Frankly I had hoped for a day or two off the station, perhaps a quick sortie to London,' he wrote later. 'I was pretty sore and a bit shaken but quite obviously I couldn't be spared.'

Deere's commander, Leathart, admitted that he, too, was exhausted and hoping fervently that they would be taken out of the line before long. The calculation of how much flying a squadron could endure and how many losses it could sustain before its morale buckled and it became ineffective was a fine one, and a peculiar combination of ruthlessness and sensitivity was needed to judge it correctly. The decision, in the case of 54 Squadron, belonged to Dowding and Park, both of whom were trusted by their pilots. Dowding was approaching sixty. He had come to flying late, qualifying as a pilot in 1914 after serving around the fringes of the empire in the artillery. With his feathery moustache and pained demeanour he was an unlikely aviator, but he had a good war with the RFC in France, serving as a squadron leader and ending up a brigadier general. Dowding had a dashing side. Apart from flying, a dangerous and romantic occupation when he took it up, he was a good and brave skiier. In general, though, he seemed grave, careworn and short of friends – 'stuffy' as the universal nickname acknowledged. The loss of his wife after only two years of marriage and the responsibility of bringing up their son, Derek, himself a Fighter Command pilot with 74 Squadron, added another layer of seriousness to a solemn nature. These were not traits normally appreciated by fighter pilots. Then and later, though, his 'Dear Fighter Boys', as he addressed them, felt affection for him, and more importantly assurance. 'Even junior people like myself had enormous confidence in him,' Christopher Foxley-Norris said later. 'He was a father figure. You felt that as long as his hand was on the tiller all was going to be well.'[3] Dowding in turn felt a strong paternal bond with his men. Later on, when he turned to spiritualism, he claimed to be in communication with the souls of dead pilots.

The women who worked with Dowding at his headquarters at Bentley Priory could sense warmth behind the stiffness. 'We all admired our Stuffy enormously,' said Elizabeth Quayle, a Waaf operations room plotter. 'We had great loyalty to him. I think you might call it affection. He built up a tremendous *esprit de corps* among us. He was very remote, but if you met him he was always very considerate.'[4] These qualities did not necessarily recommend him to his senior colleagues and superiors. Dowding's heavily worn sense of duty and touch of lugubriousness – what Trenchard had called his 'dismal Jimmy' side – brought out the bully in some of those above and around him. When his big work was over, he would be disposed of with a bad grace that dismayed the men and women who served under him.

Keith Park was less taut, more approachable, but still someone who glowed with discipline and purpose. He was a New Zealander who had been wounded at Gallipoli, then transferred to the RFC in France, where he shot down twenty Germans. He made a point of showing himself to his men in 11 Group, flying around the bases in his own Hurricane, listening rather than talking. Many seem to have seen the long, lined face, which made him look much older than forty-four, at some time during the summer months of 1940.

Dowding's chronic lack of pilots was alleviated a little by the arrival of foreign airmen now entering the system. Most were Polish pilots, a large number of whom had managed to escape through Romania at the end of 1939 and made their way to France, where they carried on fighting. Altogether 145 of them served in Fighter Command between July and October 1940. Billy Drake, after recovering from his injuries, helped to train them up. He found them, as most did in the RAF, 'very independent minded. They were all a touch older than we were and a touch more experienced.' They could also 'be a handful . . . they wouldn't take any orders except from their own people'.[5]

Discipline was less strict in the Polish air force, and divisions between ranks less marked. Officers and crews socialized with each other in a way never seen in a British squadron. The reputation for hot-headedness and indifference to air drill was soon established and stuck with them until long after the war. Language difficulties explained some of the Poles' alleged reluctance to follow orders. There were also deeper reasons. Experienced pilots were unhappy with the formation tactics that persisted throughout the summer, believing them to be stupid and dangerous. Contrary to another popular myth, the Poles were not particularly reckless, and their casualty ratios were in line with those of British pilots. It was true, though, that they hated the Germans with an un-Anglo-Saxon vehemence. Some pilots found this aggression admirable. To others it could seem embarrassing, even distasteful. Stories circulated accusing Polish pilots of shooting at Germans as they floated down on parachutes, but there is little hard evidence to show this was a regular practice. The leading historian of the Polish air force in Britain, Adam Zamoyski, does concede that 'it is true that some pilots still finished off parachuting Germans by flying directly over them; the slipstream would cause the parachute to cannon and the man would fall to the ground like a stone'.[6]

Given the differences of language, culture and approach, the Poles and the other Continental pilots, Czechs, Belgians and French, fitted surprisingly easily into the fabric of the fighter squadrons. British pilots did not try to master the consonant clusters of the Slavic names, simplifying and jollifying them instead, so that Karol Pniak and Boleslaw Wlasnowalski, two of the three Polish pilots who joined 32 Squadron, became 'Cognac' and 'Vodka', and the new soubriquets slotted democratically in alongside the other squadron nicknames. Pete Brothers found the newcomers 'very good value . . . socially everybody mixed in'. However, there was some unease when a German pilot who had been shot down was brought to

Biggin Hill. 'The police captured the chap and stuck him in our guardroom,' he said. 'In the evening we were still at readiness in the dispersal hut and we had him brought over. We had the wing of a 109 propped up against the hut, which [Flying Officer Rupert Smythe] had shot down ... He'd come back to Biggin Hill with it on the roof of a car. We said to the German, "One of your 109s," but he wasn't going to commit himself. We had a chat to him in dispersal and decided we'd better keep our eyes on the Poles, who were sitting all three together some distance away. We thought, "If we take our eyes off them they'll probably murder him," which I would have done, given the chance in their circumstances, most certainly.' The German, who spoke English, was led away for a drink in the mess. 'He said could he have paper and a pencil. We said, "Why?" He said, "I want to write all your names down because tomorrow the Luftwaffe will blacken the skies, you will have lost and I want to make sure you are all well-treated." He couldn't understand why we fell off our stools laughing.'[7]

Not all foreigners in 32 Squadron were popular. Comte Rudolphe de Hemricourt de Grunne was a twenty-eight-year-old Belgian who had gone to Spain and fought for Franco as a pilot in the civil war alongside the Luftwaffe. He claimed to have shot down fourteen Republican aircraft. He later joined the Belgian air force, and when the country was overrun made his way to Britain. He arrived at Biggin Hill early in August. Brothers considered him to be not a 'Nazi sympathizer so much as a mercenary', but he was regarded as too boastful for the squadron's liking. The 32 Squadron pilots were very impressed when he told them he had flown an Me 109 in Spain and they expected him to have no problems when encountering one from the other side. He managed to shoot one down on his second day in action, but a week later was shot down by another, an event that caused some amusement. De Grunne was to meet his death at the hands of a 109, drowned after a fight over the Channel in May 1942.

Virtually every squadron was enriched by a dash of overseas blood. Of the 2,917 airmen who flew in Fighter Command between 10 July and the end of October 1940, 2,334 were British, 145 were Polish, 126 from

New Zealand, 98 from Canada, 88 from Czechoslovakia, 33 from Australia, 29 from Belgium, 25 from South Africa, 13 from France, 11 from the United States, 10 from Ireland, 3 from Rhodesia and 1 each from Jamaica and Newfoundland. Some pilots liked the mix of nationalities. With him in 92 Squadron Tony Bartley had South Africans, Canadians, Australians and New Zealanders. 'I felt,' he said later, 'that when someone lacked something, the other compensated for it, because of the different part of the world they came from . . . We had Czechs and Poles who were very brave and we had a Frenchman . . . Together it made an absolutely indestructible team . . . Everybody's morale was [compensated] by each others. The whole thing, put together, was undefeatable.'[8] Dowding was less convinced, at least as far as the Poles were concerned. He worried about their numbers diluting squadron identities and from the end of July began making plans for separate Polish squadrons.

Manpower was more of a concern than machines. The appointment of Lord Beaverbrook as Minister of Air Production in May had an almost immediate effect in galvanizing manufacture, and by July the flow of Hurricanes and Spitfires off the production lines was sufficient to keep pace with losses. The fighters had proved their flying ability against the aircraft of the Luftwaffe. But the early summer fighting had increased doubts about the effectiveness of the British fighters' armament of eight machine-guns when compared to the combination of cannon and machine-guns carried by the Me 109.

The Colt-Browning guns in the Hurricanes and Spitfires carried 2,660 rounds in total, enough for fourteen seconds' firing. The bullets were only 7.7 mm in calibre, the same as the ones used by infantrymen, though the introduction of the De Wilde incendiary type had increased their effectiveness. The Me 109 had two wing-mounted Oerlikon cannon and two 7.9 mm machine-guns sited above the engine. There was only enough room in the wings to carry sixty cannon rounds per gun, but they were 20 mm in calibre and usually explosive. The machine-guns each carried 1,000 rounds.

It seemed clear early on that the Me 109 carried the heavier punch. It

bove: The deadly schoolboy. Albert Ball, ıortly before leaving for France. The glossy air and blank stare disguised a strange :mperament. He shot down 43 German eroplanes and won the Victoria Cross, yet the ›eastly killing' filled him with disgust.

ight: Mick Mannock in the fur-lined kit viators on both sides wore to combat the itter cold in the winter skies over the trenches. gave them a primitive look that heightened ıe illusion of belonging to a classical warrior adition. Mannock was a complex man who ›se from humble beginnings to exemplify the ›irit of the Royal Flying Corps. He died in one f the 'flamerinoes' that haunted his ightmares.

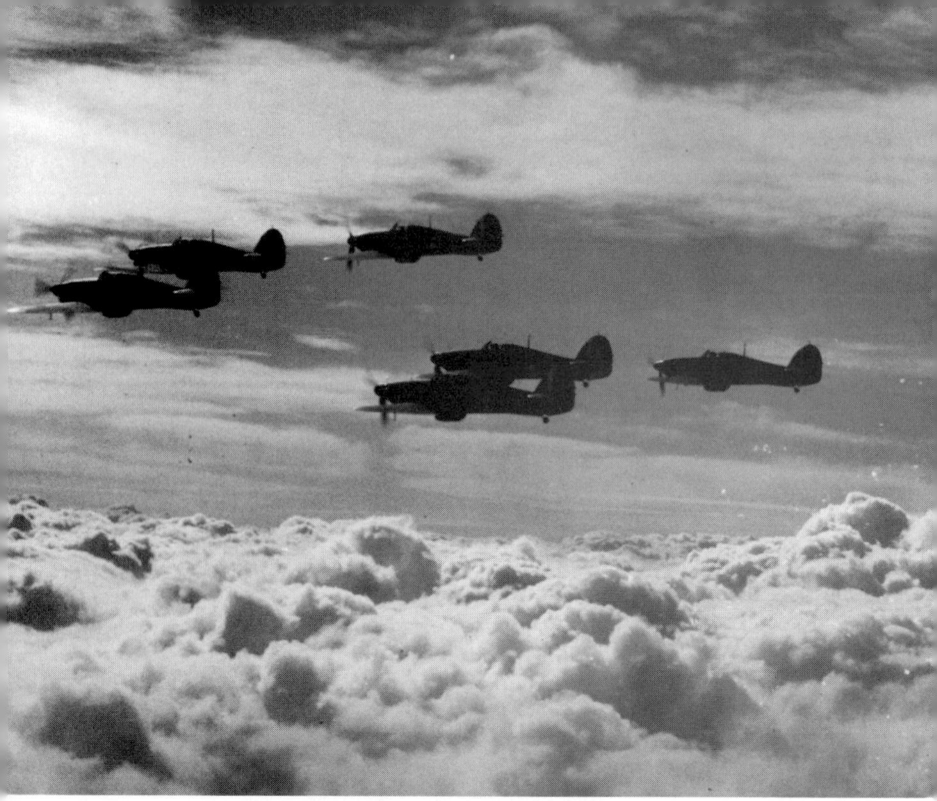

Above: Hurricanes flying in 'vic' formation.

Left: Pilots spoke of the Spitfire in the language of love. It was beautiful, fast and elegant and it had almost no vices.

Right: Number 1 sqn in France. Bull Halahan (in sheepskin flying jacket) surrounded by his pilots front of the Mairie at Vassincou winter 1939/40.

Above: 'Black wavy hair and chiselled good looks.' John 'Killy' Kilmartin.

Above left: Squadron stalwart Billy Drake.

Above right: Paul Richey was as good a writer as he was a pilot. His book on his experiences in France rang with authenticity.

Left: The Ju 87 Stuka dive bomber. It terrified ground troops but its lack of speed and vulnerability when diving made it an easy target for British fighters if only they could get at it.

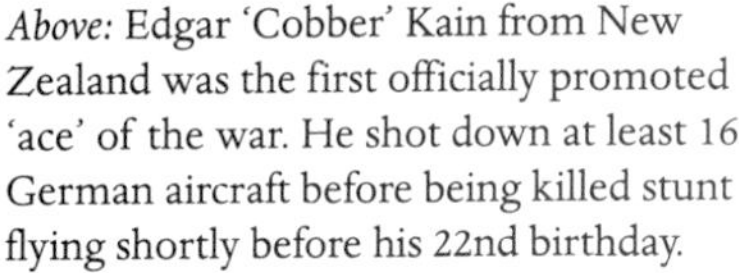

Above: Edgar 'Cobber' Kain from New Zealand was the first officially promoted 'ace' of the war. He shot down at least 16 German aircraft before being killed stunt flying shortly before his 22nd birthday.

Above right: Pete Brothers learned to fly at 16 and chose the RAF over the family business.

Above: Al Deere. Tough in the air, kindly on the ground.

Left: Peter Townsend. A pre-war regular who learned to appreciate the newcomers.

Above: Looking the part. Robert Stanford Tuck with swastikas recording his successes.

Left: Michael Crossley later in the war.

Above right: Tough Tyke. George Unwin clambering out of his Spitfire while a membe of the ground crew stands by to get to wor

Right: Brian Lane (left) and two other 19 sqn pilots are debriefed by a intelligence officer on returning from a sortie

Above: The main threat — the Me 109.

Below: 'Sailor' Malan. Hard on himself and hard on his pilots.

Below: Geoffrey Page, aged 17.

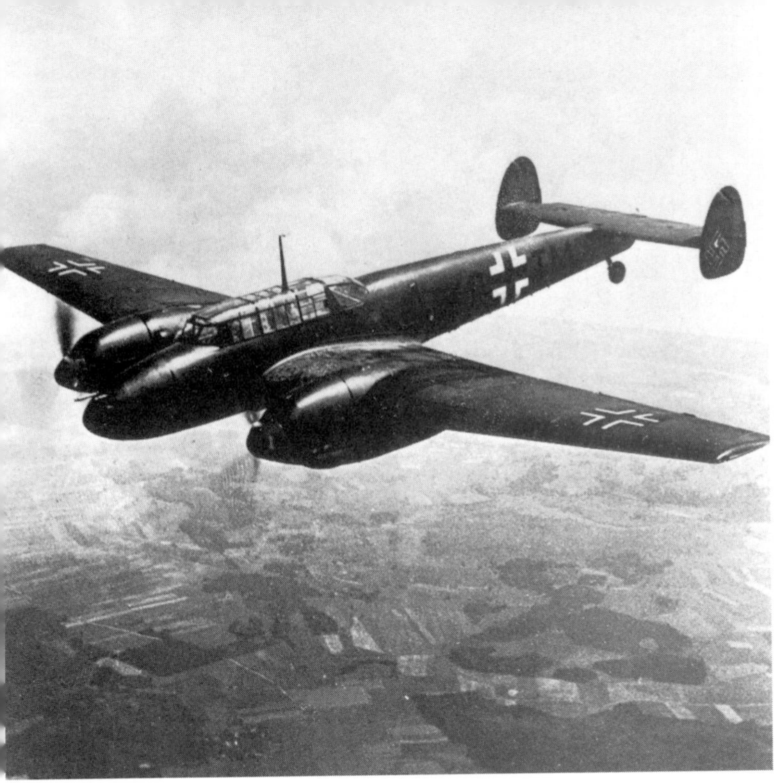

Above: Me 110 fighter-bomber.

Below: Dornier 17 medium bomber.

Right: Ground staff swarm over a Spitfire refuelling and rearming. Without the skill and bravery of the ground crews, the Battle of Britain could never have been won.

Above: Adolf Galland. 'Complicated and deceptive.'

Below: Heinkel 111s raked by fire from fighters. German bombers could withstand a huge number of hits without being brought down.

Below: Pilots from 610 sqn grab a brief respite from the fighting. The airfield is Hawkinge and it is the middle of the day.

Above: Nearly a third of the Fighter Boys in the summer of 1940 were NCOs.

Below: 'Some of the boys,' it says on the back of the snapshot. Members of 66 sqn in late 1940. Robin Appleford is on the far right.

Left: Fighter Boys and their girls. Rob, Pamela, Christine and Robin.

Middle: A jaunt in the freezing winter of 1941. Robin Appleford is in the front with Christine. Pamela is looking at Rob Bodie, who took the picture.

Below: 'Tall, elegant, sophisticated and beautiful.' The Belles of Biggin Hill. The Macneal twins, Moira and Sheila, outside the White Hart.

Above: Tony Bartley, aged 23, leading a squadron in North Africa.

Far left: Decent, vulnerable and doomed. Denis Wissler in the last year of his short life.

Left: Edith Heap, Denis Wissler's fiancée.

Below: Brian Kingcome before 92 sqn moved to Biggin Hill.

Above: A Heinkel 111 silhouetted over Docklands.

Below: A Heinkel gunner tries to bring his gun to bear on a Spitfire which has just flashed past after a rear attack.

Above: The end of the line. Paddy Barthropp (right) after being shot down in May 1942.

Right: 'This is it, chaps.' Paddy Finucane in the cockpit of his Spitfire, not long before his death.

Below: Johnny Kent (centre) with FO Zdzislaw Henneberg (left) and FO Marian Pisarek, two of the 145 Poles who, with 88 Czech pilots, fought with Fighter Command in the summer of 1940.

has been calculated that a three-second burst from an RAF fighter weighed about thirteen pounds. In the same time a Messerschmitt could deliver eighteen pounds.[9] The rate of cannon fire was much slower – only 520 rounds a minute against 1,200 for a machine-gun – but the shells exploded on impact and one or two hits could bring down a metal-skinned Spitfire (though the Hurricane's old-fashioned fuselage construction of struts, formers and fabric made it less vulnerable). This was an advantage in circumstances where a fighter pilot chasing another fighter pilot could expect to have his target in his sights for only a few seconds. To be effective, machine-gun fire needed to smash the engine, set it on fire, shoot off a vital control or kill the pilot. The greater size of the bombers, with their extra structural strength and armour plating, meant that thousands of rounds fired by several fighters might be needed to bring one down. One of the most dispiriting experiences a fighter pilot could have, captured on many a camera-gun sequence, was to catch and hold a bomber in a perfect deflection shot only to watch it cruise blithely through the blizzard of tracer.

The German bombers had steel plates that offered partial protection to their crews and self-sealing fuel and oil tanks with membranes that melted when the metal was pierced, automatically plugging leaks. But the engines were unprotected from the rear, making an attack from astern the fighter's most profitable line of approach. If armour plating was fitted to cover this vulnerable spot, shooting down a bomber would become a very difficult task for a fighter armed only with machine-guns. To penetrate armour and redress the balance, cannon were needed.

This realization produced a flurry of belated activity. Experiments had been going on for at least two years to fit cannon to fighters. Formidable engineering problems were involved. The Hispano guns were potentially excellent weapons, with a high muzzle velocity delivering a powerful and penetrating blow, but the fighters' wings had to be able to absorb the recoil. The armament also needed to be fixed in such a way that the magazines did not create too much drag and impede flying performance. One solution was to fit the guns so they lay on their sides. But this had the effect of slowing the flow of shells to the breech and interfering with the cartridge-ejection system. Also, despite their bulkiness, the magazines held only sixty rounds each, giving the fighter a negligible six seconds of firing time.

These problems were well known. None the less work began on fitting the guns to a new Spitfire type, the Mk IB, with a view to putting them into service. At the end of June the first three were delivered to 19 Squadron at Duxford, which as the most experienced Spitfire squadron in Fighter Command was given the task of trying them out. 'They had to have special wings with this huge blister on top where the magazine fitted,' said George Unwin, who was one of the first to fly them. 'They were absolutely useless. You could only fire [when] absolutely straight and level.' Pilots found that the mildest G forces were enough to make the nose of the bullet dip and jam in the breech when they pressed the firing button. Air-gunnery tests were very disappointing, with guns misfiring constantly. When the more experienced pilots lined up to shoot at a towed aerial target, only one direct hit was scored.

Dowding was under pressure from the government to send 19 Squadron into action as soon as possible to test the new weapons in battle conditions. He resisted deploying it in the 11 Group area, where it was certain to encounter 109s. In the next six weeks, operating mainly out of Fowlmere in the less hazardous air of 12 Group, the squadron had five encounters with German formations. When the cannon shells struck the raiders they did spectacular damage, shooting away propellers and tailplanes and setting engines ablaze. But virtually every aeroplane suffered stoppages on every outing. On 31 August, eleven Spitfires from the squadron went up to intercept a large force of bombers and fighters to the south. In the clash Flying Officer James Coward was shot up, losing a foot, but managed to bale out. Pilot Officer Raymond Aeberhardt, nineteen years old and new to the squadron, was forced down, turned over on landing and was killed. Again many guns had jammed and only two probable Me 110s could be claimed against the losses.

Squadron Leader Philip Pinkham, who had struggled throughout the summer to make the new armament work, had had enough. Strongly backed by his pilots, he petitioned Dowding for the return of their old machine-gun equipped fighters. 'The next day the great man was there and he listened to what we had to say,' George Unwin remembered. 'He had a miserable face. He said, "I won't teach you to suck eggs. You shall have your eight-gun Spitfires back by tomorrow morning." And we did, except that they were all clapped-out Spitfires from an Operational Training Unit, shedding oil all over the windscreen.'[10]

On the morning of 5 September, Pinkham, who had not flown in the operations of the previous weeks, led his men off in these machines with orders to patrol Hornchurch aerodrome at 15,000 feet. On the way, and while still climbing, they saw a mass of forty bombers escorted by the same number of Me 109s above them to the south, approaching the Thames estuary. Before they could reach them another group of RAF fighters attacked the formation, turning it southwards. To the dismay of some of the experienced pilots, Pinkham ordered five Spitfires to follow him up into the bombers while the rest of the squadron took on the escorts.

They were attacking from almost the worst possible position, lacking height and blinded by the glare from the south. 'He flew straight into the sun,' said Unwin later. 'It was a pretty incompetent thing to do.' Pinkham was last seen flying towards a group of Dorniers before apparently falling victim to the Messerschmitts. David Cox, a twenty-year-old sergeant who was flying with him that day, described the decision as 'tactically wrong but morally right . . . The squadron had been told to intercept this formation which was coming in to attack Hornchurch.'[11] What Pinkham should have done, he believed, was to have flown a dog-leg to gain height and bring the squadron in at a speed and position to have taken on both escort and bombers.

Pinkham, though, lacked the tactical experience to see this. He was popular with his men. Cox thought him 'a very fine chap, a real gentleman. He treated a sergeant pilot the same as he would treat an air marshal'. Born in Wembley and educated at Kilburn Grammar School, he joined the RAF on a short-service commission and as a result of his outstanding flying skills had been selected first for the Meteorological Flight and then posted as an instructor. He was twenty-five when he died. Despite his sense of duty and diligence, his lack of combat experience meant he was a poor choice to command a fighter unit.

The cannon problem was eventually overcome by the installation of a belt-feeding system, a solution that had been under consideration from the outset. The decision to persist with an unpromising experiment meant the squadron had been sent into action with guns that were known to be faulty. Thanks to luck and skill, losses had been relatively small, but it had also deprived Fighter Command of the full use of a seasoned unit which would have inflicted much more damage on the Luftwaffe during the middle passage of the summer if it had been armed with its old weapons.

Despite Dowding's reluctance to commit resources in the opening stages, the Germans were now arriving in such numbers that it was impossible to ignore them. Fighter doctrine as laid down by the pre-war planners, based on the premise that bombers would arrive unescorted, had been shown to be utterly unrealistic. Unruffled by this failure, the revived analysis by the senior officers of Fighter Command continued to be based on cheerful hypotheses that bore little relation to what was happening in the skies. Pilots were told that 'whenever possible, fighters should attack enemy bomber formations in equal numbers by astern and quarter attacks at the same level'.[12] At the same time the memorandum was written, fighter squadrons routinely found themselves outnumbered by bombers by five or ten to one. As for the accompanying fighters, the same document suggested that half the flight or squadron should 'draw off their escort and if necessary to attack them'.

These instructions were meaningless by the middle of July. On the 13th, six Hurricanes from 56 Squadron led by Flight Lieutenant Jumbo Gracie took off from Manston to protect a convoy coming through the Straits of Dover. Gracie, according to Geoffrey Page, was 'far from being the popular conception of a fighter pilot. He was fat and pasty and had a high-pitched voice, more of a Billy Bunter than a Knight of the Air.' Despite his appearance, he was famously energetic and aggressive. The controller told them twenty bombers on their way to attack the ships had been picked up on the radar, protected by sixty fighters flying above them. Gracie ordered Pilot Officer Taffy Higginson to take his section off to deal with the bombers. He meanwhile led his section, including Page, up into the midst of the fighters where they prepared to do battle at odds of twenty to one. 'I suppose with hindsight I should have been scared stupid,' Page said later. 'But I think I was so busy getting my aircraft ready, making sure the camera gun was switched on and the safety button on the guns was on "fire", generally trimming up the aeroplane for the approaching combat. Then suddenly there was this enormous swarm of aircraft above us and we were climbing up.' When they reached the height of the fighters, they found both Me 109s and Me 110s. The latter reacted to the arrival by going into a waggon-circling manoeuvre, following each other around to give their rear gunners the chance to provide maximum defensive firepower. Page felt his mouth go dry, but still found the Germans' caution when faced by three Hurricanes funny. He 'dived into the circle, firing rather wildly .. then the 109s came down on us'. For the next few minutes he 'registered nothing but flashing wings bearing Iron Crosses, and streaks of tracer'. Then came the phenomenon that never ceased to amaze: the sky was completely empty 'as if the hand of God has wiped the slate clean'.[13]

Page was regarded by his colleagues as an exceptional fighter pilot. The line dividing the merely good from the outstanding was a fine one. Sailor Malan, considering the qualities needed to fly fighter aircraft successfully, reckoned that, unlike among the First World War pilots,

> courage, these days, is a minor talent. No man is braver than the next . . . the air raid wardens in Coventry or Plymouth, these men do things under fire which we fighter pilots can only regard with awe. A fighter pilot doesn't have to show that kind of courage. Unreasoning, unintelligent, blind courage is in fact a tremendous handicap to him. He has to be cold when he's fighting. He fights with his head, not his heart. There are three things a first-class fighter pilot must have. First, he must have an aggressive nature. He must think in terms of offence rather than defence. He must at all times be an attacker. It is against the nature of a Spitfire to run away. Second, both his mind and his body must be

> alert and both must react instinctively to any tactical situation. When you are fighting you have no time to think. Third, he must have good eyes and clean hands and feet. His hands and feet control this plane and they must be sensitive. He can't be ham handed. When your Spitfire is ambling along at 390 miles an hour a too-heavy hand on the rudder will send you in an inadvertent and very embarrassing spin. Your hands, your feet, your mind, your instinct must function as well, whether you're right side up or upside down.[14]

Malan might have added to his list, possession of very good eyesight. He himself was said to have been able to spot 'a fly on the Great Wall of China, at five miles'.[15]

Page was certainly aggressive. Writing to a friend from his days at Cranwell, late in the evening after a night in mess, he confessed: 'I enjoy killing. It fascinates me beyond belief to see my bullets striking home and then to see the Hun blow up before me.' But the sight, he admitted, 'also makes me feel sick. Where are we going and where will it all end? I feel I am selling my soul to the devil.'[16]

Given the disparity in forces it is remarkable that more pilots were not killed in the Channel battle of July. As it was seventy-nine died. The worst losses came on the 19th, the disaster resulting from the failure of machines rather than of men. The Boulton Paul Defiant was a strange conception from the outset. It had no fixed gun that fired forward. Instead, a gunner swivelled around in an electrically powered turret sunk into the fuselage behind the cockpit. The extra weight meant it was slow, managing just over 300 m.p.h. The four Browning guns could generate a reasonable rate of fire, but this only counted if the pilot manoeuvred his partner into a good position. The aeroplane was an anachronism before it ever went into action, reflecting thinking about aerial fighting that had gone out with the First World War. It was the very weirdness of its design that explained the Defiants' brief success. During the Dunkirk campaign, the Germans had at first mistaken them for Hurricanes and, going in from the rear, were unpleasantly surprised when they spat back bullets. On one day, 29 May, 264 Squadron claimed to have shot down thirty-five German aircraft. It was an exaggeration, but there was no doubt that they inflicted significant losses. The Germans soon learned the difference.

On 19 July, the Defiants of 141 Squadron were moved forward to Hawkinge at breakfast time and sent off on patrol. The crews had never been in battle, had only arrived in the south from Scotland a week before and were unaccustomed to 11 Group control procedures. At 2.30 p.m., twelve Defiants were ordered off to patrol just south of Folkestone. Three machines had to be left behind with mechanical trouble. There was no warning from control when, a quarter of an hour later, a swarm of Me 109s from the Richthofen Geschwader crossed the path of the squadron in the air and, identifying them correctly, moved in efficiently for the kill, attacking from below and astern where they were at no risk from the guns. Four Defiants were shot down in the first attack. The gunners, clamped into their claustrophobic turrets, went down with their aeroplanes. One pilot baled out and was picked up wounded from the sea. The remaining Defiants tried to hide in cloud, but one was caught and set on fire. The gunner baled out but was drowned and the pilot was killed on crash-landing. Four made it back, two of them damaged, one beyond repair. Altogether, in the space of less than a quarter of an hour, six machines had been destroyed and ten men killed. The losses would have been even greater if Hurricanes from 111 Squadron had not arrived to scare the Messerschmitts off. Two days later what was left of the Defiant squadron was sent back to Scotland.

Some of the losses of July seemed particularly wasteful. Fighter Command insisted on mounting night interceptions even though the chances of catching anything were tiny. Seven pilots were killed in accidents during the hours of darkness. Most pilots feared flying at night. It was very dangerous and the results were almost never worth the risk. Stephen Beaumont, the most uncomplaining of pilots, was told, one night at Middle Wallop at the end of July, to hold his flight at readiness. He was exhausted, there was no moon and it was pitch-black.

As they settled down at dusk in the dispersal hut they devoutly hoped they would not be required. Half an hour before midnight the operations room ordered one pilot up to investigate an unidentified aircraft near Ringwood. Beaumont thought this was 'stupid, ineffective and potentially dangerous', and said so. He contacted his commander, George Darley, but was told, with some sympathy, that orders were orders. Flying Officer Jarvis Blayney, the son of a Harrogate doctor and one of the pre-war squadron members, was sent up first. He set off with a heavy heart but his engine overheated and then it was Beaumont's turn. He trundled down the runway, swinging his Spitfire from side to side to see the line of the flarepath and managed to take off and climb to 1,000 feet. He cruised overhead, desperate not to lose sight of the dim glow of the lights below, and was greatly relieved to be told to forget the interception and come back and land. He suspected afterwards that Darley 'had been to the Operations Room, expressed his views on the futility of this order and got the controller to recall me'.[17]

July had been unsettling for the pilots, just as the Luftwaffe intended it to be. Kept in the dark about Fighter Command's assessment of the Germans' intentions, the pilots had no idea as to how the battle would develop. Most seem to have shared Brian Kingcome's feeling that what they were engaged in was 'part of a continuing routine, certainly not . . . an isolated historic event . . . merely part of the normal progress of the war, which we assumed would continue unabated until final victory.'[18]

The pilots understood, though, that for the coming weeks and months they were the most important people in Britain. All eyes were on them. Since May the BBC had been broadcasting morale-boosting talks by fighter pilots. On 14 July, Harbourne Stephen of 74 Squadron went on the radio to describe how his squadron, though greatly outnumbered at Dunkirk, had escaped unhurt and knocked down several bombers in the encounter, and recounted Malan's exploit of bringing down the two bombers at night over Essex. The day before, a team from *Life* magazine turned up at Debden to shoot a feature on the fighter pilots who were beginning to be famous across the Atlantic. Denis Wissler was one of those ordered up to provide some formation flying pictures for them. Afterwards the 17 Squadron pilots were called to the mess and posed for a picture. The pilots stand around in frozen, monumental poses. Only one is looking at the camera as the mess steward in a starched white jacket distributes 'half-cans' of beer in silver mugs. The effect is stilted, straining to be epic. One of the subjects is starting to look bored. Denis Wissler, in the centre of the shot, planted squarely in a leather armchair, is scratching his nose, beer in hand as he skims a magazine. Later, the caption reports, 'everyone joined in a harmless battle, hurling the flashbulbs of *Life*'s photographer at one another'. The article did not appear for another year, by which time half the men in the picture were dead.

Were they supermen, the journalists wondered, or the boys next door? Godfrey Winn, a star writer for the *Sunday Express* who visited 54 Squadron on 18 July, decided they were both. The article was called 'Portrait of a Miracle Man'. 'He has captured the imagination of the whole world . . . What is he like as a man?' asked Winn. He went on to provide a composite profile.

> First of all he is a very ordinary fellow. He keeps on stressing that over and over again to you. And if you press him he will assure you that only with the greatest difficulty he reached certificate standard at school and never got his colours as if that had anything to do with it. He roars with laughter at all the references to himself as a knight of the sky and he tells you that the reason why he is a fighter and not a bomber pilot is because they discovered he was better at flying upside down.

Typical pilots laughed a lot, were addicted to music, playing Connie Boswell singing 'Martha' over and over again on the gramophone. They didn't read much, except for thrillers like *No Orchids for Miss Blandish*, a risqué bestseller. They were ordinary, until they stepped outside. 'The moment that he starts to walk towards the flarepath you see the transformation take place before your eyes . . . He becomes impersonal, merciless and completely self-disciplined.'

And, Winn did not need to add, more than a match for the Germans. Unofficial propagandists were already reassuring the public that any imbalance in the odds would be compensated for by the superiority of

British machines and men. The air reporter of the *Daily Express* revealed that the Luftwaffe 'use machines with a life of 50 flying hours. That is as long as they are made to last . . . staking all on numbers they don't attempt to train their crews carefully.' O. D. Gallagher in the same paper declared that 'our Spitfire boys enjoy a confidence in themselves that the Luftwaffe pilots cannot have'. He told a recent story of an intelligence officer going over to debrief a pilot who had just returned from a sortie. 'It was some minutes before he could get anything out of the fighter. He sat in his cockpit, eyes bright, grinning, saying: "God they're easy! God they're easy!"' These fantasies provided the pilots with a cynical laugh as they read them in the mess. Only they knew how far they were from the truth.

12

The Hun

The German airmen attacking Britain respected the enemy they were facing and liked to think the feeling was mutual. Contacts between the two air forces in the approach to the war had been frequent, cordial and remarkably open. In October 1938, General Erhard Milch, one of the main architects of the reconstructed German air force, led a senior Luftwaffe delegation to Britain and was given a tour of important installations. His hosts were nothing if not hospitable. When Milch went to Hornchurch, the pilots were told they could answer any questions put to them by the visitors except those concerning defensive tactics, the control of operations and the recently arrived reflector gunsight. Inquiries about the latter were to be turned aside with the reply that it was so new they had not yet learned how to use it.

General Milch chose Bob Tuck's aircraft to clamber on to. He peered into the cockpit, noticed the gunsight and asked how it worked. Tuck prevaricated, as ordered, only to be interrupted by an air vice-marshal accompanying the Germans who offered a detailed demonstration. Tuck said later he had to stifle the urge to ask: 'Sir, why don't we give General Milch one to take home as a souvenir?'[1]

The visit followed several encounters in which each side had tried to intimidate and deter the other by 'revealing' the extent of their preparedness in the air. It was a phoney exercise in which candour was mixed with deception, leaving everyone suspicious and confused. Milch did take away with him a strongly favourable impression of the cadets he met during a trip to Cranwell and told Hitler of their high quality. Afterwards he sent a thank-you gift, two fine, modernistic portraits of Richthofen and the first German 'ace' Oswald Boelcke, which still hang in the college library. With them came a letter expressing the hope that the images 'might encourage the feeling of mutual respect and help to prevent that our two Forces have to fight each other again as they were unfortunately forced to do some twenty years ago'.[2]

But less than three years later they were fighting each other once again, and British pilots who had served in France could feel little respect for men they had seen machine-gunning and bombing refugees. Brian Kingcome's sardonic style wavered when it came to Stukas. It was, he said later, 'a great tragedy in my life' that he had never had a chance to shoot one down. He had conceived 'a special hatred' derived from images of them 'strafing the endless queues of refugees'.[3] For pilots who had not seen such sights in France, the July battles over the Channel were straightforward military encounters which did not strongly engage their emotions. They were shooting, as they often said later, 'at the machine not the man'. This attitude was to harden when the focus of the German attack shifted inland and over the homes of those they loved.

Many German airmen believed that they shared with British pilots an experience and outlook that transcended differences of nationality and the fact that their governments were at war. Some of those who survived were to claim they had no desire to fight Britain, had assumed the war was over with the fall of France and were saddened when told they would now have to try and kill men whom, from a distance, they admired.

Their feeling that they had much in common with their British counterparts was to some extent justified. The pilots facing Britain in 1940 in both fighters and bombers had mostly been attracted to the Luftwaffe, not by ideological reasons, but because they loved flying, or the idea of it. 'Flying brought me a lot of happiness,' Georg Becker, who piloted a Junkers 88, said later. 'I knew I was good at it.' The air offered him an escape from genteel poverty. He was the son of a civil servant who died in a train crash, leaving his wife struggling to bring up four children on a state pension. It was also 'a glamorous thing to do . . . more romantic than being a foot soldier'.[4] For Gerhard Schöpfel, who was to become famous for shooting down four Hurricanes in three minutes in August, flying in the Luftwaffe was 'new and exhilarating'.[5]

Many aspects of the pre-war existence lived by German airmen would have been recognizable to their British counterparts. Off duty, Becker and his comrades 'went to the officers' mess and drank. We had breakfast, lunch and dinner all together. We had the week planned out so we knew when we would be working and we arranged our free time around that. In Brandenburg, we had a boat and would take it out with friends. Some of us had cars. We'd drive to the coast or into Berlin at weekends.'

They called each other by nicknames and enjoyed dogs, cars, sport and jokes. Like the pre-war RAF, they thought of themselves as an élite, semi-detached from the drab, terrestrial world. But this was Germany in the 1930s. At Becker's base they 'had dances where the officers could invite girlfriends but they also had to invite people like the town council and the mayor who we used to call the little Nazis. They had joined in 1933. We used to get them drunk and stick them in a corner and basically ignore them. There were some nice Nazis there too, people who didn't really believe it. We used to stick them in the corner as well.'

German airmen were required to take an oath of personal loyalty which committed them to 'yield unconditional obedience to the Führer of the German Reich and Volk, Adolf Hitler'. So did every other member of the German armed forces. Few of the pilots were active Nazis. That did not mean they were reluctant to fight. As with the expansion of the RAF, the birth of the Luftwaffe offered young, modern-minded German men an opportunity for adventure and an escape from mundane lives. They had not joined the air force necessarily to go to war, but inside its ranks war became simply an extension of duty.

The Luftwaffe had been conceived in subterfuge. Civil aviation in the inter-war years was developed with one eye on military potential. The bombers and fighters of 1940 took their names from men – Claude Dornier, Hugo Junkers, Ernst Heinkel, Willy Messerschmitt – whose companies started out manufacturing commercial aircraft. A state airline, Deutsche Lufthansa, was created in 1926, and its training schools were to provide the Luftwaffe with many of its pilots. The government encouraged youth to be 'air-minded' through gliding clubs which provided a cheap and practical way of teaching the elements of flying and by 1929 had 50,000 members. Some of the preparations were secret. In 1923 Germany negotiated a hidden agreement with Soviet Russia to supply military training at the Lipetsk air base, south-east of Moscow, an arrangement that lasted ten years. By the time the Luftwaffe's existence was officially announced in March 1935, it could rely both on the design teams and factories of the strongest aircraft industry in Europe to provide machines and a large reserve of young air enthusiasts to supply pilots and crews.

Adolf Galland, one of the two most famous of the German pilots of 1940, first took to the air in a glider. The flight lasted only a few seconds and carried him only a few feet above the ground near his home in Westphalia, but it was enough to persuade him he had found his vocation. The family were descended from a Huguenot who had left France in 1742 and become bailiff to the Graf von Westerholt. Successive Gallands had held the post ever since. Adolf's father was a traditionalist, an authoritarian who administered discipline with his fists. His mother was profoundly Catholic, so much so that her devotion was to get her into trouble with the Nazis.

Like some of the most successful Fighter Boys, he learned to handle a gun early, and by the age of six he was shooting hares on the Westerholt estate. At school he was dull. When he read anything, it was war stories, particularly the sagas of Boelcke and Richthofen. At the local glider club, the Gelsenkirchen Luftsportverein, he shone and became the star pupil. Later he would claim that pilots who served a long apprenticeship on gliders 'felt' the air better. In 1932, aged twenty, he was accepted for pilot training at the commercial air school at Brunswick. His talents were recognized and he was summoned to Berlin to ask if he was interested in undergoing secret military training. He spent a few, mostly wasted months training alongside Mussolini's air force. There was a stint as a

Lufthansa pilot flying airliners to Barcelona. Then, at the end of 1933, excited by the prospects opening up in military aviation after the Nazis came to power, he joined the air force. In April 1937 he went back to Spain as a pilot in the fighter section of the Luftwaffe-directed Condor Legion, flying inferior He 51 biplanes. By the time the new Messerschmitt 109s were arriving in sufficient numbers to dominate the air, he was back in Germany in the Air Ministry. It was not until May 1940 and the blitzkrieg that he started to do what he became famous for.

Galland had a complicated and deceptive personality. He seemed, at first glance, to resemble some of the more flamboyant of his RAF counterparts. He liked wine, women and cigars. He appeared good-humoured, gregarious and relaxed in his attitude to discipline and senior officers. All this was true. But Galland also brought a chilly analytical intelligence to the war against the British and was harsh with pilots who failed to reach his standards. He was one of the boys, but also intimate with the big men who ran the war. He was an admirer of Goering until his chief's intolerable behaviour made admiration impossible. He admitted to his biographer that, after leaving his first private meeting with Hitler, 'he felt a mutual respect had been forged . . . for the rest of his life [he] would remember how on that Wednesday afternoon he had been drawn under the intensely focused spell of Hitler's personality'.[6] His high-wattage bonhomie allowed him later to play the part of a professional Good German. He was a prominent guest at post-war fighter-pilot reunions. He and Douglas Bader were photographed together and he enjoyed a sort of friendship with Bob Tuck. Some pilots were never persuaded. In the view of Christopher Foxley-Norris, 'Galland was a shit.'[7]

At the start of July, Galland was still in the shadow of Werner Mölders, who, flying an Me 109, had shot down fourteen aircraft in Spain followed by a further twenty-five during the French campaign. Mölders was tactically intelligent and in Spain developed the system of flying in pairs that was eventually adopted by the RAF. He was introverted and grave-looking, a serious Catholic who passively disliked the Nazis. This did not prevent them loading him with honours and high rank, nor him from accepting. He was the recipient of the first Knight's Cross to go to a fighter pilot and became a general of fighters before he was twenty-nine. Mölders had been shot down early in June by a young French pilot and taken prisoner but released after the armistice was signed between Germany and France. At the end of July he was put in command of the fighter wing, JG51. On Sunday, 28 July, he made his first outing at its head. He shot down one Spitfire from 74 Squadron but was then engaged by Sailor Malan. His Messerschmitt was badly damaged and he received leg wounds that kept him out of action for a month. He was, however, to make his presence felt later on.

He was inspirational and a good teacher. Galland acknowledged that much of his skill was learned from Mölders. Another successful pupil was Helmut Wick, whom Mölders instructed during advanced training and who ended the French campaign with fourteen 'victories', just behind his mentors. Galland, Mölders and Wick shared the same, atavistic approach. When they wrote, they expressed themselves in the same language, drawn from forest and hillside, as that used by Richthofen, whom they regarded as a spiritual forebear (although Mölders saw himself more as Boelcke's successor). Wick declared that 'as long as I can shoot down the enemy, adding to the honour of the Richthofen Geschwader [his fighter unit] and the success of the Fatherland, I am a happy man. I want to fight and die fighting, taking with me as many of the enemy as possible.'[8] A Spitfire from Fighter Command fulfilled one of these wishes by shooting him down and killing him near the Isle of Wight in November. Galland saw his task as being 'to attack, to track, to hunt and to destroy the enemy. Only in this way can the eager and skilful fighter pilot display his ability. Tie him to a narrow and confined task, rob him of his initiative, and you take away from him the best and most valuable qualities he possesses: aggressive spirit, joy of action and the passion of the hunter.'[9]

Such words could never have been spoken or written by a pilot of Fighter Command without provoking bafflement, embarrassment or derision. Then there were the medals. The leading German pilots were encrusted with layers of Ruritarian decoration. They started off as holders of the Knight's Cross, rising through clouds of glory to acquire the Knight's

Cross with Oak Leaves, Knight's Cross with Oak Leaves and Swords, culminating in the highest honour of all, the Knight's Cross with Oak Leaves, Swords and Diamonds. These honours were worn prominently at the neck, and the condition of wanting one but not having one was known as 'throatache'. The RAF had the Distinguished Flying Cross, to which further exploits might add a bar or two, and which was signalled by a scrap of cloth sewn over the left-hand breast pocket of the tunic. Only one Victoria Cross, the highest gallantry award, was won by Fighter Command in 1940. To qualify for consideration for the honour, candidates had to have demonstrated outstanding courage in the face of overwhelming odds. It might have been argued that most pilots in 11 Group in the summer of 1940 were doing this most days.

When the *Kanalkampf* began in earnest, the German pilots were rested, warm with the afterglow of a succession of victories and enjoying the fleshly comforts of a sybaritic country which had come to a fairly rapid accommodation with its occupiers. It was perhaps with some reluctance that they resumed operations. But they went off cheerfully enough and morale remained high as the scope of the campaign widened, deepened and lengthened. Partly by design, partly by force of circumstances, the German air campaign would climb an ascending scale of violence. The bombing attacks on shipping and the free hunts to draw up the British fighters would give way to raids on aerodromes and defence installations, culminating in an all-out air assault. The escalation, in theory, would deliver one of two results. Either Britain would be beaten into submission, making a full-scale invasion unnecessary. Or it would hold out, forcing a landing, in which case much of the preparatory destruction would already have been achieved.

After the war Galland and several other leading veterans of the campaign would claim that they knew from the beginning that the Luftwaffe on its own could not achieve a strategic victory in the air. 'We didn't believe at any time that we could win the battle, to the effect that Britain would surrender,' he said. 'We couldn't force England to surrender by attacking without any operation from the army or navy . . . We were asking that the High Command order the invasion.'[10]

But the army and navy commanders, even the Luftwaffe's own leader, agreed that the invasion could not go ahead until Germany had air supremacy, or at least air superiority. The chances of resolving this conundrum were reduced by Goering's ignorant, impetuous approach. The gap between the airmen's understanding of their own capabilities and their commander's expectations was wide. Goering had latched on to the most optimistic pre-war feasibility study to persuade himself that a war of attrition was winnable and had gone on to assure Hitler that the air force was capable of bringing Britain to negotiations. The pilots and crews learned early that praise was abundant when the going was good, abuse lavish as soon as the momentum faltered. 'At the beginning we had great respect for him,' said Gerhard Schöpfel, 'but later our feelings changed. He began to complain that we were not doing enough, but we needed far more machines and manpower to achieve what he wanted.'[11]

It would not take long for it to become clear that the Luftwaffe was facing a daunting task. But that was not how it seemed at the outset. Many of the men arriving at the airfields of northern France in July believed their superiors' predictions that the campaign would last only a few weeks. The operation was not being mounted from a standing start, but in the flush of several victories won with relative ease.

The German bombers and fighters had suffered steady losses during July – 172 from enemy action and 91 in accidents – but their pilots and crews were confident that when the big push came they would be able to overwhelm the British defences. The fighter squadrons accepted that they were facing the most difficult opponent to date, but were none the less sure they could wipe the Hurricanes and Spitfires from the sky. 'We wanted to make the invasion work and we were sure it would work,' said Schöpfel, who was serving with Galland in Jagdgeschwader 26. 'We believed that we had beaten the English over France and we did not think that here was a force which could defeat Germany. We believed the landing would be possible with our help and that our wings would be able to reach out to London. We thought it would be possible to beat the English in England the way we had beaten them in France.'

The build up of Luftwaffe forces in France was to continue into August, but on the morning of 24 July, before the full wing apparatus was in place, Galland announced that his three squadrons were ready for operations. At 11 a.m. a British convoy nosed out into the Channel from the Medway and a force of eighteen Dornier 17s was sent to bomb it. With them went an escort of forty Me 109s, led by Galland. Spitfires of 54 Squadron at Rochford were ordered up to meet them. At the same time, a further nine Spitfires, of 610 Squadron, took off from Biggin Hill to patrol over Dover and cut off the raiders' retreat. Another six Spitfires, of 65 Squadron, which was operating from Manston, were also sent into the area, and seeing the Messerschmitt escorts were preoccupied with fending off 54 Squadron tried to attack the bombers, but were driven away by fierce and well coordinated fire from their gunners.

No. 54 Squadron was pleased with its showing in its first encounter with Galland's fighters, which went down in the unit's history as the 'Battle of the Thames Estuary'. The squadron diary described it as 'the biggest fight since the second day of Dunkirk and in the face of considerable odds the casualties inflicted on the enemy by the squadron (including three new pilots) can be considered eminently satisfactory and most encouraging'. A claim was made for sixteen Me 109s destroyed; a great exaggeration, as it turned out. The more likely figure was two. One was shot down by Colin Gray; another by Sergeant George Collet, who then ran out of fuel and was forced to land on the beach, writing off his Spitfire.

In the clash the squadron lost one of its best-liked and most prominent members. Johnny Allen was attacked by an Me 109 near Margate. Another pilot saw him putting down in a forced landing with his engine stopped but the aeroplane under perfect control. Then the engine started again and he turned towards Manston, but it cut out a second time. The Spitfire flicked on to its back and went into an uncontrollable spin. Allen crashed to earth near Cliftonville. He was twenty-four-years-old and had been the first member of the squadron to fire a shot in anger almost exactly two months previously. In the meantime he had destroyed seven German aircraft, winning a DFC. The story of how he had been shot down over the Channel during the Dunkirk evacuation, been miraculously picked up by a naval corvette and appeared in the squadron mess later the same evening dressed in naval uniform and carrying a kitbag had been recounted in Winn's article in the *Sunday Express* three days before. The photographs show an open-faced, shyly smiling youth. Deere remembered him as 'quiet and religious . . . out of place' in the boisterous squadron atmosphere, yet an elemental part of the unit. The normally undemonstrative diarist noted that 'the loss . . . will be greatly felt by the squadron'.

Despite this death and the over-optimistic assessment of the damage inflicted on the 109s, the squadron was right to regard the encounter as a moral victory. Its pilots had been considerably outnumbered but had stayed to fight, refusing to be driven off. The over-claiming may have been a result of the fact that, with their fuel warning lights glowing red, many of the German pilots had used their Messerschmitts' superiority in the dive to drop steeply down to sea-level before racing for their home field.

The German pilots returned home to the base at Caffiers to be harangued by Galland, who was dismayed by his men's lack of discipline and apparent unwillingness to engage the Spitfires. This first sortie over England, he told his biographer, had come as an unpleasant surprise. 'The tenacity of the RAF pilots, despite being heavily outnumbered and relatively inexperienced, had been remarkable. It had shocked him to see how inept his own pilots were; and that would have to change. This was no sudden blitzkrieg, bundling a disorganized enemy backwards across indefensible plains; this was the real business of hardened air combat, against an enemy who was going to stand and fight.'[12]

13

Hearth and Home

Early in the summer, as a wave of Germans closed over the Channel ports, Pete Brothers was flying low over Calais when he looked down and saw a cinema belching smoke and flame. In that moment his attitude to the war changed. 'I suddenly thought that the Odeon in Bromley could be next. It came home to me that this was deadly serious.'[1] By the middle of August, bombs were falling every day on placid coastal towns and suburbs where, until then, nothing much had ever happened. This was not the terror bombing that Hitler had reserved the right to order if Britain remained obstinate. It was unintended and accidental, the inevitable consequence of the stepped-up attacks on factories and defence installations prior to the big assault. Civilian casualties were small compared with what was to come. But the sense of violation was great. Bombs tore away walls, opening up homes as if they were dolls' houses, putting all the ordinariness of family life on intimate display. Twenty-five years before, if the wind was in the right direction, the inhabitants of Dover and Folkstone could sometimes just hear the faint rumble of artillery on the Western Front and feel a slight thrill of proximity. Now the sound of gunfire was all around, and for the first time in a thousand years the enemy was visible.

The defenders fought the battles of high summer in view of the people they were defending. Often the pilots were diving and shooting over their childhood homes. Roland Beamont could see his family house in

Chichester every time he took off from Tangmere. John Greenwood, a pilot officer with 253 Squadron, flew head-on into a formation of Ju 88s over Surrey and was horrified when 'they jettisoned their loads which fell between Epsom and Tolworth. My family lived in Tolworth and seeing the bombs exploding I went down to ground level to have a look.'[2] The nearest bomb had been several hundred yards away from his home. When he got back to Kenley he telephoned his mother, who told him she had been sheltering in the cupboard under the stairs during the raid. Peter Devitt of 152 Squadron was flying near Sevenoaks one Sunday evening when he saw Dorniers fleeing from a raid dropping their last bombs on Young's depository, where all his furniture was stored.

In some extraordinary cases, parents watched their sons fighting. On 16 August an intense engagement broke out between a large German formation and Hurricanes from 1 Squadron. One of the British fighters was hit in the fuel tank by a cannon shell and burst into flames. The pilot, Pilot Officer Tim Elkington, managed to bale out and was drifting down into the sea when Sergeant Frederick Berry swooped past him and used the aircraft's slipstream to blow the parachute over land. Elkington landed safely at West Wittering and was whisked away to hospital. The whole event was witnessed by Elkington's mother watching from the balcony of her flat on Hayling Island.[3]

Until August the fighter bases had been insulated from the violence of the war and the comfort and orderliness of mess, living quarters, flower beds, tennis courts and squash courts were undisturbed. The calm was about to be smashed. The mess waiters, batmen, clerks, Waafs, fitters and riggers; the great host of supporters who sustained the men in the sky, were now in as much danger as the pilots themselves. Watching the Germans swarming across in ever-bigger concentrations, many pilots felt a sense of revulsion they had not experienced before. The urbane Brian Considine 'hated them . . . thinking of what they were going to do if they were allowed to do it and what they had already done'.[4] Christopher Foxley-Norris described the sentiment as 'the sort of wave of indignation you get if you find a burglar in your house'.[5] No matter how the feeling was expressed, it gave an edge to the pilots' courage, driving them on to make greater efforts and take bigger risks.

August had opened quietly. Dowding and his senior commanders correctly interpreted the lull as the harbinger of a new and more intense phase. He could view the coming clash with some confidence. Factories were producing more fighters than the Germans were destroying and production targets were being overtaken. On 1 August he had roughly 650 combat-ready aircraft. In contrast to only a month before, he also had an adequate number of pilots. By trying to fight only when strictly necessary, he and Park had kept most of the squadrons relatively fresh. Some, like 54, had done a disproportionate amount of the fighting. But in all only a quarter of the strength of Fighter Command had been on extended duty during July. The problem, as the weeks ahead were to show, was not the quantity of pilots available but the quality. Many of those swelling the ranks had been hurried through training and were still not fully familiar with their machines. The accelerating pace of the battle meant that these novices would be thrown straight into aerial fighting of unprecedented intensity.

Hitler had set the date for the start of the new phase as on or after 5 August. Another directive, expressed in general terms and without naming specific targets, called for the air force to attack 'flying units, their ground installations, and their supply organizations [and] the aircraft industry'. This was in keeping with the imperative to destroy the Royal Air Force before any invasion could begin. In another document he told the three services to be ready to launch *Seelöwe* by 15 September if, by then, a landing had become necessary. Field-Marshal Kesselring, the leader of Luftflotte 2, which covered a line drawn east to west just above Paris, and Field-Marshal Sperrle, commanding Luftflotte 3 below it, differed over the approach. Kesselring favoured a dispersed campaign that would reduce the risk of concentrated, heavy losses. Sperrle backed a short, furious effort, hurling bombers, dive-bombers and fighter bombers en masse to smash the British defences.

Both agreed a sledge-hammer blow should start the assault. The operation was given the Wagnerian code name of *Adlerangriff*, the 'Attack of the Eagles', and *Adlertag* ('Eagle Day') was eventually set for 13 August. The preceding days were filled with dress-rehearsal raids and attempts to knock out radar stations to weaken the defenders' capacity to respond. On the morning of 12 August, Dover radar station was bombed, then a few minutes later those at Rye, Pevensey and the Kentish hamlet of Dunkirk. The damage looked spectacular but was quickly repaired and all stations were back on the air within six hours. The installations were small and well tucked away. The very flimsiness of the criss-cross construction of the transmitter towers made them remarkably resilient to blast. The Luftwaffe was never to achieve its aim of a total blackout of radar, but raids could result in dangerous blind spots in the cover that could last several hours.

While the radar was down, bombers raced in to exploit the advantage, attacking Lympne and Hawkinge airfields on the Kent coast. The decision to target Lympne, which since June had only been used as an emergency satellite field for fighters in trouble, was an early indication that the Luftwaffe's information about the nature and importance of RAF installations might be faulty or incomplete. A few hours later, Manston, sitting vulnerably on the crown of the North Foreland, was strafed by Me 110s closely followed by Dornier 17s dropping 150 high-explosive bombs. The landing ground was pitted with craters and four of the ground staff were killed. Once the smoke cleared and the chalk dust settled, it was seen that the damage was not catastrophic. None of the Spitfires caught on the ground was badly damaged and ground crews laboured to fill in the holes so that the airfield was in action again within twenty-four hours. The raid gave an unpleasant foretaste of what pilots, and particularly the ground staff of Manston, would have to suffer over the next weeks as the aerodrome was hit again and again.

The temporary loss of radar meant that a huge fleet of bombers protected by a fighter escort launched later that morning was already well on its way to its target before it was picked up and a force of forty-eight Hurricanes and ten Spitfires, operating in separate squadrons, sent up to confront it. The bombers were heading for Portsmouth. The bomber force split into two. The first group swung in through a gap in the balloon barrage defending the city and ploughed through a storm of anti-aircraft fire. Bombs hit the Royal Dockyards and the railway station and sank some small ships in the harbour, killing twenty-three people and wounding a hundred. The second group of fifteen Ju 88s turned for the Isle of Wight and dived on the radar station at Ventnor.

The German fighters circled behind and above the bombers, tempting the British fighters to come up. It was an invitation that they were learning to resist. Instead, the Hurricanes of 213 Squadron waited for the first group to emerge from the Portsmouth defences and pounced on them, shooting down the machine of Oberst Johannes Fisser, who was leading the attack. The second group was also set upon by Spitfires from 152 and 609 Squadrons, as it turned for home from Ventnor. Three 609 pilots, Noel Agazarian, James 'Butch' McArthur, who before the war had been a civil aviation pilot, and David Crook had been about to set off from the forward base at Warmwell, Dorset, where they were living under canvas, for London on a twenty-four-hour leave when the order to go to readiness came through. They took off immediately, except for Crook, who was delayed by a faulty radio. He arrived over the Isle of Wight to find 'circling and sweeping all over the sky at least 200 Huns . . . "My God," I said to myself, "what a party!"'[6]

The circling aircraft were the Me 110s on station to protect the bombers. They found themselves in a tactical dilemma. The British squadrons were launching small, successive attacks on the bombers. The escorts faced the choice of coming down in twos and threes to try and chase away the attackers, in which case they would be engaged by other British fighters; or they could descend in a great flock, which meant breaking up the defensive umbrella and creating a free-for-all in which the Spitfires and Hurricanes could get among them relatively unmolested. The raiders had lost ten bombers before their fighters, circling 10,000 feet ahead, could react. When they finally arrived they were punished, and four Me 110s and two Me 109s were destroyed in the space of a few minutes. Agazarian shot down two and Crook one. After landing the British pilots resumed their plan to set off for London, arriving five hours later than intended, and were back in the battle again the following day.

The toll among the defenders had been high, with eleven pilots killed and six wounded. Among the injured was Geoffrey Page. He was sitting on the grass in front of the dispersal tents at Rochford having afternoon tea after a long day of fighting when the field telephone rang and the order was given to take off in squadron strength to meet ninety bandits approaching from the south at 15,000 feet. Only ten aircraft were available. They caught up with the Dorniers as they were heading north past the mouth of the Thames, having dropped their loads. As Page, in the leading section, closed on the nearest Dornier 17, he saw 'all this tracer ammunition coming from the whole formation. They'd singled me out as the target . . . all these things that looked like lethal electric-light bulbs kept flashing by until suddenly there was an enormous bang and the whole aircraft exploded'.

Like most of the pilots Page had never made a parachute descent. The drill was taught in training, however, and now it came to his rescue. Instinctively he released the heavy webbing Sutton harness strapping him to his seat, slid the cockpit hood open and rolled the Spitfire on to its back. He remembered 'popping out of the aircraft like a cork out of a toy gun'. It was not fast enough to save him from the flames. Page was not wearing gloves. His hands, and the area of his face not protected by the oxygen mask, were terribly burned.

Free of the machine, he found himself 'tumbling head over heels through space. I remember seeing my right arm extended and I sort of looked at it. My brain ordered it to bring itself in and pull the metal ring of the rip cord on the parachute, and that was agony because with this cold metal ring and badly burned hand it was like an electric shock.' Somehow he yanked the cord and looked up to see the parachute blossom overhead. A ball-crunching shock between his legs as the harness arrested his descent told him he was safe for the moment, and drifting down he took stock of his situation. 'I noticed quite a funny thing had happened. My left shoe and my trousers had been blown off completely by the explosion. I was just about almost naked from the waist downwards. My legs were slightly burnt and I could hear the fight going on all around.' It was a sound he had never heard before. Engine noise blotted out the noise of fighting.

It took Page ten minutes to drift down into the sea. As the water came up to meet him, he ran through what he was meant to do next. The drill taught him he should twist the release catch on the harness through ninety degrees, then bang it to make it spring open. His roasted hands would not obey. As he settled in the sea the parachute silk and shrouds sank down on top of him 'like an octopus's tentacles. I knew that if I didn't get away from the parachute quickly it would get waterlogged and sink and take me with it.' Desperation numbed the agony and somehow the metal disc flipped open.

The next thing was to inflate his lifejacket, the Mae West that every pilot wore over his tunic. He blew into the rubber tube and was dismayed to see bubbles frothing through the holes where the fabric had been burned through. There was nothing to do but swim for it. Through swelling eyes, he could just see the English coast, and weighed down by his waterlogged uniform and a helmet which his fingers could not unbuckle, he struck out. He remembered that in his jacket pocket was a brandy flask given him by his mother.

'Quite often in the mess over the previous weeks when the bar had closed my fellow pilots had said, "Come on Geoffrey, you've got a flask there, let's have a tot of brandy," but I said, "No, one day I may have an emergency." As I was swimming along I thought that this probably qualified.' There was a further agonizing tussle as he unbuttoned his tunic flap and extracted the flask. He wrenched the cap off with his teeth when 'a dirty big wave came along and knocked it out of my wrists and the whole lot went to the bottom of the Channel'.

Despairingly, he floundered on. He had been in the water half an hour and almost given up hope when he heard the chug of an engine. His descent had been spotted by the coastguards, who sent a launch to search for him. After he persuaded his rescuers, with a stream of obscenities, that he was not a German he was dragged out of the sea and taken back to Margate where the mayor, strangely attired in a top hat, greeted him on the quayside.[7]

Page was very lucky. Fighter pilots on both sides hated the Channel. To the Germans it was the 'shit canal'. To the British it was 'the dirty ditch'. Bomber pilots had a second engine to get them home if the other was shot up or failed. Hurricanes, Spitfires and Me 109s had only one. Putting down on the sea was almost invariably catastrophic. The air intake slung under the fuselages of all three types dug into the water, sending the machine cartwheeling in a curtain of spray before it sank within seconds. Parachuting was barely less hazardous. The further away from land you were, the slimmer your chances of being picked up. British safety equipment was primitive and inferior to that of their enemies. Mae Wests relied for their buoyancy on wads of kapok and a rubber bladder that had to be inflated by mouth. The Germans had rubber dinghies and dye to stain the water to signal their whereabouts to rescuers.

The pilots made great efforts to pinpoint downed comrades. The day before Page was shot down, another 56 Squadron pilot, Sergeant Ronald Baker, was seen parachuting into the sea near a British destroyer. Michael Constable Maxwell recorded in his diary how Flying Officer Percy Weaver '(circled) round keeping him in sight – a most difficult thing to do as the turning circle of the Hurricane is too big and the aircraft is on the verge of spinning all the time. Another tried to get the ships over while I fly overhead watching for any hostile aircraft. It is extremely hard to keep an eye on a Mae West in the water as it is so small.'[8]

When, after an hour, a motor boat finally picked him up, Baker was dead. Many a pilot spent the last minutes of his life savouring the bitter knowledge that he had escaped death in the air only to meet it in the water. Three pilots drowned that day. A week later Park drafted revised orders to his sector controllers, instructing them to send up fighters to engage large formations only over land or within gliding distance of the coast as 'we cannot afford to lose pilots through forced landings in the sea'. Belatedly, a committee was set up at the Air Ministry to establish an RAF air-sea rescue organization with spotter aircraft and launches. But the incompetence of the Air Ministry in failing to put efficient rescue arrangements in place before the fighting began would come to be regarded by the pilots as shameful.

'Eagle Day' began inauspiciously for the Germans. The fine weather of the preceding days faltered. There was cloud over the Channel and a thin drizzle fell patchily on southern England. Goering hesitated. The weather reports predicted the skies would clear in the afternoon. That would still leave time, he decided, to deliver the smashing blow that would begin the final destruction of Fighter Command. The decision to postpone operations was slow in passing down the line. The first scheduled raid of the day was already forming up when it arrived. Sixty Me 110s, led by the *Kanalkampfführer* himself, Colonel Johannes Fink, had taken off early in the morning and climbed to an assembly point where they had been told fighters were waiting to escort them. But instead of slotting in alongside them, 'they kept coming up and diving down in the most peculiar way. I thought this was their way of saying they were ready. So I went on and found to my surprise that the fighters didn't follow . . . I didn't worry much.'[9] The fighters, it seemed, had received the signal changing the orders, but with no radio link between them and the bombers were unable to pass it on.

On reaching the English coast, the formation split, with one group heading for the naval base at Sheerness and the other for Eastchurch aerodrome on the Isle of Sheppey. It was a strange choice of target. Eastchurch was primarily a Coastal Command station, of little importance given the Luftwaffe's current preoccupations. By chance, fighters were present. Dowding had began to shift rested squadrons down from the relative quiet of the north to fill gaps in the front line. At Wittering in the Midlands 266 Squadron had been passing a pleasant summer. On 11 August its members spent the day bathing and boating on the lake next to their dispersal point and were drinking in the mess in the evening when the message came through that they were to prepare to move south at dawn. 'After two months' intense inactivity there was much excitement and speculation,' wrote Dennis Armitage, who had joined the squadron from the RAFVR the previous December. 'I went out to warn the ground staff, the bar was reopened and the news celebrated until about 3 a.m. when we all retired for an hour's shuteye.'[10] A month later, many of those toasting the approach of action were dead.

The squadron was supposed to go to Northolt for the day and return to Wittering in the afternoon. Like so many plans of the time, it had no sooner been made than desperate circumstances rendered it redundant. In the hectic weeks of the summer, squadron leaders would get used to responding to constantly changing orders as Dowding shifted Fighter Command's stance to meet each German feint and lunge. The pilots of 266 ended up spending all day at Northolt before being ordered on to Tangmere, where they arrived in the early evening. The following morning they were told to prepare to fly to Eastchurch the next day, where they were to escort Battles – the sluggish, death-trap bombers that had fared so badly in France – on raids on E-boats in French and Dutch ports. No one had brought a razor or a toothbrush so an aeroplane was dispatched to base to fetch basic kit.

Before they left they were ordered up to patrol over Tangmere, but with strict instructions not to engage the enemy unless absolutely necessary. Twenty minutes later that changed to an order to head south and attack the large bomber formation approaching Portsmouth. It was the first time the squadron had been properly in action. 'Having done so much messing about, waiting, wondering what was going to happen, getting your teeth into something was a great thrill,' Armitage remembered.[11] He shot down one of the three German machines claimed by the squadron. But there was a price to pay. Pilot Officer Dennis Ashton, who the day before had been celebrating the move south, was shot down in flames. He was twenty years old. His body was found a month later by a naval minesweeper and buried at sea.

Armitage finally arrived at Eastchurch that afternoon to find 'an odd place built on a bog with a small, L-shaped, undulating landing ground'. The officers' mess was 'an enormous erection of light girders and plywood. You entered by some steps onto a great verandah running the full length of the ante-room, which was big enough to have housed a dozen full-sized billiard tables.' In the middle was a wide chimney and four cavernous fireplaces. It was rumoured that the building had been designed for use in India but had somehow been misplaced. That evening after supper there was a conference at which the station commander explained the plan. Armitage and the others were told that the planned dawn take-off had now been cancelled because there was no precise intelligence on the whereabouts of the E-boats and that as yet there were no bombs for the Battles. He promised more information at 10 a.m., when everyone had had a good night's rest and enjoyed a late breakfast.

This pleasant prospect was disrupted by the arrival of the Germans led by Fink. The first bomb landed shortly after 7 a.m. Armitage 'awoke to find my bed waltzing about the room, which seemed most unpleasant but was caused by what in reality was a blessing . . . the bogginess of the land. The whole place shook as if we were having a major earthquake, but the bombs . . . buried themselves deeply before exploding, leaving nothing but a little pile of earth.' One bomb struck one of the ground-crew huts, killing sixteen men and injuring several more. Armitage was slightly hurt from a bomb which struck the gutter above the room where he was sleeping and exploded before it hit the ground. The same blast shook the chimney and monumental fireplaces in the mess, where several pilots ducked for shelter as the raid began. They emerged smothered in soot. Another bomb demolished a hangar, exploding the squadron's stock of ammunition, already preloaded in metal trays ready to slip into the guns when the fighters returned to rearm. But only one Spitfire was destroyed and the rest of the fighters, carefully dispersed around the airfield, were untouched. After the engine notes of the departing Germans had faded and the initial relief subsided, the 266 pilots recognized that the squadron had got off lightly. The dead airmen were a tragedy, but the brutal truth was that airmen, even highly skilled riggers and fitters, could be more easily replaced than pilots. Such relative good fortune could not last.

Hurricanes from 151 Squadron at North Weald were sent up to harry the raiders as they headed home. Fink's early unconcern about the lack of fighter protection faded. 'The RAF fighters attacked only singly, but we were a bit scattered, so we simply used the cloud layer. If the fighters were up top we dived down. If they were below we climbed up. But we lost five aircraft . . . I was furious.' After landing 'in this over-excited condition I went straight to the phone, got on to Kesselring and shouted down the line exactly what I thought about it. I asked what . . . the people at HQ thought they were doing to send us out unprotected. Poor old Kesselring was so overwhelmed he was unable to get a word in edgeways. Eventually he said, "All right, all right, I'll come over personally."'

'Eagle Day' may not have started well for the Luftwaffe, but the brightening weather offered a second opportunity. By early afternoon the meteorological reports proved correct. The sky cleared. The order was given for the main attack to begin. It was launched, not directly from across the Channel but from the south-west. A huge mass of aircraft began forming up above the Cherbourg peninsula, made up of 120 twin-engined Ju 88s and nearly 80 Stukas, protected by about 100 Me 109s and 110s. At 3.30 p.m. they began to appear as a thick cluster of blips on radar screens, stretched out across a forty-mile front and coming from the direction of the Channel Islands. The blow seemed to be aimed at the ports and air bases of the West Country, 10 Group's area. Nearly eighty Hurricanes and Spitfires from Exeter, Warmwell in Dorset, Middle Wallop in Hampshire and Tangmere were scrambled to intercept them. This was, by Fighter Command's standards, a very large number of fighters to commit to one action. The momentum of the raiding force carried it through. One group pounded Southampton. Another split off and headed for Middle Wallop, but failing accurately to locate the base dumped its bombs around the village.

10 Group was a quiet sector. Most of the pilots had never seen such an array of enemy aircraft. Kenneth Gundry, who had only arrived at 257 Squadron as a pilot officer ten days before, tried to describe the nature of the experience in a letter to his parents.

> We separated as a flight and found ourselves sitting under about eighty Me 110 fighters milling around in a huge circle. Above them were about fifty or more Me 109s. Two of our five got split away by a few stray Jerries buzzing around and then the next thing I knew was a ruddy great earthquake in my A/C [aircraft] and my control column was almost solid. On my left another Hurricane was floating about over a complete network of smoke trails left by cannon shells and incendiary. We had been attacked by another unseen bunch of Me 110s . . . [After] shaking

> the bleeder off my tail I managed to get some fairly close but ineffective deflection shots into him, but he used his extra speed and dropped clean away, down out of range leaving me with plenty of others to contend with. I joined up with another Hurricane and Jerry just seemed to dissolve. We just couldn't find any at all.[12]

When he landed he found that the tail of his Hurricane was 'shot to hell' and his starboard aileron was splintered in two and hanging off.

Despite its schoolboy language, Gundry's account must have given his parents some feeling of the frenzied struggle going on over their heads and added to their burden of worry. It also reflected the vengeful mood gripping the pilots. Later in the letter he described how 'one poor swine of a Ju 88 was spotted while going back from a raid . . . and about seven of us whooped with joy and dived on him from all directions. His rear gunner put up a marvellous show and was replaced later by the observer, I guess, but he finally went down in a complete inferno of red-hot metal and we could see the column of smoke rising from where it crashed . . . from our 'drome at Tangmere for several hours afterwards.'

The satisfaction of downing a German bomber was enormous. As one Stuka squadron left the Dorset coast for home it ran straight into the guns of 609 Squadron pilots, who shot down six of the dive-bombers, despite the presence of a fighter escort. The attack was led with customary icy professionalism by George Darley, who described later how he 'managed to slip the squadron through the fighters then went right through the Ju 87 formation, taking potshots without throttling back. This enabled the chaps behind to position themselves without having to avoid me.'[13] John Dundas, who claimed one of the victims, wrote in the squadron diary: 'Thirteen Spitfires left Warmwell for a memorable tea-time party over Lyme Bay, and an unlucky day for the species Ju 87.'[14]

'Eagle Day' ended as an anticlimax. It had decided nothing. Fighter Command could feel some satisfaction at its performance. Initial assessments put the German losses at sixty-seven with thirteen on the British side. In fact forty-seven Luftwaffe aeroplanes had been destroyed. The human cost had been greatly disproportionate. The Luftwaffe lost eighty-nine pilots and crew killed or taken prisoner, while only three British pilots died. In a war of resources these ratios were comforting.

The Germans were more successful, though, in their new aim of destroying Fighter Command's infrastructure. Despite the early warning and the large numbers of fighters put up to block the raids, the bombers had managed to get through. It was the Luftwaffe's bad judgement that had averted a catastrophe. An afternoon raid devastated the aerodrome at Detling, near Maidstone, killing sixty-seven people, military and civilian, demolishing messes crowded with airmen and flattening hangars. Once again it seemed an unlikely target to choose. It was not a Fighter Command base and its destruction had no effect on the fabric of the defences. None the less it provided a stark demonstration of the havoc that could be wrought if the bombers were directed on to an important target, such as the sector bases which acted as the synapses for the fighter control system.

Luftwaffe activity slackened off on 14 August. A raid was launched at noon that resulted in a swirling dogfight involving 200 aircraft over Dover. Manston was attacked again, and Middle Wallop, this time with more success. A month previously such action would have been memorable. At this frenetic phase of the battle it counted as a lull. Dowding took the opportunity to rotate tired and battered units out of the 11 Group area and bring fresh ones in.

The following day was bright and clear, not what the Luftwaffe's experts had forecast. In the expectation of bad weather, Goering had summoned his commanders to Karinhall, his princely hunting castle near Berlin, for an 'Eagle Day' post-mortem. The intended spectacular assertion of power had flopped, achieving little but losses. It was time to try something different. When reconnaissance flights over Scotland reported clearing skies, Goering decided to press on with another full-scale attack. This time it would be made on two fronts, taking the battle for the first time to the north of England. The forces of Luftflotte 5, based in Denmark and Norway, had taken little part in the fighting so far. Now they were to be brought into play. At the same time virtually every unit of Luftflottes 2 and 3 in France was brought to readiness. The aim was to breach and overwhelm Britain's air defences down the whole eastern and southern flanks of the island on an 800-mile front stretching from Edinburgh to Exeter.

The numbers the Germans were able to muster were greater than anything ever seen in aerial warfare. On the German side were 1,790 bombers and fighters arrayed in a huge, ominously curved crescent. Set against them Dowding had 233 serviceable Spitfires and 351 Hurricanes. The battle opened just after 11.30 when Stukas, strongly protected by an umbrella of fighters, bombed Hawkinge and Lympne on the Kent coast. At Hawkinge they dropped heavy bombs which destroyed a hangar and damaged a barracks block. They also scattered small fragmentation bombs, but the aircraft they were designed to destroy were no longer there, having by chance been ordered off half an hour earlier by the Biggin Hill commander, Group Captain Grice. There was a separate raid by Me 110s on Manston, the third in four days, and two Spitfires belonging to the luckless 266 Squadron, which had moved on there after being bombed out of Eastchurch, were destroyed on the ground. As well as being the target for snap attacks, Manston's position in the Germans' path meant that any enemy aircraft with bombs or ammunition remaining was likely to use the station as an opportunity target before racing home across the Channel. This vulnerability, the base's historian remarked, 'created an atmosphere of danger in which death could come without warning at any time of the day'.[15]

The first force from Luflotte 5 set off from Stavanger on the Norwegian coast in mid-morning. It was made up of seventy-two Heinkel bombers, protected by twenty-one Me 110s. Their targets were aerodromes in north-east England, particularly Dishforth and Usworth. A group of Heinkel seaplanes flew ahead of them, heading for Dundee, hoping to draw away the defending fighters. The ruse worked, and when the aircraft showed up on the radar, squadrons at Acklington, Drem and Catterick were brought to readiness. Once again luck came to the aid of the defenders. As a result of a navigation error, the bombers had been drifting steadily northwards as they crossed the North Sea, so they neared the coast at the point at which the feint attack had successfully lured the

British fighters. When they realized their mistake, they turned quickly southwards, but by now the fighters were in the air and heading towards them. Led by Squadron Leader Ted Graham, 72 Squadron intercepted the raiders twelve miles out to sea over the Farne Islands in Northumberland. 'None of us had ever seen so many aircraft in the sky at one time,' wrote Robert Deacon Elliot, a twenty-six-year-old pilot officer. Faced with so many choices, Graham took time to giving his order. When he tried to speak he was hampered by his chronic stutter. 'By the time he got it out,' Elliot remembered, 'the attack was on. There was a gap between the lines of bombers and the Me 110s coming up in the rear, so in there we went. I do not think they saw us to begin with. When they did, the number of bombs rapidly jettisoned was fantastic. You could see them falling away from the aircraft and dropping into the sea, literally by the hundreds. The formation became a shambles.'[16]

It was, he recorded, 'a terrific scrap'. He saw 'two separate Huns literally disintegrate'. One, a Me 110, had fallen victim to Despond Sheen, who 'fired at it and it just blew up'. His shot appears to have ignited a long-range tank fitted underneath. He was enveloped in a cloud of black smoke from the explosion, but 'started to climb up again and have another go and a 110 came straight down, head-on at me and I shot at it head-on climbing up, and its port engine went up in flames and it went over my head about ten feet away.'[17] The squadron claimed fourteen destroyed without loss. As usual, the whirling confusion of the engagement made accuracy impossible and the score would later be revised considerably downwards. But there was no doubt that serious physical and moral damage was inflicted on the raiders. A few pressed on courageously. Others scattered their bombs in the Newcastle area before turning out over the daunting expanse of the North Sea. Squadron after squadron came up to hound them on their way. A second large raid, launched from Ålborg in Denmark, was also heavily punished.

The losses suffered by Luftflotte 5 effectively removed it from the battle. It was never again to mount a significant daylight attack from the north on Britain's defences. The Germans had lost 20 per cent of their aircraft, with eighty-one air crew killed or missing. In the north there was little to show for it. Driffield airfield had been hammered, but it was a bomber base and the destruction made no difference to the immediate battle. In the south, the raids did much more damage. The airfield at Martlesham, used as a forward base for squadrons from Debden, was heavily bombed and knocked out for forty-eight hours. Middle Wallop was attacked but escaped lightly. Croydon was the worst hit. The bombs smashed into the terminal buildings, where smart travellers had presented themselves in the inter-war years for flights to the Continent, and destroyed hangars and stores. Some bombs had delayed fuses, exploding hours after the aeroplanes had gone. They killed sixty-eight people and cast a pall of nervous gloom over the base. The destruction was terrible but not catastrophic. Croydon was of secondary importance, unlike Kenley, which had apparently been the real target.

The fifteenth of August became 'Black Thursday' in the folklore of the German air force. It was a tribute to the Luftwaffe's morale that the attacks of 16 August were almost as heavy and were pressed home with the same energy as the day before. But, to the increasing concern of the German commanders, the spirit of the defenders appeared as resilient as ever. If anything, resistance seemed to have taken on a more bitter quality, with the British pilots eager to inflict as much punishment as possible. When a raid came in close to Hornchurch just after noon, the nine Spitfires of 54 Squadron sent up to meet it not only prevented the bombers from reaching the aerodrome, but chased them all the way back to the French coast, shooting down three on the way without loss. For once Al Deere was not with them. He had been forced to abandon his machine the previous day after being shot up on a similar sortie, pursuing an Me 109 all the way back to the Pas de Calais.

The grimness of the defenders' determination was evident in a new tactic, the head-on attack, which began to be adopted by some pilots. It required exceptional sang-froid and was fatal if misjudged. When bombers crossed the Kent coast at Dungeness at noon, 111 Squadron, which had been one of the first units to develop the technique, climbed up to meet them. Among the pilots was Henry Ferriss, who had abandoned his medical studies to take up a short-service commission before the war and had just celebrated his twenty-second birthday. He was one of the most tenacious and experienced pilots in the squadron and had shot down at least nine enemy aircraft. On this day he flew his Hurricane straight towards an approaching Dornier 17 and opened fire. Neither pilot turned away and the two collided and crashed to earth. This event did not dissuade 111 Squadron from continuing with the tactic. Ben Bowring, a Blenheim pilot who answered a call for volunteers for single-seater fighter units, arrived at the squadron a few days afterwards. His motivation was to avenge the death of his best friend, a fellow pilot, George Moore. 'I didn't really think of having any fear at the time,' he said later. 'What had overcome it was the desire to get one's own back for everything that was being done to your friends.'[18] He found the head-on attacks 'nerve-racking' but worth while. The pilots were grimly pleased to notice that, unlike beam or rear attacks, head-on assaults produced an immediate and dramatic effect. 'You could see the front of the aircraft crumple,' Bowring said. He also noticed that the bomber pilots reared up from their seats and stumbled backwards in a futile attempt to escape the stream of bullets.

Sheer weight of numbers meant that the Germans still got through. At 1 p.m. on 16 August it was the turn of Tangmere, most bucolic of Fighter Command's bases, to feel the full force of the German attack. A raid the day before had done some damage before being beaten away by 43 Squadron. This time the Stukas, escorted by Me 109s, gathered in a great buzzing mass over the Isle of Wight. Then, as a signal flare looped down from the lead aircraft, they closed on Tangmere, just across the water, and tipped into their dives. The remaining hangars were flattened, along with the officers' mess, the station workshops, stores, sick quarters and shelters. Six Blenheims belonging to the fledgling Fighter Interception Unit were wrecked. The bombs killed ten of the ground staff and three civilians.

Most of the Hurricanes of 1, 43 and 601 Squadrons were already in the air, but too late to block the attack. They managed to destroy seven dive-bombers as they fled. Two Hurricanes were shot down during the interception. One of these was flown by Billy Fiske, of 601 Squadron.

William Meade Fiske was the son of an international banker from Chicago, an Anglophile who had gone to Cambridge University, married the former wife of the Earl of Warwick, set a record on the Cresta Run and moved in the sporting circles from which 601 Squadron drew its pre-war members. He had volunteered for the RAF two weeks after the outbreak of war and was posted to join his friends in 601 Squadron at Tangmere on 10 July. Fiske was an above-average pilot and a fast learner. He had never flown a Hurricane before making his first flight with the squadron. How he was shot down was never established. He managed to crash-land on the aerodrome and was carried out of the cockpit by an ambulance crew, who reported that he was suffering only from superficial burns on the face and hand. The following day he was visited in hospital by the squadron adjutant who reported that he was 'perky as hell'.[19] But later that day he was dead, apparently having succumbed to shock. Fiske's social standing and American citizenship ensured that his death was extensively reported. The tragedy also had propaganda uses to a government intent on drawing America into the war. Fiske was presented, plausibly enough, as an idealist who had defied the neutrality laws to fight in the cause of humanity. A plaque was placed in St Paul's Cathedral to commemorate 'an American Citizen Who Died That England Might Live'. He was one of eleven pilots from the United States who flew with Fighter Command that summer.

Death was now becoming as familiar to Fighter Command's rear echelon as it was to the pilots. The ground crews were proving themselves as courageous under fire as the men they supported. When a raid warning was sounded at Warmwell, three 609 airmen, Corporal Bob Smith and Leading Aircraftmen Harry Thorley and Ken Wilson, ran out to wind down the thick steel-plated doors on a hangar to protect the Spitfires inside. A bomb smashed through the roof and all three were killed. The pilots using the airfield as a forward base felt particular sympathy for the airmen stuck on the ground under continuous threat of bombardment but unable to defend themselves. John Nicholas of 65 Squadron watched an airman grimly driving a petrol bowser out to a refuelling point during a raid. The driver was decapitated by a salvo from an Me 109 and the bowser went up in flames. Al Deere and the other 54 Squadron pilots were baffled by the insistence on keeping Manston operational, and hated flying from there. Its advanced position was no advantage. It was too far forward to allow a straight climb up to interception height. It was a great relief to pilots and ground crew when, by the end of the month, the airfield was virtually closed down as a fighter base. 'There seemed no tactical advantage in continuing to use an airfield so far forward, especially when it had such a damaging effect on the morale of the pilots and ground crews,' Deere wrote later.[20] The suspicion was that Fighter Command believed that to pull back would have handed a moral victory to the Luftwaffe. If so, it was uncharacteristically stupid and wasteful thinking on Dowding's part.

Civilians, too, had now made their first chilly acquaintance with the meaning of aerial warfare. On 16 August bombs fell on the suburbs of south London. The following day the BBC broadcast an eyewitness account by a young woman, Marjery Wace, who had been in Wimbledon when Dorniers passed overhead. She refused to go to a shelter, instead keeping company with a bedridden old lady. 'The house absolutely shook as if it was made of cardboard,' she told listeners. 'It was horribly alarming while it lasted, and I found myself longing to be in the open. I expect if I had been in the open I should have been longing to be in the house.' After dark she went out to inspect the damage. It was 'a beautiful August night. I could just see a dim outline of a few people sitting in front of their houses . . . as I arrived a stream of people began to enter further up the street . . . they came quietly in groups of three or four. The only sound was from small children crying from sheer weariness as they were carried home by their fathers. And what homes to have to come back to. It was just a small street of small houses, but now the glass had been blown in and the whole insides of the rooms destroyed.' Two things struck Miss Wace as she walked around. One was that 'there was a great deal of truth in the soldiers' attitude to the chances of being hit . . . it's simply a question of luck.' The other was the sight of women patiently cleaning up. 'There's a strange impulse in every housewife to go on sweeping whatever state the world is in,' she observed. 'For quite a number of people explained to me how they had swept up rooms that they agreed no one could possibly live in again.'[21]

The violence was widening and deepening, but the pilots could take comfort in the thought that the Germans, in inflicting it, were paying a high price. On 18 August they at last had their revenge on the Stukas. At about 4 p.m. nearly thirty Ju 87s approached the radar station at Poling on the Sussex coast and prepared to attack. The sun was in their eyes, blinding them to the presence of the Hurricanes of 43 Squadron, who swooped in, to be joined by fighters from four more squadrons. The Stukas were just going into their dive when the attack was launched. In the fight that ensued, sixteen dive-bombers were shot down and two more crashed on the way home. The escorting Me 109s offered little protection. Once the Stukas plunged, it was impossible to keep up with them. They managed to catch up with the British fighters after the damage was done, shooting down four Hurricanes and two Spitfires, but losing eight of their own in the process.

The episode persuaded Luftwaffe commanders to withdraw the Ju 87 from the front-line bombing strength for the remainder of the summer fighting, though a few more sorties were flown. News of the losses stoked Goering's anger at the lack of progress and the elusiveness of the swift victory he had predicted. Once again he called his chief officers to Karinhall to harangue them and issue new directives. Dowding, too, was looking back over ten days of heavy fighting and trying to guess how the battle would develop. Both commanders now knew that the fight would be long and that stamina and morale would decide it.

14

Attrition

Life for the squadrons based in the south was, by the end of August, being lived in a daze of exhaustion, exhilaration and fear. Duty now stretched from dawn to dusk. The day started when the pilots were woken at 4 a.m. and driven out to dispersal, where they ate breakfast in the half-light. Pilots made two, three and four sorties a day, lasting up to an hour each, and on bad days could expect to be in combat on half of them. The weather provided no respite. Of the thirty-seven days from 1 August, twenty-two were 'fine' or 'fair', culminating in a glorious spell at the end of the month when the summer reached its zenith. There were only ten days during which cloud or rain were recorded anywhere. The pilots came to hate the sight of another cornflower-blue morning and yearned for fog and drizzle.

The fatigue was paralysing. Moving to Kenley from the north, Christopher Foxley-Norris was struck by 'how incredibly tired people were. They would go to sleep while you were talking to them.'[1] Al Deere, sitting down at breakfast after a morning flight, noticed that George Gribble 'had dropped off to sleep and with his head nodding lower and lower was gently swaying to and fro in his seat, his bacon and eggs untouched in front of him. As we watched, his face pitched forward into his eggs, much to the amusement of the assembled pilots.'[2] These blackouts could have potentially fatal results. Denys Gillam was one night ordered up to investigate a raid despite the fact that he had been flying all day, and fell off to sleep in the cockpit. 'The next thing I knew the speed was building up and there were lights in front of me and I couldn't make out what it was, and I realized I was upside down diving hard for the ground.'[3]

In the hectic weeks from August to mid September days off were rare. When they came, many pilots simply went to bed. Sleep came down like a coma. Frank Usmar of 41 Squadron woke up, after ten blissful hours unconscious, to learn that a full-scale raid had taken place while he was out. The hours waiting at dispersal appeared to offer the chance of rest. The pilots lounged in Lloyd Loom chairs or deckchairs, reading magazines, playing chess or draughts or cards, occasionally kicking a football or tossing around a cricket ball or dozing in the heat. There was tea to drink, sometimes beer, and a Naafi van would deliver sandwiches. The smell of cut grass and hedgerow flowers mingled with the stink of high-octane fuel, and the drone of insects overlaid the twanging of plates and wires as the Hurricanes and Spitfires baked in the sun.

But the imminence of danger made it impossible to relax. Every pilot had one ear cocked for the jangle of the telephone and the order to scramble. 'Hanging around was the worst part, waiting for the bloody phone to ring,' Robin Appleford, a pilot with 66 Squadron and, at eighteen years old, one of the youngest men flying that summer, said later.[4] For years after the war, the sound of a telephone bell would bring a rush of anxiety. But the call did at least dispel the vapour of unease that clung to the dispersal hut in the hours before action. Appleford found that 'at readiness . . . you were never actually ready when the order came, but as soon as you started running out to the aircraft, once you started the engine, it was all right'. Frank Usmar also hated the sound of the operations phone. He too noted that 'when you were running to your machine, the adrenaline took over . . . Once you got in your aircraft and were roaring away you seemed to have another feeling altogether.'[5]

The apprehension was sharpened by the knowledge of what lay ahead. Some glimpses of the fighting of August and September have come down to us through snatches of cine-film shot by the few camera-guns to be mounted on fighters at the time. Most of the sequences are only seconds long, but they manage to convey something of the confusion and desperation that flooded each high-velocity encounter. They also make it clear how crowded the sky would become when large numbers of aeroplanes clashed inside a few cubic miles of air. In one clip, filmed by Noel Agazarian as he closed on a bomber, the wing of what looks like an Me 110 flashes out of nowhere across the path of his fighter, missing it by a matter of feet, creating a jolt of shock that carries down the years. Despite the shakiness of the images, we can see the essential drama. The cameras were activated when the guns were fired, so the first thing the viewer notices are the white smudges of tracer crawling out towards the hunted aircraft. Often the intended victim seems oblivious, or impervious, ploughing on through the sky while the skein of bullet trails floats harmlessly by. Sometimes the camera records a kill. The fatal moment is instantly recognizable. A piece of debris detaches itself from the enemy machine and goes spinning by, or a gust of flame flares from an engine. A very few sequences last long enough to record the moment of complete destruction when the bomber erupts in a banner of smoke and fire, blotting out the attacker's vision as he swoops through the cloud of debris and burning fuel that is all that is left of his victim.

Official words, particularly the formulas employed by the pilots when, arriving back exhausted after a sortie, they were required by the intelligence officer to fill in an 'F form' combat report, were inadequate to describe the extraordinary drama of what was happening. Even afterwards, the participants often found it hard to find language powerful enough to describe the things they had seen and done.

Tom Gleave, who led 253 Squadron at Kenley, succeeded with a vivid account of an encounter with an enormous force of Me 109s cruising above Maidstone at 17,000 feet. 'Shown up clearly by the sun,' he wrote, 'and stretching fore and aft as far as the eye could see were rows of 109s riding above the haze, each row flying in line astern and well spaced out – all of them heading south south-east. It was a fantastic sight.' Gleave, until now untested in a full-scale battle, was in a section of three Hurricanes. Undeterred by the ludicrously uneven odds, he charged in. Flying into the rows of Messerchmitts, he lined up a target and fired at 175 yards range.

> The thin streaks of yellow tracer flame ran parallel for what appeared to be about seventy-five yards and then bent away to the left in a succession of curves. The hiss of pneumatics, the smell of cordite in the cockpit and the feel of the nose dipping slightly under the recoil all lent excitement to the first real combat in my short-lived career at Kenley. Most of my shot appeared to be going into the engine cowling and cockpit. It was the tracer, fired on a turn, which produced the strange illusion of the shot entering at right angles. The Hun flew straight for a while and then turned gently on to his back. After a short burst of about four seconds I stopped firing and as I did so, I saw sunlit pieces of shattered perspex spiralling aft like a shower of tracer. The Hun slewed slightly while on his back, his nose dropped and he dived beneath out of my sight, going straight down.

Gleave himself came under fire immediately afterwards and discovered he was in the midst of a mass of 109s. 'Tracers passed above and below, curving downwards and giving the impression of flying in a gigantic cage of gilt wire.'[6]

The large numbers of aircraft increased the rawness and intimacy of combat. Dennis Armitage remembered 'the flick of an aircraft's belly as you shot underneath not ten feet below at a relative speed of ten miles a minute'.[7] The fighter pilots were shooting at machines, but at such close quarters it was impossible to ignore the fact that inside them were men. 'It was really quite a shock,' Brian Kingcome said later, 'when suddenly an aeroplane you were firing at would erupt bodies. It brought it home to you . . . that there were actually people in there who you were killing.'[8]

To the novice fighter pilot, the overwhelming feeling when confronted by all this apparent chaos was bewilderment. Non-aviators, when taken through the manoeuvres of a dogfight, are made immediately aware of how extraordinarily disorienting even the most basic moves can be. Sky and earth, left and right, up and down, alternate at intervals of fractions of a second, allowing no time for adjustment. Thought, in fact, has little part in the proceedings. Fighter pilots *in extremis* operate on instinct. Flying a hugely powerful, nimble and sensitive machine is a feat in itself. Flying one in such a way as to bring guns to bear on another fast and manoeuvrable target, while avoiding being shot oneself in the process, is considerably more difficult.

Many of those now sitting at dispersal were attempting to do the second while still having barely mastered the first. The squadrons were better manned than they had been at any time since the spring. Dowding got 53 volunteers from Bomber Command and the Army Co-operation squadrons, and the Fleet Air Arm also contributed. But the high number of pilots 'on state' had still mainly been achieved by compressing training courses and rushing novices into action. It was painful but unavoidable. No amount of practice was sufficient preparation for battles that were unprecedented in size and intensity and whose tactics evolved every day.

Inevitably the untried pilots were often quick to fall. There were at least two cases of pilots being killed on the day they reported to their squadron. Flying Officer Arthur Rose-Price arrived at Kenley on the morning of 2 September to join 501 Squadron and was immediately sent on patrol. In the afternoon he went off on another sortie and was shot down over Dungeness. Pilot Officer Jaroslav Sterbacek turned up at 310 Squadron at Duxford on 31 August. Within a few hours he was over the Thames estuary, attacking Dornier 17s. By the evening he was dead, shot down by Me 109s. Both men were practised pilots. Rose-Price held a short-service commission before the war and had been an instructor. Sterbacek had served with the Czech air force and later with the Armée de l'Air. Neither of them had any real combat experience. As was shown repeatedly, flying skill alone did not guarantee success as a fighter pilot, nor necessarily improved chances of survival.

Terence Lovell Gregg, a New Zealander, who at seventeen was the youngest pilot to receive a flying licence in Australasia, had spent the war as an instructor and on operations room duties when he was given command of 87 Squadron in the second week of July. He was acutely aware of his lack of practical knowledge and allowed his flight commanders to lead the squadron until he felt he was ready. On 15 August an order came to intercept a formation of a hundred Stukas and Messerschmitts. Lovell Gregg felt the time had come to take command in the air. He took off with eight of his pilots, including Roland Beamont, who was surprised to find they were setting course directly for the approaching Germans. 'I just had time to think, "I wonder what sort of tactic he's going to employ. Is he going to turn up-sun and try and dive out of the sun at them or go round to the right and come in behind?"' To his pilots' alarm it became clear he was going to do neither. Instead he 'bored straight into the middle . . . we seemed to be going into the largest formation of aeroplanes you ever saw. Then his voice came on the radio and said: "Target ahead, come on chaps, let's surround them!" Just nine of us.'[9] Lovell Gregg's Hurricane was soon in flames. He tried to land, crashed into a copse and was killed.

Most of the victims of the fighting of August and September had joined their squadrons before July, and had at least had some time to learn control procedures and get a taste of what was coming before the all-out assault began. But among the dead there were also those who had gone into battle hopelessly unprepared. Many were sergeants who had come through the RAFVR, like Geoffrey Gledhill, who arrived at 6 Operational Training Unit at Sutton Bridge on 6 July for his fighter training. After only four weeks he was posted to 238 Squadron at Middle Wallop. A week later he was shot down and killed.

Pilot Officer Neville Solomon, another RAFVR graduate, was particularly unfitted for action. After basic training he had been taught to fly Blenheim fighter bombers, then abruptly sent on 19 July to join 17 Squadron at Debden. When it became clear he had no Hurricane experience, he was sent back to Sutton Bridge for a conversion course. He was back after twenty days, on 15 August. Three days later, apparently after his first sortie, he was reported missing. He was not around long enough for the squadron diarist to learn to spell his name correctly and is referred to as 'Soloman' in the three sparse mentions he receives.

In 54 Squadron Al Deere received two replacement pilots from New

Zealand who had never previously flown a Spitfire and made just two trips in a Hurricane. There was only time to take them up in a Miles Master trainer, then brief them on the controls of the Spitfire. 'They'd go off for one solo flight and circuit. Then they were into battle . . . These two lasted two trips and they both finished up in Dover hospital. One was pulled out of the Channel. The other landed by parachute.'[10] During the phoney war, pilots would get at least twenty-five hours' experience on a Spitfire before being posted. Some of the longer-serving pilots tried to pass on what knowledge they could. In 87 Squadron, Roland Beamont would 'take our new pilots and put them in the hands of our most experienced pilots and send them off to do dogfight practices . . . The experienced pilot by demonstration would show the junior just how little he knew about it and give him tips as to what he could do to improve his skills, because there were ways you could use your aeroplane to better advantage once you knew it very well. The essence of combat flying was to know your aeroplane's absolute limits so that when you were called upon to use them you could actually get to the limits of the performance without endangering you or the aeroplane.'[11]

For most incoming pilots, though, the learning process was not so gentle. In 616 Squadron, where Denys Gillam was a flight commander, an effort was made 'to give replacement pilots a sporting chance. I always had one as my number two. The trouble was that they had too little experience. The average amount of flying they'd done was about 100 to 120 hours only and their entire attention was focused on the ability to fly the plane rather than to fight. One could get them to the battle reasonably well, but once it was joined they were sitting ducks.'[12] David Cox, a sergeant pilot with 19 Squadron, was taken under the wing of Flying Officer Leonard Haines. 'I can give credit to him for the fact that I stayed alive as long as I did,' he said later. 'He used to say, just keep my tail wheel in front of you and just stick to me. Don't worry about shooting things. If you can follow me, you'll learn to throw a Spitfire about, which I did.'[13]

Others doubted the value of the practice. Bob Doe, who had spent the summer with 234 Squadron in the West Country and destroyed at least five German aircraft, noticed that 'when action happened an experienced pilot would treat his plane purely as a gun platform, which meant that he wouldn't know what was happening to his plane or his number two . . . Although this phase only lasted for a matter of seconds, his poor number two would be concentrating on staying with his leader, who was doing impossible things with his machine, and at the most dangerous time he would not be seeing the enemy around him.'[14]

John Worrall of 32 Squadron rejected three newcomers who arrived without having passed through an Operational Training Unit, considering they would weaken the unit and that sending them into action was tantamount to condemning them to death. Sailor Malan took a tougher view. One of his young pilots was clearly never going to succeed as a fighter pilot. He was, he told his biographer, 'a boy born to be killed. You knew or felt that it was only a question of time before he was picked off.' But Malan felt that 'the cruellest thing in the world would have been to tell him to drop out of the flight, and recommend him for an operational training unit. He had lots of guts. He struggled very hard to be a good pilot. But everything was against him.'[15] Fate took its course. 'We were on patrol one day with this boy flying No. 4 astern. Then suddenly, looking round, he had gone. A Jerry must have sneaked up behind and picked him off.'

The demand for pilots meant standards, inevitably, were relaxed. Candidates who would have been rejected before the war now made it into Fighter Command. Eustace Holden, a twenty-eight-year-old flight commander with 501 Squadron, remembered a new arrival who was 'nice enough, but it was easy for me to see that he shouldn't have been there . . . He thought it was marvellous to be in this front-line squadron, but he wasn't good enough. I could see him being shot up in no time at all.' Holden took him to one side and 'had a few words . . . I said that I wasn't at all sure that he was up to it and I thought it better if he left the squadron. The poor chap was very nearly in tears and it made me feel awful but I still thought that he should go.' Later, the whole squadron took off on an interception. 'This one chap was lagging behind, why I don't know. There were three Messerschmitts up above . . . I kept telling him to come on, come on, catch up. And sure enough one of these chaps came whizzing down and shot him down in the Channel, and he was never seen again. I blamed myself for that.'[16]

Bad weather between 19 and 24 August brought a respite from the grinding routine of daily heavy raids. The pause coincided with another reassessment by Goering of the direction the battle was taking. The impression of overwhelming force created by masses of aircraft moving inexorably in rigid formation towards their targets was misleading. The Luftwaffe was suffering badly. On 15, 16 and 18 August it lost more than fifty aircraft each day and human losses were heavy. Among the casualties were 172 officers, dead, seriously wounded and missing, including 23 of senior rank. The morale of the crews was fraying. The German fighter pilots were at least as tired as their British counterparts. They got little leave or time off. One commander, Oberst Carl Viek, based at Wissant overlooking the Channel, tried to keep his men on the ground in bad weather and send them off for a swim, and forbade those he judged to be closest to cracking up from flying. This attitude earned him a reprimand from his headquarters for 'softness'.

On 19 August Goering summoned his commanders for another conference and another blast of criticism. He blamed the bomber losses on the failure of the fighters to give proper protection, only just stopping short of an outright accusation of cowardice. The charge ignored the by now obvious fact that it was impossible for an Me 109 to keep up with a Stuka once it went into its dive. Also, as he must have known, the fighters were severely restricted in the time they could spend shepherding the bombers by the amount of fuel they could carry. Bomber crews often watched in dismay as the Messerchmitts left them to their fate and turned away to run for home before their petrol gave out.

Goering insisted that the fighters' main task now was the close escort of the bombers. He dismissed the expert view of experienced men like Galland that the most effective way of dealing with the British fighters was free hunts, which by some estimates accounted for the majority of the RAF's losses. The Me 109s would now also have to cover the Me 110s, which had proved themselves vulnerable. Fighters would be protecting fighters. The Stukas, Goering conceded, were fatally unsuited for the job. They would be withdrawn until they could fulfil their proper role of supporting the army when it finally blitzed a path across Britain. The performance would not have been complete without some bloodletting. Several commanders were dismissed, and younger more aggressive officers promoted, among them Galland.

On the same day, Dowding and Park conducted their own analysis. Following the meeting, the sector controllers in 11 Group were issued with new instructions that augmented other orders issued two days previously, designed to close the loopholes in the defence revealed by the preceding ten days of heavy fighting. Between 8 and 16 August, Fighter Command had lost about ninety pilots and another fifty had been wounded, many of them seriously. With the aircraft problem on its way to being solved, pilots were Dowding's most precious resource. The ability to resist depended on suppressing losses to a level that maintained continuity and experience in squadrons, allowing them continuously to regenerate themselves and maintain their effectiveness. It was essential to reduce casualties, impossible to halt them. Dowding and Park resolved that the lives that were going to be lost should be expended in the most effective manner possible.

Preventing pilots from flying over the sea was one way of stemming losses. In addition, orders were again issued to controllers and commanders to stop squadrons taking on German fighters as they swooped in over the coast on free hunts. Park had tried to hold his fighters back from these costly clashes, but the encounters had persisted. It was now emphasized heavily that the overwhelming priority was to knock down the bombers, an approach which, it was hoped, would limit the damage done to the airfields, further injure the Luftwaffe's morale and on the British side slow the attrition of fighters, and more importantly of pilots.

The survival of the fighter bases, particularly the 11 Group sector aerodromes, Northolt, Tangmere, Kenley, Biggin Hill, Hornchurch, North Weald and Debden, had become an overwhelming concern. They were the junction boxes in Fighter Command's control system in the south-east. They housed the sector operations rooms which responded to the information coming in from radar and the Observer Corps and juggled the available resources to meet each threat. Their destruction or serious disruption would paralyse Fighter Command's protective reflexes. The British inferiority in numbers meant survival depended on advance knowledge of the direction and dimensions of German attacks and a command and control structure that made the most efficient use of assets. Without it, the RAF would be fighting blind and weight of numbers would inevitably carry the day.

The key stations had got off lightly in the opening phase of the assault as the Luftwaffe's faulty intelligence and misconceptions directed it to RAF bases which were unconnected with the immediate defensive effort. But the devastation done to Tangmere on 16 August, and the raid on Kenley two days later, which destroyed most of the hangars and forced the evacuation of the sector operations room, suggested the German aim was improving. Park ordered the controllers to ensure that, when the squadrons based around London were in the air fending off mass attacks, 12 Group be asked to provide patrols to protect the sector bases north of the Thames at Debden, North Weald and Hornchurch.

On 24 August, with Goering's admonitions ringing in their ears, the Luftwaffe commanders in France resumed their attack on the RAF in the air, and now increasingly on the ground. The first targets were Hornchurch, North Weald and Manston. Air Vice-Marshal Trafford Leigh-Mallory, the commander of 12 Group, was called on to provide cover in keeping with Park's new directive. Only 19 Squadron turned up at North Weald in time to get in a few shots with their still-malfunctioning cannons before the raiders departed. The rest were guided to their destinations by the columns of smoke and fire rising into the clear afternoon sky. The raids destroyed messes, stores and living quarters and a few aircraft, but barely affected the bases' ability to operate.

The disappointing performance by 12 Group was to mark the start of a feud fought out at the highest levels throughout the rest of the summer, and it opened a debate on tactics that rumbled on into the post-war years. Leigh-Mallory believed that the most effective way to deploy fighters was *en masse*, grouped together in what came to be known as a 'Big Wing'.

He had tried to assemble such a force over Duxford before sending it to the rescue of the north London stations, but there had been confusion over the order. It took time to put a formation of fifty to sixty aircraft together – at least three-quarters of an hour, even when conditions were ideal. The delay meant that, according to Tom Gleave, speaking later as a distinguished RAF historian, 'of thirty-two Big Wings launched by 12 Group, only seven met the enemy and only once did a Big Wing arrive first at its intended point of interception'.[17] Despite this dismal record and the almost universal scepticism of the pilots, Leigh-Mallory and Douglas Bader, regarded as the author of the idea, persisted in championing the tactic after the war and insisting that a battle-winning innovation had been wilfully neglected.

On the night of 24 August bombs fell on central London for the first time since 1918. Goering had given his commanders the right to choose where they should aim their attacks, reserving for himself the right to order the bombing of Liverpool and London. Hitler did not, at this stage, wish to jeopardize the chance of a political settlement by a massacre of civilians. On the night of 24th/25th a fleet of more than a hundred bombers set off westwards across the Channel to resume their bombardment of Short's aircraft factory at Rochester and the oil storage farm at Thameshaven. Instead of unloading their explosives, however, they flew on, unmolested by night fighters, and dumped their bombs on the department stores of Oxford Street, City offices, the terraced streets of Stepney, Finsbury, Bethnal Green and East Ham. The breach of orders was blamed on an error in navigation. Goering, anticipating a storm of rage when Hitler heard the news, demanded to know who was responsible and threatened the guilty with a transfer to the infantry. The error detonated an explosive chain of events. The following night, eighty-one Wellington and Hampden bombers flew to Berlin and dropped incendiary bombs, most of which landed in open country and allotments, and leaflets. The raid was followed, on Churchill's orders, on 28, 30 and 31 August, and would accelerate a dynamic that was to have dire consequences for Londoners in the months ahead.

For the moment, though, the bombing of central London appeared an aberration. The Luftwaffe continued its daylight pounding of the airfields. On 25 August the weight of the attacks shifted to the south and west and attacks were launched on Portland, Weymouth and Warmwell airfield in Dorset. The raid on Warmwell was intercepted by Hurricanes from 17 Squadron and only a handful of bombers got through, hitting two hangars and destroying, with a lucky bomb, the station's telephone and teleprinter cables. On the morning of 26 August the attacks swung back to the 11 Group airfields, with a formation of forty Heinkels and twelve Dorniers making for Biggin Hill. In keeping with the new orders, they were protected by eighty Me 109s and some Me 110s, a ratio of almost two to one. Park sent up seventy Hurricanes and Spitfires and a handful of Defiants to block them, and the raid was eventually turned away without reaching its target. The second wave was aimed at Debden and Hornchurch. This time forty Dorniers were protected by eighty Me 110s and forty 109s. By the time they approached their targets, however, the escorts were running low on fuel. The increasingly apparent vulnerability of the Me 110s meant that the effective strength of the fighter screen was the forty Me 109s, who had the schizophrenic task of fending off attacks on both bombers and their fellow fighters.

The raid began to falter before it reached Debden, with most of the bombers turning south shortly after crossing the Essex coast. Half a dozen Dorniers pressed on unprotected, and dropped bombs that killed three airmen, destroyed buildings and severely damaged an aircraft. The Hornchurch raid was aborted before it reached its target. A third wave was launched in the afternoon against Portsmouth and Southampton, and was also repulsed without significant damage being done to targets. Fifteen bombers had been shot down for no real result. The bomber crews and their commanders complained that they were still not receiving adequate protection, a charge that cannot have been amiably received from the fighter units, which lost fifteen Me 109s and five Me 110s, the former paying the price of trying to protect the latter.

But this was a battle of attrition. Fighter Command's satisfaction at having beaten off the attacks was tempered by the knowledge that victory or defeat would be determined by the ability of Fighter Command to absorb protracted punishment. At its simplest that meant having a steady supply of men and machines to replace losses. But equally important was the quality of morale and the maintenance of squadrons as functioning fighting units.

A day like 26 August could have a devastating effect on the fabric and spirit of a squadron. No. 616 Squadron had arrived at Kenley on 19 August, having spent most of the summer in Leconfield in Yorkshire, and was anxious to get into the action. Hugh Dundas recorded that, 'Joy and jubilation marked our last hours at Leconfield'. Before setting off there was a genial lunch in the mess with plenty to drink. Most of the original auxiliary pilots were still there. Dundas reflected afterwards that 'it never occurred to us that we should not continue together indefinitely'.

They arrived at the new station to a sobering scene. Kenley had been blitzed the day before. Wrecked aircraft and lorries littered the edge of the field and the landing ground was dotted with newly filled craters. The atmosphere in the officers' mess 'was taut and heavily overlaid with weariness. Both the station operations staff and the pilots of 615 Squadron [who were based there] . . . showed signs of strain in their faces and behaviour. The fierce rage of the station commander when a ferry pilot overshot the runway while landing a precious replacement Spitfire was frightening to behold.'

On 26 August, Spitfires of 616 were scrambled and directed to Dover and Dungeness in anticipation of the first raid of the day. They arrived too late to attack the incoming Heinkels, but were quickly set upon by the accompanying Me 109s. George Moberly's aircraft was hit and he baled out. His parachute failed to open and he plunged into the sea to his death. Sergeant Marmaduke Ridley, an ex-apprentice who had joined the squadron early in 1940, was also killed. Teddy St Aubyn, the aristocratic ex-Guards officer and ante-room wit, was shot down and badly burned.

Moberly had learned to fly privately after leaving Ampleforth, the Catholic public school, and had been one of the first two officers to join the squadron. He visited Dundas the day before in hospital at Canterbury, where he was recovering after being shot down. 'He talked to me about personal affairs, about his family and his property,' Dundas wrote. 'He told me that he wanted me to have his personal belongings if he were killed. I had a strong feeling that he had a premonition that he would be.'[18] Moberly's death was particularly painful for Denys Gillam, who counted him as his best friend in the squadron.

Two other pilots, Roy Marples and William Walker, were shot down the same day. Walker, who had been posted to the squadron from the RAFVR, which he joined while a young trainee executive at a brewery, had been woken that morning at 3.30 a.m. by his orderly with a cup of tea. There was a first breakfast at 4 a.m., the usual sombre affair eaten in silence. If pilots were still at dispersal at 8 a.m., a second breakfast – eggs, bacon, sausages, coffee – would be brought out. Walker was to be grateful for his second breakfast that day. He took off with Yellow Section, made up of himself, St Aubyn and Ridley, and was caught when the Me 109s pounced over Dungeness. He decided to bale out, but when he tried to leave found he was still attached to the cockpit by the radio lead fixed to his flying helmet. 'I took off my helmet and fell out. I was still at 20,000 feet and pulled the ripcord. The sky, which moments before had been so full of aircraft, was now without a single plane in view. I had no idea where I was and 10/10th cloud below obscured any view of land. It seemed to take ages to reach the clouds, and eventually on passing through them I was concerned to see that I was over the Channel.' Walker sensibly kicked off his heavy flying boots and watched them spiral down for 'what seemed like ages'. Splashing down and releasing his harness, he looked around, saw land, but did not know whether it was England or France. He noticed the hull of a wrecked boat protruding from the water, swam to it, clambered up and awaited rescue. He was now very cold and very tired. He was, in fact, close to the Kent coast. The wreck he was sitting on was one of many that had come to grief on the Goodwin Sands. After half an hour a fishing boat appeared and he was helped aboard and given tea and whisky.

He was taken into Ramsgate harbour, cheered by a small crowd of civilians, given a packet of ten Player's cigarettes – the Fighter Boys' favourites – and taken to hospital, where his injured leg was examined. He was put to bed under a canopy of electric lights, which it was hoped would thaw his hypothermia. It was eight hours before he warmed up. The hospital had been bombed and the kitchen was out of action. The only food available was two slices of bread and butter. The following day he was put in an ambulance to be taken to the RAF hospital at Halton in Buckinghamshire. On the way they had to pick up an airman from Manston, shell-shocked after the almost constant bombardment. They passed by Kenley so Walker could pick up some kit. He then told the driver to take him to dispersal so he could bid *au revoir* to his comrades. To his dismay, 'hardly any pilots remained. I had not heard of the appalling losses . . . nor had I heard of what had happened to the other members of Yellow Section'. The ambulance picked its way across London, taking detours where the roads were closed by bombing. The seventy-mile journey from the coast took almost twelve hours.[19]

Within eight days of arriving at Kenley, 616 Squadron lost five pilots killed or missing, with five others hospitalized. Half of the pilots who had flown down in high spirits from Leconfield were gone. Denys Gillam, who although only a flight commander was effectively leading the squadron, asked for it to be given a week's rest to train up replacement pilots. 'It was very unpopular to suggest that the squadron should be taken out of the line for a short time to give them the chance to recover,' he said later. 'They wouldn't do it and Dowding was very put out by this and kept us there another week. By then we were down to about four pilots.'[20] On 2 September, Gillam was shot down and wounded, and the following day the remaining pilots moved to the relative safety of Coltishall, near Norwich, to re-form.

The blitz on airfields continued on 28 August. By now a pattern had developed in which Luftwaffe attacks came in distinct phases. The first wave arrived over the Kent coast at breakfast time and split up, with one formation heading west and the other turning north towards Rochford. Fighters were sent up, including twelve Defiants, which went in to attack the bombers, oblivious to the Me 109s hiding in the sun. Four Defiants were shot down and three damaged. Five of the crew were killed. One,

Flight Lieutenant Robert Ash, who had given up a risk-free job in the general duties branch at the relatively advanced age of thirty to volunteer for air-crew duty, had baled out but was found dead. There was a strong suspicion that he had been shot while dangling from his parachute. When a second raid approached Rochford later in the day, the remaining crews clamoured to go into action, but this was refused. The inevitable, lethal consequences of deploying Defiants in daylight were at last recognized. Henceforth, they would only fly at night.

The third phase, as shown on the radar, appeared to be another bombing attack aimed at sector airfields, and six groups of fighters were ordered up to intercept. Instead of bombers they found Me 109s and 110s, and the Hurricanes and Spitfires were lured into just the sort of costly and unproductive clash Dowding and Park were so desperate to avoid. Six German machines were shot down, but so, too, were six British fighters and four pilots killed.

Among them was Noel Benson of 603 Squadron. After the war, it was the thought of the novice pilots going unprepared to their deaths that the public found particularly poignant. The fact was that in the fighting of August and September death came evenly, falling on the experienced and the débutant alike. Benson went into battle fully trained, with only some inkling of the nature of what he was confronting but touchingly eager for the fray. He had been to Sedburgh public school before Cranwell, from where he graduated in October 1939. Benson, nicknamed 'Broody' because he got despondent if not flying, finally got his wish for action when the squadron moved to Hornchurch from Turnhouse in Scotland on 27 August. It had been engaged until then in night flying and occasional attempted interceptions of German intruders. Benson's impatience glows through one letter home. 'I am enclosing a photo that a chap took at Montrose,' he wrote. 'I am in the cockpit starting up the engine to go off on a genuine interception. I believe that at the time some trawlers were being attacked but as usual, the enemy went into the low clouds as soon as we appeared.'

Benson was as well prepared as it was possible to be without having experienced full-scale combat. His commanding officer wrote to his father after his death: 'Your son was an excellent pilot with all his wits about him and he was the last of the squadron I had expected to lose.' He lasted just one day. George Prior, an ex-serviceman who had served at Gallipoli, was standing outside his cottage at Leigh Green near Tenterden in Kent on the evening of 28 August, watching seven German aircraft overhead. He later described in a letter how 'a single British plane suddenly dived into them from above, the pilot tackling them single handed. He was hit at once by one of the enemy and I saw smoke pouring from his machine. He then turned and dived towards the ground to about 1,000 feet to save himself, then straightened out.' Prior believed that Benson had deliberately stayed with his aeroplane to steer it away from farm buildings. 'He could certainly have saved himself before his plane got further alight: instead he went on, avoiding the farm etc. and all the houses and the post office and a large Army Service Corps depot . . . he drove on with his machine now ablaze. I saw the flames yards behind it and he had no chance then. He gave his life to save us all at Leigh Green.' He finally crashed a few fields away. By the time Prior reached the spot, 'his machine was a charred mass of metal . . . he met his death in this last act of self-sacrifice'.[21]

Mr Prior wrote his letter at the request of another resident of Leigh Green, Mrs Marguerite Sandys, who campaigned for several months for Benson to be awarded some posthumous medal, but the request was turned down by the Air Ministry. The gratitude of the villagers was an indication of how civilians and airmen were being drawn closer together. Ordinary people were in the war now. Many knew all too well what aerial bombardment was like. On 24 August Portsmouth had been subjected to a four-minute blitz by 250-kilo bombs dropped by Ju 88s, which slipped through a fighter screen and laid waste the naval base as well as the town, killing 107 civilians and injuring 237.

The advent of night-time raids disrupted the lives of millions. Fighter Command issued warnings to local defence authorities of likely raids, classed from yellow, the lowest threat, through purple, to red. Officials erred on the side of caution. The bombers roamed far and wide as they reached out beyond coastal cities to the industrial Midlands and the north. The sleep of everyone in their paths was ruined as people made their way to shelters and the war production effort slowed as factories switched off the electricity until the raiders had left.

Nowhere in the south-east felt entirely safe. Bombers would jettison their loads at random when running for home. Pete Brothers moved his wife away from Biggin Hill to what he thought would be the safety of the small town of Westerham, about five miles away. One late afternoon in August she was preparing for a visit from her husband. 'She was getting ready, sitting in her bedroom with the windows open putting on her lipstick and so on, when someone dropped a bomb and a splinter came in through the open window and smashed her mirror. That got me pretty angry. It could have gone into the back of her head.'[22] Brothers moved her to Lancashire to stay with his parents.

Fighters on free hunts occasionally strafed roads and villages. Joan Lovell Hughes, who was later to marry Christopher Foxley-Norris, was working on a farm at Penshurst in Kent. The excitement of watching the fighting overhead was tempered by the danger from the Luftwaffe. 'The boys, when they'd downed somebody, used to come low over the field, waggling their wings and we would shout, "Well done!" But there were also nasty times when the Germans came over and they would drop their bombs and shoot at anything that moved . . . One night I was cycling alone on my own and a lone raider came along, low, so I flung myself in a hedge and it fired at me and missed . . . They fired at anything that was moving.'[23]

Despite the increasing threat they had posed to the civilian population, crashed German crews could expect decent treatment. Oberleutnant Rudolf Lamberty was forced to crash-land his Dornier 17 near Biggin Hill on 18 August. Climbing out of the flaming wreckage, he saw some 'very excited Home Guard men with shotguns . . . they pointed their guns at me. I was busily engaged in putting out the fire on both my sleeves.' During the confrontation, another raid came in, and everyone threw themselves to the ground while bomb splinters tore the air around them. When the German aircraft had departed, Lamberty and the rest of his crew were led along a road to the entrance to the base. On the way they met some civilians. 'The first question they asked was: "Are you glad it's all over for you?" But we weren't and said so.' Lamberty wanted to get rid of his parachute and offered it to one of the curious civilians, telling him it would make good silk shirts. He asked for help getting his cigarettes as his hands were too badly burned to open his tunic pocket. Someone retrieved them, put a cigarette in his mouth and lit it for him. They were surprised to see the cigarettes were English. Lamberty had bought them in Guernsey a few days previously. He was driven to the base hospital, where he was given a cup of tea with a straw to drink it through. His face was smeared with Tannifax anti-burn cream and he was brought food. Lamberty was unable to eat it as the inside of his mouth was burned. The nurses misunderstood and brought him a different dish to see if that would tempt him. He and another officer were taken to a room for a mild interrogation, but 'they saw we were not capable and left it'.[24] Next day he was transferred to a civilian hospital.

Such courtesy was conditional on the defeated behaving themselves. After a raid on Tangmere in which two airmen were killed, a captured German crew happened to be marched past the bodies. One of the Germans, 601 Squadron's historian recorded, was imprudent enough to laugh. 'A senior RAF officer who was walking to meet them lengthened his stride and punched the German on the nose. That evening the prisoners were given brooms and made to sweep up the bomb debris in the hangars.'[25]

The method of dealing with the German raiders, as they threw themselves repeatedly against Fighter Command's defences, evolved continuously, refined and adjusted by bitter experience. Whatever Park might say about the necessity of concentrating on the bombers, it was impossible to do so effectively without protection. By now a rough division of labour had evolved between Hurricanes and Spitfires. Hurricanes, it was agreed, were slower, but in compensation were sturdier in construction and provided a more stable gun platform. To them fell the job of shooting down bombers. The Spitfires, with their greater speed and manoeuvrability and higher operational altitude, were more suited to fending off the Me 109s and 110s hovering overhead.

The defending fighters were almost invariably greatly outnumbered by those they were attacking. As always, a fighter pilot's tactical position was greatly improved if he was flying higher than the enemy and coming at them from out of the sun. It was a constant complaint by squadrons that they were scrambled too late to climb to an ideal attacking height. Pilots operating from the forward coastal bases were at a particular disadvantage as they had even less time to react before the raiders were overhead or gone. Some commanders used their own initiative and flew inland to gain height before turning back in the direction of the enemy. The first aim of the attacks was to try and split up the disciplined ranks of the bombers. This disrupted the field of covering fire the gunners could provide for each other, churned up the formation into smaller and less defensible groups and separated individual machines from the warmth of the pack, making them much easier to pick off.

'If you could break up the leaders, that was the ideal situation because we knew that they were the pathfinders for the bombing raid,' Harold Bird-Wilson, a Hurricane pilot with 17 Squadron, said later. 'The bomber formations were very good and they [followed] their leader's bombing. The leader dropped his bombs followed by everyone else.' When the protecting fighters saw a Hurricane attack go in, 'they used to come hurling down at us and through us and then back up again . . . "yo-yo" tactics.'[26]

The effectiveness of head-on attacks was now established. Brian Kingcome, who arrived with 92 Squadron at Biggin Hill at the beginning of September from the relative tranquillity of Pembrey in South Wales, discovered that the escorts 'never had time to get to you if you attacked from head on before you had managed to have at least one good solid go at the bombers'.[27] The attacker had a good chance of shooting down the leader, thereby removing the raiders' controlling intelligence as well as unnerving the following pilots. The tactic, though, required tungsten nerves. Its invention was sometimes attributed to Gerry Edge, who had been an auxiliary officer before the war. He flew in May with 605 Squadron over France, where he showed exceptional aggression, shooting down at least six aircraft and damaging many more. Count Czernin of 17

Squadron was another practitioner. He used it not only against bombers but also against Me 110s, as a means of overcoming their habit of forming a defensive circle to enable the rear gunners to put out a retaliatory curtain of fire. The trick was to get in and out with the maximum speed before one or other of the Messerschmitts in the circle broke off to fasten on to the attacker's tail. Czernin's commander Squadron Leader Cedric Williams, tried a head-on attack on an Me 110 on 25 August. His left wing was shot off by the forward fire from the German and he crashed into the sea off the south coast.

The squadrons being fed in to replace exhausted and depleted units had been training hard during their time out of the front line and gaining what experience they could from the interceptions they were called on to make against intruders. But little effort seems to have been made to pass on systematically to the squadrons waiting their turn in the front line the tactical lessons that had so far been drawn from the fighting. On 30 August, 222 Squadron, which had arrived from the north the day before, began operating from Hornchurch. By the end of the day eight Spitfires had been shot down, one pilot killed and three wounded. They had been flying in tight formation and using a weaver to protect their tails, tactics recognized as faulty months before. Individual squadrons did what they could to modify their techniques, trying out flying patterns which allowed more flexibility and a greater field of observation. But in October squadrons were still flying in V-shaped 'vics', in which the leader was supported by two wingmen, each formated closely on him. When Archie Winskill joined 72 Squadron, they 'still hadn't got out of this rather archaic business of flying in tight formations of three, which was ridiculous. It meant . . . keeping in formation and watching your leader rather than flying in the loose two formations which the Germans did which left you completely free to roam the skies.'[28]

The German formation, known as 'finger four' by the RAF pilots who experimented with it and eventually adopted it, was the one developed by Werner Mölders in Spain. The basic unit was the pair: a leader and a wingman who flew roughly two hundred yards behind on the sunward side and slightly below so his partner did not have to look into the glare to see him. The wingman's job was to protect the leader. The formation was known as a *Rotte*. Two *Rotte* made up a *Schwarm*. The tactic was basically protective, and if efficiently applied would give early warning of an attack coming out of the sun. Once battle was joined, however, both sides found that cohesion and control vanished and most of the time pilots had only themselves to rely on.

Since the end of the brief pause lasting from 19 to 24 August, the Luftwaffe had been launching several major raids a day involving hundreds of aircraft. On the first day of the resumed assault, there were six large attacks by a total of at least 500 bombers and fighters lasting from 6 a.m. to 6.45 p.m. After night fell the Germans returned and the residents of southern and western England, South Wales, the Midlands, East Anglia and Yorkshire heard the drone of enemy engines overhead. As well as the raid on London, bombs fell on Liverpool, Sheffield, Bradford, Hull and Middlesbrough and were scattered over areas of Kent, Hampshire, Reading and Oxford.

On the 25th there were no mass attacks until the afternoon, when two were launched by at least 400 aircraft, and once again there was a full programme of night attacks, concentrating on the Midlands. On the 26th there were three main phases directed against the Dover–Folkestone area, then Kent and north of the Thames estuary, then the Portsmouth–Southampton area, involving nearly 500 aircraft, followed by a widespread night bombing. Bad weather on the 27th brought a respite. The following day there were four main raids and a 150-bomber raid on Liverpool by night. The 29th brought a momentary shift of tactics. A huge force of several hundred aircraft appeared on radar screens, building up over the French coast. It turned out to be a ruse. Most of the force were fighters and the small number of bombers were clearly intended as bait to lure up the British fighters, a stratagem which did not succeed.

Given the weight of German numbers and the strains imposed on pilots and controllers alike, it was inevitable that breakthroughs would occur. On 30 August, the Luftwaffe succeeded in pressing home a devastating attack on Biggin Hill. The base had been heavily bombed twelve days before but had remained operational. As one of the key bases in 11 Group's defences, strategically positioned at the gates of London and facing the main direction of the Luftwaffe attack, it was inevitable that further intensive efforts would be made to destroy it.

The first raid came in just before noon, when a group of ninety bombers and an equal number of fighter escorts crossed the Kent coastline and peeled off to attack the London perimeter airfields. Park ordered almost all his fighters into the air and two squadrons were sent down from 12 Group to patrol Kenley and Biggin Hill. A group of Ju 88s nonetheless slipped through and dropped more than thirty bombs, most of which fell in the cornfields around the base and the village next door.

Once again the station's luck seemed to have held. Instead of waiting a few hours to launch the next phase, the Luftwaffe maintained the pressure with successive waves of bombers rolling over the south-east all afternoon. In two hours from 4 p.m., about 400 aircraft swept in over Kent and the Thames estuary, confusing the controllers trying to plot so many courses and direct fighters towards them. At about 6 p.m. a small group of eighteen Ju 88s suddenly appeared, flying very low over Biggin Hill. No warning was given and there was no one overhead to stop them, 79 Squadron being on the ground at the time and 610 Squadron patrolling elsewhere. When the raid swept in, airmen were just leaving the mess after their evening meal. Only sixteen 500-kilo bombs were dropped, but the effect was devastating. One bomb landed directly on a trench crowded with airmen, killing many. One of the four remaining hangars was destroyed, as well as workshops, the armoury, storerooms, the sergeants' mess, the Waaf quarters and airmen's barrack blocks. All gas, electricity and water mains were cut and telephone lines severed. The walls of one shelter caved in under the shock, burying a group of Waafs, all but one of whom were later dug out alive. Altogether thirty-nine ground staff were killed and twenty-six wounded.

The following day 610 Squadron was moved north to Acklington, to be replaced by 72 Squadron. At noon, while the squadron airmen were waiting with their kit to be picked up, the noise of anti-aircraft guns signalled another raid, which left the runways so badly cratered that they were unusable and 79 Squadron, returning from operations over Dover, had to be diverted to Croydon. The ground crews worked themselves to exhaustion during the afternoon, filling in the holes so that when 72 Squadron arrived they were able to land. 'The amazing thing about it,' wrote Robert Deacon Elliot, one of the new pilots flying in, 'was the human factor – no panic, everyone doing their utmost to keep the aircraft in the air. Bomb craters in the airfield being quickly filled in, food being delivered to dispersals to avoid waste of time returning to messes. Land lines installed to run out from ops to squadron dispersals to replace those lost.'[29] The base was to be attacked five times in forty-eight hours, one raid arriving as the station commander, Group Captain Grice, led the burial service for fifty Biggin Hill staff at the small cemetery at the edge of the aerodrome. Despite the effort and the stoicism, the base was no place to leave precious pilots and aeroplanes. The day after it arrived, 72 Squadron shifted a few miles away to Croydon, which, though damaged, was in better shape than Biggin Hill and had the added advantage of the Airport Hotel, where the pilots took their first baths for three days.

The squadron it had replaced, 610, had been pulled out of the line after being at Biggin Hill and Gravesend since July. At the start the unit had twenty pilots 'on state'. Over the two months, nine pilots were killed and six seriously wounded. In addition there were numerous shootings down, crash-landings and balings out. Such figures were high but not unusual. Between 1 July and 6 September, 501 Squadron lost twelve pilots, and 601, squadron of the dashing pre-war auxiliaries, whose insouciant ranks were filled with sportsmen, playboys and adventurers, lost eleven. By the time it was taken out of the line most of its original pilots were gone, dead or posted away. Two of the pre-war members, Carl Raymond Davis and Willie Rhodes-Moorhouse, son of a First World War RFC pilot and winner of a Victoria Cross, were killed on the day before they were due to move to the relative quiet of Exeter. Rhodes-Moorhouse had obtained his pilot's licence aged seventeen at Heston, near Eton, where he went to school, had been engaged at every stage of the war, and was an outstanding pilot who had shot down at least nine bombers and fighters, shared in the destruction of several more and been awarded the DFC. His death was a reminder that skill and experience were no protection against the inevitable shortening of the odds that each combat brought.

Squadrons like 501 and 601 absorbed their losses over a relatively lengthy stay in the line. With others the heart was torn out of the unit in a few nightmarish days. Between 12 and 16 August, 266 Squadron, which had arrived in such good spirits, determined to do well after a summer of relative inactivity in the Midlands, had suffered six pilots killed, including the squadron leader, and two badly wounded. Next it was caught in a bombing raid on Manston on the 17th, the second time the pilots had been battered on the ground since their arrival. There had been twenty-three pilots when they came south. By the end they were down to nine, which meant that every fit man had to go on every trip. Dennis Armitage, wounded in the left leg, walked with a stick and had to be helped into his Spitfire. Fortunately, as he observed, 'there is no place other than bed where full use of the legs is so unimportant as when driving a single-engined aeroplane'.[30] Twelve days after arriving in the south, they were sent back to Wittering to lick their wounds.

Pilots died horribly, riddled with splinters from cannon shells, doused in burning petrol, dragged down into the chilly depths of the Channel by the weight of their parachutes, heavy boots and fur-lined flying jackets. Unless they were killed outright, they had time to recognize they were finished. Often they died in front of their friends, who witnessed the strike of fire, the faltering engine and the long inexorable dive, trailing smoke and flame. On a few occasions, when the R/T was switched to 'on', they heard them die, screaming prayers and curses as they 'went in'. The survivors reacted to the losses in the only way they knew how, with nonchalance and a touch of manufactured, protective heartlessness. There was no open grieving. 'You didn't spend days moping around,' said George Unwin. 'You just said, "Poor old so-and-so's bought it," and that was it.'[31] In 32 Squadron there was a black tradition of inking in devil's horns on the dead man's picture in the squadron group photograph. Pilots in some squadrons put money into a kitty kept behind the bar in the mess so they could be toasted on the evening of their death. There was hardly ever time to attend a funeral. Burial arrangements were often complicated by the absence of a body. The dead men were burned to cinders, or at the bottom of the sea, or still welded, phantom-like, to the controls of their beloved Hurricane or Spitfire buried in mud or sand or water.

Death was 'the chop' and all that was left behind of those who got it were memories and a handful of young man's possessions: cigarette case, cuff links, perhaps a tennis racket or a set of golf clubs. The RAF bureaucracy listed personal effects with poignant precision. Among the effects left behind by Paddy Finucane were: '1 blue leather wallet contg. – 2 snapshots; 2 Religious illustrations, 2 Religious emblems. 1 Black Cat Mascot. 2 silver cigarette cases. 2 cigarette lighters. 3 cabinet photographs (1 with glass broken). 1 Eversharpe pencil.'[32] The melancholy business of sorting out kit was described in a poem by Flight Lieutenant Anthony Richardson:

The officer in charge
Made out the inventories, point by point –
Four shirts, six collars and nine pairs of socks,
Two uniforms complete, some flying kit,
Brushes and comb, shaving gear and shoes –
(He tried a jumper on which didn't fit!)
There was dirty washing, too, which was a bore,
Being certain to get lost in the delay.
A squash racket with two strings gone, and a cap
That like himself, had seen a better day.
Then there were letters, beginning 'Darling Dick',
Photos and snapshots all of the same girl,
With a pale, eager face and fluffy hair. . .[33]

Frequently there was a car, which would be auctioned at a convenient moment, or driven around until claimed by a relative. Geoffrey Page bought a 1938 Ford convertible that had belonged to Ian Soden, who was killed in France. Soden had acquired it from the estate of another dead pilot. After Page was shot down and badly burned, a fellow 56 Squadron member, Mark Mounsden, wrote to him in hospital asking him what he wanted him to do with it. Page replied that it was his for five pounds. Later he saw the jinxed vehicle being driven through Torquay, where he was recuperating. A badly burned officer was at the wheel.

There was no point in brooding about death. It was too commonplace, and in all likelihood soon to be encountered by those who were left behind. 'The death of a friend or enemy,' wrote Page, 'provided food for a few moments of thought, before the next swirling dogfight began to distract the . . . mind from stupid thoughts such as sadness or pity . . . the art was to cheat the Reaper and perhaps blunt his scythe a little.' Events such as being shot down and crash-landing or baling out were almost too commonplace to merit mention. 'Something more spectacular was necessary to draw anything greater than a passing comment.'[34]

Behind the blank exteriors, though, they felt the ache of loss. David Crook was with Peter Drummond-Hay, a 609 Squadron original who had amused his fellow officers with his aspirations to a life of landed leisure, when he was shot down. Returning to their shared room the following day, he saw 'Peter's towel was still in the window where he had thrown it during our hurried dressing eighteen hours before. Now he was lying in the cockpit of his wrecked Spitfire at the bottom of the English Channel . . . I took my things and went to sleep in Gordon's room next door.'[35]

Inside the squadron, the emotional burden of the losses fell most heavily on the leader. It was his melancholy duty to write the letters informing parents that their sons were gone. Dennis Armitage took over 266 Squadron after Squadron Leader Wilkinson was killed and the senior flight commander was shot down and severely burned. At the end of a day's flying from Hornchurch, while the other pilots made off to the pub, he would be left with the paperwork. 'I would get down to the awful job of writing to the parents or wives – not often wives I'm glad to say – of the lads who had not come back . . . I tried hard at first, tearing up several letters before I was satisfied, but I am afraid before the end I had developed a more or less stereotyped letter which needed little more than the name and address adding.'[36]

Some squadron commanders made great efforts to comfort grieving families. No. 603 Squadron had been too occupied with the fighting to send a representative to Noel Benson's funeral, which took place in St Mary's Church in the Bensons' home village of Great Ouseburn, and wreaths from his brother officers and the sergeants' mess were delivered instead. They did, however, invite his father, a Yorkshire doctor, down to Hornchurch for lunch, which was disturbed when the squadron was scrambled. Writing to his brother, Dr Benson described how he had last seen his son only two days before his death when, by a happy chance, the squadron stopped overnight in the neighbourhood on its journey from Scotland to Hornchurch and he had been able to come home for supper. 'You can imagine our joy at the chance of seeing him again, tho' both we and he knew full well what it meant! That "they were flying South".'

Dr Benson's grief was all the more moving for its understatement.

> We have no regrets for him. He was happy at school, at Cranwell and with his squadron, on service. He loved every minute he was flying. He was devoted to his home and to his father and mother, loved by all who knew him. He never gave us a moment's anxiety except for his safety and *that* was inseparable from the career he had chosen. I have never known a finer character. If he had been spared he would have achieved eminence in his profession of that I'm certain. Early he has been killed and gladly he has made the supreme sacrifice, but we are left to miss him very, very sorely.[37]

Dr Benson lost only one son. The Woods-Scawen family lost two, on consecutive days. On 1 September, Patrick, a twenty-four-year-old flying officer with 85 Squadron, was shot down in the skies over Kenley, within sight of his old school, the Salesian College, Farnborough. He baled out but his parachute failed to open. The following day his younger brother, Charles, a pilot officer with 43 Squadron, was cornered by Me 109s near

Folkestone and badly shot up. He also baled out, but too low for his parachute to work. He was twenty-two.

The ability of units to absorb deaths and injuries was reinforced by the knowledge that, however heavy their own losses, the German toll in men and machines was greater. The daily official tally put out by the Air Ministry and reported in the press and on the BBC was invariably exaggerated, inflating the number of German aircraft destroyed and minimizing the wastage on the British side. The pilots, who contributed to the inflation by their own understandable habitual overclaiming, believed them, and the figures were an important factor in maintaining morale. But it was essentially true that the balance of destruction lay in the RAF's favour. On only one day in August the 29th, were German and British losses roughly equal.

The Luftwaffe was suffering. The crews had been told regularly by their superiors that Fighter Command was down to its last handful of fighters, yet every day the Spitfires and Hurricanes were still there waiting for them, aggressive and unbowed. They began to wonder how much longer they could go on. Being shot up in a bomber, limping home over the hated sea, was a harrowing business. The Heinkel of Major H. M. Wronsky was hit by anti-aircraft fire near Portsmouth on the night of 31 August/1 September. 'We saw flames right away; the starboard engine was on fire and we thought the whole machine must burn.' They turned back out to sea and smothered the engine with foam from extinguishers, scrabbling for their parachutes that were stacked up against a bulkhead. As they approached the French coast, they saw a British bombing raid in progress near Calais and swung away so as not to be mistaken for a raider. It was clear that they would never make their home base at Villacoublay near Paris. The decision was made to jump, but in their haste they had put their parachutes on upside down and no one could locate their ripcord. By the time the mistake had been sorted out they were too low to bale out.

> The ground rose up in front of us – a hill. The machine struck and tore across the top of the hill, ploughing through bushes. We lay there all

> injured. One man had been so badly cut on the head that he died later. Another man had been hurled right through the perspex of the nose . . . I had a broken nose, broken foot, broken arm. We lay there in the sudden quiet, listening to a hissing noise. We thought it was fire, that trapped and injured as we were, we should be burned to death. But it was only the oxygen bottles. The port engine had been hurled right out of the machine and was lying eighty yards in front.[38]

Day after day the British pilots were inflicting heavy punishment on the raiders. But the Germans continued to come. As August turned into September there appeared no let-up in the grinding, sapping routine. On 31 August the British fighters suffered their heaviest losses so far, with forty aircraft destroyed, nine pilots killed and eighteen badly wounded, half of them burnt. On 1 September Biggin Hill was hit again. The following day there were four major attacks on airfields and aircraft factories. The pattern was maintained until 6 September. Among the 11 Group squadrons absorbing most of the violence, exhaustion was now a permanent condition. 'The Luftwaffe,' wrote Peter Townsend, leading 85 Squadron from Croydon, 'by sheet weight of numbers . . . was wearing us down; we were weary beyond caring, our nerves taughtened to breaking-point.' Townsend was one of the victims of 31 August. The Germans arrived while the pilots were grabbing lunch. 'Their bombs all but hit us as we roared, full-throttle, off the ground. The blast made our engines falter.' For once, Townsend gave way to his emotions. Until then he had 'never felt any particular hatred for the German airmen, only anger. This time, though, I was so blind with fury that I felt things must end badly for me. But I was too weary and too strung-up to care.'[39] His instinct was accurate. His Hurricane was hit and he was forced to jump. That evening doctors at Croydon hospital extracted a heavy-calibre bullet from his foot. A few days later the squadron, after its two senior flight commanders were killed, was taken out of the line.

The most buoyant and resilient personalities were now suffering moments of doubt. In Al Deere's squadron there were only four pilots who had been with him at the start of the summer. His confidence in victory began to falter as he considered the stark reality that he was 'fighting a war with very inexperienced chaps. That could only get worse, progressively worse.'[40] Even Sailor Malan's granite imperturbability could crumble. One night, he told Archie Winskill later, he was overwhelmed by despondency as he sat in his room in Hornchurch and began to cry. Then he dried his tears, persuaded himself they were only a sign of his extreme tiredness, pushed away the images of the day and tried to sleep.[41]

15

Brotherhood

Despite the desperation of the situation, the level of optimism among the pilots had remained remarkably high throughout the summer. Fortitude was a Fighter Boy virtue. In its short life the RAF had established a light-hearted tradition of assuming the worst and mocking misfortune. Underneath the careful insouciance lay a thick seam of resolution. The German attack had uncorked something old and potent. 'It's surprising how fierce one's protective instincts become at the sight of an enemy violating one's homeland,' Brian Kingcome remarked.[1]

Many felt honoured to be fighting, though the conventions of un-seriousness meant that few would have admitted as much at the time. The quality of morale varied from squadron to squadron and base to base depending on how much of the fighting they had had to endure. The strain was greatest in 11 Group. Further out in 10 Group and 12 Group there were longer gaps between engagements and the tension was less acute. 'Nevertheless,' Roland Beamont said afterwards, 'no matter where you were, there was this extraordinary spirit. The squadron pilot was encouraged to believe that there wasn't anything special about the task he had been asked to do – which he had been trained for – and that he was extremely privileged to be in one of the key units in the defence of this country because that was what it was all about . . . the battle for Britain. Without any exhortation at all, the pilots, all the ground staff, all the people concerned were just reminded quietly by the squadron commanders and the flight commanders, whenever it was necessary, that this was the finest job anybody could have in the world and we were extremely privileged to be doing it.'[2]

These softly spoken appeals worked because they were addressed to a fraternity which had already in its short life developed a singular identity and adopted clear values and attitudes. Hectoring, when it was tried, usually had limited results. There were exceptions. Sailor Malan, when he took over 74 Squadron in early August, was regarded as a hard master. 'Sailor was a very tough nut indeed,' said Christopher Foxley-Norris. 'He gave no quarter. If you failed once, you failed.'[3] Tony Bartley remembered Malan explaining how he led his men: 'I kick their arses once a day and I've got a good squadron. Otherwise they'd wind up nothing.'[4] It was in sharp contrast to the approach adopted by another outstanding leader, Al Deere. 'Al was a kindly man,' said Foxley-Morris. 'Extremely tough but prepared to make allowances and concessions.'

Discipline, of a traditional military type, was necessary for much that was done in the air. On the ground it jarred. None of the pilots had joined because they were attracted by convention and the comforts of blind obedience. Relations inside squadrons, more than in any other service units, were based on tolerance and *laissez-faire*. Individualism was respected. At the same time, mutual reliance and the shared dangers inherent in flying tied individuals together. Each unit had a personality and style of its own that its members made an effort to sustain. There was a spirit of collectivity. In the best squadrons there was no room for the self-important. Yet equally, no one was allowed to think themselves insignificant. Doing his rounds of the fighter stations the war artist Cuthbert Orde came to the conclusion that 'a squadron of pilots can be divided into three groups: natural leaders and fighters at the top; then the main body of solid talent containing the germ of leaders of the future, chaps whose qualities will develop with experience; and then I suppose a tail, two or three perhaps, who will never be quite good enough to earn distinction but who nevertheless are pulling their weight for all it may be worth'.

What social distinctions had existed before the start of the summer were eroded by the fighting. The auxiliary squadrons lost their exclusive character as pilots were killed, wounded or posted away. 'Eventually we got pretty well used to everybody,' said Peter Dunning-White, an old Harrovian member of Lloyd's and one of the blades of 601 Squadron before the war. 'It didn't matter what kind of type you were as long as you behaved well.'[5] The new pilots came from everywhere and every class. Death rubbed out the last traces of the line dividing the pre-war short-service officers and the part-timers from the volunteer reserve. The members of 66 Squadron were, according to Hubert Allen, who served in it, 'a truly motley throng, consisting of young men from every walk of life. Regular air force officers, sergeant-pilots who had in peacetime been dockhands, clerks, motor-mechanics; there was even an ex-dirt-track motor-cycle expert with us. Every conceivable type was represented.'

Some of the 'Clickety-Click' personalities were revealed in an unsentimental book which came out in 1942. Ten pilots were asked to write a short chapter about themselves and their war. Three others were killed before they could get started. Of those who did contribute, three were dead before the book was published. The pilots appeared under pseudonyms. 'Bob' was Flying Officer Bobby Oxspring, the son of an RFC veteran, who joined the RAF on a short-service commission in 1938. Allen described him as 'a tallish, good-looking, fair-headed bloke, with a typical schoolboy complexion, liable to blush every now and then . . . he can take his beer like a man, comes from the north and has a typical Yorkshire outlook. A little shy he may appear off-hand at first, but having broken down his barriers of reserve, you would find a loveable, gay, carefree youth of twenty-two years.' 'Bogle' was Flying Officer Crelin Bodie, nineteen, also known as 'Rob', who joined on a short-service commission the month after war broke out. He was 'a strong individualist . . . decidedly unconventional in appearance, usually wearing a uniform which would not pass muster on a ceremonial parade, with a colourful scarf around his neck and a large sheath-knife in his boot. His language is foul but he possesses more character than anyone I can remember.'

Pilot Officer John Kendal – 'Durex' – who had gone through the RAFVR, was 'young and noisy . . . he can imitate every noise conceivable, from an underground train pulling out of a station to the ricocheting of a rifle bullet. Something had to happen before he would shut up. A little of Durex went a long way.' Sergeant Douglas Hunt, 'Duggie', an apprentice at the Bristol Aeroplane Company who joined the RAFVR, had 'a very droll manner and a terrific scheme about a revolution after the war so that the whole of the country can be governed by pilots'. Last on the list was Sergeant William Corbin, known as 'Binder' because he was 'always moaning, usually about leave. He was the image of George Formby except that he was born in Kent and proud of it.'[6]

Corbin was from Maidstone, a builder's son who had gone to a technical school, then trained to be a maths and science teacher. He had joined the RAFVR in April 1939 and arrived at 66 Squadron at Coltishall on 28 August as a sergeant. His first impression was that the officers were all public-school boys, an observation that did not bother him. His academic abilities, he felt, made him their equal. The distinction in status and privilege between men who were doing the same job and taking the same risks would appear unreasonable and unjust in later years. At the time it seemed much less remarkable and most accepted it, illogical though it clearly was. The maintenance of the division between officer and NCO pilots was a hangover from the inter-war years, when the majority of sergeant pilots were ex-apprentices who had been accepted for flying training but might at any stage be required to return to their old trades.

By the late summer just under a third of the pilots flying were sergeants, many of them products of the RAFVR. Their duties were indistinguishable from those of officers. They were there, principally, to fly and fight. The decision whether or not to award a commission to a pilot on completing initial training was based on obscure criteria. One consideration was their leadership potential. The practice seems to have been to commission those who fitted most easily into pre-war conceptions of what constituted an officer and a gentleman. That meant public schoolboys and those who looked as if they belonged to the middle or upper class. Even here the formula was shaky. Don Kingaby, who turned out to be one of the best pilots in Fighter Command, was a vicar's son, and was educated at a public school – King's, Ely – yet was classed as a sergeant when he finished training in the early summer of 1940. Many sergeant pilots shared the same backgrounds as those who had been classified as their superiors.

The nature of the RAF required it to be a meritocracy. Its technical essence made it more egalitarian than the other services. In the RAF, more than in the army or navy, it was possible for an expensively educated son of privilege to be under the command of a man who had emerged from the working class. In 74 Squadron Tony Mould, who went to Mill Hill public school, was a sergeant. His squadron leader, Francis White, started his RAF career as an apprentice fitter. The war accelerated the rationalizing process, but in the summer of 1940 odd gradations remained.

Sergeant and officer pilots went to separate messes and enjoyed different levels of comfort. Away from the front-line stations, in properly appointed bases, officers could still have their own batman or orderly, a privilege which did not extend to the sergeants. Ian Hutchinson was posted from the RAFVR to 222 Squadron in February 1940. At that time, he said later, pilots arriving by that route were 'regarded as the lowest of the low,' particularly by the regular sergeant pilots who had arrived in the squadron from the workshops. 'They treated us differently at first, but when it came to the action then everything disappeared.'

Hutchinson noted that 'as an officer you lived rather better. You had a nicer uniform. [As a sergeant] you had a scratchy uniform, although the scratchiness wore off eventually. Your accommodation was not so grand, although you did get individual or double rooms. You didn't have a batman to wake you up in the morning and make your tea or press your trousers or polish your buttons. You did it yourself. You envied the officers their privileges but nothing more. Nobody felt aggrieved.'[7] Maurice Leng, a sergeant with 73 Squadron, agreed. 'We were very close. There was no officers *versus* sergeants nonsense. Just a marvellous camaraderie.'[8]

Some officers, like Geoffrey Page, found the division stupid. 'I felt it terribly wrong that a man who hasn't got an officer's rank is asked to do exactly the same thing as the officer. You can't climb out of your aeroplane and then say "Cheerio" and you go off to the officers' mess and he goes off to the sergeants' mess. I always thought that it was a very wrong system.'[9] Once at dispersal distinctions usually, but not invariably, disappeared. In 41 Squadron under Squadron Leader Hilary Hood, differences between pilots were minimal. Sergeant Frank Usmar remembered Hood as 'a lovely chap. When you were at dispersal it was nothing for him to say, "Well, if you've got half-a-crown, let's have a game of cards." And we'd play this innocent game and we'd be one big happy family . . . We were sitting there waiting for the telephone to ring and to keep your mind off what's going to happen you play cards and make fun of things.' Hood was killed on 5 September when his Spitfire collided with that of another squadron member, Flying Officer John Webster, while they were attacking bombers over the Thames estuary.

The new squadron leader was less convivial. 'One day the NCOs – that was about half a dozen of us – were sent for to report to the orderly room with our greatcoats on and buttoned up above the throat and buttons polished. We were told by the CO that it was a court martial offence for officers to play cards with the NCOs but they were too much gentlemen to tell us to stay out.' He ordered them to stop. When the sergeants returned to dispersal, the officers asked why they had been summoned. When they heard the story, they glumly accepted the decision. 'So we used to lay on our bed in the corner or in the armchair waiting for the bell to ring to scramble, feeling cheesed off and miserable, and the same thing applied to the officers at the other end of the room, longing to play cards or something, but unable to do it.'[10]

Off the base, where there was no one to object, sergeants and officers often drank together. The social gap between pilots and ground crews was wider, though some pilots reached across it. John Coghlan, a flying officer with 56 Squadron, known as 'Slim', was, according to Corporal Eric Clayton, who maintained his Hurricane, 'a friendly, amusing and unflappable character, overweight and unfit he perspired freely and had a prodigious intake of ale'. Clayton and his fellow airmen would often bump into him with his girlfriend in their favourite Ipswich pubs, 'which resulted in beery and jolly evenings'.[11] The pointlessness of the distinction was evident from the fact that almost every sergeant pilot flying in the summer of 1940 was sooner or later commissioned. Many sergeant pilots went on to high command. Neil Cameron, a bank clerk who joined the RAFVR and was posted to 1 Squadron at the end of September, ended up Marshal of the Royal Air Force.

It was in the air that rank held the least meaning. On the occasions when Flying Officer Ben Bowring was called on to lead 111 Squadron and 'felt he wasn't qualified', he asked Sergeant William Dymond, a regular, to take over instead, while he followed behind.[12] Yet on the ground flying and fighting prowess did not necessarily increase the standing of those who possessed it. An egalitarian spirit and a propensity for knockabout humour and mickey-taking made the establishment of hierarchies of esteem difficult. Pilots admired success but did not subscribe to the notion of 'aces' or show deference to outstanding performers. When an interview with Count Czernin appeared in the London press, in which he spoke freely about his successes, his colleagues in 17 Squadron organized a mock ceremony and awarded him a large cardboard medal. The fact was that most pilots never shot anything down. Fewer than 900 of the 2,330-odd pilots who flew in Fighter Command between July and November claimed victories. There was no shame in that. They knew among themselves that the simple presence of a Hurricane or Spitfire, even if its bullets were not striking home, had a demoralizing effect on the enemy. And they understood very well the courage that was needed simply to maintain yourself in the air.

Brian Kingcome was not a self-effacing man, but he resisted attempts to establish an order of precedence among pilots based on the number of 'kills'. He qualified as one of the most successful pilots of the period. Between 2 June and 13 October he is credited with shooting down at least seven enemy aircraft and damaging many more. The true figure is almost certainly considerably higher as he was careless about recording claims. Kingcome was tall, amused, sceptical, slightly offhand. He had a flattened nose and droopy eye, the result of a pre-war car crash, which did nothing to reduce his attractiveness to women. These were attributes that might make him an object of envy to other men. Yet he was popular and respected. He was convivial and loved a party. He gave credit where it was due. His irritation with attempts to classify him as a hero was genuine. So, too, was a bluntness that could disconcert. 'He didn't suffer fools, there's no doubt about it,' said Sergeant David Cox, who flew with him in 72 Squadron and liked him.[13] He worked hard at insouciance. Geoffrey Wellum, nicknamed 'Boy' because of his youth and innocence, described waiting at dispersal and thinking, in an atmosphere thick with anticipation, that 'only . . . Brian Kingcome, who is reading and sucking a matchstick, looks relaxed. But on second thoughts, when did he last turn a page? I watch quietly and he doesn't.'[14]

The Fighter Boys cultivated ironic modesty. Those who became well known to the public during and after the war were regarded with some reserve. Unlike Kingcome, Bob Stanford Tuck advertised his successes and painted swastikas on the fuselage of his Spitfire marking the number of Germans he had knocked down. This practice, according to Birdy Bird-Wilson, was regarded by the majority as 'a bit of a line shoot'. Douglas Bader, the most famous fighter pilot of the period, aroused mixed feelings in those who fought alongside him. His bombastic nature and tendency to dramatize was in many ways the antithesis of the Fighter Boy ethos. All paid tribute to his courage, aggressive spirit and ability to enthuse those who followed him. There was reticence, though, about his sharp tongue and fondness for the limelight. David Cox regarded him as 'a good leader, there's no doubt about that. I think you could say you admired him. To like him, though, would be a little difficult.' Dennis David, a generous-hearted man, found him, 'very apt to being a bit smart, a bit short'.[15] Christopher Foxley-Norris thought he was 'a show-off', but 'enormously inspirational'.[16] To the ground crews he could be arrogant, bullying and foul-mouthed.[17]

The worst criticism, made all the more damning by its apparent mildness, was that a pilot was 'not entirely genuine'. To be a 'gen man' meant that you knew what you were doing and did it well, honestly and without fuss. Some of those who fell most emphatically into this category were unknown outside the ranks of Fighter Command. Johnny Dewar, who lead 87 Squadron, was at least ten years older than most of his pilots. He was a member of the whisky family and renowned for his hospitality. After graduating from Cranwell, his career had taken him to every corner of the inter-war RAF. He took the squadron over after it was posted to France and fought all through the summer until he was reported missing on 12 September 1940, shortly after being promoted wing commander. His leadership impressed Dennis David, who found him 'full of common ordinary decency'.[18] Roland Beamont, who also served with him, thought 'he might have been a rather paternal type of schoolmaster in his manner, gentle, quiet mannered resolute and totally unflappable. He was all of thirty-two at the time. We thought he was an old man.'[19]

Most of the pilots were between nineteen and twenty-six years old. The extreme circumstances they found themselves in made them more appreciative of father figures than they might have been in peacetime. Among the most popular men in Fighter Command were several station commanders who were admired for their good nature and efficiency in keeping the bases going and the pilots properly looked after. Wing Commander Victor Beamish ran North Weald for the worst part of the summer. Cuthbert Orde, the former RFC pilot turned war artist, described him as 'unique as an individual and probably the best-loved man in Fighter Command'.[20] He was charming and slightly eccentric, roaming the base in mechanic's overalls. He had been the RAF's heavyweight boxing champion in India in the 1930s and had narrowly missed being selected to play rugby for Ireland, where he had been born, in Dunmanway, County Cork, in 1903. While his pilots were standing at the bar with their 'half-cans' in the evening, he would trot around the aerodrome, trying to keep fit. He flew continuously throughout the summer, shooting down about a dozen bombers and fighters and earning the respect of pilots almost half his age. 'I don't think any pilot would dare to do less than his best if Victor was about,' wrote Orde. 'Not because he might get ticked off but because he would feel ashamed.' The ground staff liked him too. To Eric Clayton he was 'a large burly figure with a friendly face and a ready smile . . . energetic with a powerful sense of duty; hot-tempered but quick to apologize. He was a pugnacious but warm-hearted Irishman. He was also ready with his praise, altogether a great leader.'[21] Beamish resisted the pull of desk and office to the end and died in the air, shot down over the Channel in 1942.

The personality of Group Captain Richard Grice dominated Biggin Hill. Dick Grice was a veteran of the RFC and had won a DFC in the First World War. He was a comforting presence during the repeated blitzes of the base. Pilots, ground crews and station staff, men and women, were reassured by the sound of his calm voice over the Tannoy warning of an imminent raid then announcing the all-clear, and afterwards the sight of the slim, concerned figure picking his way through the smoke and flame to check on the welfare of his 1,000 charges. He was particularly solicitous towards the female staff, the 200 Waafs who were now indispensable to the functioning of the place, and the women who manned the Naafi. He praised their courage and nourished their morale. When the manageress of the Naafi appeared on the point of collapse through overwork, he overrode her demands to stay at her post and sent her on leave. When she returned she found he had arranged for a pullover she left behind, embroidered with the names of European capitals she had holidayed in, to have the name of Biggin Hill added.

It was natural that inside each squadron pilots made special friendships or formed little groups who would sit together at dispersal or return to each others' rooms for a last drink after a night in the mess or down at the pub. In 17 Squadron Denis Wissler was particularly close to Birdy Bird-Wilson, and 'Pitters' – Geoffrey Pittman – his favourite companions on trips to bar, cinema or hop. Robin Appleford and Rob Bodie gravitated naturally to each other, both the babies of 66 Squadron, both good-looking. They teamed up for forays into London in an unlicensed, untaxed banger, once piling into a bomb crater as they raced home through the blackout. Like inclined to like. George Unwin formed an alliance with Frank Steere; both were pre-war sergeants and superb pilots. Richard Mitchell and George Johns, West Country boys and ex-Halton apprentices, teamed up together in 229 Squadron. It was also inevitable that there would be outsiders, those who somehow never managed to cross the low threshold that led to acceptance. On 16 October, Wissler noted the departure of two pilots who had been with the squadron for several months, but until then had failed to feature in the dramatis personae of his diary. They were 'both dim types whose posting was expected'.

Fitting in was made easier by the very difficulty of becoming a fighter pilot in the first place. Being posted to a squadron meant that the first and most important test had been passed. The new pilots were joining an élite. Like all élites, it was indulgent towards its own. The social matrix was elastic, stretching to accommodate differences of personality and background. There were common attitudes that were reasonably easy to embrace. Fundamental to the outlook was humour. It was black, broad, coarse or feeble, usually schoolboyish but constant and all-pervasive.

The practical joking and ragging traditions of pre-war days survived and, when the situation allowed, evenings regularly ended with boisterous mess games. 'A wonderful evening terminating at the Schooner,' wrote the unofficial diarist of 73 Squadron of a night in late July. 'The CO, strong as he was, failed to prevent a not unusual ceremony of being debagged.'[22] Ian Hutchinson was playing the piano in the mess one night when a raid came in. He reached for his steel helmet, but another pilot beat him to it. When he placed it on his head, beer cascaded over his shoulders. In 74 Squadron Peter Chesters bombarded his fellow pilots with meteorological balloons filled with water as they ran from the dispersal hut in response to a phoney scramble. The trick only worked once. Later the pilots had their revenge when, while again fooling about on a roof, he managed to get wedged between the walls of a hut and the surrounding blast barrier. His comrades relieved themselves on him before helping him out. Chesters was high-spirited until the end. He was killed when he misjudged his height doing a victory roll over Manston after shooting down an Me 109 the following year.

Mishaps that ended short of death were a subject of hilarity, such as getting shot down by a bomber rather than by one's equal, an Me 109. The joking, as was recognized, served a need. 'One of my greatest recollections of the time was laughter,' Roland Beamont said later. 'Obviously there was a release of tension in seeing the funny side of things. Maybe sometimes the laughter got a little high. Perhaps there was a bit of hysterics in it somewhere . . . We saw things in very sharp outline. If you saw a chum on a parachute, the fact that he landed with a bit of damage was thought of as really rather amusing. The fact that he wasn't killed was extremely satisfactory for all concerned and a cause of merriment.'[23]

The pilots were further bound together by their own argot, a mixture of public-school slang, technical jargon and transatlantic coinages picked up from films and records. The public-school contribution included boyish expressions of enthusiasm as well as boredom (a very British preoccupation). Anything tedious, a broad category, was a 'bind'. Pilots would complain of an uncongenial activity that it 'binds me rigid'. Inevitably, when it came to serious matters, understatement was obligatory. 'Walking out' was parachuting out from a burning aeroplane. Colliding with the ground or sea at several hundred miles an hour was 'going in'. Many a pilot's death was announced with the laconic news that he had 'had it', or 'bought it', or 'gone for a Burton'. The Fighter Boys' enthusiasm for Hollywood movies and American singers and bands provided them with a rich new word-hoard. To the more traditional types, girls were still 'popsies'. But among the racier pilots, young women became 'dames' or 'broads'.

Most pilots were on the look-out for fun, and fun was almost invariably accompanied by alcohol. Fighter Boys were drinkers. Despite the obvious unwisdom of the combination, pilots and alcohol had always gone together. Beer, the tangy sudsy bitter of the county breweries that covered the country, was what they customarily ordered, served in dimpled mugs or pewter tankards, up to eight pints a night. They drank it, when they were not in the mess, in pubs whose nostalgia-wreathed names became as fondly remembered by the pilots as the airfields at which they served: the Red Lion at Whittlesford, the Old Ship at Bosham, the White Horse at Andover, the Golden Cross near Canterbury.

At the height of the summer battles, every effort would be made to get to the pub before closing time no matter how hard the day had been. Pilots at Biggin Hill welcomed the shortening of the days as the summer wore on, as it meant they could reach the brass rail sooner. Often they would be driven there by the station commander. 'Dick Grice had a tannoy speaker mounted on his car and we'd be down at the White Hart and you could hear him coming from a mile away,' said Pete Brothers. '"This is the CO. I want three scotches and two pints of bitter." He'd got a bunch of chaps in the car and and was calling up the bar. You could hear this booming across the countryside.'[24]

The White Hart at Brasted, a pleasant village that straggles along the road from Westerham to Sevenoaks, became the most celebrated of the Fighter Boys pubs. There had been an inn on the site since the seventeenth century. It had steep-pitched tile roofs and thick lintels, large rooms made cosy with beams and fireplaces and stone-flagged floors. The White Hart was not the nearest pub to Biggin Hill, seven miles away across the fields, but it was the most attractive. The bar was presided over by a reserve navy officer, Teddy Preston, and his wife Kath. Among the customers were Moira and Sheila, handsome twins and the daughters of Sir Hector Macneal, a friend of Beaverbrook who lived near by at the Red House. They were, in Brian Kingcome's description, 'tall, elegant, sophisticated and beautiful young women . . . They exuded the indefinable quality that comes from impeccable taste'.[25] Moira, the elder, was married to an air commodore on duty posted to the Middle East. Sheila was the widow of a fighter pilot who had disappeared after being sent on a hopeless mission on a winter night at the start of the war. She was left with a small daughter, Lesley.

Behind the blackout curtains the pilots would banter among themselves and with local customers, flirt with the Macneal twins and, when gently moved on by the local policeman at closing time, look for somewhere else to drink. Tony Bartley recorded the last frantic minutes of a typical session.

> 'Time gentlemen please,' yelled the barman.
>
> 'Who's for the Red House?' said one of the twins . . . There was a unanimous howl of approval . . . We piled into the station wagon like sardines again, and after a short drive arrived in front of a fine old

> red-brick manor house. The twins had gone ahead and were waiting for us at the door. I was shown into the drawing room and had a very large whisky thrust into my hand. Someone put on the radiogram.[26]

After its move to Biggin Hill in September, 92 Squadron ensured there was always somewhere to go by creating its own club in Southwood Manor House, to where the pilots had been moved by Grice, who dispersed the squadrons around surrounding country houses because the incessant bombing made it too dangerous to stay on the base at night. The squadron had a jazz pianist of professional standard in Bob Holland. Other musicians from among the Biggin Hill staff would be drafted in for jam sessions. Writing to a Waaf friend, Holland enthused about their 'wizard billet which is in a fairly large country house we have taken over with a dance floor, piano, drums, double bass and plenty of VR musicians to go with it. We just have a night club here every night. Our drink bill is mounting up to something terrific, but still, what the hell!' Fun was necessary to forget what was happening. The next line in the latter reads: 'Poor old Bill Williams and Drummond were killed this morning. They must move us soon for a rest.'[27]

Pilots pursued fun with the same enthusiasm that they brought to flying. Even at the height of the battles, pilots at the London perimeter bases would manage sorties to the West End. 'There was almost a daily routine at the height of the summer,' remembered Geoffrey Page, who was with 56 Squadron at North Weald. 'We'd land, having been based all day at somewhere like Manston, trying to get on the ground in time . . . to get to the pub. The pubs closed at 10.30, so the rush getting from your aircraft to the local tavern was enormous. We'd make it. The landlady would give us some extra time, then some idiot would suggest we went up to London. We'd bundle into various cars, drive up and stay in a night club until two in the morning. We had to be back on readiness at four. Back we'd come, really not in 100 per cent condition to be doing the job we were doing but happy about it.' They went to the Bag o'Nails in Beak Street or Hatchett's in Piccadilly to bask in the admiration of the young hostesses. These encounters never 'led to anything because you had to get back to the airfield . . . It was just schoolboy enthusiasm and mirth.'[28] Back at North Weald, Page would sober up in the pre-dawn light by walking around the perimeter, acting the part of the keen young officer by pretending to inspect the men guarding the fence.

Some pilots in Al Deere's squadron would dispense with bed altogether after a very late night and simply don their flying jackets and doze on deckchairs in the dew-laden grass at dispersal, waiting for the first scramble of the day. Archie Winskill, based at Hornchurch, would go to Romford with his squadron friends and take the tube to Piccadilly Circus 'to hit the high spots. Often we stayed all night at the Jermyn Street Turkish Baths, which were open all night, and then after a few hours' sleep, went back on the tube to Romford and into the cockpit.'[29] The Antipodeans would meet up at the Tivoli bar close to Australia House and New Zealand House in the Strand. Irving Smith, a New Zealander with 151 Squadron had arranged to meet some friends there one evening but was delayed. His quarters at North Weald had been bombed. He was separated from his kit and had been moved to Stapleford Tawney. He sent a message to the bar saying he would not be coming, but then discovered there was a train that could get him to London by closing time. He arrived to find them holding a wake. 'My message was garbled,' he said later. 'They all thought I'd been shot down and was dead. After that there was a great thrash.'[30]

Away from the metropolis the fun was less sophisticated. No. 87 Squadron, based in Exeter, lived in two hotels but had little contact with the local people. Their main social contacts were with the police and the Royal Marines, who invited them to drinks at headquarters. Internal squadron celebrations could have the quality of a provincial Rugby club piss-up. The unofficial diary of 73 Squadron, based at Church Fenton in Yorkshire, records a dinner held to mark the departure of one of the pilots on 29 August.

> Throughout dinner Henry sat miserably, tugging at a large hydrogen balloon tied to his VR collar badge. After he had eaten his fill he was duly escorted to The Ship by the CO and Reggie Lovett [a flight

> commander], in company with several other members of the sqn. What a night! At 11.30 p.m. he was duly carried out of The Ship screaming loudly for assistance. After several unsuccessful attempts he was inserted into the awaiting vehicle where he peacefully passed out on the floor while being driven back to the mess. On arrival he was carted up to his room where we at last fulfilled our promise and put Henry to bed with his boots on. During the night sundry untoward incidents occurred about which the less said the better! However at 5 o'clock the following morning a certain very soiled-looking figure was seen searching for his teeth with almost frantic energy. They were eventually found in a place where they were very nearly washed away for good, and as a result they spent the rest of the night in strong disinfectant![31]

The authorities took a sympathetic attitude to drink. In July 1940 the Judge Advocate General of the RAF, Foster MacGeagh, pointed out that the Air Force Act had purposely avoided precision over what exactly constituted drunkenness. He drew attention to the observation of his predecessor that it was 'one of those things that it is easier to recognize than to define comprehensively'. He concluded that 'the only safe rule is that no person should be convicted of drunkenness . . . unless the court is satisfied that he was so much under the influence of drink as to be drunk according to the view of ordinary, reasonable men'.[32] In fighter squadrons, that allowed considerable leeway.

Commanders understood the need for release. When his pilots grew more and more fatigued Beamish arranged the rota to try and give everyone one day in four off duty. Sometimes he would accompany them to town, impressing the younger men with the familiarity with which he was greeted by the female habituées of the night clubs. Peter Devitt, commanding 152 Squadron, would send exhausted pilots off to a pub in Swanage to rest for forty-eight hours. Staying in with a cup of cocoa did not guarantee either success or survival. Charlton Haw found that 'throughout the war, people in squadrons who used to go to bed early and not go out and chase a few pints were far more likely to buy it than people who were a little bit on the wild side'.[33]

Laughter and drink edged out thoughts of death. The lowest hour of the day was always the first, sitting at dispersal in silence, smelling the familiar smells of crushed grass, metal, oil and high-octane fuel, waiting for the arrival of the coffee wagon to dispel the beer taste lingering from the night before, nervous sickness stirring in the bowels in anticipation of the first scramble. This was the time when courage was most fragile. Each pilot braced himself to face a day which might bring death or horrible injury. If he survived it was only in order to face the same ordeal the next morning. The ring of the ops telephone was almost welcome. Then, an hour later, they were back on the ground and if everyone had made it home the mood was transformed. It was as if the sun had emerged from behind a cloud. So far, so good. The first, the worst, was over. Having got through it, the pilots' natural optimism persuaded them to hope that the end would not come that day. Clambering out of the cockpits, the relief showed in the shouted banter and the sudden appetite for bacon and eggs swimming in greasy Naafi trays by the dispersal hut. But towards the close of day the foreboding returned. The pilots were strained and tired. Their nerves were on the surface now, exposed by the constant ebb and flow of emotions and sensations: fear, hatred, anger, satisfaction. So many had gone up on the last sortie of the day and not returned. It seemed to be tempting fate. It was without eagerness that they trotted out across the lengthening shadows towards their Hurricanes and Spitfires, and with thankfulness that they bumped down over the grass or concrete and headed for the pub.

The resolution of the pilots, their ability to keep going up day after day, over and over, with each trip shrinking the odds of survival, was sustained by interlocking feelings and convictions. The essential sentiment was loyalty, and it came in several forms. There was loyalty to the country and its inhabitants. Noisy expressions of patriotism were considered bad form in Fighter Command. It took outsiders to see how deep and passionate the attachment was. Tim Vigors had been schooled in England and spent much of his youth there, but considered himself an Irishman to the extent of having a tricolour painted on the nose of his Spitfire. He wrote later that he was 'not possessed of that uncaring patriotism which caused so many young Englishmen . . . unselfishly to lay down their lives for their country'. But he believed that had the battles been fought 'over the green fields and purple mountains of Tipperary, in all probability I would have been fired with the same wild, protective feeling for my country which was responsible for the deaths of so many of my brave friends and almost certainly would not be alive . . . today'.[34]

Next to this lay loyalty to comrades. The determination not to let down the man next to you is the main ingredient of military courage and the dynamo that drives all wars. 'The strongest feeling was not to disappoint your friends,' said Peter Dunning-White. 'There was no question of not flying. You daren't not take off.'[35] This was particularly true of the leaders. It was impossible to funk it without everyone seeing you turn away. Belonging depended on sharing the risks and the dangers, and also, though it was by no means essential, achieving some success. No matter how fearful they might be, pilots wanted very much to fly and to succeed, even the least experienced. As the attrition of the summer ground on, Ian Hutchinson ended up as the most senior sergeant pilot in his squadron, able to decide for himself whether or not he would fly. 'We were flying from a base near Southend and the scramble call came. One chap came to me and said, "Can't I fly?" I had been flying all the time so I said OK. He went up and he was killed. It was such a shame. He was a lovely chap. I hadn't allowed him to gain enough experience so I blamed myself.'[36]

The pilots were fighting a battle for the survival of Britain. It was only afterwards that the significance of their effort started to become apparent. Most pilots held the silent conviction that they were engaged in a struggle between good and evil. That feeling intensified the longer the war continued. Beyond their allegiance to hearth, home and squadron, a loyalty to humanity drove them on. Brian Kingcome remembered looking at the body of a dead German airman, a member of the crew of a Ju 88 he had helped shoot down near Minehead. 'Gazing at the young man lying in front of me I could not accept that he had been some kind of non-political combatant. He seemed too close to the ideal Aryan mould cherished by Hitler to be a coincidence or accident, and any charitable . . . thoughts I might normally have harboured simply remained frozen . . . I found myself looking at him with loathing.[37]

Stories circulated of German breaches of the unwritten conventions of aerial war, in particular the cold-blooded shooting of pilots as they dangled defencelessly on the end of parachutes. The pilots of 266 Squadron believed that their commander, Squadron Leader Rodney Wilkinson, had been killed in this way on 16 August. 'He was seen to bale out of his crippled aircraft apparently unhurt but his body was found, so we were told, as full of holes as a sieve,' Dennis Armitage reported. 'This incident stirred up intense hatred of the Germans. Perhaps they had some justification in that a fully trained and experienced pilot was far harder to replace than the machine he was flying, but our "Wilkie" was much loved and the thought that he was shot up while dangling helplessly from a parachute filled us with a vindictive hate that had not been there before.'[38] Other accounts say he died colliding with a Me 109. Squadron Leader Harold Starr of 253 Squadron was certainly machine-gunned to death by a Messerschmitt after he baled out over Eastry in Kent on 31 August. Flight Lieutenant Robert Ash, flying as gunner with a Defiant of 264 Squadron, baled out after being hit on the morning of 28 August. The pilot also jumped and landed with minor injuries, yet Ash was found dead with bullet wounds in his body. Dennis David believed Johnny Dewar had been shot while descending.

There were no accusations that British pilots had ever responded in kind. There were some suspicions, though, that Polish pilots were less fastidious. Peter Matthews was on leave at the beginning of September and went home to Ewell. He was teaching his wife to drive on Epsom Downs when he looked up to see 'Hurricanes shooting down Germans in parachutes. I knew jolly well who they were. They were 303 Squadron boys. Poles. They owned to it.'[39]

As the German attack widened to include civilians, British sensibilities hardened. Pilot Officer Richard Barclay of 249 Squadron reported in his diary how he had led a chase of two Me 109s, one of which tried to crash-land near Manston. 'Just as he was at tree-top height Sergeant X shot at the E/A [enemy aircraft]. It flew straight into some trees and crashed in flames. On returning Butch [Flight Lieutenant Robert Barton] tore a terrific strip off Sergeant X about his unsportsmanship, etc., and we all heartily agreed.' The following day the squadron heard of the bombing of Coventry. Barclay noted: 'We are inclined to think that perhaps Sergeant X's action yesterday wasn't so bad after all.'[40]

Paddy Finucane's detached attitude towards the Germans changed after he visited Southampton to see friends shortly after a blitz. When he returned he was visited by a Polish pilot friend, Boleslaw 'Ski' Drobinski, at his room in the country house near Tangmere where he was billeted. Finucane stood shaving while Drobinski listened. 'It was the longest shave I can remember,' he told Finucane's biographer. 'We talked for about an hour. Speaking slowly to ensure I understood, Paddy said: "Listen, Ski, when this war is over we must make sure there will not be another one. It is a terrible way to settle anything. Until it is, we must shoot down every bloody Jerry from the sky."'[41] For some, the point of the fighting now was to hurt as well as to kill. Sailor Malan told Geoffrey Flavell, a doctor acquaintance, that he changed tactics and now tried to avoid shooting down bombers outright. 'If you shoot them down they don't get back and no one in Germany is a whit the wiser. So I figure the right thing to do is let them get back. With a dead rear gunner, a dead navigator, and the pilot coughing his lungs up as he lands . . . I think if you do that it has a better effect on their morale.'[42]

Killing and maiming were none the less not things to boast about. Most pilots told themselves and the outside world that, when they shot at a German aeroplane, they were aiming at the machine not the man. George Bennions 'was relieved when they baled out'. Another 41 Squadron pilot, Tony Lovell, who was a devout Catholic, 'used to go and see the RC padre and pray for forgiveness . . . He used to get very upset when he'd shot something down, very upset.'[43] Michael Constable Maxwell of 56 Squadron, another fervent Catholic, left behind in his diary an account of the complex evolution of his feelings as he closed in on a Dornier that he had managed to isolate from the fleet.

> While attacking the formation I was frightened and excited, but once it had left the others I began to experience the most wonderful and jubilant excitement imaginable. I took a joyful pleasure in the thought that I had made it leave the formation, and all I wanted to do was close in and kill. I had no fear of his bullets, even though a shower of tracer came at me whenever I got within range, and I felt no compunction in shooting something damaged. I just felt a primitive urge to chase and to kill . . .
>
> [But then] suddenly all this changed. I saw that he had had enough and merely wanted to land. The fight was over. He had given in and all he wanted was a safe place to get down. Four humans were in that plane. They were up in the air and in a damaged machine that the pilot was heroically trying to land. This last few minutes [were] the most unpleasant I have experienced in this war. I was safe, they were in danger of death. They crashed and no one got out.

The next day's entry describes an encounter he had with some other pilots with a local lawyer who was friendly with the squadron. 'He is told of the Dornier. "Oh how absolutely splendid of you, I do hope they were all killed!"' Constable Maxwell found this 'the filthiest remark I have ever heard and I was staggered by its bloody sadism . . . it is this loathsome attitude which allows papers to print pictures of wounded Germans. They must be killed and I hope to kill many myself . . . but the act is the unpleasant duty of the executioner which must be done ruthless and merciless [*sic*] – but it can be done silently.'[44]

No matter how powerful the pilots' motivations might be, they could not dispel the surges of fear that rose and fell with the stresses of the day. Robin Appleford 'got that sort of sick feeling all the time. I think most people if they were honest would confirm this.'[45] Peter Devitt was 'scared bloody stiff most of the time and anybody who says he wasn't frightened . . . was just as frightened as everybody else'.[46] Even Wing Commander Teddy Donaldson, who was notably unsparing of his pilots in 151 Squadron, admitted that the experience of tackling enemy aircraft when hugely outnumbered was 'very, very, frightening'.[47] But the level of fear climbed and fell away. In between the peaks were periods of excitement, even of boredom. No pilot could have operated if gripped by terror.

Few were ever overwhelmed by fear, but for some the struggle was fearful. One pilot in 501 Squadron would pause to vomit as he ran out to his aeroplane. One of George Unwin's sergeant pilots was 'terrified not of the Germans but of the Spitfire. I used to say, look, would you like me to have a word with the CO, and get you on to bombers. "No, no," he said, "that shows I'm a coward." I said, "Be buggered, it doesn't show you're a coward at all if you're prepared to go on bloody bombers." But he wouldn't and eventually he killed himself landing.'[48]

Constant exposure to fear, though, inevitably caused psychological damage. Pete Brothers came across one of his pilots sitting on the grass bathed in sweat and ordered him to report to the medical officer. Later 'the doc appeared and said: "This chap's sick. He's not to fly again. I'm grounding him."' He had been suffering the delusion that he had been shot down in flames, the fate of another squadron member the day before.[49] Fatigue, Birdy Bird-Wilson remembered, 'broke into a chap's mentality in the most peculiar ways. Some really got the jitters . . . others, as I did, had nightmares at night. I used to wake up in the dispersal hut . . . and I was night-flying my Hurricane. This went on for quite a long time.'[50]

Good squadron leaders understood when a man was at the end of his limits and had him posted away for a rest, usually as an instructor at an Operational Training Unit. Peter Down recognized the symptoms in himself. In the middle of September, though he was only a pilot officer, he led the remnants of 56 Squadron out of the line to Boscombe Down. They were given a week's leave, but Down knew that would not be enough. He asked to see Air Vice-Marshal Sir Christopher Quintin Brand, the commander of 10 Group. 'To my surprise he appeared two days later and led me under a tree near our dispersal point away from everybody else and said, "What do you want to see me about?" And I just said I wanted a break . . . I seemed to be doing all the work because of the lack of experience of anybody else. I knew my England without looking at a map and could fly anywhere within reason, whereas the squadron commander at the time didn't have the ability to do so . . . He said, "All right, nice to have spoken to you," and he gave me a pat on the shoulder and left. Three or four days later the signal came through saying I could take myself off as an instructor to Sutton Bridge.'[51]

The training units at Sutton Bridge and Aston Down were staging posts for many strung-out pilots. 'You saw chaps who had really taken shock extremely badly,' said Birdy Bird-Wilson, who instructed in both. 'They'd come into the bar and they'd have a terrible facial twitch or a body twitch and there was nothing you could do to help them except to act back again the same twitch. If they had a facial twitch, while you're drinking your drink, whatever it might be, you did the same back to them. And so they realized they were doing it – it's a very cruel way to be kind . . . It cured chaps in the end, it really did, and they returned to operations thereafter.'[52]

In a small number of cases a pilot's inability to fulfil his duty could not be overlooked and action had to be taken. One pilot came to Donaldson and 'admitted to me that he was a bit terrified and so I said, "Right then, off."' He had already noticed 'too many engine failures. He'd just disappear in the middle of a battle and go home.'[53] Denys Gillam witnessed one pilot who 'went to pieces on the ground, just as he was getting into his aeroplane. The doctor [was] seeing us off. He hit this chap on the chin, hard, knocked him out. He didn't fly again.'[54]

In one case it was the commander himself whose nerve was suspect. In early September Pete Brothers and Bob Tuck were posted to 257 Squadron at Martlesham Heath to replace two flight commanders who had been killed on the same day on the same operation. Brothers discovered that 'morale in the squadron was . . . way down the bottom, naturally. They were a bunch of young chaps, only two of them with pre-war experience. The others were chaps with minimum training. Naturally they were thinking, if these two experienced chaps can be shot down, what sort of chance have we got?'

On the first sortie they flew with the squadron leader, the ground controller ordered them to patrol a line above Maidstone at 20,000 feet. As they did so they saw a large formation of bombers with fighter escorts approaching and alerted the squadron leader. 'He said, "We've been told to patrol the Maidstone line and that's what we'll do until we've been told to do otherwise." So we all pissed off and left him and got stuck in.' Later Brothers worried that perhaps he had made a misjudgement. 'But then this happened a second time, then a third time, and we decided that this chap just wanted to avoid combat at all costs.' A few nights after they arrived, after fortifying themselves with beer, they rang up Keith Park and asked for him to be sacked.[55] The squadron leader was immediately posted away to a training unit. Other pilots deemed to be suffering from 'lack of moral fibre' were put on menial duties like towing drogues.

The pilots' resolution was fortified by the knowledge of the admiration they were held in by everyone in the country. Churchill had acknowledged the nation's debt in a speech on 20 August in the House of Commons, when he expressed the thanks of 'every home in our Island, our Empire, and indeed throughout the world', towards the pilots, who were 'turning the tide of world war by their prowess and devotion. Never in the field of human conflict was so much owed by so many to so few.' This gratitude was already visible to the pilots every time they ventured off base.

Yvonne Agazarian became the most envied girl in her convent school, which had been evacuated to Rugby, when her handsome, adored brother Noel arrived to visit her during a leave. 'The girls were gaga about him,' she said. 'He seemed a wonderful, incredible figure.'[56] Tom Bartley found that after the Churchill speech fighter pilots were 'the epitome of glamour. It was unbelievable. They loved us, and I mean loved. They bought us drinks, appreciated everything.'[57] On trips to London, Robin Appleford and Rob Bodie would wear their flying boots, ensuring a flow of free drinks and the undivided attention of the girls. The practice of wearing the top button undone was now well known. When men in air force blue walked into a pub, eyes would stray to their tunics and the word would go around that there were Fighter Boys in the bar. The pilots were polite to civilians, sometimes actually welcoming the chance to talk about things other than the fighting. Mostly, though, they preferred the warmth and security of their own company.

The great exception to the rule was women. The attitude of the pre-war RAF had been courtly and correct. At Tangmere, the young women Billy Drake met were the sisters of brother officers or the daughters of family friends. They would attend balls at the station, be entertained to drinks in the ladies' room in the mess, and in the summer sail and swim. It was all very proper. 'These were very innocent affairs. You knew the parents. They knew you.' The raffish life of the RFC pilots was alien to the modern young men of Fighter Command. 'There was no bought sex as such. If anybody was oversexed they dealt with the situation but they didn't talk about it.'[58]

For most respectable young men in 1940 the world of sex was remote and mysterious. War would bring it closer, but for many it would remain out of reach. No one knows how many of those who died in the battles of the year went to their deaths without having slept with a woman. The pilots liked to portray themselves as men of the world. Their upbringings, however, had given them little chance to acquire much sophistication in matters of sex. Most of them had passed their adolescence in classrooms and playing fields before entering service life. The majority of RAFVR entrants had been in conservative jobs where there was little opportunity for revelry. The conservative mores of the time swamped their outlooks, ladled on thickly by the heavy hands of their parents. Paddy Finucane wrote home reassuringly to his mother and father from Rochford on 9 August, after a party at a local hospital, 'We had a rattling good time and the nurses were a jolly decent lot and thought the boys in blues [*sic*] were all heroes. They could not do enough for us. It got rather embarrassing. After a while they all wanted to go for a walk round the grounds. Yours truly played the game and admired the beauty of the evening but not letting myself in for anything.'[59]

Time, everyone knew, was short. Perhaps there was no time at all. It was the classic chat-up line of the military seducer. But it was affection, if possible love, that most pilots seemed to be looking for. Striking up any kind of relationship was difficult in a life of constant geographical shifts, a heavy weight of duty that kept you occupied for all the hours of daylight and which was punctuated by only brief and unpredictable periods of leave. Keeping in touch by telephone required serious dedication. Three-minute calls were all that wartime restrictions allowed and they could take hours to be put through. Robin Appleford and Rob Bodie were lucky. One night at the Tiger's Head in Chislehurst they fell in with two wealthy civilians who had two young women, Christine and Pamela, in tow. By the end of the evening the women had switched allegiances and the four spent several happy weeks together, until the pilots were posted away.

An RAF uniform, a pilots' wings, could be a passport to sex in the summer and autumn of 1940. Charles Fenwick went to the aid of a young woman who was being pestered by an army officer in the bar of a London hotel. The intervention led to drinks, lunch and a trip to the cinema. 'As soon as we had settled down to watch a flick I put my arms around her shoulders . . . then before I can say Jack Robinson, she slips her hand under my raincoat and into my trousers nearly shooting me through the roof with surprise.' Fenwick had already lost his virginity to a thirty-five-year-old woman married to a wealthy industrialist who lived in the north and left his wife to her own devices. She collected Fenwick from the Tangmere mess and drove him around the surrounding pubs, embarrassing him by leaving her Dutch cap on the bar while she rummaged in her handbag for cigarettes.[60]

The most obvious source of women was the WAAF. By the middle of the summer Waafs were to be found on most of the main fighter bases. The girls of the first war-time intakes were adventurous, reasonably educated by the standards of the time, anxious to show they could hold their own in a man's world, yet also alive to the possibilities of romance. Edith Heap, a well-brought-up young woman from Nun Monkton in Yorkshire, arrived at Debden in the autumn of 1940 to work in the motor transport pool, driving Albion two-and-a-half-ton lorries and the tractors which laid out the flare paths to guide the pilots in at night. The women worked hard, their hours were long, and the airmens' married quarters they lived in three to a billet were cold and damp. Both the RAF commanders and their own female officers imposed strict discipline, wary of the consequences of having young men and women in close proximity, and they did what they could to limit their social lives. The Waafs were only allowed off the base with permission and had to be back by 10.15 p.m.

It was impossible, of course, to keep the Waafs and airmen apart. Edith Heap and her friend Winifred Butler came across the pilots, mostly public-school boys of their own age, as they drove them around the base or ran them to the satellite station at Martlesham Heath. The friends were attractive, funny and independent-minded. Edith had her own car, a baby Jaguar, a classier motor than most pilots could afford, which she sometimes let them borrow for trips to London. The girls were popular and often taken out to dinner at the Red Lion at Duxford or the Rose and Crown at Bishop's Stortford. They had two particular admirers, Jerrard Jefferies, tall, 'quite knockout to look at', with a silver streak in his dark hair, and Richard Whittaker. The relationships never had time to develop. 'Jeff' was posted as flight commander to a Czech unit, 310 Squadron at Duxford. Whittaker was killed over France.

One day Edith met Denis Wissler of 17 Squadron. He was eager, particularly boyish-looking, but perhaps slightly more sophisticated than most. On his first trip to France with 85 Squadron in May, he confided to his diary, he had visited a 'place of doubtful virtue' in Le Havre. But the impression shining from the diary's pages is of an innocent young man, anxious to meet the right girl, fall in love, marry and live happily ever after. His and Edith's first encounter was gauche. He playfully threw some sand at the tractor she was driving and the engine stopped. She offered him the crank handle and ordered him to start it again, which, sheepishly, he did.

Wissler's months at Debden and Tangmere after his return from France were dominated by the desire to succeed as a fighter pilot and the search for a nice girl. His keenness was unquestionable. But he never seemed to be there when the squadron did well. '"A" Flight were over at Martlesham and shot down five machines,' he wrote on 12 July. 'What a party they had.' He, though, was in 'B' flight, which did not get into the action. On the 28th he practised aerial gunnery shooting at a drogue. 'The scores were awful,' he recorded. 'I failed to hit the thing at all.' The following day he had better luck. 'Up at 4.30 and forward to Martlesham Heath. I was with Flight Lieutenant Bayne and Flying Officer Bird-Wilson and after one uneventful patrol we met a Heinkel 111 which was being half-heartedly attacked by Spitfires. We made a head-on attack and then an astern attack, pieces and oil coming out in all directions. The E/A slowly went down to the water, I thought it was trying to get away low down and made another head-on attack. This time in [it] went into the water.' He was credited with a share in the destruction of the Heinkel.

Many of the diary entries, though, fizz with mild dissatisfaction. On 9 August he broke his wireless transmitter and was fined ten shillings and later, while watching the daily inspection of his Hurricane, got himself covered in oil. He went to bed 'in a damn bad temper . . . everything has gone wrong today'.[61] His days were spent in long periods at readiness, followed by frustrating patrols and interceptions in which little or nothing happened. On the 20th the squadron moved briefly to Tangmere and at last he was deep in the action. On the 25th he was in 'a hell of a scrap' over Portland. He saw two Me 110s he had fired on going down, but the operations record book notes just one 'probable' and only gave him a share. When the squadron learned that it was to return to Debden at the start of September, it was rumoured this would precede a further move out of the firing line to Northern Ireland. 'I hope not,' he wrote.

The squadron stayed in East Anglia. One night his friend Birdy Bird-Wilson asked him to come out to dinner with a girl he knew and her friend. The girl was Winifred Butler. Bird-Wilson was keen on her but was already engaged, an arrangement that was stalled until his situation became less precarious. He thought Denis might take her mind off the loss of Richard Whittaker. The friend was Edith Heap. Both women had by now graduated from driving to the highly responsible work of plotting, shifting the indicators around the map table in the control room to show the progress of the raids and battles. As they drove away from the base for dinner in Bishop's Stortford, Birdy sat in the front with Winifred, and Denis and Edith were in the back. 'We got on like a house on fire and gradually the conversation became two tête-à-têtes,' Edith remembered.[61]

Driving back, they heard a colossal bang, saw flames leaping up from some distant fields and went to investigate. In the excitement, Denis held Edith's hand. They found a stable block ablaze where a departing night raider had jettisoned his bombs. The fire brigade was already there, so they resumed the journey to Debden. 'That seemed to be that,' Edith thought at the time. 'Denis was taking out someone else. It had been a lovely dinner, he had been attentive and fun but not specially interested.' The woman in question he had met not long before at a party in the sergeants' mess. She was, he reported in his diary, 'a sweet little Waaf called Margaret Cameron'. They had 'quite a kissing session after the party was over'.

On the morning of Tuesday, 24 September, 17 Squadron was ordered south to intercept bombers approaching the Thames estuary. Their Hurricanes were still climbing when they saw the formation. As they closed on it, they were surprised to find a gaggle of Spitfires diving towards them, followed closely by a large number of Me 109s. Denis made one attack, broke it off, then climbed to make a second on a group of four Messerschmitts above him. Realizing he was about to stall, he levelled off. 'There was a blinding flash on my port wing and I felt a hell of a blow on my left arm and then blood running down. I went into a hell of a dive and came back to Debden. A cannon shell hit my right wing and a bit of it had hit me just above the elbow and behind.' Somehow he got the Hurricane down, but the shell had blown away most of the port flap and he was unable to stop, slewing off the runway into a pile of stones and cutting his face.

He was taken to Saffron Walden hospital. The following day he had visitors. Edith and Winifred came to see him. He was hungry and the girls went out to buy cakes and sandwiches. The following day he was released and spent the evening at 'a hell of a party in the sergeants' mess'. He also, as he recorded ruefully, 'put up a hell of a black with Margaret [Cameron], as I rather deserted her for two other friends'. On Sunday, before going off on seven days' sick leave, there was another bash in the sergeants' mess. The pilots would arrive after dinner in the mess for the arrival of the band and the dancing would carry on until 10.30 when the Waafs had to leave. Denis was delighted to see his hospital visitor among them. 'Met Edith Heap and fell in love with her at sight,' he wrote before going to bed that night.

When he returned from visiting his parents in London there was yet another party, this time at the 'B' Flight dispersal hut to mark 17 Squadron's imminent move to Martlesham. Edith and Winifred were there, with 'Jeff', who was visiting the base, in attendance. Denis, Edith wrote later, 'just commandeered me. We danced and chatted all evening.' In honour of the occasion the Waafs were allowed to stay until midnight. 'Just as we had to go a rather stormy Jeff arrived in front of me, furious because I had not gone to find him. I told him it was up to him to do that, not me.' Edith felt he was being unreasonable. He had not written while being at Duxford, and anyway had spent most of the evening dancing with Winifred. Edith didn't care. 'I was bowled over. Denis and I arranged to write each day and meet again as soon as our duties allowed it.' Denis was now smitten. 'My God it seems to be the real thing this time,' ran the awestruck entry in his diary. 'She is so sweet and seems to like me as much as I like her.' It was ten days before they saw each other again. Edith managed to arrange a twenty-four-hour pass. They decided to spend the night at Cambridge. 'We couldn't get into the Garden House Hotel,' she recalled. 'Denis came back saying, "We can only have a double room and that's not right, is it?" And I said, "No, it isn't."' They found two rooms at the Red Lion at Trumpington.

During dinner he told her he had something to say to her. They went upstairs to her room. 'He sat on the bed and I leaned against the dressing table. He just said, "Will you marry me?" And I said, "Yes."' Champagne was ordered. They drank it and went to their separate beds. The next day Denis insisted they drive to London to break the news to his family. His parents had moved to Dolphin Square, across the Thames from the Marmite factory which 'Pop' Wissler ran. On the way they stopped off in Cambridge to order an engagement ring. Edith telephoned the base to plead for an extension to her leave, which was granted as long as she was back for duty the following day. Denis rang ahead to Dolphin Square to say he was bringing a friend. When they arrived, Edith 'got ever so apprehensive. I think he did as well. On the way down the corridor to the flat he held my hand. I was in a blue funk by this time.'[62] Denis had said nothing in letters and calls home about Edith and was worried in his diary about keeping them in the dark. 'I don't want to hurt them,' he wrote, 'for I love them so.' There was no cause for concern. 'Denis shot me into the bathroom while he told them the news. I just stood there shaking in my shoes. A yell from the sitting room and I emerged to be hugged and kissed. I belonged to the family from that minute.' There were drinks, then dinner. Despite a bombing raid, everyone 'laughed all through dinner till we ached, completely ignoring all the banging and crashing going on outside'.

Edith took him to Yorkshire to meet her family. Then they spent another forty-eight-hour leave together at Dolphin Square, planning the wedding, set for 4 January, the date of the Wisslers' own anniversary. Denis had been anxious to get married as quickly as possible, and was delighted that she had already applied to leave the WAAF as the regulations demanded. 'Oh my darling it is grand you putting in your discharge now,' he wrote. 'We might speed up getting married a little if you say the word, but it all rests with you, my sweet. I wonder what you bought yourself while you were in Cambridge. I am living for the time I shall find out. Oh darling, I do miss you so, I do so love to be with you. Oh, I need you by me, I love you so, so much.'[63]

Three days after he returned from London, on the morning of 11 November, Denis landed at Martlesham Heath from an uneventful patrol over a convoy. Towards noon the squadron was scrambled again to intercept sixty dive bombers apparently heading for the same ships. Denis was in Blue Section. Edith and Winifred were at work in the control room, which had been moved to Saffron Walden after the summer blitzes of Debden. The 17 Squadron Hurricanes were vectored on to a plot that would bring them into contact with the Germans over Burnham in Essex. Edith tracked the fighters, Winifred the raiders. 'We could hear everything that was going on and all the battle that took place,' Edith said. Over the tannoy came a voice yelling that Blue Four was going down into the sea. 'I knew who that was. It was Denis. I didn't say anything. I just sat there because we had finished our work. They were coming back.' She went off duty but was unable to eat lunch, still forcing herself to hope it wasn't true. She tried to stifle her fears by going to the motor depot to talk to her old colleagues. 'When I got back to Saffron, Bill [her former superior] was waiting for me . . . Yes it was true, he was missing. No parachute.'

The following day she went to break the news to the Wisslers. Pop Wissler's grief was savage and shocking. A little later she was invited to lunch at Martlesham and to pick up Denis's belongings. His body had not been found. He had apparently been shot down by Me 109s while flying into the bombers, after the order to break off the attack had been given. Three days before, while on leave, he made his last diary entry. Once again he had been absent during a day when the squadron had done well. 'Each of the blokes got at least one,' he wrote. 'Total score fifteen destroyed and some probable. Oh God, fancy missing a party like that.'

16

'The Day Had Been a Year'

Saturday, 7 September, like all the preceding days of the month, was sunny, cloudless and hot. It was perfect bombing weather. In the early morning the Germans flew the usual reconnaissance missions to note the damage from the raids of the day and night before. Fighter Command braced itself for the first wave of what was expected to be another series of attacks on the bases. But no bombers came. For six hours the radar screens remained blank. Out at dispersal the pilots wondered at the inactivity, then gratefully took the opportunity to doze in the glowing sunshine. It could not last. Dowding and Park listened to the silence with foreboding. Clearly something ominous was brewing. At 3.54 p.m. the spell was broken. The first report came in that aircraft were forming up over the Pas de Calais. On the cliffs below, Hermann Goering, dressed operatically in a powder-blue uniform clustered over with gold braid, looked up at his aeroplanes. His dissatisfaction with the performance of his commanders and crews had driven him to take personal charge of the last phase of the air attack before the invasion of Britain was launched. The first formation of bombers swept overhead, nursed by an escort of Messerschmitts. It was followed almost immediately by another; then another. In his headquarters, Dowding looked at the counters crowding the table map and guessed that every aircraft the Luftwaffe could muster was heading for Britain's shores.

By the time the last German pilot had taken off, there were nearly

1,000 machines in the air: 350 bombers and more than 600 fighters stacked up in towering ranks. At the bottom were the Dorniers, Heinkels and Junkers cruising in layers that began at 14,000 feet. At the top were the Messerschmitts, ready to plunge on the British fighters, which would have no choice but to accept the challenge and come up to be annihilated. The enemy force moved through the still, warm air across a front twenty miles wide in a tight, throbbing grid, the biggest mass of aeroplanes ever till then to be assembled. Dowding had only one course of action open. At 4.17 p.m., twenty-three minutes after the first radar sighting, he ordered eleven squadrons to scramble. By 4.30 every Hurricane and Spitfire fighter within a seventy-mile radius of London was in the air or awaiting the order to take off.

Pilot Officer Richard Barclay of 249 Squadron was already airborne. He had been patrolling over the Essex coast, looking down at Clacton, Burnham-on-Crouch, Westgate, places he knew from childhood holidays, baking in the haze. When the alert came, he told his parents in a letter home, the squadron 'started to climb hard, turning to get a good look around and there several miles away was a black line in the sky – 35 Hun bombers in close formation – and I gradually began to distinguish about 70–100 other little dots: Hun fighters.' As the squadron turned to attack, he

> switched on the electric sight and turned the gun button from 'SAFE' to 'FIRE'. And then things began to happen. We went in at the bombers and as I broke away I saw two dropping back from the formation streaming white smoke from one engine but before I could take stock of the situation the Messerschmitts were on me. I say 'me' rather than us because from this time on I never noticed another Hurricane in the sky until the end of the fight . . . I turned quickly to see if there was anything on my tail and at the same moment two Messerschmitt 109s went past beneath my nose. I turned quickly diving on one and gave him a burst. Nothing happened. Presumably I missed him but the noise of my 8 guns gave me great confidence. I gave the second Me 109 a burst and whoopee! A sudden burst of brilliant flame, a cloud of smoke

> and a vast piece flew off and down he went, but no time to watch because there's something behind me shooting . . . I turned to the right and saw [an] Me 109 go past with a vicious yellow nose and the large black crosses on the fuselage.'[1]

Barclay dived away from the German fighters, levelling off at 6,000 feet. Ten thousand feet above he could see the bombers beating inexorably on. He climbed up, keeping his distance so as not to be spotted. As he approached, the formation swung towards him and he raced into the leader in a head-on attack, but had to break off when he ran out of ammunition. He thought he had hit an engine. His own had certainly been damaged. Oil obliterated his windscreen. He switched off and glided down over the Thames estuary. Thick coils of black smoke hung over the water from oil-storage tanks blazing from an attack the previous day. There was no chance of making it back to North Weald. He slid the Hurricane into a belly landing on a field five miles from the base. When he got back the squadron had landed, rearmed and refuelled and was setting off again. There was no aeroplane for Barclay and his fighting was over for the day. The squadron had spent much of the summer in the north and had only arrived in Essex a week before. The sights he had seen that afternoon disturbed him. 'The odds today have been unbelievable,' he wrote in his diary, 'and we are all really shaken.'

Similar frantic scenes were taking place inside an 800-square-mile block of summer sky as hundreds of aircraft clashed. The cerulean blue over the fields of Kent and Essex was scribbled with the white curlicues of condensation trails and stitched with the glitter of cannon and tracer. Alone, frustrated, awaiting the return of his comrades, Barclay saw three bombers approaching the aerodrome at 16,000 feet. He assumed they 'had come back to finish the job they had started on the 3rd' when 200 bombs had been dropped on North Weald. But the bombers sailed on. They were no longer interested in the airfields of Fighter Command. Their target was London.

The decision to attack had been made inevitable by Churchill's ordering of retaliatory raids on Berlin for the Luftwaffe's mistaken bombing of the capital on the night of 24/25 August. Hitler was at Berchtesgaden when the RAF Wellingtons and Hampdens arrived over Berlin early the following morning. They returned two days later, then again on the 30th and 31st. Hitler went to Berlin and promised in a speech on 4 September: 'If they attack our cities then we will wipe out their cities.' Earlier General Jodl, Chief of Staff of the OKW, the Armed Forces Supreme Command, had warned his deputy that Hitler now intended to strike back 'with concentrated forces when the weather is favourable'. Considerations of revenge, taken in hot blood, should not have been allowed to alter the course of the invasion preparations.

The climate of sycophancy pervading Hitler's court and the desire for self-preservation meant that no one would contradict the Führer. Goering, anyway, seems to have approved of the plan. The mass raids could have several beneficial effects. They would continue the campaign of destruction of Britain's infrastructure. Inevitably, they would draw the RAF even more tightly into the war of attrition. Fighter Command had no choice but to defend the capital. It was now becoming obvious to the Germans that Churchill's government was unlikely to seek negotiations without further, more violent coercion. A devastating attack such as those that had traumatized Warsaw and Rotterdam might fatally undermine civilian morale and turn the population against its political and military leaders, forcing them, essentially, to surrender.

Almost every bomber unit in France was thrown into the attack. General Fink, the forty-five-year-old veteran at the head of Kampfgeschwader 2, told his men to make their wills before they took off. So much time was spent forming up that the fighter escort had run out of petrol by the time it reached Sevenoaks and had to turn back. The bombers' target was the Victoria Dock. The huge bend in the Thames at Docklands, the *U-Bogen* as the Luftwaffe called it, glinted treacherously in the sunlight, pointing the way. Despite the lack of an escort, Fink's formation was relatively untroubled by British fighters on the way in. The order to scramble had been given too late for many of the squadrons to reach attacking height by the time the first waves of bombers crossed the coast. Once over London, though, the Spitfires and Hurricanes began to appear.

'They dived through the bomber formations from a terrific height,' Fink remembered. 'Obviously we had too many machine-guns for them to attack any other way. We had the impression that each fighter had chosen one bomber and was diving to attack it . . . It was a horrible feeling when they came down on you.'[2] But the fleet succeeded in dropping its bombs and got away still holding formation. The fighters inflicted some damage. Fink was the only one of his four-man crew not to be wounded and it was a tribute to the sturdiness of their Dornier 17 that it managed to make it back to the base at Arras.

Oberstleutnant Paul Weitkus was commanding 11 Gruppe of the Geschwader with orders to attack Tower Bridge and the docks. 'We all had sketches of our targets. When we reached [the] Docks there were not many fighters but the guns seemed quite good.' They 'placed the bombs very well and large fires started'. Weitkus had time to take photographs of the burning docks, for his own amusement, with his Leica. By the time they had finished, the sky over London was chaotic. 'You couldn't tell a 109 from a Spitfire in the chaos of diving machines and bursting flak. Whoever saw who first was the victor.'[3]

Coming in to land at Arras, Weitkus swung round and there, 150 miles distant, a great banner of smoke stained the horizon above the stricken city. The sirens had sounded at 4.43 p.m. People were slow to move to the shelters, reluctant to leave the sunshine. The first bombs to ripple across the docks were incendiaries that started blazes that acted as beacons to the bombers that would flow in an almost continuous stream throughout the evening and early morning. The first raid lasted less than half an hour. The all-clear was sounded at 6.15 p.m. The shattered streets were full of rescue workers when the next bombers arrived at 8 p.m., dumping their loads of high explosive into the churning smoke and flame beneath. The docks were hit again, and the Royal Arsenal near by at Woolwich. Bombs landed on Victoria and Charing Cross stations and Battersea power station. Those who had remained in the city centre ran for the steps of the underground stations. Hours passed without the comforting wail of the siren announcing the Germans had gone, the air continuing to get heavier and more foul. People spread out newspapers and tried to sleep. The banter slackened and conversation turned serious. A raid as heavy as this must surely mark the start of the invasion. Even below ground in the shelters they could hear the noise and vibration of the anti-aircraft batteries.

The gunners were unable to identify their targets as it was impossible for the searchlights to penetrate the filth and murk that rolled overhead. The warehouses and stores around the Port of London were stacked with combustible goods which, as the bombs landed, blossomed into flames that ran hungrily from each dry, flammable structure to the next. A Thameside refinery disgorged a torrent of molten sugar that covered the river in burning sheets. A rum store caught fire, the barrels exploded like bombs and the streets ran with blazing spirit. The air was choked with soot, oil, chemicals, burning paint and rubber, bound together into a slimy viscous vapour by the water of hundreds of hoses playing on the inferno as ineffectually as a shower of rain on a volcanic eruption. Firemen were surrounded, cut off, vaporized by the superheated oxygen. Whole areas were abandoned to burn themselves out. This was the hell that the pessimists peering into the future of war in the 1920s and 1930s had predicted, the proof of what would happen when the bomber got through. London was experiencing a firestorm. The fire rose, sucking in huge draughts of cold air at its base that fed its intensity, giving it a demonic life of its own that could only end when there was nothing left to nourish it.

It was the poor quarters, clustered around the Port of London where the work was, that suffered most: Bermondsey, Woolwich, Deptford, Polar, Wapping. It was easy for the bomb-aimers. They had only to wait for the sight of the big bend in the river, then release their loads. They were almost bound to hit a worthwhile target. If not, the bombs tumbled into the blank, terraced workers' streets, toppling the thin walls, pulverizing the little houses into dust and splinters. That day and night 306 people were killed in London and 1,337 seriously injured. Another 142 died in the suburbs. This was just the beginning. The raids would continue, with one exception caused by bad weather, for seventy-six consecutive nights.

The fighters had been unable to provide any serious protection for the population of London or prevent the German bombers from smashing and disrupting vital installations. Once night fell, the Luftwaffe was free to bomb unmolested and flew hundreds of sorties. The RAF had only two squadrons of Blenheim night fighters at its disposal, one of which, 600 Squadron, had been prevented from taking off by the clouds of smoke blanketing Hornchurch.

Even in the daytime fighters had performed poorly. The order to scramble had been given late. The caution was understandable. Until now the practice had been to hold back until the direction and size of an attack had revealed itself before committing resources, a tactic designed to make the most effective use of Fighter Command's ragged assets. By the time the nature of the first raid of the afternoon of 7 September became clear, the fighters were too late to position themselves to block the air armada or to scatter the formations and dilute their destructive power. They were able to inflict a certain amount of punishment as the first raiders turned for home, usually with their defensive formations intact. But by then the damage was done. The final total for the day was unimpressive. They shot down thirty-eight German bombers and fighters. But in the process they lost twenty-eight machines. More important were the pilots who had been killed.

But to Dowding and Park, standing at Bentley Priory on the western edge of London and watching the fires reflecting off the underside of the smoke *massif* rising over the city, the day offered hope. The Germans appeared to have shifted the focus of violence away from the airfields and defence installations towards the commercial and political target of the capital. But was this a permanent change, or merely a fluctuation? It seemed unlikely that the Luftwaffe would concentrate its effort on London without first having satisfied itself that it had ground down the RAF to the point where it no longer posed an insurmountable obstacle to an invasion.

The destruction of the air force, and in particular Fighter Command, was the starting point for all German planning for a landing. Goering had consulted the two Luftlotte commanders about the attack on London. Sperrle was dubious but easily persuaded. Kesselring was supportive. He assumed that if the southern fighter stations were obliterated, the squadrons would merely be evacuated to bases further north, so the destruction of airfields was not a vital objective. The doctrine prevailing in Goering's headquarters was anyway that the RAF was down to its last handful of men and machines, posing only a minor threat to the bombers. This misapprehension was understandable. Dowding and Park's tactics of using limited numbers of fighters meant the Luftwaffe rarely encountered large defensive forces. The Germans' inclination confronted with a similar situation would have been to have used whatever machines were available en masse. The assumption was that the RAF's resources were draining away and the residual resistance could be swept aside in the fighting over the capital. The timetable for 'Operation Sealion' was pressing. A decision on the announcement of the final preparations was imminent. The barges and boats that were to carry the Wehrmacht across the Channel were clogging the ports. It was time to move on.

It was true that the RAF pilots were weary and apprehensive. The week before the London attack the strain was becoming intolerable. They were under attack in the air and on the ground, flying three or four missions a day before returning to shattered bases where they were always half-listening for the whistle of falling bombs. When Sunday, 8 September, dawned cloudy, the relief among pilots and commanders was profound. 'The weather was bad today, thank goodness, so we had a reasonable rest,' wrote Richard Barclay. 'I think we are all still a bit shaken after yesterday.'[4] It had been a bad day for 249 Squadron. Pilot Officer Robert Fleming had been shot down and managed to bale out, but was severely burned and died of his wounds. Flying Officer Pat Wells was missing, though he was located five days later, burned and in hospital. Two others were wounded. But the pilots were young and recovered quickly. Two days later Barclay was recording his pleasure that he was now 'on state' almost all the time, an improvement on the beginning of the month when a surplus of pilots meant his flying opportunities were limited.

Dowding and Park had placed their faith in a system of rotation, moving squadrons out of the front-line stations of 11 Group when they judged they had had enough and replacing them with units which had benefited from a period in the relative quiet of a base in the north or west. It was the only way to approach an open-ended struggle which would be decided when one side or the other recognized that its losses were unsustainable. There had been times when the temptation had been strong to throw all Fighter Command's resources, dispersed round the country, into one great confrontation with the Luftwaffe. But Dowding had resisted.

Nor was there any question of falling in with the German assumption and withdrawing the main fighter force from its positions in the south-east around London to less vulnerable bases well behind the capital. Whatever the military logic, political considerations, and above all the morale of the civilian population, would not allow it. It was for this reason, it was said, that Dowding had clung to exposed satellite bases like Manston until they were impossible to hold, to the dismay of even such lion-hearted pilots as Al Deere. It was an approach that required strong nerves and a fine appreciation of each unit's stamina and ability to absorb punishment. The system functioned more smoothly if there were occasional gaps in the intensity of the fighting to allow redeployments to be made with a minimum of difficulty. Its existence depended on the bases in the south-east actually being able to operate.

Only two raids were launched during the mainly cloudy daylight hours of 8 September: on the Kent coast and the Thames estuary. The controllers ordered a limited response, which allowed most squadrons a day of partial respite. Pilots flew 65 patrols involving 215 sorties. The previous day there had been 143 patrols involving 817 sorties. In the evening the bombers returned to London in force and pounded the city until dawn. On the 9th there was a flurry of attacks in the late afternoon on the suburban belt south of London, apparently mainly directed at aircraft factories. Once again the damage was limited. The defenders were given good warning and at least twenty-six bombers and fighters were shot down.

Park was now using his squadrons in pairs, throwing them into the formations in concentrated force. The tactic had a demoralizing effect, causing the Luftwaffe commanders to modify their orders. A signal was intercepted from *Gruppe* headquarters directing crews to 'break off task if fighter opposition is too strong'.[5] The decision to combine squadrons was welcomed by advocates of the Big Wing as a tacit admission of the value of the tactic. Several squadrons from Duxford led by Douglas Bader had arrived to take part in the fighting of the 9th. Once again they were slow forming up and were low on petrol by the time they sighted the enemy. They claimed to have destroyed nearly twenty aircraft, but there was little evidence from ground observers or debris to support this. What was certain was that five Hurricanes were lost in the encounter and two pilots killed.

On the 10th poor conditions kept German activity to a minimum. The following day bomber formations managed to penetrate to London in the afternoon and bomb the docks, but when fear of running out of fuel forced the fighter escorts to withdraw they were harried by the British fighters and ten bombers were shot down on the way home. The next two days saw another daytime pause. On Saturday, 14 September, a week after the first big blitz of London, the tempo picked up again with random raids on south London and coastal towns which did little damage to any significant target but killed civilians, nearly fifty of them in the tranquil suburbs of Kingston-upon-Thames and Wimbledon.

It was a different story at night. The raiders returned again and again, but the RAF was not there to meet them. A night fighter, equipped with airborne radar and capable of intercepting intruders, had yet to be perfected. A handful of patrols were dutifully mounted, each of only one or two aircraft. Their presence could only be symbolic. London would have to rely on anti-aircraft artillery, and the number of guns was doubled in the two days following the blitz. The inability of the air force to mount a nocturnal defence was a blessing. It spared the fighters from having to operate on another front, so deepening their exhaustion and accelerating the rate of attrition. The great strategic necessity was the preservation of Fighter Command. Set against that, the bombing of the city was tragic. But in the end it was a lesser tragedy than the destruction of Britain's fighter strength.

Unlike the soldiers on the beaches of Dunkirk, Londoners seemed to accept the RAF's limitations. Tim Vigors shot down an Me 109 on 9 September and was then shot down himself and crash-landed, unhurt, in an allotment plot in Dartford. He salvaged his parachute and was given some tea and whisky by a friendly lady. Unable to make it back to Hornchurch, he arranged to stay with his aunt at her flat in Tite Street and called a girlfriend, Jill, to invite her to dinner. He met her at the Berkeley Hotel and took her on to supper. It was only when it was over that he remembered to call the squadron. His voice was met with relief. His comrades had assumed he was dead. He promised to be back first thing in the morning and resumed enjoying the rest of the evening. They spent an hour dancing at the Four Hundred Club in Leicester Square, then he escorted Jill to the station and the last train home. On the way back to Tite Street, he had a taste of what Londoners were going through. 'Sirens were wailing. Searchlights were lighting the sky over to the East and the thuds of exploding anti-aircraft shells blended ominously with the screech of the sirens. The drone of bombers could be heard above the racket and then the bombs started to rain down. They fell in sticks of three or four and one could judge from the explosions of the first two in each stick where the subsequent ones were going to fall.'[6] Early the following morning, parachute slung over his shoulder, he set off for Fenchurch Street to catch a train to Hornchurch, passing through streets littered with debris and lined with smouldering buildings. No trains were running but there was a bus service. He asked two policemen for directions to the bus stop and they offered to show him the way. 'We walked through the arch onto the road and there was a queue of about a hundred people lined up by the bus stop. As we approached a number of people started looking at us curiously. "There's a bloody Hun!" said one of the leaders.' The crowd surged forward and Vigors realized what was happening. 'The blue/grey colour of my uniform was not dissimilar to that worn by pilots of the Luftwaffe . . . My head was covered by a crop of light blond hair. My parachute, helmet and flying boots made me look like somebody who had just got out of an aircraft. With a policeman on each side of me, they had taken me for a captured German.' The three backed against a wall while the policemen yelled that the pilot was one of their own, but nobody was listening. 'Now there were about forty around us and those at the back of the crowd were pushing forward on the leaders. I was suddenly scared. These wretched people who had seen their homes going up in flames meant business. "Hell," I thought to myself. "What a way for a fighter pilot to get killed: lynched by a bunch of East Enders."' But then those at the front of the mob realized their mistake. 'The ferocious hatred in their eyes turned to horror. "He's RAF," they yelled and started to try and push back the crowd behind them . . . then the reaction set in. I was quickly hoisted on to the shoulders of a few of the front division and carried through the crowd with everybody cheering and trying to clap me on the back.'

Compared to the days of July, the fighting had been hectic. Compared with the relentless activity of the first week of September, the pace had definitely slackened. In the six days before the blitz, Fighter Command flew 4,667 sorties. In the six days after it flew only 2,159. Some squadrons were as occupied as ever, but many in the front line were allowed a brief, longed-for spell of semi-relaxation. The pilots were young, strong and fit, and even a small respite had a powerful restorative effect. More welcome still was the slackening of attacks on the airfields. The Luftwaffe's attention seemed definitely to have shifted. Between 8 and 14 September there were only token raids on RAF bases. The work of repair could go relatively unmolested and unit rotations take place without the fear that newcomers would be arriving and exhausted units leaving in the middle of a raid.

Such was the rate of pilot losses before the blitz began that Dowding had been forced to reconsider the system of rotation. Inexperienced squadrons arriving from the north were suffering heavy casualties in short periods that shattered their cohesion as a unit and forced their early removal from the line. Dowding had reluctantly devised a system to keep seasoned squadrons for longer than he wished at the forefront of the battle, replacing losses with veterans from other squadrons. Units were to be divided into three categories. All those in 11 Group, the most important sector, were classed as category 'A' and were kept up to strength with fully trained pilots, as well as those units in 10 or 12 Group which would be the first to be called in as reinforcements. Squadrons that were fully equipped and up to strength and held as a second-line reserve were 'B' class. 'C' squadrons were those which had suffered the heaviest losses and were to be kept out of the fighting while pilots rested and new ones were trained. Veterans who had survived could, after recuperating, be posted away to replace losses in squadrons in the first two categories.

Dowding had held back a few strong assets. No. 92 Squadron, home of some of the most aggressive and skilful pilots in Fighter Command, had spent most of the summer in Pembrey in South Wales, and was impatient to get properly to grips with the Luftwaffe. On 8 September it arrived in Biggin Hill. Over the next few days, despite the lull, it still lost six aircraft, with two pilots killed and two seriously wounded. Even for a well-rested unit, manned by experienced pilots, the skies over south-east England continued to be a very dangerous place.

The diminished daytime presence of the Luftwaffe was assumed to be an indication that the last touches were being put to the invasion preparations and a landing was imminent. Church bells, the signal that the Germans were coming, had been rung, mistakenly, on 7 September and Local Volunteer Reservists had gamely set off to their roadblocks to stem the German advance. The continental Channel ports were choked with barges and boats and every night the RAF went to bomb them. 'The invasion is expected any moment now,' wrote the politician and diarist Henry 'Chips' Channon on Thursday, 12 September, 'probably some time during the weekend.'[7] In fact Hitler's plans were undergoing another revision. On 14 September, unpersuaded that the preparations were complete, he decided to put off his decision to give the order for the invasion to proceed until 17 September. Before that could happen, though, another great effort was required from the Luftwaffe.

The morning of Sunday, 15 September, was fair in contrast with the thundery, showery and unsettled weather of the preceding days. A warm sun burned off the light haze hanging over the coast. Dowding assumed the change in the climate would mean a busy day and at each sector station a full squadron was kept at readiness from first light. At North Weald Richard Barclay was woken at 4.30 with a cup of tea by an orderly. He was sleeping with the rest of the squadron in the dispersal hut. It was cold and he dressed quickly. He put on an Irvine flying suit over his pyjamas, which acted as insulation against the chill felt at high altitude in the unheated cockpit of his Hurricane, also a sweater, scarf and flying boots, and finally his yellow Mae West. He took down the blackout from the window and saw it was 'a lovely autumn morning with a duck-egg blue sky half covered with high cloud'. He wondered what he would be doing in peacetime: probably preparing to drive over to a relation's estate to shoot partridge and then sit down to a hearty lunch. He reflected that 'now a fine sunny day meant flying, flying, flying and terrific tension all day, gazing endlessly into the burning sun to see what wily Hun was lurking there, a fight or two perhaps, and someone not there to join the drinking in the bar that evening'.[8]

Outside he greeted Airman Barnes and Airman Parish, who were running up the engine of his Hurricane. He climbed into the cockpit and glanced over his instruments, checking that the petrol gauge was showing full and the airscrew set at fine pitch. He made sure that two pairs of gloves were stuffed where he knew where to find them and that his helmet was sitting on the reflector sight, with the oxygen and R/T leads connected up, ready for a fast getaway. He lay down on the grass and 'immediately became unconscious, as if doped'.

In what seemed like only a few moments he was awake again. 'I woke with a terrific start to see everyone pouring out of the hut, putting on Mae Wests, silk gloves . . . I could hear the telephone orderly repeating, "Dover, 20,000 feet, fifty plus bandits approaching from SE."' He ran, still half asleep, to his machine. The crew had already started the engine. They helped him into the cockpit and tightened his straps. He taxied out into position No. 2 in Yellow Section and took off, only full waking up when he switched on his R/T to hear the orders. His mouth 'was like the bottom of a birdcage from last night's party'. It was too early in the morning and he was 'not in the mood'.

The first blips indicating a raid had appeared on the screens of radar stations near Dover at about eleven o'clock. They represented a smallish formation of twenty-seven Dorniers from a base near Paris. Their appearance was passed on immediately to the control room at the Uxbridge headquarters of No. 11 Group, which Winston Churchill, on a whim, had decided to visit that day. The Dorniers had been late arriving at Calais, having had to re-form after scattering while climbing through cloud. When they got there their escorts, three *Gruppen* of twenty 109s each, were waiting for them, circling impatiently and wasting precious fuel. They knew that the extension of the raids to London meant that their already limited time over target was further reduced and they were operating at the outer reaches of their capacity. A further force of twenty-one Me 109s equipped with underslung bombs, protected by a similar escort, was due to overtake them and carry out a nuisance raid that would distract the defenders before the arrival of the main force.

To the controllers, the force of a hundred-plus aircraft now showing represented two possibilities. It might be another major raid aimed at London. It could equally be simply a large group of fighters preparing a free hunt to lure up the British fighters. Park judged, emphatically, that it was the former, and decided to bring all his forces to bear. He immediately ordered two squadrons up from Biggin Hill; then, ten minutes later, nine more squadrons from the airfields around London, eight of them arranged in pairs. He also requested a squadron from 10 Group to cover the south-west approaches to London. Finally, he ordered five squadrons from Duxford, massed in a Big Wing, to take off and be at 20,000 feet by the time they were over Hornchurch. Thirteen minutes after the first scramble order, a second set of orders was issued ordering another ten squadrons to climb to different heights in defensive positions around the capital. By midday, there were fifteen squadrons of Hurricanes, totalling 167 aircraft, and eight squadrons comprising 87 Spitfires in the air.

Park's responses had been developed from nearly two months of intensive decision-making while dealing with daily attacks and refined with the grim experience eight days previously of the first major raid on London. His plan was arranged in three phases. The first bombers would be attacked by Spitfires shortly after they crossed the coast in an attempt to try and break up the formations before they got near the targets. The Messerschmitts would then be expected to come to the rescue. By doing so, though, they would be burning fuel at four times the cruising rate in high-speed chases, further reducing the time they were able to stay with their charges. After the first jarring impact would come a relay of assaults by Hurricane squadrons arriving in pairs from all directions. The last phase would take place in the skies over London, when the remaining squadrons would descend on what it was hoped would by then be a battered and demoralized bomber force and a dwindling fighter escort as, out of ammunition and low on fuel, the Messerchmitts broke off and ran for home.

The advance guard of German fighters crossed the Kent coast just after 11.30 p.m., followed by the Dorniers. The Spitfires of 72 and 92 Squadrons were stationed on their right flank, just to the north and east of Ashford, waiting for them. For once the pilots had the greatly desired advantage of height. The early decision to scramble meant they had reached 20,000 feet. It was freezing up there even at the height of summer, and the cold bit through sheepskin jackets and fur-lined boots and silk gloves. The discomfort was forgotten as the pilots looked down at the Dorniers cruising westwards 9,000 feet below, then looked up to check that the sky was clear of escorts. In fact the German fighters were 3,000 feet underneath. The twenty Spitfires were led by Flight Lieutenant John 'Pancho' Villa of 72 Squadron. He ordered the two squadrons into line astern, then swung his machine over on to one wing and peeled off into a steep dive, followed, in a long chain, by the others. The sight of the British fighters galvanized the Messerschmitts, who turned to meet them. The Spitfires failed to break through to the bombers, although another Spitfire unit, 603 Squadron, which arrived to reinforce, shot down three Me 109s in the space of a few minutes.

But the action had succeeded in drawing some of the German fighters away from the bombers they were supposed to protect. The Dorniers flew on straight into the path of two Hurricane squadrons from Kenley, 501 and 253, who attacked them head-on. Two of the bombers were shot down, a third so badly damaged that it immediately turned for home. Those remaining held their formation, bunching up to maximize their formidable defensive firepower. As they moved westwards another twenty-four Hurricanes from 229 Squadron and the all-Polish unit, 303 Squadron, joined the mêlée. The body of aircraft crawled across the sky towards London. At the bottom were the bombers, plodding stoically on to their targets. Above and around them darted the rival fighters, wheeling, twisting and plunging, scrabbling for an advantage that it was only rarely possible to seize.

The sound of the battle drifted down to the placid fields and villages to a population which, despite the expected invasion, were engaged in the old rituals of a Sunday morning: returning from church or preparing the roast beef for lunch. The action looked far off and unreal. Yet the distant violence would intrude from time to time. Metal and flame would descend out of the azure, bringing with it death. Just after midday a Hurricane detached itself from the turmoil over the village of Staplehurst and dropped, spinning earthwards. The Belgian pilot, George Doutrepont, was dead. The machine roared down, the engine note rising ominously, and smashed into the green-and-cream painted railway station, killing a young ticket clerk and severely wounding the station master, sending flaming debris flying through the village.

The formation butted on. As the first British fighters turned away to rearm and refuel, four more Hurricane squadrons moved in from around the capital to block its path, some engaging the escorts while the rest tried to crash inside the bombers' ranks. Again the Dornier crews held their nerve. By now the Messerschmitt fighter-bombers had overhauled the main body of aeroplanes and reached south London, and were scattering bombs over the Victorian streets of Penge, Dulwich and Norwood.

The main body arrived a few minutes afterwards. By now the German fighters who had shepherded their charges through successive waves of Spitfires and Hurricanes were reaching the end of their reserves of petrol and ammunition and were faced with the choice of crash-landing or running for their lives. As the fuel gauges sank lower and the red warning lights began to glow, they started to swing away. By the time the bombers arrived over their targets, their formations were still intact but the phalanx protecting them had dwindled alarmingly. Through the Plexiglass canopies the bombers could see an unexpected – almost unbelievable – sight. The sky ahead, the air around, was dotted with small shapes that were rapidly getting bigger. Having survived some of the heaviest concentrations of British fighters they had ever encountered, they were now faced with a huge force of yet more Hurricanes and Spitfires, fighters which they had been told by their superiors did not exist.

The anti-aircraft batteries, which had begun to fire as the bombers crossed into the great brick bowl of south London, ceased their barrage for fear of hitting the approaching fighters. The Germans were now in the very unusual position of being significantly outnumbered. Six squadrons, Nos. 17, 41, 66, 73, 257 and 504, were over the city, a stirring sight to the population craning its necks below. More were on their way. A Spitfire squadron, No. 609 from 10 Group, was stationed in the west. And approaching from the north were five squadrons from Duxford, formed in a Big Wing.

The Hurricanes of 504 and 257 Squadrons were the first to engage. Sergeant Ray Holmes followed his leader, Squadron Leader John Sample, who 'more or less took us slap across the centre of the formation. The Dorniers didn't fly particularly tight, which was to their disadvantage. If they had done, they'd have had better fire power to beat off the fighters. But our CO went at them in a quarter attack and more or less went through them and spread them out a bit.'

Holmes discovered again that it was 'surprising how quickly you lose your overall view of a lot of aircraft. We were travelling at 250, 300 m.p.h., and at that sort of speed the air clears very quickly. You make one attack, turn round and come back again and you wonder where everyone's gone. Then, if you're lucky, you see one or two that you can go for, if you've broken them up.'[9] He fastened on to the rear of a bomber and began firing. His windscreen was drenched in flying oil. By the time it had cleared he was on the point of collision and dived steeply to flash underneath its belly. The Dornier had been hit and turned desperately for home. As it struggled out of London, it was attacked again, its second engine failed and it crash-landed in a field near Sevenoaks.

Ray Holmes now turned on a lone bomber and attacked it from head-on. After a few seconds his ammunition was exhausted, but he was determined to hold his course. The left wing of the fighter and the tail wing of the bomber struck with what Holmes later considered was a surprisingly slight shock. Almost immediately the Dornier began to break up, crashing to earth in front of Victoria Station. As it fell, two bombs and a canister filled with incendiary devises tumbled into the gardens of Buckingham Palace. The bombs were not fused but the incendiaries ignited, setting the lawns on fire. Despite the apparent gentleness of the collision, the controls of Holmes's Hurricane were gone. When the nose dipped he baled out. He landed on a block of flats, slithered down the roof and was saved from serious injury when his parachute snagged in the guttering and he found himself suspended a few feet above a dustbin.

With extraordinary determination, the Dorniers had persisted with their bombing run, aimed at the railway viaducts at Battersea. After releasing their bombs, the pilots threw their machines into the tightest turns they could manage and tried to flee the fighters. As they did so, the Hurricanes and Spitfires of the Duxford wing tipped down from 25,000 feet. The confusion was total. The British fighters were getting in each other's way in their determination to get a shot in, and there was a real danger of them shooting each other down. Richard Barclay turned to confront what he thought was an enemy fighter, only to identify it, just in time, as 'one of those confounded Spitfires again'.

As the formation fled, the fighters moved in to pick off stragglers. Rob Bodie attached himself to a crippled bomber limping along with a damaged engine. He raked it with fire and it slipped into a long shallow glide. He watched the gunner bale out, then flew alongside to inspect the damage. The pilot 'sat bolt upright in his seat, and he was either dead or wounded for he didn't even turn his head to look at me, or watch out for a place to land, but stared straight ahead. Suddenly a pair of legs appeared, dangling from the underneath hatch. The other gunner was baling out. He got out as far as his waist, then the legs kicked.' Bodie realized the man was stuck and felt a momentary spasm of pity, then 'thought of the people down below, wives, mothers, kiddies, huddled in their shelters, waiting for the "All Clear".'

But the sight disturbed him. 'The legs still wriggled and thrashed, 2,000 feet above the cool green fields, trapped in a doomed aircraft, gliding down, a dead pilot at the controls. First one boot came off, then the other. He had no socks on, his feet were quite bare; it was very pathetic.' The bomber was down to 1,000 feet. Bodie had an image of the gunner being cut in half when they hit the ground, scraped away like grated cheese. 'In spite of all he stood for, he didn't deserve a death like that. I got my sights squarely on where his body would be, and pressed the button. The legs were still. The machine went on. The pilot *was* dead. He made no attempt to flatten out and land, but went smack into a field and the aeroplane exploded. I saw pieces sail past me as I flew low overhead. I didn't feel particularly jubilant.'[10]

David Cox, who had arrived with 19 Squadron, engaged some of the remaining Me 109s but broke off to attack a fleeing Dornier, which escaped by ducking into a convenient cloud. Keen to shoot something down, he carried on. 'I had plenty of ammunition and flew south a bit. To my right I saw six single aircraft which I thought were Hurricanes. We were always told you shouldn't fly around on your own and you should always try and join up with any friendly aircraft.' The angle he had been approaching from was deceptive. As they approached he realized they were Me 109s. 'Four of them dived away and I saw nothing more of them. Of the others, one climbed behind me and one climbed in front. The one behind attacked and I turned very violently and he just carried straight on . . . but the one who had been above me turned. As he was coming at right angles I fired a ninety-degree deflection shot and he went down and crashed.'[11]

The reluctance of the other Me 109s to engage was an indication of their desperation to get back to their bases. All the remaining raiders were heading for France. A Messerschmitt escort was waiting to shepherd them home. Despite the great concentration of force and the huge expenditure of ammunition, only six of the Dorniers had actually been shot down. The remaining nineteen struggled back some way or another, most of them sieved with bullets, frozen air whistling through the holes in the Plexiglass canopies, their interiors stinking of cordite and petrol, the wounded moaning or unconscious, the dead slumped, still strapped in where the fighters' bullets had caught them. It was not the damage that had been inflicted that was significant. It was the story the survivors had to tell.

The bomber crews were shocked at the strength of the British resistance, their superiors at first disbelieving. While they were being debriefed, another attack was already under way, bigger than the last. This time there were 114 bombers, Heinkels and Dorniers, which had taken off from bases in Holland and northern France to form up over Cap Gris Nez, half-way between Boulogne and Calais, and set course for the pebble promontory of Dungeness, thirty miles across the Channel. They arrived in two waves. In the first were three formations of sixty-eight bombers. The second was smaller, two formations of forty-six bombers. Each formation had an escort of about thirty Me 109s. Another 150 fighters cruised in a loose box around the core of the force, throttling back, swinging from side to side so as to remain just above stalling speed and not outstrip the bombers, with a similar number roaming ahead and on either side to sweep the way clear. Once again the target was London, this time the Royal Victoria and the West India Docks.

The British pilots had landed, spoken to their intelligence officers, briefed the crews on the performance and needs of their machines and flopped down for a few moments' rest while their machines were checked, refuelled and rearmed. Many fell straight to sleep. Richard Barclay and the other 249 pilots 'had a rotten lunch in our dispersal hut sitting on our beds'. The excitement of the morning had not subsided before they were in the air again. At 2 p.m., Park ordered eight squadrons off in pairs to patrol over Sheerness, Chelmsford, Kenley and Hornchurch. Five minutes later he scrambled four more; then a further eight. Reinforcements from 10 and 12 Group were summoned to come to the defence of the capital, including a Big Wing of five squadrons from

Duxford, comprising twenty-seven Hurricanes and twenty Spitfires.

The first clash took place over Romney Marsh. As the Germans crossed over land, the advance guard of twenty-seven fighters from 41, 92 and 222 Squadrons sailed in to the attack. The escorting Messerschmitts broke off to confront them. Pilot Officer Bob Holland, 92 Squadron's brilliant pianist, was shot up from behind. The German pilot watched him slide back the canopy and step out into space. He landed, unhurt, near Staplehurst. Park ordered 303 and 602 Squadrons to scramble. With that, every one of 11 Group's units were now engaged. With outside reinforcements, 276 Hurricanes and Spitfires were facing or approaching the enemy, slightly more than had been in action in the morning. This time, though, the odds were not so favourable. Their task was to stop the bombers, which, if they maintained their formations, were capable of defending themselves strongly. To get to them they had to break through a defensive screen of 450 fighters. With height, the British pilots had the tactical advantage over those providing the close escort. But once they went in to attack they were vulnerable to the German outriders, flying high and wide to swoop as soon as they saw a British fighter commit himself to the dive.

As the German formations breasted the first wave of attacks, they were confronted with the second line of defence, Hurricanes from 213 and 607 Squadrons, who flew straight into them. Pilot Officer Paddy Stephenson of 607 Squadron was unable to avoid a collision, smashing into a Dornier and sending his own and the other machine spinning out of the sky. Tom Cooper-Slipper, a nineteen-year-old pilot officer, after being shot up while closing on another Dornier and realizing he would have to bale out, decided to ram it before jumping. Appalled crews saw him overhaul the bomber and turn into it, knocking it into an uncontrolled dive. Astonishingly, both Stephenson and Cooper-Slipper survived.

The German force was now arranged in three groups approaching London down an air corridor that took it past Maidstone, reaching the widening mouth of the Thames as it flowed past Gravesend, where it would swing left towards Docklands. But before the bombers and fighters reached the targets, they had to fight their way through the third and thickest line of defence, the squadrons now massed before the south-eastern approaches to the city. The bombers cruised on, in bright sunshine one minute, the next tunnelling through the clammy grey of towering stacks of cumulus that reared up from 2,000 feet. Just after 2.30 p.m., ten minutes away from the bombing zone, the British fighters plunged into their third major assault. Bobby Oxspring with 66 Squadron was detailed to watch for fighters while the rest of the squadron tried to get among the centre group of Heinkels. With no threat apparent, he dived towards the action, where he found a bomber which had been chiselled away from the formation and was 'getting a hell of a plastering by four or five Hurricanes and Spits'. He 'gave it a squirt for luck just before he went into cloud. When last I saw him his wheels had come down and he was looking awful sick. My number 3 followed him through the cotton wool . . . along with several of the other fighter boys wasping around. He told me afterwards they succeeded in making [it] crash on a nearby aerodrome.'[12] The Heinkel put down on West Malling, with the fighters still in hot pursuit. It was to be claimed as a 'definite' in numerous individual combat reports.

The presence of the German fighters made such unrestrained behaviour extremely dangerous. Pilot Officer Tom Neil, a friend of Richard Barclay's in 249 Squadron, had just shot down a Dornier and been momentarily mesmerized by the sight of 'spreadeagled arms and legs as two bodies flew past my head, heavy with the bulges that were undeveloped parachutes . . . the crew! Baling out!' Then he was engulfed by Me 109s arriving to take revenge. 'In a frenzy of self-preservation, I pulled and pushed and savagely yanked my aircraft about, firing whenever I caught sight of a wing or a fuselage in my windscreen. They were not sighted bursts, just panic hosings designed to scare rather than kill and directed against aircraft that were often within yards of me . . . a murderous, desperate interlude.'[13]

Such encounters imposed huge physical strains. The crushing G forces endured in steep dives induced blackouts so that in any combat a pilot might be unconscious for several seconds, then come to find he was upside down or screaming towards the ground. At high speeds a fighter's delicate controls became stiff and leaden and it took real strength to shift the stick so that after a fight the pilot's right arm would be throbbing. The layers of warm clothing needed against the intense cold of high altitudes, the oxygen mask that enveloped half the face, became horribly restricting in the intense physical exertion of a dogfight and pilots climbed out of the narrow cockpits soaked in sweat. Almost everyone, even the 'Tubbys' and the 'Jumbos', lost pounds during periods of action.

Despite the vicious attentions of the fighters, the German bombers held their formations and pressed on doggedly through the flowing, incandescent line of tracer and the foul black mushrooms of flak. Now and then a machine would dip earthwards or slip behind, engine coughing, away from the comforting embrace of the pack. But at 2.40 p.m. most of them were still there, approaching London and preparing to go into their bombing runs. The two formations aiming for the Royal Victoria Docks were unable to find the target, which was hidden under a bank of cloud. Just beyond, though, to the north and clearly visible, lay railway lines and a gasworks. They would have to do. The lead bombers tilted towards them. The bomb doors opened and the crews behind watched a ripple of white explosions race across the dingy townscape of West Ham thousands of feet below. The second formation's target, the Surrey Commercial Docks on the south side of the river, was also cloaked in cloud. Three Hurricane squadrons coming in to intercept watched the Dorniers swing into a right turn and head away, scattering bombs as they departed over the suburbs of south-east London.

On the way back they were harassed constantly by fighters and flak. The most vulnerable were the strays, deprived of the reassuring crossfire that a well-maintained formation could put up, reliant on the protection of any Messerschmitts which had noticed their plight and had sufficient petrol remaining to go to their aid, ducking wherever they could into cloud. Some were fortunate enough to meet up with a force of fifty Me 109s that arrived over the middle of Kent to help the bombers home.

As the retreating bombers crossed the beaches of Kent, fringed with barbed wire, scored with trenches and sown with mines in preparation for the invasion, the attacking fighters fell away. Everywhere now the fighters were coming in to land. During the ninety minutes of the action, twenty-eight squadrons had been ordered off and every one of them had been in action. As the pilots reached for mugs of tea and lit up cigarettes, Fighter Command was potentially at its most vulnerable point in the entire summer. For the first time in their handling of the battle, Dowding and Park had thrown all their immediate resources into one fight. A second German raid now, aimed at the airfields, would have caught almost every man and machine in 11 Group and the neighbouring sectors defenceless on the ground. Park had gambled that the thunderclouds which blessedly sprawled over nine tenths of the sky above his main fighter stations would make it very difficult for an accurate attack. The anxious moments passed. One by one the squadrons came back to readiness, waiting for another onslaught that never came.

The combined fighting of the main action of the day, from first sighting to the last bomber trailing over the coast, had lasted less than five hours. In the midday and afternoon engagements the Germans had lost fifty-six aircraft in action and 136 men were either dead or missing. It was the worst day they had suffered so far. The RAF losses had been relatively slight: twenty-nine aircraft, which were easily replaceable, and twelve pilots killed. The pilots could afford to feel a sense of profound satisfaction. Rob Bodie was exhausted when the order came to return to base. 'The day had been a year. I flew to the coast and set course for home. Passing low over fields and villages, rivers and towns, I looked down at labourers working, children at play, beside a red-brick schoolhouse, a bomb crater two streets away; little black heads in the streets turning to white blobs as they heard my engine and looked up. I thought of workers in shops and factories, of stretcher-bearers and ARP wardens. I hoped the 'All Clear' had gone. I was tired. I'd done my best for them.'[14]

17

Autumn Sunset

There were many parties that night as the pilots celebrated the unusual feeling of being in control of their own skies. The next day's newspapers presented 15 September as a great victory for the RAF and one of the most severe defeats the Luftwaffe had yet suffered, and they carried hugely inflated figures of the German losses.

The following morning, rain clouds covered much of south-east England and the bombers stayed away. No one yet felt, though, that the battle was ebbing. There was little sign that the German invasion preparations had been affected by the setback. In the Channel ports the build-up of boats and barges continued, despite a nightly RAF bombardment. Throughout the early autumn, tension remained high. Richard Barclay wrote in his diary on 25 September that 'everyone was rather expecting an invasion to break out at dawn this morning because it was said that the Boche was sweeping the Channel of mines yesterday. Everyone was therefore very much at readiness at 5.50 a.m.' In his squadron there was concern at civilian complacency. On 29 September there was a rare political discussion between the pilots. Among their conclusions were that 'the British people are still fast asleep. They haven't begun to realize the power of our enemies and that they have to give their all, as well as the Forces, to win . . . That the threat of invasion is very real and not a sort of flap or bluff . . . that we need dictatorial methods to fight dictator . . . that 1 German is nice, 2 Germans are swine.'[1]

The caution seemed justified when, on 18 September, the bombers returned. During the morning there had been several combats at high altitude between German fighters and ninety Hurricanes and Spitfires sent up by Park, who thought the formation showing on the radar screens might indicate a bombing raid. Five Spitfires were shot down, and a pilot killed, a pointless waste of resources. When, later, a small force of bombers heavily escorted by Me 109s appeared over Dover, Park ignored the provocation, and it went on to bomb Chatham and Rochester. When a third, larger force appeared, apparently heading for London, he had to react. At its core were two formations of Junkers 88s flown by inexperienced crews, drafted in to replace the losses. Fourteen squadrons went up to meet them. Geoffrey Edge, the master of the head-on attack, was at Kenley when the order came through, playing a post-lunch game of squash after being released at midday. He managed to assemble six other pilots and they took off hurriedly to be vectored on to a course by the controller that took them into an excellent attacking position. They lay back in the sun, invisible to the bombers and the Me 109s flying closely round them and overhead. Edge ordered his men into a diagonal line, a wingspan apart and two aeroplane lengths between them. He selected the bomber to the left of the leader for himself. They were to try and attack any bomber that had not been hit. The two groups of aircraft were now approaching each other at a closing speed of 180 to 200 yards a second. Edge calculated that would allow five seconds of firing time before he would have to drag back on the stick and roll to the right to avoid collision. He opened fire at 1,000 yards.

'Almost instantly,' he wrote, 'his cockpit starts to disintegrate. His plane swerves towards his leader, crashing into the tail plane. I leave my guns firing on the port side of the formation. The bombers are breaking up and I have moved my aim to my starboard and at this range I just left the guns firing as I aimed at one cockpit after another.' Just before a crash became inevitable, he pulled up, then threw his machine into a steep dive and felt G forces drain the vision from his eyes. As it returned he saw dark shapes flashing past his wings. The Germans were jettisoning their bombs. He had seen no incoming fire from the bombers, who appeared to have been oblivious to the attack until it was too late.[2]

Such encounters could not be endured repeatedly by the Luftwaffe without serious damage to morale. Seventeen aircraft were lost and forty-one men were dead or missing as a result of the day's action. Members of a bomber flight that had lost four of its six aircraft in the raid on London got drunk that evening in memory of their dead comrades and sang a defiant dirge, 'Es blitzen die stahlernen schwingen, Uns hat der Tommy verfehlt' ('The steel wings are flashing, the Tommies have missed us again'). But implicit in the song was the recognition that, despite the assurances of the commanders, the RAF was far from beaten. Each night the bombers were bringing fire and death to London. But the violence seemed to be leading nowhere. Goering assured the crews that their attacks 'at the heart of the British Empire . . . have reduced the British plutocracy to fear and terror. The losses which you have inflicted upon the much vaunted Royal Air Force with your determined fighter combat are irreplaceable.'[3] If the first assertion was true, there was no sign of a British surrender. The second, they knew from harsh experience, to be false.

The pilots and crews were as patriotic as their British counterparts. Their doggedness and determination were testimony to their conviction that they could win. But that assurance was fading. 'At the beginning we weren't particularly taken aback at the resistance,' said Gerhard Schöpfel. 'We thought it wouldn't last. But as it continued we became more and more surprised at how resilient they were and the fact that they didn't back down.'[4]

By the time Goering delivered his morale-boosting address, plans for the invasion had undergone further modification. On 19 September the decision was taken to postpone the issuing of orders for the final preparations once again, this time without setting a new date for the question to be reconsidered. As the other service chiefs pointed out forcefully, the Luftwaffe had failed to deliver the conditions necessary for a successful operation, and was even unable to protect the transports waiting to carry the Wehrmacht to England's shores.

The problems facing 'Sea Lion' were not discernible to British pilots, who felt themselves to be in a limitless conflict. The desperation felt in the squadrons during the end of August and the first week in September had eased, however. Aircraft production was booming and the new Hurricanes and Spitfires were the more powerful Mark II models. By the third week in September, almost every squadron in 11 Group had a full complement of pilots. Fresh pilots were arriving in the system in quantity, allowing the creation of six new fighter squadrons. Veterans of the fighting of the early part of the summer, who had spent the months from June to September serving as instructors, now rested, were volunteering to return to operations, among them Killy Kilmartin and his old No. 1 Squadron comrade, Billy Drake, who joined fighter squadrons in September and October.

But even with the slight relaxation, the pilots were still suffering. As September wore on the Luftwaffe began altering its tactics. The frequency of daylight bombing raids by large formations fell away, though they continued to be launched intermittently, sometimes with considerable success. On 25 September a fleet of Heinkels devastated the Bristol Aeroplane Co. factory at Filton. The following day the Supermarine works at Woolston, near Southampton, was hit. Production was disrupted, but there was no lasting effect on the supply of machines. On 27 September there was a daytime raid by Ju 88s aimed at London which was beaten back with heavy losses on both sides. Three days later, 100 bombers and 200 fighters launched another attempt to reach London, which again was forced back.

The Luftwaffe was adjusting to the fact that, since 15 September, its circumstances had changed, significantly and for the worse. If it persisted with mass raids in daylight it would face devastating punishment. Instead, Fighter Command was now increasingly having to contend with precision attacks by Me 110s using their speed and their bomb-carrying capacity to hit important targets. At the beginning of October there was a further refinement when each fighter wing was ordered to adapt thirty of its new generation of Me 109s to carry an underslung bomb, thus transforming them into *Jabos* or fighter bombers. The Luftwaffe commanders also took to sending masses of regular Me 109s on high-altitude sweeps over southern England. In his previous, reduced condition,

Dowding would have chosen not to react. Fighters on their own could do little damage except to other fighters. As his forces recovered their strength, however, he decided to confront them in a further assertion of Fighter Command's growing control of British skies.

As the days went by, the pilots flew higher and higher, outbidding each other in the search for altitude and the tactical advantage. Only the Spitfires could get near the Me 109s. Flying at 25,000 and 30,000 feet in an unheated, unpressurized cockpit meant new discomforts. Pilots experienced the illusion that their stomachs were inflating grotesquely. They felt intense pain in their elbows, knees and shoulders caused by tiny bubbles of gas in the blood. The prolonged inhalation of oxygen created a burning sensation when they breathed and the skin around their mouths became raw and tender. Most pilots switched it on at 15,000 feet. Above 20,000 feet it was an absolute necessity. Without it they quickly developed anoxia, or oxygen starvation. It induced feelings of giddiness, nausea, sometimes rapture, then insensibility. A fault in the oxygen supply at great height often meant death. On 10 October two pilots, Sergeant Edward Bayley of 249 Squadron and Sergeant H. Allgood of 253 Squadron died within a few minutes of each other in crashes that were attributed to unconsciousness brought on by oxygen failure.

Leave became more regular, but the hours at readiness were still long and the yearning for rain and cloud that would limit flying was frequently thwarted by the fine weather that annoyingly reappeared just when it seemed that an English autumn had finally set in. The prolonged contact with danger meant that, sooner or later, even the most experienced pilots ran out of skill or luck. Birdy Bird-Wilson was unfortunate to meet Adolf Galland over the Thames estuary on 24 September and was forced to bale out, becoming his fortieth victim. The insouciant spirit cultivated by 92 Squadron was severely tested by a spate of casualties. 'First Norman Hargreaves had gone,' wrote Tony Bartley. 'Then Sergeant Eyles. Gus Edwards was found dead a week after he'd gone missing, in the middle of a forest. Similarly Howard Hill, after three weeks, lodged in the top of a tall tree, decomposing in his cockpit, his hands on the controls and the top of his head blown off by a cannon shell.'[5]

Bartley wrote to his mother on 19 September that, despite the losses, 'the morale of the Fighter Boys is terrific. We will crack the German air force at all costs. This is our greatest and diciest hour but we are proud to have the chance to deal with it.' He made a thoughtful but futile appeal for her not to worry. 'I am safe until my predestined time runs out. I am happy and almost enjoying myself. In these times of danger one gets drawn much closer to one's friends, and a great spiritual feeling of comradeship and love envelops everyone. I can't explain, but everyone seems much better men somehow.'[6]

It seemed to Bartley that the only one unaffected by the searing events was Brian Kingcome, for whom 'the war in the air seemed just an incidental interruption which kept him occupied during the day'. Even Kingcome's composure was disturbed when he was shot down on 15 October, apparently by Spitfires who had either mistaken him for a Messerschmitt or who hit him while attacking a German who was on his tail. He jumped and survived.

But survival meant many things. George Bennions had been patrolling high at 25,000 feet and was about to return to base with the rest of the squadron when he saw a group of Hurricanes being pursued by some Me 109s. He dived towards them and found he was on his own. 'I thought, "I'll just try to attack the rearmost one of the squadron, shoot him down if I can and then get away." It didn't happen like that.'[7] He made one attack and saw his bullets striking the German fighter. Then his machine shuddered with the impact of a cannon shell hitting the right-hand side and exploding inside the cockpit. He found he could not see and felt terrible pain in his right arm and leg. Blinded, he groped at the canopy to push it back one handed as his right arm was useless. So was his right leg. The clarity that seems to have flooded the thinking of many pilots as they faced death came to his rescue. He undid the small hatch on the left of the cockpit, tipped the machine to port and tumbled out. Now the problem was getting the parachute to open. The release cord was on the right of the harness. He reached around with his good hand feeling for it and somehow grasped it, pulled and felt the kick of the harness between his legs as the parachute opened, then blacked out.

He came to in a field, told his rescuers who he was and lapsed into a coma.

He woke up in the Queen Victoria hospital, East Grinstead. While he was unconscious he had undergone preliminary operations performed by the plastic surgeon Sir Archibald McIndoe for severe burns received during his struggle to get out of the cockpit. Bennions was unaware that he was burned. When he tried to open his eyes he thought he was blind. An awful depression descended. 'I felt terribly isolated. I couldn't see. I couldn't hear very well. I couldn't recognize people unless it was somebody very close to me. My wife came down and my mother came down. I felt so deflated, just as though half of my life had been taken and the other half wasn't worth bothering with.' He was told that he had lost the sight of one eye. To save the other, the damaged one would have to be removed. Bennions resisted, knowing this would mean the end of the flying life he loved, but in the end was forced to agree.

He was 'feeling extremely sorry for myself' when he got a message from another patient, a friend who had joined the air force with him from school. He had badly burned legs and asked Bennions to come and see him. Bennions

> was on crutches at the time, but I managed to get over there with a hell of a lot of struggle and self-pity. As I opened the door in Ward 3 I saw what I can only describe as the most horrifying thing I have seen in my life. [There] was this chap who had been badly burnt, really badly burnt. His hair was burnt off, his eyebrows were burnt off, his eyelids were burnt off. You could just see his staring eyes. His nose was burnt, there were just two holes in his face. His lips were badly burnt. Then, when I looked down, his hands were burnt. I looked down at his feet also. His feet were burnt. I got through the door on the crutches with a bit of a struggle. This chap started propelling a wheelchair down the ward. Half-way down he picked up a chair with his teeth. Then he brought this chair down the ward, threw it alongside me and said: 'Have a seat, old boy.' I cried. I thought, 'What have I got to complain about?' From then on, everything fell into place.

The man was Sergeant Ralph Carnall of 111 Squadron, who had been shot down on 16 August. He underwent a year of treatment by McIndoe and eventually went back to flying.

For the burns cases, the relief of having escaped death did not survive the first look in the mirror. Lying on the operating table shortly after being shot down, Geoffrey Page caught a glimpse of himself reflected in the overhead lights. He saw 'a hideous mass of swollen, burnt flesh that had once been a face'.[8] Arriving at East Grinstead for reconstruction surgery, he met the other patients, including Richard Hillary, who had been shot down and baled out into the sea on 3 September. 'Standing at the foot of the bed was one of the queerest apparitions I had ever seen. The tall figure was clad in a long loose-fitting dressing gown that trailed to the floor. The head was thrown back so that the owner appeared to be looking along the line of his nose. Where normally two eyes would be, were two large bloody red circles of raw skin. Horizontal slots in each showed that behind, still lay the eyes. A pair of hands wrapped in large lint covers lay folded across his chest. Cigarette smoke curled up from the long holder clenched between the ghoul's teeth. The empty sleeves of the dressing gown hung limply, lending the apparition a sinister air. It evidently had a voice . . . it was condescending in tone. "Ah! Another bloody cripple!" '[9]

The victims were acutely aware of the effect they had on others. Page was taken to the pub by two squadron friends. For a moment he felt he was back to normal life until he overheard the landlord's wife whispering loudly to her husband. 'The poor dears, and them so young and all. Quite turns me stomach.' The barmaid at the Red Lion in Basingstoke, where patients from the hospital at Park Prewett nearby would go for a drink, was by contrast magnificently humane, welcoming burned pilots with a kiss and a greeting: 'My darling, how lovely to see you.'[10] As a Waaf, Edith Heap frequently encountered the ravaged faces, and made sure to always look them, unflinchingly, in the eye. But the sight was desperately upsetting. In 1942 Richard Hillary visited an old comrade, Ron Berry, who had been a sergeant in 603 Squadron with him and was now commanding a fighter squadron. In other circumstances it would have been normal for Hillary to have been introduced to the pilots. 'It was a very difficult decision I had to make,' Berry said later. 'With my young flock I'm afraid I denied him the pleasure of going round the squadron . . . I think one or two of them would have felt it very difficult to stomach.'[11]

As October wore on, the number of daylight bombing raids dwindled but the fighter sweeps persisted, requiring the squadrons to maintain a high level of vigilance. The Hurricane units could do little against them. No. 249 Squadron was still awaiting its Mark II replacements and its aeroplanes were showing their age. Most of them had developed oil leaks that blotted out the windscreens after half an hour in the air. On many patrols the pilots sighted the condensation trails of Messerschmitts high above. They were unable to reach them but lived in fear of them swooping down. On the third trip of the day on 30 September, Richard Barclay noted that 'we had hundreds of 109s above us. We were too high for the Hurricane anyway . . . an awful trip as we were quite helpless, just waiting to be attacked.'

On 12 October the squadron was

> up before breakfast, climbing up to 23,000 feet and patrolling all over Kent and south London. We were looking for some 109s which for once were said to be below us. But no luck in the first hour. We were floating about over Dover with 257 Squadron, who were meant to be guarding our tails, below us, when I happened to look back to the left and there was a glistening yellow nose pointed very much in my direction about fifty yards away. I immediately took action to avoid his quarter attack in the shape of a violent turn to the left and lots of bottom rudder. The inevitable result at that height was a flick roll and spin. I got out, had a good look around and saw three 109s 2,000 feet above. I kept a good eye open for the 109s and rejoined the squadron. Unfortunately my No. 2 has not been heard of since this short mêlée.[12]

Nothing had gone right. On the second scramble a wireless fault meant that the pilots were unable to hear the controller and the sortie was abandoned. The replacement pilots arriving at the squadron were proving slow to learn. Barclay complained that 'the new sergeant pilots, of whom we have all too many, didn't take off in their right sections, the resulting chaos taking some time to sort out. We've almost got to train them in formation flying.' The third operation was also 'a farce. As we took off we saw the trails of the Me 109 bombers over London . . . we were scrambled twenty minutes late! As usual this was due to Group's slowness . . . it was ridiculous taking off at all.'

The new tactic of sending off squadrons in pairs that Park had introduced at the beginning of September was proving difficult to operate, as he had known it would be. There were further frustrations as the brother squadrons tried to work out new flying formations to reduce their vulnerability to fighter attack, slowly moving away from the reliance on 'vics' and moving towards the *rotte* system of covering pairs used by the Germans. But the uncharacteristic note of irritability in Barclay's diary had deeper causes. He had arrived at the height of the battle on 1 September. He got his first proper break on 27 October. He was, as he admitted, in need of it. 'I'm glad I've got some leave coming along,' he wrote a few days beforehand. 'I'm getting so intolerant of the shortcomings of the new pilots.' Here and there, between the accounts of beery nights in the mess and at the Thatch in Epping to celebrate a clutch of medal awards, a touch of sadness creeps in. After he heard of the death of his friend Percy Burton he noted: 'I am now the only one left of the five Cranwellians of the squadron.'

Almost everyone had lost a dear friend by now. Tim Vigors spent most of his evenings with Hilary Edridge. Their backgrounds were different. Edridge came from Bath and was interested in music. Vigors was steeped in the horsy traditions of the Anglo-Irish upper class. But, since meeting at the start of the year, they had become inseparable. Almost every night they would drink beer and play darts with the locals in the pubs around the base. Once or twice a week they went to London for dinner and a tour of the nightclubs. On the morning of 30 October, shortly after they had returned from a trip to town, together with Vigors's other constant companion, his lurcher Snipe, they took off together from Hornchurch. They attacked a formation of Dorniers coming in north of Dover and were immediately bounced by Me 109s. A cloud of smoke engulfed a Spitfire on Vigors's right. He knew it must be Edridge. Back at Hornchurch he 'waited in dread. Still no sign of Hilary. All the rest of the squadron were home . . . an hour passed and still no news. I had no appetite for lunch and waited by the telephone at dispersal. At about 2 p.m. the news came through from Group Headquarters. The wreckage of a Spitfire bearing Hilary's markings had been found in a field near Sevenoaks. The pilot was dead.'

Vigors felt something he had never felt before.

> A wave of misery swept over me. Up till now I had been able to shrug off the deaths of even my close friends. But this was different. Hilary had been like my brother for the past nine months. We had pooled all our hopes, thoughts and fears and had somehow managed to support each other through the trauma of those times. Now he was gone. I just couldn't get my mind to accept it. I called Snipe and together we walked off down the airfield. I tried to explain what had happened, but he just wagged his tail and didn't seem to understand. Then something occurred which had not happened in years. I started to cry. Snipe realized there was something wrong. I sat down on the grass and he nuzzled up to me. I pulled myself together and suddenly a different emotion took hold of me, an emotion which I had not experienced before in my life. Cold, impossible to control, hatred.[13]

The Fighter Boys had grown up. The days were cooler and darker now. The fabulous summer flickered and died. Lightness of heart was harder to sustain. At Biggin Hill, 92 Squadron fought hard and then drank, joked and flirted at the White Hart or in their improvised nightclub at Southwood Manor. But there was melancholy behind the laughter. At the end of October, Pilot Officer Roy Mottram sent a letter to Bunty Nash, a much-loved Waaf officer known by the squadron from its time at Pembrey, with news of her friends. The old gang were going; dead, wounded or posted away.

> 92 has a number of strange faces these days [he wrote]. One or two of them are real good types well up to standard! Bill Watling rejoined us a couple of days ago and everybody was pleased to meet him again. He seems little the worse for his experience, but has rather an ersatz healthy look about his face – the result of his burns – but that will vanish with time. He is simply itching to be back and wipe off the 'black' as he calls it, and I feel sorry for the next Hun he has in his sights. Alan is on sick leave at the moment . . . Brian is going on famously, but the powers that be want to move him to Halton and he definitely objects in no small manner. X has been having a pretty rotten time of it and his nerves have been in a pretty shattering state for some time. He came back today from seven days' leave and I hope he is much better. He took to the bottle in no small degree and quickly earned the nom-de-plume 'Boy Drunkard'. That is one of the little things that war does and is quite beyond the ken of the average layman who fondly believes the Fighter Boys can stand anything without it showing.[14]

Bill Watling was killed four months later. Mottram survived until the following August, when he was shot down over France. The Boy Drunkard sobered up and survived the war.

The strain was continuous, the German attacks relentless. But now they lacked purpose or meaning. The daylight raids could never change the course of the war. The nightly blitz caused grief, misery and discomfort, but never the 'mass psychosis and emigration' the Germans desired. 'Operation Sealion' remained technically alive, but the autumn gales waiting to sweep the Channel made its implementation unlikely, at least until the New Year. On 12 October, Field-Marshal Keitel, the head of the OKW, informed the Wehrmacht that the plan would remain in effect only as a means of exerting political and military pressure on Britain, though its execution would remain as a possibility for the spring or early summer. The great battle faded. Its actual end was never clearly discernible to the pilots. On 31 October, though, it seemed that some climacteric had been passed. For the first time since anyone could remember, neither side lost a man or an aeroplane in battle.

18

Rhubarbs and Circuses

The glorious summer died and autumn faded into winter. Fighter Command changed with the seasons. There were new faces at the top. On 25 November, as soon as it was safe to do so, Dowding was removed and the Deputy Chief of the Air Staff, Sholto Douglas, put in to replace him. At the same time, Keith Park was shifted from 11 Group to make way for Trafford Leigh-Mallory, his old antagonist and a man he detested. The departures were expected, yet the pilots felt unhappy at the speed with which Dowding and Park were sent on their way. They were a distant, unconvivial pair, but their dedication and decency, and the intelligence of their handling of the summer fighting, had won them the admiration, even affection, of those they sent into battle. The official explanation was that they were tired and the circumstances of the war had altered. Dowding went off on a mission to the United States. Park was given a training command. Most in 11 Group felt that the two were the victims of jealousy and intrigue. It seemed to Al Deere that they had 'won the Battle of Britain but lost the battle of words that followed, with the result that they . . . were cast aside in their finest hour'.[1]

It was true, though, that the air war had taken a different turn. From the end of the year, as Luftwaffe daytime activity fell away, Fighter Command increasingly took the offensive. The roles were gradually reversed. Now it was British fighters escorting bombers to strike German targets in northern France, or wheeling provocatively over the Luftwaffe bases, trying to tempt the Messerschmitts up to fight in the RAF's adaptation of Jagdgeschwader free-hunt tactics.

The squadrons had also changed. Many now contained only a handful of the original members who had been there when the serious fighting started. Of the twenty-two pilots who had been with 32 Squadron when it celebrated at the White Hart in Brasted on 15 August, only four, including Michael Crossley, remained at the end of the year. In between, at least a dozen had been posted away. Six had been badly wounded. Another six had been killed. When Al Deere's squadron, 54, was finally moved out of the line, only four of the pilots who first went into battle were left. Its character was modified further when the unit was designated as category 'C'. Its more experienced members were sent off to stiffen front-line units and Deere was given the job of training up novices.

The few were becoming many. The pilot shortage was solved. Young men were pouring out of the operational training units. At the beginning of July there had been forty-four Hurricane and Spitfire squadrons in Fighter Command. By the end of 1940 there were a total of seventy-one squadrons, with a secure supply of ever-improving aircraft. Many of the newcomers, as the months passed, came from abroad. During 1941, 609 Squadron had pilots from Belgium, France, Poland, Canada, the United States, New Zealand and Rhodesia pass through its ranks. The most cosmopolitan squadrons distilled a new spirit from the mix of nationalities and it was noted that they were often the most happy and successful. But it was clear that the old intimacy was cooling.

With the slackening of the crisis, military discipline, eroded by the frantic conditions of the summer, began to be reasserted. No. 92 Squadron was only a year old, but in its brief life it had cultivated an air of separateness and indifference to the rules that had been tolerated or overlooked because of its great success in destroying German aircraft. Its self-absorption had been reinforced during September and October by heavy losses that bound the survivors together, darkened their mood and increased their resentment of outsiders.

During much of the heavy fighting, the squadron had operated without an effective permanent commanding officer. Squadron Leader Phillip Sanders, who had led the squadron from the relative quiet of Pembrey into the heat of Biggin Hill at the beginning of September, set himself on fire lighting a cigarette after returning, soaked in petrol, from a sortie on the 15th. He was succeeded by Robert Lister, a Cranwell graduate and pre-war career officer, who had spent most of the war encased in plaster after a flying accident. Shortly after taking over he was shot down, badly wounded and declared unfit for flying. Instead of choosing a successor from the squadron's veteran pilots, the authorities defied the lessons of the summer and inexplicably went for a relatively elderly and inexperienced outsider, Alan MacLachlan, who had been commissioned into the reserve in 1930. He lasted a week before being shot down and wounded and Brian Kingcome became the de facto squadron commander. The recommendation was finally made that he should take over. Before it could be implemented, Kingcome, too, was out of action, after being wounded and forced to bale out on 15 October.

Eleven days later a new commanding officer arrived at Biggin Hill. Johnny Kent was a Canadian, an outstanding pilot who had gained his licence at sixteen and been an RAF test pilot in the pre-war years. It had been hair-raising work. On 300 occasions he was required to fly into barrage-balloon cables to calculate the damage they did to aircraft and try out devices for cutting through them. He came from a Polish squadron, No. 303, where he had been a flight commander, helping in a short time to turn it into one of the most effective units in Fighter Command.

Kent reached Biggin Hill at tea time, and the mess sergeant pointed out the officers of his new squadron, sitting together at one table. He joined them without telling them who he was. 'My first impressions,' he wrote later, 'were not favourable and their general attitude and lack of manners indicated a lack of control and discipline. I realized I was going to have my hands full.'[2]

Kent was astute enough to understand there were reasons for the pilots' truculence. Despite their impressive performance, they had suffered shocking casualties and were 'disorganized, undisciplined and demoralized'. There was a move to post the squadron north for a rest, which he resisted, arguing that if this was done it would be finished as a fighting force. Instead, he 'begged to be allowed to keep it at Biggin as that would give me the chance I needed to get it into shape – while the stigma of having "had it" could not be attached to it'.

A few days after he took over and was leading the squadron on patrol, they encountered high-flying Me 109s, but several pilots, instead of turning to face them, broke formation and headed for home. It was a case, Kent concluded, of '109-itis'. On landing he threatened to shoot down the pilots himself if there was a repetition. A few weeks later, a weaver failed to break up a formation of German fighters attacking the squadron from the rear. This provoked another tirade. The senior NCOs were summoned and accused of being slipshod and insubordinate. There were some words of praise for the pilots' record in the air, but then he moved on to attack their conceit, indiscipline, drinking habits and clothes. The parties at Southwood House would have to be scaled down and women guests out by 11 p.m. Check shirts, old school ties, suede shoes and pink pyjamas worn under tunics would no longer be tolerated. The theft of aviation petrol to fuel their uninsured, unlicenced cars was to stop.

Kent reckoned later that 'this action made me even more unpopular and I am sure many dire threats were made behind my back, but nothing came of them and gradually it began to dawn on them all that the squadron had become more efficient and that perhaps my tirade had not been delivered simply because I was an unpleasant bastard but because I had done it for their own good'. He appealed to Tony Bartley to help him win the squadron's cooperation. Bartley agreed. Kent's success in the air and willingness to join in the fun at the White Hart hastened the process of reconciliation, and by the time he was posted away six months later to command a training unit, he was held in great affection by most of the pilots.

It was clear, though, that the days of informality were over and the grip of convention was tightening on the Fighter Boys. From the outside it seemed that little had changed. Propagandists continued to present the pilots in the light-hearted image they had created for themselves. Biggin Hill became a centre for media visitors. Sailor Malan, Al Deere and Bob

Tuck became celebrities. The BBC leant heavily on fighter pilots to make broadcasts harking back to the great events of the summer. The scripts were mostly written for them by Ministry of Information apparatchiks, in a Hollywood-tinged style that sounded strange when spoken in the clipped line-by-line delivery the novice broadcasters invariably used. A typical 'talk' was made in December 1940 by James Nicolson of 249 Squadron, describing the action in August in which he won Fighter Command's only Victoria Cross of the war. Speaking in a public-school accent, he described how he chased after his quarry, 'shouting out loud at him when I first saw him, "I'll teach you some manners you Hun!"' The form was to regard broadcasts as a 'line shoot'. Any embarrassment was offset by a fee, from which the Air Ministry insisted on taking its cut.

The old reluctance to promote 'aces' had gone. Certain pilots were pushed towards the newspapers. Paddy Finucane, the good-looking, slightly gauche Irishman who, once the duffer of his training intake, had gone on to become one of Fighter Command's most successful pilots, became a favourite. His crinkly hair, square jaw and faraway look made him a favourite with women readers. Recovering in hospital after accidentally breaking an ankle while jumping over a wall in the blackout in the autumn of 1941, he was inundated with get-well letters. 'I guess you've received tons of fan mail from hero-worshipping dames all over the country,' wrote a land girl who gave her address as 'Amongst the turnips, Wiltshire'. She signed off, 'Boy, don't I wish I'd been a nurse.' Another from 'an admirer', Miss Rose Layton of Heathstan Road, Shepherd's Bush, began: 'Dear Paddy, I read of your accident in the *Daily Herald* and I am very sorry and hope you will get well again soon [as] I know how anxious you must be to get up there again. They can't keep a good man down. Don't think this silly of me Paddy but I would like you to carry or wear this horseshoe I am sending you for luck.'[3]

The zenith of the Fighter Boys' fame coincided with a relative decline in their military importance. Heavy raids by the Luftwaffe in daylight virtually stopped. Instead there were fighter-bomber raids and a continuation of the night offensive. This lasted through the winter, killing 18,000 civilians in the first four months of the new year. Some pilots were diverted to flying night fighters, which slowly became more effective as the radar needed to locate the raiders improved.

Having fought off the Luftwaffe and ensured its own survival, Fighter Command took on a secondary role. From the end of 1940 it served as an adjunct to the British bomber offensive being launched against German targets in northern France. The pilots went from attacking bombers to defending them. They were required to fit into complex tactical arrangements designed to shield Bomber Command aircraft on their way to their targets, to cover them while they did their work and to hold off attackers as they headed home. The missions were called 'Circuses' and could involve a hundred or more fighters, organized into wings, escorting small numbers of bombers. Many pilots realized from the outset that the importance of these operations was slight. They were aimed at appropriate targets: marshalling yards, workshops, refineries and the like. But the number of bombers involved and the loads they delivered meant that the effort was disproportionate to any results. The real purpose was to use the bombers as bait to entice the German fighters into the air with the aim of destroying as many as possible.

As well as the escort duties, the pilots were tasked to fly 'Rhubarbs', low-level attacks against targets of opportunity such as bridges, locomotives, convoys, flak batteries and barges. Sometimes they were ordered off on anti-fighter sweeps, with the hazy instruction from Leigh-Mallory to 'seek and destroy the enemy'. Some of the inspiration for the offensive had come from Trenchard, still a brooding presence. Before taking over Fighter Command, Sholto Douglas had been informed of the old man's view that the time had come to 'lean towards France'[4] with aggressive sallies over the enemy lines like those flown by the RFC above the Western Front.

Both Douglas and Leigh-Mallory had served with the RFC in the First World War and were disposed to listen. Douglas wondered at first whether the likely casualties would justify the results. Leigh-Mallory was persuaded from the outset. Thus began a phase of fighting which killed hundreds of pilots for negligible results. Between November 1940 and the end of 1941, nearly 470 pilots who had survived the Battle of Britain were killed. The campaign got off to a poor start with even the official arithmetic weighing in the Germans' favour. Between January and June 1941, there were 2,700 sorties by fighters, during which fifty-one pilots were lost. Only forty-four German aircraft were claimed destroyed. Inevitably, the real figure was lower, probably about twenty.

The initiative might have fizzled out had it not been for the German attack on the Soviet Union in June. The Circuses and Rhubarbs gained a new ostensible purpose: to force the Luftwaffe to pull back assets from the Eastern Front, or at least to make life in northern France so difficult as to prevent a transfer of the men and aircraft stationed there. The offensive was stepped up. This time the balance seemed more acceptable. Fighter Command claimed to have shot down 731 German aeroplanes while losing 411 itself. The true score was 154 including 51 losses unconnected with British action. 'The combat balance sheet would thus appear to be about four to one in Germany's favour,' judged John Terraine, in his classic history of the RAF in the European war.[5] Nor could the Russians be said to have benefited. The activity persuaded the Luftwaffe to keep a force of fighters in France and the Low Countries. But it consisted at any time of about 260 single-engined aircraft which would have had little effect on the fortunes of the war in the East.

For many veterans of the summer fighting of 1940, flying Circuses and Rhubarbs was more nerve-racking than anything they had experienced during the Battle of Britain. Flying close escort to the bombers meant crawling along at their speed, rocking in the shock waves from the exploding flak and waiting to be pounced on by the German fighters. Now the British pilots were experiencing the same dread that their Luftwaffe counterparts had felt the year previously. To Paddy Finucane, close escort duty was 'murder'. The Rhubarbs were less feared, but were still regarded with apprehension. Al Deere later described them as 'useless and hated'. At best they 'served only as a means of letting off steam in that [they] enabled pilots to fire their guns in anger, more often than not against some unidentified target'. Deere confessed that on the few Rhubarbs in which he was engaged he could not 'truthfully say that the vehicles and the train which I attacked were strictly military targets'.[6]

A graphic account of the experience and the psychological aftermath, written for the psychologists who were by now being used to study aircrew personnel, was given by a pilot who had been shot down and seriously wounded after taking part in fifty sweeps.

> On September 17, 1941, after getting separated from the wing during a spot of confusion near Lille, I began returning home alone at 18,000 feet, weaving hard and losing height gradually to keep my speed up. Over St Omer, two Me 109Fs passed 1,000 feet above me and slightly to the left, going the opposite way. I was then at 13,000 feet. I climbed into the sun, intending to beat these two up as soon as I was alone, but I soon ascertained just the opposite and immediately became the centre of a large gaggle, consisting of nine or ten MEs and one Spitfire. I don't remember feeling frightened, only highly interested and thoroughly keyed up . . . I took a lot of evasive action and the Huns did a lot of inaccurate shooting, till it began to look as though I could float about all afternoon without being hit.

Then, as he neared the French coast,

> there was a terrific bang inside the cockpit and something feeling like a steam hammer hit me on the back of the head and knocked me for six. I don't think I was ever quite unconscious, or if I was it was only for a few seconds, but complete darkness descended and I hadn't the energy to move a finger. I felt myself fading away, as though going under an anaesthetic. There was nothing left but pitch-darkness and a pain behind my right ear. But a tiny corner of my mind, aloof from everything else, still seemed to be functioning, and I remember thinking detachedly in the dark: 'So, after all it's happened to me too . . . it's come to you who always told yourself there's a way out of every scrape. But there's no way out of this one, buddy, because you are quite blind and you haven't the strength to move a muscle and you are diving down towards the sea with a lot of 109s which are ready to polish you off as soon as you show any signs of revival.

'So there! I wish I could have had a word with the chaps, just to explain how it happened, instead of simply vanishing like so many others. And there are a lot of people I'd like to say goodbye to . . . And you're a clown to be shot down by a bloody Hun anyway. But it's too late for regrets now. It can only be a few seconds now . . . just one almight holocaust as we hit the sea; then no more fighting, no more fear, no more pain in [the] back of the head. Just peace . . . God, how marvellous!'

At the last second he pulled out of the dive, shook off his pursuers and made a good landing at Hawkinge, despite a terrible head wound and the loss of one and a half pints of blood.

Convalescing in the Palace Hotel, Torquay, he was told that he would not be able to fly for three months.

I pretended to be alarmed but was secretly very glad. For a couple of weeks I slept no more than an hour at a time. When I did there were awful dreams such as being towed around the sky by my foot . . . After I had been on leave for a couple of weeks, I settled down, slept most of the night and ate fairly well. The kindness of my wife and the loveliness of my little boy took things off – made me forget for quite long periods. Then the sleeplessness and the dreams came back and while reading I would suddenly see myself having to bale out of an aircraft. I shivered with fright.'

After a particularly harrowing night he reported his dreams to a doctor. He was referred to a wing commander who reassured him he would not have to go back to flying for several months.

I felt better for a day or two. Then it returned. I began to think perhaps I should have to go on bombers and stick it out for eight or more hours. Rather than that I will go back to my night fighters now where we seldom do more than a 3-hour stretch. Supposing I was petrified with fear and could not fire a gun or read my special equipment instruments,

> I should be letting my CO, my squadron, and my country down, and again if I did not go back to my job I am letting them all down and myself by being a coward.[7]

Many of the moral and material advantages the British pilots had enjoyed the previous summer had disappeared. They were no longer flying over friendly fields and beaches within reach of rescuers, but ranging with limited fuel into hostile territory where the Germans' increasingly efficient radar system gave plenty of warning of their approach. It was up to them whether or not they took the bait. Frequently they chose not to and preserved their resources. The enemy then became the light flak guns, which accounted for a large number of casualties. From late September onwards, the German pilots became more aggressive with the arrival into service of the new Focke-Wulf 190s, which, it quickly became clear, had the edge over the improved Spitfire Vs.

The sky over northern France was a very dangerous place. It was the Fighter Boys' turn to experience the desolation of the journey home on drying tanks, the wind thrumming in shrapnel holes and the cold and empty sea below. Baling out unharmed over land during the defence of Britain usually meant an unpleasant shock, rescue with a cup of tea or a shot of whisky, transport back to base and the joyful greetings of friends. Now it signalled the end of the line: imprisonment until the war was over. The apprehension mounted as the French coast approached and the leader's voice crackling over the R/T announced the start of the ordeal with the words: 'Corks in, boys!'

Some were pleased with the opportunity to go onto the attack. Douglas Bader had had a frustrating time during the summer of 1940 and took to the 'sweeps' with impatient energy. In March 1941, he was posted to Tangmere to command a wing of three Spitfire squadrons. With his arrival the pace of activity rose sharply. By mid June his pilots went to France almost every day, except when the weather was bad, flying up to three sweeps. Bader's difficult personality was redeemed by a gift for leadership. The shift from defence to offence might have been expected to weaken morale and motivation, but Bader created in his wing a spirit of cheerful aggression and dedication. Cocky Dundas, a perceptive and humane observer, was seduced by the mercurial, unconventional 'DB'.

'There was a close bond between the three Spitfire units at Tangmere that summer,' he wrote. 'Bader welded the wing into a single unit and we all knew each other well, so that the losses sustained by the other squadrons were almost as painful as our own.' And the losses were heavy. Between 20 June and 10 August, Dundas's squadron, 616, lost twelve pilots, more than half its establishment. Dundas found that, unlike the previous August, when a spate of casualties dented the squadron spirit, 'morale was sky high'.[8]

Dundas found Tangmere in the high summer of 1941 an enchanted place where fear of death heightened the intensity of his joy at living. His memory was of 'sharp contrasts; of the pleasure of being alive and with friends in the gentle Sussex summer evenings; of visits from Diana, when we would dine and dance in Brighton, or sit long on the balcony outside the Old Ship Club at Bosham watching the moon on the water and listening to the tide lapping against the wall beneath us and memories of tearing terror when, at the end of a dogfight, I found myself alone with fifty miles of hostile sky between me and the Channel coast and the hungry 109s curving in to pick off the straggler'.

The era came to an end with Bader's fall. He was shot down in a dogfight with 109s between Boulogne and Le Touquet early in August and taken prisoner. When Dundas returned from leave after Bader's capture, he was dejected at the thought of the endless fighting that lay ahead. 'I knew in my heart that I had little enthusiasm for the prospect,' he wrote later. It took an enormous effort of will to keep going.

There was no disguising the changed nature of the struggle. Dennis Armitage, who arrived at Tangmere later in the summer, felt that it 'wasn't like fighting a battle on your home ground. It seemed to us very pointless . . . it was a political, psychological exercise so that the French could see British aircraft overhead. I didn't enjoy it. I didn't enter into the spirit of it in the same way as I had at the Battle of Britain.'[9] Armitage was shot down on 21 September while trying to keep the formation he was leading on bomber escort duty together. He was hit by an incendiary round, which set his tank and his oxygen supply on fire, but he somehow managed to bale out. The Germans were waiting for him when he landed and 'horribly cocky'. As they stepped forward to arrest him they announced, without apparent irony, that for him the war was over.

And so it was, for Armitage, for Bader and for many others, among them some of the outstanding pilots of the previous summer. Bob Tuck was shot down in January 1942, not by fighters but by flak outside Boulogne during a Rhubarb, and spent the next three years in prison before he escaped and after a dreadful journey reached the Russian lines. Paddy Barthropp had only been back on operations for two days after a six-month spell instructing when he was shot down near St-Omer, baled out and was captured.

At least they were alive. Hundreds who survived the Battle of Britain were to die in Circuses and Rhubarbs. Paddy Finucane lasted until July 1942. Like Tuck he was brought down by ground fire. On the way back from shooting up shipping and a German airfield, the wing he was leading passed over the beach at Pointe du Touquet. Pilot Officer F. Aikman, who was flying as his number two, described how, as they flew over the beach, he saw a small machine-gun post perched on a ridge of sand. 'We were almost on the post before Paddy realized it was there and the soldiers opened up at point blank range.'[10] The radiator of Finucane's Spitfire was hit and he prepared to bale out. He was too low. The engine stopped. He knew what was coming. His last words over the R/T before he hit the sea in a curtain of spray were: 'This is it, chaps.'

Others were killed in the new theatres opening up, in the Mediterranean, North Africa and the Far East. Noel Agazarian volunteered for duty in the Middle East and was shot down in his Spitfire over the Libyan desert in May 1941. The life of the man his family loved as 'Le Roi Soleil' was snuffed out. His sister, Yvonne, was devastated. 'But I didn't cry,' she said later. 'It wasn't done.'[11]

Death seemed very much closer now. The folklore of the mess taught that acceptance was often the precursor to the chop. 'If one once doubted that one was not going to survive then the way downhill was pretty quick,' said Denys Gillam.[12] The fatalism was cumulative. After his first tour flying offensive operations, Al Deere was 'always confident that I would come through all right'. On his second one, 'although it was far less hectic, there was always uppermost in my mind the thought that I would be killed'.[13] Pete Brothers, later in the war, 'reached the stage where I thought there was no question of surviving. It was either going to happen today or it was going to happen tomorrow.'[14]

Yet, despite the ever-shortening odds, the compulsion to 'go back on ops' repeatedly dragged men who had demonstrably done their bit away from safe and comfortable desk jobs and instructing posts and back into the realm of danger. Richard Barclay, the earnest Cambridge economics graduate who kept a diary during the late summer of 1940, was shot down at the end of November that year. He was wounded in his legs, ankle and elbows and spent two months in hospital. There was a brief spell as an instructor before he was back in action with 611 Squadron. During a sweep over St-Omer he was attacked by Me 109s and forced to land. He escaped and met up with local resisters, who passed him down the line to the Pyrénées. Once in Spain, he presented himself at the British Embassy and made his way back to Britain via Gibraltar after an eleven-week odyssey. He was given a cushy headquarters job, but was soon agitating to be back in action. At the beginning of July 1942 he was in Egypt commanding 238 Squadron. On the evening of 17 July he was dead, shot down while patrolling in the Alamein area.

Many of those who died and those who expected to die were already embarking on the next phase of their lives. Paddy Finucane had just got engaged before his death to Miss Jean Woolford, a typist at the Ministry of Agriculture. Al Deere's anxiety to get back into the fighting was mixed with tender thoughts about his fiancée, Joan. Richard Barclay, whose diary is interspersed with wistful speculations about how he would be enjoying the perfect autumn days if he was not waiting at dispersal, knew what he was missing. But they went on. 'You didn't stop because you were tired or you didn't like it,' said Denys Gillam afterwards. 'You just kept going.'[15]

By the time the end came the Fighter Boys had long since split up. Those who survived were scattered throughout the now sprawling RAF empire. The others were dead, lying in English country churchyards and sun-baked military cemeteries, buried in estuary mud or North Sea strands or long dissolved in the Channel tides. Of the 2,917 men who fought in Fighter Command the air battles of the summer of 1940, 544 were killed. Another 795 died before the war was over. On 15 August 1945, those who were left were able to believe for the first time that they might live the natural span of a man. Few had any idea of what awaited them as they stepped out into the mysterious world of the normal. But all knew they could never forget what they had left behind.

Epilogue: The Last Note

On 17 September 2000, a chilly Sunday morning tinged with intimations of death and winter, hundreds of guests filed through the west door of Westminster Abbey for a service of thanksgiving to mark the sixtieth anniversary of the Battle of Britain. The rows of hard, narrow chairs were packed with RAF members of all ages and ranks accompanied by their wives, sons and daughters.

After the readings the congregation rose. As the scraping of wood on stone and the coughing died away a towering silence settled over the abbey. Then the Central Band of the Royal Air Force struck up the opening notes of the Battle of Britain March and down the aisle, moving with slow dignity, came eight white-haired men bearing the Roll of Honour inscribed with the names of the airmen who died in the summer of 1940.[1] Pete Brothers lead the procession alongside Christopher Foxley-Norris, with Paddy Barthropp and Tom Neil among those following behind. They were escorted by a phalanx of junior officers, slim and upright, a reminder of the men the survivors had once been. When the service was over, the crowd stood for a while outside, greeting friends, lighting cigarettes, making plans for lunch or preparations for the journey home. A familiar noise cut through the hubbub and all heads tilted upwards. A Spitfire slid out of the low, greyish murk, hung for a few seconds overhead, then disappeared back into the cloud.

At the time about 300 veterans of the fighting were still alive. Two years later the number had fallen to 231. There was a feeling that the service marked the last occasion when the event being commemorated would remain moored to the recent past. Soon death and time would loosen the bonds of memory and it would slip into the realm of history.

The Fighter Boys had already passed into legend. Churchill had created it before the fighting had even properly begun and reinforced it before the outcome was known. The 'Battle of Britain' was his invention. Long before its outcome was decided, the men fighting it had been eulogized as 'The Few'. Despite the power of the rhetoric, the pilots seem to have been only half-aware that they were involved in a historic struggle. It was only when it was over that they began to discern the epic dimensions of the event they had been engaged in.

For most of the pilots the battle had a deep personal significance. For some it was the most important experience of their life, shaping for good or bad everything that came afterwards. For all of them, their participation was a badge of honour that they would wear until they died, arousing an admiration, respect and gratitude that took precedence over all subsequent achievement.

The great question of what to do when it was all over was perhaps harder to confront for the Fighter Boys than for any other serviceman. Staying on in the RAF gave the opportunity to carry on flying and to remain in a familiar world, even if it had become more petty and mundane. Many chose to continue. Dutiful, conscientious Al Deere carried on for another twenty-two years, ending up as commandant of the apprentice school at Halton, and retiring to live nearby until his death in 1995. Christopher Foxley-Norris finished with the rank of air chief marshal and a knighthood. Birdy Bird-Wilson became an air vice-marshal. Dennis David had a long and satisfying career and was air attaché in Prague during the Soviet crushing of the 'Prague Spring' in 1968. Pete Brothers joined the Colonial Service and went to Kenya, but after a few years reapplied to the RAF, commanded a bomber squadron during the Malayan emergency and ended his distinguished service as an air commodore. Billy Drake held a number of staff appointments, retiring as a group captain in 1963 and starting a new life as a restaurateur and property developer in Portugal.

But there would never be another summer of 1940. It was a truth that the routines of peace-time service underlined. Sailor Malan went to staff college for a year, then decided, in the words of his biographer, that 'the air no longer held out anything that would retain his interest and enthusiasm . . . He saw the magnificent combative spirit of the Air Force turn flaccid now the challenge was gone.'[2] He returned to South Africa with his wife and two children to work for the Anglo-American mining heir, Harry Oppenheimer, bought a huge farm and plunged briefly into politics, defending the constitution against Afrikaner extremists. Before he left England he made a last trip to the White Hart to unveil a memorial in the bar parlour, a blackout blind that had been signed in chalk, over the years, by many of the pilots who had passed through the inn door. A replica is there still. Malan died young, aged fifty-two, in 1963, brought down at last by Parkinson's disease. Michael Crossley also ended up in South Africa, where he grew tobacco before his death in 1987. So did Robin Appleford, before moving on to Rhodesia and Kenya, where he worked for a British company for fifteen years before returning to Britain. His friend Rob Bodie was killed in a flying accident in February 1942.

Some found jobs in civil aviation. Paul Richey was European area manager for BP, then took up an offer from his old Fighter Command comrade Max Aitken to work as air correspondent on the family-owned *Daily Express*. He continued to live an adventurous life. He climbed mountains, sailed racing yachts and went deep-sea diving with Jacques Cousteau. To add to the broad row of decorations, there was a medal from the Royal Humane Society, awarded after he dived in to rescue a woman drowning in heavy seas off the Ligurian coast at Portofino. He was working on a definitive history of Anglo-French relations when he died in 1989. Hugh Dundas also joined Beaverbrook Newspapers and moved into television in the 1960s, ending up as chairman of Thames Television. He was knighted in 1987 and died in 1995.

Tim Vigors, after an extraordinary series of narrow escapes, survived the war. In peacetime he pursued the loves of his life, going into the bloodstock industry and breeding some notable champions and founding his own aviation company. Douglas Bader left the RAF in 1946 to work for Shell who awarded him his own aeroplane. The appearance of Paul Brickhill's biography, *Reach for the Sky*, which was turned into a film, established him as a post-war celebrity. He enjoyed his fame and made some good use of it, encouraging disabled people to believe that they could lead, as he had done, not a normal but an exceptional life. He died in September 1982 on his way back from a dinner in honour of Sir Arthur 'Bomber' Harris.

Roland Beamont became a test pilot, then an aviation executive. Tony Bartley also started a peacetime career as a test pilot before following his wife, the actress Deborah Kerr, to Hollywood. He had met her at a film studio in 1941. She was starring in a costume drama. He was doing the flying stunts for *The First of the Few*, which told the story of the Spitfire's inventor, R. J. Mitchell. They married in 1947. Dowding, by now a peer, was among the guests. He alarmed Bartley's father during the service by asking him if he could feel, as he could, the presence of his son's dead comrades. The marriage lasted until 1959, by which time Bartley had launched into a career in television. He died at his home in Ireland in April 2001.

Brian Kingcome found the transition to peacetime service difficult. He tried several times to resign his commission, but was told that, as an ex-Cranwell cadet, he owed it to his country to stay on. In September 1950 he contracted tuberculosis, which he blamed on a bachelor lifestyle of steady drinking, late nights and irregular meals. He spent three years in a sanatorium. On leave, in a bar, deciding what to do next, he ran into an American acquaintance who worked for Twentieth Century-Fox. The man asked Kingcome to be his assistant on the film he was working on. Kingcome resigned his commission the same day. Later he tried to get a management job in industry but was disappointed by what he found. His mistake, he said, was to assume that the ethical standards and codes he had been brought up with at home, at schools and in the RAF would apply equally in commercial life. This misapprehension cost him a lot of money.

At one point Paddy Barthropp provided a solution. He had left the RAF in 1958 and used his severance money to set up a Rolls-Royce hire firm. He invited Kingcome to be his partner. Kingcome wrote of Barthropp, that 'underneath a façade of eccentric inanity there lurked one of the kindest, most generous and warm-hearted of men, and everyone sensed it'.[3]

Kingcome's bachelor life came to an end when, with forty approaching, he fell in love with a young woman almost half his age called Lesley. She was the daughter of Sheila, one of the beautiful Macneal twins, and he had known her since she was a child. They had a long, happy marriage, presiding over a successful furniture business until they retired to Devon. Their neighbours there included Killy Kilmartin, who on leaving the RAF in 1958 had started a chicken farm. After fifteen years he had sold it, shifted around Europe for more than a decade and then returned to Devon. With Barthropp, who bought a retreat locally, they formed a convivial trio. Kingcome died in 1994, and Kilmartin in 1998. Cocky Dundas gave an address at Kingcome's funeral. His four chief attributes, he said, were 'courage, determination, a total lack of pomposity or self-importance and an everlasting lightness of heart and touch'.

This approach to life was evident in Kingcome's attitude towards the Battle of Britain. 'Why can't they just talk about B of B pilots?' he once complained in a letter. 'Why does it always have to be heroes? I think it devalues the word and denigrates all those others who were called on to face just as great odds and whose contribution and sacrifices are just as great, but whose exploits hadn't been pushed into the public eye by Churchill's splendid oratory. Dying is what's important, not the time and place you did it.'[4]

It was a typically generous sentiment. By the time it was expressed it was far too late to change things. The event achieved its cinematic apotheosis in 1969. The film *The Battle of Britain* was a serious, almost reverential work. Even after this time, Hollywood was not prepared to tinker with the myth. The technical advisers included Bob Tuck, and on the German side, Adolf Galland. Galland had ended up a much-decorated air force general. He professed to know nothing about Nazi atrocities until learning of them after the war. He was released after a long interrogation and went to Argentina to help train its air force before returning to Germany to start an aviation consultancy. In his autobiography, *The First and the Last*, which appeared in 1953, he presented himself as an amiable, apolitical professional soldier, who brought a touch of chivalry to a nasty business. He was widely accepted as such. He was on good terms with Bader, whom he had treated well after his capture. He was particularly close to Tuck, visiting him at his mushroom farm in Kent and inviting him to his home near Bonn to go boar shooting. Tuck's death in May 1987 affected him strongly. His own, in February 1996, was marked in the British media as the passing of a Good German.

When the war finished many pilots were left with the suspicion that the most exciting and important passage of their existence was over, even though they still had most of their lives left to run. It was equally true for some non-combatants. Edith Heap never forgot Denis Wissler. She married a doctor after the war, but they were divorced after five years. Occasionally, during the intervening sixty years, she is convinced she has felt Denis's presence. 'Once,' she told me, 'I was sitting up in bed, reading, and suddenly there was Denis. He bent down and kissed me. I felt it. It was a lovely warm feeling. Then he smiled at me and faded away.'[5]

Despite their tendency to understatement and self-mockery, it was hard for the pilots to escape the realization that they had been involved in something great. The Battle of Britain, inevitably, underwent historical revision. Doubts have been cast on the seriousness of the German invasion plan and adjustments have been made to the odds that Fighter Command was facing. These re-examinations have done nothing to diminish the pilots' achievement. More than sixty years later it seems as remarkable as ever.

Fighter Command dealt Hitler's forces the first defeat they had suffered since the war began. The battle of attrition that the Luftwaffe was forced to fight had a profound effect on its future efficiency. A Luftwaffe general, Werner Kreipe, later judged that the decision to try and destroy the RAF had marked 'a turning point in the history of the Second World War. The German Air Force . . . was bled almost to death and suffered losses which could never again be made good throughout the course of the war.'[6]

The victory was of colossal importance. 'Our battle was a small one,' wrote Peter Townsend, 'but on its outcome depended the fate of the western world.' It is true that Hitler spent little time on the invasion plan. But according to his assessment of the likely direction of events he did not need to. Either the RAF would be cleared from the skies, opening the way for a landing, or the Luftwaffe would inflict so much damage that the British government would be forced to seek terms. Either outcome would mean the end of effective resistance to the Nazis in Europe and the start of the 'new dark age' that Churchill had foreseen.

The fact that neither came to pass was due to the actions of 3,000 men and their machines and the intelligence of those who controlled them. The balance of forces was not as uneven as the first version of the legend suggested, though there were periodic crises of manpower and aircraft. But the battle was not to be decided by resources alone. It was, in the end, a question of character and morale. The Fighter Boys' thoughts were rarely darkened by the prospect of defeat. 'We knew we had to win,' wrote Townsend, 'but, more than that, we were somehow certain that we could not lose. I think it had something to do with England. Miles up in the sky, we fighter pilots could see more of England than any other of England's defenders had ever seen before. Beneath us stretched our beloved country, with its green hills and valleys, lush pastures and villages, clustering round an ancient church. Yes, it was a help to have England there below.'[7] George Bennions, who was badly burned in the last fighting of the summer and blinded in one eye, believed that his unit, 41 Squadron, battered though it was, 'would have fought on and on until there was nothing left'.[8]

It was a victory of spirit as much as of skill, and the spirit of the Fighter Boys was that of Britain. They came from every class and background and every area. Their values and attitudes were those of the people they were defending. It seemed to the teenage Yvonne Agazarian that her brother Noel and his comrades were sacrificing their lives to defend a way of doing things, 'fighting with a real belief and dying moderately cheerfully'.[9]

They had taken a duty and turned it into a great act, and done so with a grace and style that was almost as significant as the event itself, for it reflected the decency of their cause. The Fighter Boys are almost all gone now. One by one the last of the Few are taking off on the final flight. Their real monument is Europe's enduring peace. But long after the last veteran has departed, they will be remembered. Each September their sons and daughters, grandchildren and great-grandchildren will come to the Abbey to give thanks. Then they will file outside and listen for the pulsing tone of the Spitfire engine, like the note of a grand piano after a bass key has been struck, fading and swelling as if it is trying to tell us something, the most poignant and romantic sound on earth.

Notes and References

Prologue: The White Hart

1 'he had recorded the events of the day': 32 Squadron unofficial diary, quoted in Bob Ogley, *Biggin on the Bump*, Froglets Publications, Westerham, 1990.
2 Mr H. J. Edgerton: quoted in *Daily Mirror*, 16 August 1940.
3 'wrote a war artist': Cuthbert Orde, *Pilots of Fighter Command*, Harrap, London, 1942, p. 10.
4 'would you like to go for a flip?': Charles Fenwick, *Dear Mother*, privately published memoir.

1. Sportsmen and Butchers

1 Gierson: quoted in Nigel Steel and Peter Hart, *Tumult in the Clouds, the British Experience of War in the Air 1914–1918*, Coronet, London, 1998, p. 19.
2 Rabagliati: quoted in ibid., p. 31.
3 Loraine: quoted in Andrew Boyle, *Trenchard*, Collins, London, 1962, p. 95.
4 Lewis: Cecil Lewis, *Sagittarius Rising*, Warner Books, London, 1998, pp. 40–5.
5 'Lewis wrote': ibid., p. 45.
6 Albert Ball: Chaz Bowyer, *Albert Hall VC*, Bridge Books, London, 1994, pp. 32–5.
7 'He had but one idea': ibid., p. 81.
8 'a hero . . . and he looked the part too': ibid., p. 82.
9 'I do so want to leave': ibid., p. 76.
10 'the topping day': ibid., p. 111.
11 'May evening': Lewis, *Sagittarius Rising*, p. 174.
12 'we met Huns': *The Personal Diary of Major Edward 'Mick' Mannock VC*, introduced and annotated by Frederick Oughton, Neville Spearman, London, 1966, pp. 105 and 187.
13 'The Hun crashed': ibid., p. 187.
14 'one general reasoned': Alan Clark, *Aces High*, Cassell, London, 1999, p. 70.
15 'to finish myself': Mannock, *The Personal Diary*, p. 166.

16 'my first flamerino': ibid., p. 168.
17 'All tickets please!': ibid., p. 190.
18 'I don't feel': ibid., p. 198.
19 'saw a flame': ibid., p. 201.
20 'it gave me': Manfred von Richthofen, *The Red Air Fighter*, Greenhill Books, London, 1999, pp. 89 and 96.
21 'honoured the fallen': ibid., p. 94.
22 'The great thing': Peter Kilduff, *The Illustrated Red Baron, The Life and Times of Manfred von Richthofen*, Arms and Armour Press, London, 1999, p. 49.
23 'so you were': Lewis, *Sagittarius Rising*, p. 10.
24 'because he was': John Grider: quoted in Steel and Hart, *Tumult in the Clouds*, p. 293.
25 'Ah! Tu es pilote!': Lewis, *Sagittarius Rising*, p. 75.
26 'In such an atmosphere,' ibid., p. 60.
27 'little black and tan': Mannock, *The Personal Diary*, p. 119.
28 'My system was': Steel and Hart, *Tumult in the Clouds*, p. 310.
29 'So it was over': Lewis, *Sagittarius Rising*, p. 255.

2. Fighters *versus* Bombers

1 'Under Trenchard': H. Montgomery Hyde, *British Air Policy between the Wars 1918–1939*, Heinemann, London, 1976, p. 49.
2 'the prophet Jonah's': ibid., p. 49.
3 'the vital esential': ibid., p. 56.
4 'to really make': ibid., p. 61.
5 'less cause to': Andrew Boyle, Trenchard, Collins, London, 1962, p. 361.
6 'scene of grey corrugated': *Royal Air Force Cadet College Magazine*, September 1920, vol. 1, No. 1.
7 'Nothing that has': ibid.
8 'The first senior': See Tony Mansell, 'Flying Start: Educational and Social Factors in the Recruitment of Pilots of the Royal Air Force in the Interwar Years', *History of Education*, 1997, vol. 26, No. 1, p. 72.
9 'The Cecil Committee': ibid., p. 73.
10 'Air Ministry officials': E.B. Haslam, *The History of RAF Cranwell*, HMSO, London 1982, p. 29.
11 'The curriculum': ibid., p. 28.
12 'Fun was bruising': ibid., p. 27.
13 'In January 1921': *Flight*, 24 December 1924.
14 'The high standard': John James, *The Paladins, a Social History of the RAF up to the Outbreak of World War II*, Macdonald, London, 1990, p. 208.
15 'The policy meant': ibid., p. 113.
16 'It wanted': ibid., p. 142.
17 'Trenchard considered': Boyle, *Trenchard*, p. 519.
18 'The squadron historian noted': Tom Moulson, *The Flying Sword, The Story of 601 Squadron*, Macdonald, London, 1954, p. 22.

19 'before 1939': John Terraine, *The Right of the Line, The Royal Air Force in the European War 1939–1945*, Hodder & Stoughton, London, 1985, p. 50.
20 'As early as': ibid., p. 11.
21 'the only defence': ibid., p. 14.
22 'indicated the obsolescence': ibid., p. 23.
23 'Half an hour later': Paul Gallico, *The Hurricane Story*, Michael Joseph, London, 1959, p. 19.
24 'the sort of bloody silly name': Len Deighton, *Fighter*, Pimlico, London, 1996, p. 77.
25 'Everyone therefore started out the same': Montgomery Hyde, *British Air Policy*, p. 354.
26 'I cannot take the view': ibid., p. 410.

3. 'Free of Boundaries, Free of Gravity, Free of Ties'

1 Drake: interview with author.
2 Brothers: interview with author.
3 'as a special treat': Dennis 'Hurricane' David, *My Autobiography*, Grub Street, London, 2000, p. 11.
4 Sanders: interview with author.
5 Beamont: Imperial War Museum Sound Archive (henceforth referred to as IWM), recording no. 10128.
6 'an RAF biplane': Bob Doe, *Fighter Pilot*, Spellmount, Stapelhurst, 1991, p. 3.
7 'The fact that one was now overhead': Alan Deere, *Nine Lives*, Crécy, Manchester, 1999, p. 15.
8 'there came the drone': Brian Kingcome, *A Willingness to Die*, edited and introduced by Pete Ford, Tempus, Stroud, 1999, p. 8.
9 'were boyishly clear': Geoffrey Page, *Shot Down in Flames*, Grub Street, London, 1999, p. 9.
10 'In one story': Captain W. E. Johns, *Biggles Story Collection*, Red Fox, London, 1999, p. 40.
11 'In another': W. E. Johns, *The Camels are Coming*, Red Fox, London, 1993, p. 97.
12 'the Foreword': Johns, *Biggles Story Collection*, p. 72.
13 Brothers: interview with author.
14 Hancock: interview with author.
15 'Over tea his father': Page, *Shot Down in Flames*, pp. 8–9.
16 Doe: interview with author.
17 'Deere left Auckland': Deere, *Nine Lives*, p. 23.
18 'David had his first lesson': David, *My Autobiography*, p. 12.
19 'and was absolutely thrilled': Johnny Kent, *One of the Few*, Tempus, Stroud, 2000, p. 8.
20 Doe: interview with author.
21 'put the Tiger Moth': Wing Commander H. R. 'Dizzy' Allen, *Battle for Britain*, Corgi, London, 1975, p. 13.
22 'queasy feeling engulfed me': Tim Vigors, unpublished autobiography.

23 'Deere was so impatient': Deere, *Nine Lives*, p. 26.
24 'When the cutters': Patrick Barthropp, *Paddy, the Life and Times of Wing Commander Patrick Barthropp, DFC, AFC*, Howard Baker, London, 1990, p. 29.
25 'To some . . . it seemed': David, *My Autobiography*, p. 25.
26 'Kingcome considered': quoted in Richard C. Smith, *Hornchurch Scramble*, Grub Street, London, 2000, p. 37.
27 'Deere lost his temper': Deere, *Nine Lives*, p. 28.
28 'Kingcome enjoyed': IWM, no. 10152.
29 Brothers: interview with author.
30 Drake: interview with author.
31 Sheen: IWM, no. 12137.
32 Banham: IWM, no. 6799.
33 Nicholas: IWM, no. 12405.
34 'gone were the halcyon days': Peter Townsend, *Time and Chance*, Book Club Associates, London, 1978, p. 95.
35 Doe: interview with author.
36 Sheen: IWM, no. 12137.
37 'Deere . . . spent his first weeks': Deere, *Nine Lives*, p. 33.
38 'a school bully': Barthropp, *Paddy*, p. 20.
39 Gillam: IWM, no. 10049.
40 'Kingcome was to deliver the opinion': Kingcome, *A Willingness to Die*, p. 23.
41 Unwin: interview with author.
42 Brown: IWM, no. 12404.
43 Johns: IWM, no. 11616.
44 Haw: IWM, no. 12028.
45 Berry: IWM, no. 11475.
46 Foster: IWM, no. 12738.
47 Foxley-Norris: interview with author.
48 'Beaumont wrote': S. G. Beaumont, *The Reminiscences of S. G. Beaumont*, privately published, p. 143.
49 Barran: see Frank H. Ziegler, *The Story of 609 Squadron*, Crécy Books, Manchester, 1993, p. 49.
50 'but slow rolls I hated': Hugh Dundas, *Flying Start*, Stanley Paul, London, 1998, pp. 10–12.
51 Foxley-Norris: interview with author.
52 'Hillary was also a poor learner': David Ross, *Richard Hillary*, Grub Street, London, 2000, p. 28.
53 Yvonne Agazarian: interview with author.

4. The Fatal Step

1 Brown: IWM, no. 12404.
2 Beaumont: IWM, no. 10128.
3 Foxley-Norris: IWM, no. 10136.
4 Brown: IWM, no. 12404.

5 'never a plane "so loved" ': Dundas, *Flying Start*, p. 19.
6 Quill: IWM, no. 10687.
7 Unwin: interview with author.
8 Kingcome: IWM, no. 10152.
9 Nicholas: IWM, no. 12405.
10 Considine: IWM, no. 10961.
11 'Kingcome judged': Kingcome, *A Willingness to Die*, p. 64.
12 Drake: interview with author.
13 Deere: IWM, no. 10478.
14 'Half the pilots': Paul Richey, *Fighter Pilot*, Guild Publishing, London, 1990, p. 10.
15 'Deere wrote later': Deere, *Nine Lives*, p. 36.
16 Brothers: IWM, no. 10218.
17 Hall: IWM, no. 10342.
18 'Kingcome recalled': IWM, no. 10152.
19 'Deere wrote afterwards': Deere, *Nine Lives*, p. 36.
20 Winskill: IWM, no. 11537.
21 'Townsend also noticed': Townsend, *Time and Chance*, pp. 99–100.
22 Sanders: interview with author.
23 Hancock: interview with author.
24 'Quill wrote to his mother': letter in Quill family archive.
25 'Bartley decided to visit Germany': Tony Bartley, *Smoke Trails in the Sky*, William Kimber, London, 1984.
26 Bowring: IWM, no. 12173.
27 'Hillary went to compete in Germany': Richard Hillary, *The Last Enemy*, Macmillan, London, 1942, p. 23.
28 'At Cranwell': *Journal of the Royal Air Force College*, spring 1939.
29 Drake: interview with author.
30 Page: IWM, no. 11103.
31 'Hillary was contemptuous': Hillary, *The Last Enemy*, pp. 28–9.
32 'old-fashioned patriotism?': Beaumont, *Reminiscences*, p. 131.
33 Deere: IWM, no. 10478.
34 'spent a lot of time': see Oliver Walker, *Sailor Malan*, Cassell, London, 1953.
35 'wrote an RFC veteran': *Flight*, 18 March 1939.
36 'Kingcome was ordered': Kingcome, p. 61.
37 'Townsend recorded': Townsend, *A Willingness to Die*, p. 99.
38 'Brothers had to appear': interview with author.
39 'Vigors on leave from Cranwell': Vigors, unpublished autobiography, p. 117.
40 'the inevitable, well lubricated games': Dundas, *Flying Start*, p. 12.
41 'what a party': Townsend, *Time and Chance*, p. 102.
42 Haw: IWM, no. 12028.
43 Walker: IWM, no. 10617.
44 'one of the few to be surprised': Fenwick, *Dear Mother*, p. 36.
45 Down: IWM, no. 11449.

46 'Kingcome was struck': quoted in Richard C. Smith, *Hornchurch Scramble*, Grub Street, London, 2000, p. 51.

5. Winter of Uncertainty

1 Freeborn: interview with author.

2 'According to Eric Clayton': Eric Clayton, *What If the Heavens Fall*, RAF Museum, Hendon, ref. 34870.

3 'eighteen years old': in fact he was nineteen.

4 Deere: IWM, no. 10478.

5 'His biographer wrote': Walker, *Sailor Malan*.

6 'Al Deere noted': Deere, *Nine Lives*, p. 41.

7 Quoted in Henry Buckton, *Birth of the Few*, Airlife, Shrewsbury, 1998, p. 89.

8 Maclean: IWM, no. 10788.

9 'Townsend took part': Townsend, *Time and Chance*, pp. 105–6.

10 Bennions: IWM, no. 10296.

11 Paddy Finucane: Pilot Officer B. E. F. Finucane, letters, in IWM, documents archive, ref. 97/43/1.

12 Benson: Pilot Officer Noel Benson, letters in RAF Museum, Hendon, ref. 133331.

13 'told Benson's father later': correspondence and eyewitness account of death of Pilot Officer Benson in IWM, documents archive, ref. 133332.

14 Wissler: diary of Pilot Officer Denis Wissler in IWM, documents archive, ref, 91/41/1.

15 Earp: IWM, no. 11772.

6. Return to the Western Front

1 'wrote Paul Richey': Richey, *Fighter Pilot*, p. 19.

2 'Mould felt bad about his victory': see ibid., p. 24.

3 'Richey noticed': accidental brushes with death, it seemed, could cause more distress to a pilot than encounters with enemies who had set out to kill them. Eric Clayton, a corporal on the 56 Squadron ground staff, was at North Weald in the early spring of 1940 when Flight Lieutenant Ian Soden, a much-admired and highly experienced pilot, landed after practice formation flying with Flying Officer Illingworth and Flying Officer Rose. 'Soden got out of the cockpit looking white, released his parachute and leaned over the tailplane, clearly distressed. As the other pilots approached him, he said: "My God Illingworth! You hit me." Inspection revealed a large dent in the sternpost of the tail fin. Illingworth, a short, cocky fellow, did not seem too perturbed and Rose was slightly amused. What surprised us, though, was Soden's show of distress, for he was a man who displayed little emotion, was rather distant, and, as events proved, very brave' – Clayton, *What If the Heavens Fall*.

4 Matthews: IWM, no. 10451.

5 Paulette Regnauld: interview with author.

6 'the main attraction was the Roxy': Richey, *Fighter Pilot*, p. 29.

7 'Gallagher wrote': in *Daily Express*, 28 November 1939.

8 Foxley-Norris: interview with author.
9 'Richey pulled up violently': Richey, *Fighter Pilot*, p. 46.
10 'Beamont discovered': IWM, no. 10128.
11 Sanders: interview with author.

7. The Battle of France

1 Parrott: IWM, no. 13152.
2 Drake: interview with author.
3 'four farm hands had been working': Richey, *Fighter Pilot*, pp. 69–70.
4 'We took off': quoted in Brian Cull and Bruce Lander with Heinrich Weiss, *Twelve Days in May*, Grub Street, London, 1999, p. 48.
5 'The official RAF daily report admitted': ibid., p. 52.
6 Brothers: interview with author.
7 'Richard Whittaker's report': Public Record Office, diary of 17 Squadron.
8 'Richey had been hurrying': Richey, *Fighter Pilot*, p. 75.
9 'He described': quoted in Cull and Lander with Weiss, *Twelve Days in May*, p. 85.
10 Drake: interview with author.
11 'Richey had to collect something': Richey, *Fighter Pilot*, p. 86.
12 'David received a letter': David, *My Autobiography*, p. 26.
13 'Our nerves': Richey, *Fighter Pilot*, p. 80.
14 'Churchill was woken': see Terraine, *The Right of the Line*, pp. 135–40, for an account of Cabinet discussions.
15 'met a column of Belgian refugees': David, *My Autobiography*, p. 26.
16 'When they retold the stories': Richey, *Fighter Pilot*, p. 90.
17 'Matthews was sent one day': IWM, no. 10451.
18 'A pilot officer from "B" Flight': interview with author.
19 'Richey wrote': Richey, *Fighter Pilot*, p. 108.
20 'No. 1 Squadron took over a café': ibid., p. 112.
21 Brothers: interview with author.
22 Hancock: interview with author.
23 'He concluded that it would be "criminal"': see Terraine, *The Right of the Line*, p. 153.
24 Beamont: IWM, no. 10128.
25 'David flew to their airfield': David, *My Autobiography*, p. 28.
26 'David, who had been shot up': ibid., p. 29.
27 Drake: interview with author.
28 'Richey "noticed"': Richey, *Fighter Pilot*, p. 129.
29 Long: IWM, no. 12217.
30 Hancock: IWM, no. 10119.
31 Dawbarn: interview with author.
32 Rosier: IWM, no. 10157.
33 'one Hurricane carried a passenger': IWM, no. 10093.
34 'No. 1 Squadron diary': quoted in Cull and Lander with Weiss, *Twelve Days in May*, p. 25.

8. Dunkirk

1 'wrote Brian Kingcome': Kingcome, *A Willingness to Die*, p. 74.
2 'As Al Deere pointed out': Deere, *Nine Lives*, p. 46.
3 'Deere reported': ibid., p. 49.
4 'Deere agreed': ibid., p. 55.
5 'Leathart . . . promised': ibid., p. 59.
6 'Crossley noted': quoted in Graham Wallace, *RAF Biggin Hill*, Putnam, London, 1959, p. 116.
7 'the squadron chronicler recorded': Mounson, *The Flying Sword*, p. 51.
8 Kingcome: IWM, no. 10152.
9 Unwin: interview with author.
10 Unwin: interview with author.
11 'Leathart . . . described': quoted in Norman Franks, *Air Battle Dunkirk*, Grub Street, London, 2000, p. 27.
12 'biographer wrote': Paul Brickhill, *Reach for the Sky*, Collins, London, 1954, p. 170.
13 Kingcome: IWM, no. 10152.
14 'Malan found': Walker, *Sailor Malan*, p. 77.
15 'When Deere explained': Deere, *Nine Lives*, p. 70.
16 'Rosier . . . told how his wife': IWM, no. 10157.
17 'Kingcome saw': Kingcome, *A Willingness to Die*, p. 77.
18 Unwin: IWM, no. 11544.
19 'Malan said afterwards': quoted in Walker, *Sailor Malan*, p. 79.
20 Bartley: IWM, no. 11086.
21 Unwin: IWM, no. 11544.
22 Nicholas: IWM, no. 12405.
23 Dundas: IWM, 10159.
24 Bartley: IWM, no. 11086.
25 'Vigors . . . went off on the last patrol': Vigors, unpublished autobiography.

9. Doing It

1 'At Duxford aerodrome': Vigors, unpublished autobiography, contains the whole account.
2 'Richey found': Richey, *Fighter Pilot*, p. 114.
3 'Kingcome found': Kingcome, *A Willingness to Die*, p. 51.
4 Brothers: interview with author.
5 Freeborn: interview with author.
6 'the release from tension': Walker, *Sailor Malan*, p. 74.
7 Kingcome: IWM no. 10152.
8 Unwin: IWM, no. 11544.
9 Parrott: IWM, no. 13152.
10 Rosier: IWM, no. 10157.
11 Brown: IWM, no. 12404.
12 'I was suddenly drenched': quoted in Cull and Lander with Weiss, *Twelve Days in May*, p. 123.

13 'Just as': quoted in ibid., p. 203.
14 'Dundas was to find': Dundas, *Flying Start*, pp. 2–3.
15 'Richey . . . began to feel peculiar': Richey, *Fighter Pilot*, pp. 80–81.

10. Before the Storm

1 'Tim Vigors heard': Vigors, unpublished autobiography.
2 'Ministry of Information instructions': *The Times*, 19 June 1940.
3 'a newspaper circulating in south-east England': *Chichester and Southern Post*, 22 June 1940.
4 'in the officials': quoted in Brian Gardner, *Churchill in His Time*, Methuen, London, 1968, p. 65.
5 Brothers: interview with author.
6 'shortages were so acute': see Fenwick, *Dear Mother*.
7 Haw: IWM, no. 12028.
8 Usmar: IWM, no. 10588.
9 'Beaumont's diary entry': Beaumont, *Reminiscences*.
10 'awareness of problems': Ziegler, *The Story of 609 Squadron*, p. 99.
11 'The first person to greet him:' Vigors, unpublished autobiography.
12 'Deere was particularly proud': Deere, *Nine Lives*, p. 90.
13 Bird-Wilson. IWM, no. 10093.
14 'Fenwick . . . was in love': Fenwick, *Dear Mother*.
15 Rosier: IWM, no. 10157.
16 Unofficial diary of 72 Squadron in RAF Museum, Hendon.

11. The Channel Battle

1 'was now at': quoted in Deere, *Nine Lives*, p. 94.
2 'Deere narrowly escaped': ibid., p. 99.
3 Foxley-Norris: IWM, no. 10136.
4 Quayle: IWM, no. 10609.
5 Drake: interview with author.
6 'The leading historian of the Polish air force in Britain': Adam Zamoyski, *The Forgotten Few*, John Murray, London, 1995, p. 71.
7 Brothers: interview with author.
8 Bartley, IWM, no. 11086.
9 'the Me 109 carried the heavier punch': see Deighton, *Fighter*, p. 77.
10 Unwin: interview with author.
11 Cox: IWM, no. 11510.
12 'Pilots were told': see Anthony Robinson, *RAF Fighter Squadrons in the Battle of Britain*, Brockhampton Press, London, 1999, p. 31.
13 Page: IWM, no. 11103.
14 'courage, these days': quoted in Walker, *Sailor Malan*, p. 101.
15 'was said to have been able to spot': Allen, Battle for Britain, p. 77.
16 'Page . . . confessed': Page, *Shot Down in Flames*, p. 63
17 'Beaumont . . . was told': Beaumont, *Reminiscences*.

18 'Kingcome's feeling': Kingcome, *A Willingness to Die*, p. 99.

12. The Hun

1 'Milch chose Bob Tuck's aircraft': Larry Forester, *Fly for Your Life*, Frederick Muller, London, 1956, p. 59.
2 'Milch . . . sent a thank-you gift': Haslam, *The History of RAF Cranwell*, p. 62.
3 'Kingcome's sardonic style wavered': IWM, no. 10152.
4 Becker: interview with author.
5 Schöpfel: interview with author.
6 'his first private meeting with Hitler': David Baker, *Adolf Galland, the Authorized Biography*, Windrow & Greene, London, 1996, p. 43.
7 Foxley-Norris: interview with author.
8 'as long as I can': Wick quoted in Mike Spick, *Luftwaffe Fighter Aces*, Greenhill Books, 1996, p. 73.
9 'to attach, to track': ibid., p. 128.
10 Galland, IWM, no. 2791
11 Schöpfel: interview with author.
12 'he told his biographer': Baker, *Adolf Galland*, p. 94.

13. Hearth and Home

1 Brothers: interview with author.
2 Greenwood: letter to Dilip Sarkar, in RAF Museum, Hendon archives.
3 Elkington: interview with author.
4 Considine: IWM, no. 10961.
5 Foxley-Norris: IWM, no. 10136.
6 'circling and sweeping': quoted in Ziegler, *The Story of 609 Squadron*, p. 119.
7 Page: IWM, no. 11103.
8 Constable Maxwell: diary of Michael Constable Maxwell, in RAF Museum, Hendon, Research Department.
9 Fink: interview contained in research papers of Alexander McKee (for his book *Strike from the Sky – the Battle of Britain Story*, New English Library, London, 1969), now in RAF Museum, Hendon.
10 'After two months': Dennis Armitage, unpublished memoir.
11 Armitage: interview with author.
12 Gundry: Pilot Officer Kenneth Gundry, letters to parents, RAF Museum, Hendon.
13 'The attack was led': Ziegler, *The Story of 609 Squadron*, p. 122.
14 'John Dundas . . . wrote': ibid., p. 120.
15 'the base's historian': Rocky Stockman, *The History of RAF Manston*, RAF Station Manston, pp. 35–44.
16 'None of us had ever': Group Captain Robert Deacon Elliot, *Unofficial History of 72 Squadron*, RAF Museum, Hendon.
17 Sheen: IWM, no. 12137.
18 Bowring: IWM, no. 12173.

19 Fiske: see David Alan Johnson, *The Battle of Britain*, Combined Publishing, Pennsylvania, 1998, p. 120.
20 'Deere wrote later': Deere, *Nine Lives*, p. 142.
21 Marjery Wace: IWM, no. 2259.

14. Attrition

1 Foxley-Norris: IWM, no. 10136.
2 'Al Deere . . . noticed': Deere, *Nine Lives*, p. 136.
3 Gillam: IWM, no. 10049.
4 Appleford: interview with author.
5 Usmar: IWM, no. 10588.
6 'Shown up clearly': quoted in Francis K. Mason, *Battle over Britain*, Aston Publications, 1990, p. 256.
7 'the flick': Armitage, unpublished memoir.
8 Kingcome: IWM, no. 10152.
9 Beamont: IWM, no. 10128.
10 Deere: IWM, no. 10478.
11 Beamont: IWM, no. 10128.
12 Gillam: IWM, no. 10049.
13 Cox: IWM, no. 11510.
14 'Bob Doe noticed': Doe: *Fighter Pilot*, p. 36.
15 'Malan felt': Walker, *Sailor Malan*, p. 104.
16 Holden: IWM, no. 11198.
17 'Gleave, speaking later': Gleave made his remarks in a paper delivered at a symposium on the Battle of Britain sponsored by the Royal Air Force Historical Society and the Royal Air Force Staff College, Bracknell, on 25 June 1990. It was subsequently published in *The Battle Re-Thought*, edited by Air Commander Henry Probert and Sebastian Cox, Airlife, Shrewsbury, 1991, p. 50.
18 'He talked to me': Dundas, *Flying Start*, pp. 41–2.
19 'Walker, who had been posted': William Walker, private account.
20 Gillam: IWM, no. 10049.
21 Benson: letters of Pilot Officer Noel Benson in RAF Museum, Hendon. See also correspondence relating to the death of Pilot Officer Noel Benson in RAF Museum, Hendon.
22 Brothers: interview with author.
23 Joan Lovell Hughes: interview with author.
24 Lamberty: letter to Alexander McKee in RAF Museum, Hendon.
25 '601 Squadron's historian recorded': Moulson, *The Flying Sword*, p. 89.
26 Bird-Wilson: IWM, no. 10093.
27 Kingcome: IWM, no. 10152.
28 Winskill: IWM, no. 11537.
29 'The amazing thing': Elliot, *Unofficial History of 72 Squadron*.
30 'Armitage, wounded in the left leg': Armitage, unpublished memoir.
31 Unwin: IWM, no. 11544.

32 'The RAF bureaucracy listed personal effects': IWM, Department of Documents, ref. 97/43/1.
33 'described in a poem': Anthony Richardson, 'Because of These', in *Verses of the Royal Air Force*, Hodder & Stoughton, London, 1942.
34 'no point in brooding about death': Page, *Shot Down in Flames*, p. 69.
35 'Peter's towel': Ziegler, *The Story of 609 Squadron*, p. 103, quoting David Crook, *Fighter Pilot.*
36 'left with the paperwork': Armitage, unpublished memoir.
37 'Dr Benson's grief': correspondence relating to the death of Pilot Officer Noel Benson in RAF Museum, Hendon.
38 Wronsky: letter to McKee in RAF Museum, Hendon.
39 'Townsend gave way to his emotions': Townsend, *Time and Chance*, p. 111.
40 'Deere's . . . confidence . . . began to falter': IWM, no. 10478.
41 'he told Archie Winskill': IWM, no. 11537.

15. Brotherhood

1 'Kingcome remarked': Kingcome, *A Willingness to Die*, p. 183.
2 Beamont: IWM, no. 10128.
3 Foxley-Norris: interview with author.
4 'Bartley remembered': Bartley, *Smoke Trails in the Sky*, p. 58.
5 Dunning-White: interview with author.
6 'an unsentimental book': Wing Commander Atholl Forbes DFC and Squadron Leader Hubert Allen DFC (eds.), *Ten Fighter Boys*, Collins, London, 1942, p. 79.
7 Hutchinson: interview with Sophia Coudenhove.
8 Leng: IWM, no. 12217.
9 Page: interview with author.
10 Usmar: IWM, no. 10588.
11 'John Coghlan, a flying officer,': Clayton, *What If the Heavens Fall*, pp. 3–5.
12 Bowring: IWM, no. 12173.
13 Cox: IWM, no. 11510.
14 Wellum: Geoffrey Wellum, *First Light*, Viking, London, 2002.
15 David: interview with author.
16 Foxley-Norris: interview with author.
17 'To the ground crews he could be': see testimony of George Reid, in Dilip Sarkar, *Bader's Tangmere Spitfires*, Patrick Stephens, London, 1966, p. 51.
18 David: interview with author.
19 Beamont: IWM, no. 10128.
20 'Orde describes him as': Orde, *Pilots of Fighter Command*, p. 19.
21 'To Eric Clayton he was: Clayton, *What If the Heavens Fall*, p. 5.
22 'practical joking and ragging traditions': 73 Squadron unofficial diary, IWM, Department of Documents, Box 102.
23 Beamont: IWM, no. 10128.
24 Brothers: interview with author.
25 'in Brian Kingcome's description': Kingcome, *A Willingness to Die*, p. 177.

26 'Tony Bartley recorded': Bartley, *Smoke Trails in the Sky.*
27 Holland: letters to Bunty Nash, RAF Museum, Hendon.
28 Page: IWM, no. 11103.
29 Winskill: IWM, no. 11537.
30 Smith: IWM, no. 11754.
31 'records a dinner held': 73 Squadron unofficial diary.
32 'MacGeagh: Public Record Office, ref. AIR 71.
33 Haw: IWM, no. 12028.
34 'Vigors . . . considered himself an Irishman': Vigors, unpublished autobiography.
35 Dunning-White: interview with author.
36 Hutchinson: interview with Sophia Coudenhove.
37 'Kingcome remembered': Kingcome, *A Willingness to Die*, pp. 86–7.
38 'Armitage reported': Armitage, unpublished memoir.
39 Matthews: IWM, no. 10451.
40 Barclay: RAF Museum, Hendon, Aviation Records Department, ref. B2173.
41 'It was the longest': Doug Stokes: *Paddy Finucane, Fighter Ace*, Kimber, London, p. 43.
42 'Malan told': Walker, *Sailor Malan*, p. 99.
43 Bennions: IWM, no. 10296.
44 Constable Maxwell: Constable Maxwell diary.
45 Appleford: interview with author.
46 Devitt: IWM, no. 10667.
47 Donaldson: IWM, no. 12172.
48 'One of George Unwin's sergeant pilots': interview with author.
49 'Brothers came across': interview with author.
50 Bird-Wilson: IWM, no. 10093.
51 Down: IWM, no. 11449.
52 Bird-Wilson: IWM, no. 10093.
53 Donaldson: IWM, no. 12172.
54 Gillam: IWM. no. 10049.
55 Brothers: interview with author.
56 Yvonne Agazarian: interview with author.
57 Bartley: IWM, no. 11086.
58 Drake: interview with author.
59 'Finucane wrote': IWM, Department of Documents, ref. 97/43/1.
60 'Fenwick went to the aid': Fenwick, *Dear Mother.*
61 Wissler diary: all entries from IWM, Department of Documents, ref. 97/43/1.
62 'Edith "got ever so apprehensive"': interview with author.
63 'he wrote': letter in possession of Edith Kup, née Heap.

16. 'The Day Had Been a Year'

1 'switched on the electric sight': letter of Flying Officer R. G. A. Barclay, RAF Museum, Hendon.
2 'Fink remembered': letter to McKee in RAF Museum, Hendon.

3 'Weitkus: letter to McKee in RAF Museum, Hendon.
4 'wrote Richard Barclay': diary of Flying Officer R. G. A. Barclay in RAF Museum, Hendon.
5 'A signal was intercepted': RAF Battle of Britain Campaign Diary.
6 'a taste of what Londoners were going through': Vigors, unpublished autobiography.
7 Channon: *Chips: the Diaries of Sir Henry Channon*, edited by Robert Rhodes James, Weidenfeld & Nicolson, London, 1993, p. 265.
8 'Barclay was woken at 4.30': Barclay, diary.
9 Holmes: IWM, no. 2807.
10 'sat bolt upright': see Forbes and Allen, *Ten Fighter Boys*, p. 77.
11 Cox: IWM, no. 1150.
12 'getting a hell of a plastering': see Forbes and Allen, *Ten Fighter Boys*, p. 85.
13 'spreadeagled arms and legs': quoted in Dr Alfred Price, *Battle of Britain Day*, Greenhill Books, 1999, p. 86.
14 'The day had been': see Forbes and Allen, *Ten Fighter Boys*, p. 78.

17. Autumn Sunset
1 Barclay: Barclay, diary.
2 Edge: Flight Lieutenant G. Edge, unpublished account, RAF Museum, Hendon.
3 'Goering assured the crews': quoted in Mason, *Battle over Britain*, p. 368.
4 Schöpfel: interview with author.
5 'The insouciant spirit': Bartley, *Smoke Trails in the Sky*, p. 46.
6 'Bartley wrote to his mother': ibid.
7 Bennions: IWM, no. 10296.
8 'Page caught a glimpse of himself': Page, *Shot Down in Flames*, p. 81.
9 'he met the other patients': ibid., p. 98.
10 'The barmaid at the Red Lion': Doe, *Nine Lives*, p. 56.
11 Berry: IWM, no. 11475.
12 'Barclay noted': Barclay, diary.
13 'waited in dread': Vigors, unpublished autobiography.
14 Mottram: letters to Bunty Nash in RAF Museum, Hendon.

18. Rhubarbs and Circuses
1 'It seemed to Al Deere': Deere, *Nine Lives*, p. 172.
2 'Kent reached Biggin Hill': Kent, *One of the Few*, p. 88.
3 Finucane letters: IWM, Archive Department, 97/43/1.
4 'Douglas had been informed': Terraine, *The Right of the Line*, p. 283.
5 'judged John Terraine': ibid., p. 285.
6 'Deere confessed': Deere, *Nine Lives*, p. 211.
7 'A graphic account': Public Record Office, PRO AIR, ref. 149/357.
8 'Dundas, a perceptive and humane observer': Dundas, *Flying Start*, pp. 66–7, 70 and 79.
9 Armitage: IWM, no. 10049.

10 'Aikman described': *The Times*, 18 July 1942.
11 'His sister, Yvonne': interview with author.
12 Gillam: IWM, no. 10049.
13 'Deere was "always confident"': Deere, *Nine Lives*, p. 149.
14 Brothers: interview with author.
15 Gillam: IWM, no. 10049.

Epilogue: The Last Note

1 'Roll of Honour': the roll carries the names of 718 aircrew of Bomber Command and 280 of Coastal Command as well as those of Fighter Command who died during the period.
2 'Malan . . . decided: Walker, *Sailor Malan*.
3 'Kingcome wrote of Barthropp': Kingcome, *A Willingness to Die*, p. 176.
4 'Kingcome's attitude': ibid., p. xi.
5 Edith Heap: interview with author.
6 Kreipe: quoted in Terraine, *The Right of the Line*, p. 219.
7 'wrote Townsend': Townsend, *Time and Chance*, p. 110.
8 Bennions: IWM, no. 10296.
9 Yvonne Agazarian: interview with author.

Index